Subversive Peacemakers

Subversive Peacemakers

War Resistance 1914-1918

An Anglican Perspective

Clive Barrett

The Lutterworth Press

The Lutterworth Press
P.O. Box 60
Cambridge
CB1 2NT

www.lutterworth.com
publishing@lutterworth.com

ISBN: 978 0 7188 9367 5

British Library Cataloguing in Publication Data
A record is available from the British Library

First Published, 2014

Contents

List of Illustrations

All images provided by Clive Barrett, unless otherwise indicated.

Cover illustration: *The Conchie*, by Arthur W. Gay (1901-1958).
Used by kind permission of Penelope Gay, the Peace Museum, Bradford.
Photograph: Ben Chalcraft, Innovation and Cohesion Works. The painting
depicts a Bible-reading conscientious objector under military escort.

Abbreviations

A.P.F.	Anglican Pacifist Fellowship
C.E.M.S.	Church of England Men's Society
C.N.D.	Campaign for Nuclear Disarmament
C.O.	Conscientious Objector
C.O.P.E.C.	Conference on Christian Politics, Economics and Citizenship
C.S.U.	Christian Social Union
F.A.U.	Friends' Ambulance Unit
F.O.R.	Fellowship of Reconciliation
I.F.O.R.	International Fellowship of Reconciliation
I.L.P.	Independent Labour Party
M.T.C.I.	Movement Towards a Christian International
N.C.C.	Non-Combatant Corps
N.C.F.	No-Conscription Fellowship
N.C.F.C.	National Council of (Evangelical) Free Churches
N.M.W.M.	No More War Movement
N.P.C.	National Peace Council
N.U.W.S.S.	National Union of Women's Suffrage Societies
P.P.U.	Peace Pledge Union
R.A.M.C.	Royal Army Medical Corps
S.C.M.	Student Christian Movement
S.D.F.	Social Democratic Federation
U.D.C.	Union of Democratic Control
W.I.L.	Women's International League

Preface

We all have a tendency to let war set the agenda, and to determine our timeframes. Simply to write "1914-1918" is to define a time period with reference to war. It is, however, a distinctive and influential period in the history of war resistance. This volume chronicles war resistance in this era, including the remarkable witness and sacrifice of conscientious objectors.

When it comes to writing history, much depends on one's perception and perspective. Some pro-war critiques argue that life is cheap and that a casualty list of millions was a small price to pay for whatever it was that the war was meant to achieve.[1] Even the approach of the seemingly most "dispassionate" historians is coloured by their own personal perspective.[2] This volume has been produced with the intention of writing peace history from the perspective of contemporary opponents of war, using their words and their own, vindicated analyses. There may be a handful of stories here that are familiar, but they have previously been told by those seeking to denigrate or at least downplay the achievements of the war resisters. Original sources, however, can lend themselves to alternative interpretations. The people and events narrated may be seen in a new light when viewed from the unexpected perspective of peace history.

There are also many new stories, narratives and traditions that have either never been previously revealed, or that have never been seen in the context of an informed tradition of peace history. They have certainly never been collected together before. This volume tells these unknown stories, of peace groups campaigning against the 1914-1918 war, of individual conscientious objectors to military service, of preachers and politicians, workers and women who refused to succumb to the clamour of a society at war. In fact, there are so many stories, especially from Nonconformist and Dissenting quarters, that it has been necessary to focus not only on Christian experience, but also on the most unlikely strand within it; namely the anti-war tradition within the Established Church. We see the typical experience of many war resisters. We also sense the impact on the religious and political establishment as opposition to war moves from chapel to church, from street to state.

By way of introduction I undertake a "Cook's Tour" of key movements in western peace history, leading to a consideration of a changing peace movement that attempted to engage with the complex interplay of Empire and internationalism in the Edwardian era.

With the outbreak of war in 1914, the peace movement was completely reformed. The story of the founding of the Christian wing, the Fellowship of Reconciliation, is explored and the stories of some of the key players in it, not least Maude Royden, one of the most influential women opponents of the war. I consider a number of prominent individuals within the peace movement, including the extraordinary witness of George Lansbury, various clergy and opponents of war in the United States, India and the British Empire. The experiences of conscientious objectors, including those who heard the death sentence read out to them, are also examined; what were their stories, what was the impact of their witness on society, the state, the church? Where exactly *was* the Established Church in this opposition to war? Not at the centre, that much is clear. From the unique perspective of peace history, it appears that the religious establishment is frequently peripheral.

Finally, the lasting impact of the pacifists of 1914-1918 is explored. Their legacy continued in a peace movement that was renewed and re-shaped once again after the war. In a post-war society struggling to make sense of the slaughter of the First World War, the Church of England and other churches were forced to come to terms with pacifist insights by a remarkable international Conference on Christian Politics, Economics and Citizenship in 1923. The stand of the conscientious objectors especially came to be seen by many in post-war society as a prophetic critique of the consequences of war. Given half a chance, they might even have prevented the next one, but that was not to be.

The cost of the First World War remains evident in every community; everywhere there are memorials, often disguising slaughter as sacrifice, disingenuously reinterpreting gore and waste as glory, and celebrating the false god of patriotism. A century on, the events of 1914-1918 are still being retold and re-evaluated. That process needs to go beyond recounting the "victories", stalemates and defeats of Gallipoli, the Somme, Passchendaele et al. It must even go beyond the study of poet-soldiers, with their remonstrations in rhyme but not renunciation. It needs to include the stories of those who said "No", the stories of real resistance, of the thousands who not only rejected the official reasons for being at war, but who refused to contribute to the war effort and voluntarily carried their objection to the point where their own lives were jeopardised. Histories of the war are essential, but insufficient without engagement with the history of the war resisters. Only their stories have the power to inform our consciences, to warn us of the consequences of future war and to inspire us to work for peace in the twenty-first century.

This volume brings together the investigations, detective work, and information-gathering of twenty years. My thanks go to those, too many to identify, who have helped me along the way. Particular thanks go to Philip Dransfield, who supported this venture from the outset; to Cyril Pearce, who generously allowed me preliminary access to his remarkable database of conscientious objectors; to colleagues at the Peace Museum in Bradford, and especially to friends in the Anglican Pacifist Fellowship, www.anglicanpeacemaker.org.uk, whose practical support has brought this volume to fruition. This account reveals the underlying heritage behind their continuing witness.

1.
Introduction:
The Nature of the Church of England

The Church's Relationship with the State and the People

The Church of England is the established church of the realm. At its head is the monarch, and it has given centuries of spiritual sustenance to a militarised and imperial state. It has a history of recruitment sermons, of bishops blessing battleships, of cathedrals packed with regimental standards and war memorials, and of military chaplains in their military uniforms, receiving their military pay.

It is still the case that every person ordained as deacon, priest or bishop in the Church of England has to affirm the faith, to which the "historic formularies" of the Church bear witness. The Thirty-Nine Articles of Religion, developed in the sixteenth and seventeenth centuries, are presumed to come under this heading. The declaration of any office-holder in the Church of England at the time of the First World War was far more explicit: "I assent to the Thirty-Nine Articles".[1] Amongst these is Article Thirty-Seven, "It is lawful for Christian men, at the commandment of the Magistrate, to wear weapons, and serve in the wars".[2] That outwardly seems to imply no incongruity between the wars of the state and the Gospel of the Christian Church. Here is the church's, and the state's, justification for preparation for and participation in war. Of all human activities, warring appears to be almost the only one to be explicitly condoned by the founding documents of the Church of England. Government, the military and the church were seen to be so closely entwined that they formed the state's single trinity of power.

Complex maneuverings around the time of Henry VIII meant that political and ecclesiastical power (exerted by crown, parliament and Church) were intertwined, causing "a particular element of the Englishness of the Church of England" to be established.[3] The theologians and divines whose work developed the self-understanding and ecclesiology of the Church of England regarded membership of church and nation as inseparable, at least in their ideal model. As Richard

Hooker (1554-1600), writing in the late sixteenth century, expressed it, "We hold that seeing that there is not any man of the Church of England but the same is also a member of the commonwealth; nor any member of the commonwealth which is not also of the Church of England".[4] (What irony that this sentiment was not published until 1648, when religious as well as political divisions had reached such an intensity that the land was in the throes of civil war.)

After the Restoration, the monarch continued (and still continues) to be Supreme Governor of the Church of England. The Corporation Act of 1661 and Test Acts from 1673 ensured that officers of state were Church of England communicants. The Act of Uniformity, 1662, left no room for dissent from the doctrines and practices expressed in the Book of Common Prayer. Attempting to dissent from one part of the trinity of church, state and army would lead one to be barred from the other parts; e.g. a religious dissenter would be barred from public (civil or military) office. Over time, this discrimination diminished, and with it the Church of England's all-embracing aspirations. The (almost) Bloodless Revolution of 1688 and the Toleration Act that followed, the complexities of union with Presbyterian Scotland, and Roman Catholic emancipation in 1829 all reduced the legal reach and the claims of the Church of England, even if they left intact "the effortless superiority of the *beati possidentes*, those who occupy the high ground of English culture – or who used to".[5]

This Church of England, therefore, is the most unlikely institution in which to find war resistance and opposition to the military. The very presence of pacifists in the church was subversive, undermining the roots of the institution and challenging the entanglement of church and state. Dissenters can be expected to dissent, to refuse to conform, to be an awkward squad in more ways than one; but surely the role of members of the Church of England is to conform, to uphold the state and the status quo? For members of the Church of England to dare to resist war is to strike at the very heart of the English Establishment, to chip away at the complex binding of church and military which is at the core of the state. It is surprising to find a narrative of war resistance at the very heart of a church that is the most allied and aligned with the military organs of the state.

The parish system, whereby every person belongs within a Church of England parish and can call upon the parish church for particular occasional services, has reinforced most people's identification with the Church of England. For most of its existence, the Church of England has been "deeply implicated in the life of the English people",[6] or at least of the majority who have not taken a conscious and conscientious decision to opt out, or to dissent. For many, and for many even in a post-Christian multicultural and multifaith society, membership is still part of English identity. Some have described this as the identity of those who are religious but not necessarily Christian; those who think about God whilst refusing to be told what to think about God; or even those who don't really think much about God at all, but are content to know that others did. For centuries, "Church of England" or "C of E" was the default affiliation of anyone who had not made a deliberate choice to be otherwise.

The stories in this volume are about people with a variety of relationships to the Church of England. Some were indubitably part of the Establishment, for example a chaplain to the king. Some were immersed in Anglican faith, theology and practice, holding together both catholic and reformed traditions, fully conscious of their place within a wider Christendom. These people were Church of England to their core, being both naturally aligned with the things of Establishment and at the same time being fully at one with the Christian faith that they prayed and practised on a daily basis. In contrast, I tell of others who were, frankly, "C of E", English people who, through absorption and adoption, were Christian by aspiration and acceptance; who would not have argued with Hooker's claim but who would never have read his writings. To such people, membership of the Church of England was one of many aspects of their identity, but was not central to their self-understanding. In many ways, they were typically English.

These people, however, whether thoroughly Church of England or simply "C of E", had one thing in common: they were, perhaps against all the odds, opposed to war. At the very least, they were opposed to the war entered into by Britain in August 1914, and, in most cases, they were against all war. Theirs was not a typically English stance, and certainly not one expected of those within the established Church of England. It is precisely this incongruity, and the incomprehensibility to outsiders of the stance of Church of England pacifists, that makes that stand so important and so challenging.

Their stories are largely unknown, and are not the tales that many in the state or the church would wish to be celebrated; the individuals involved are not the kind of heroes or saints that the Establishment would revere. That is precisely why these stories have such significance. These peacemakers were subversive.

Background to Article Thirty-Seven

With the passing of the Act of Supremacy and related measures in 1534, the *ecclesia anglicana* ceased being the regional base of an international church with its headquarters in Rome. It became instead the English state's department for the religious well-being of its citizens. New definitions were needed to state, amid the turmoil of Reformation Europe, where the new Church of England stood and what its central tenets were on the great, divisive issues of the time. Such definitions were expressed in the form of articles of religion, most of which were concerned with asserting the independence of the new institution from Rome and effecting some of the reforms that had long been called for in the Roman Church. But if the Church of England was at pains to indicate that it was no longer Roman Catholic, it was also keen to indicate that there were limits to reform and that some of the ideas prevalent in mainland Europe were beyond what could be accepted. For example, the ideas of the pacifist Anabaptists were seen as threatening. Not only was re-baptism off the agenda, so too was any suggestion of pacifism. Any statement of the new church that indicated its limits of tolerance needed to make clear that not only was there rejection of papal authority, but also rejection of such pacifist movements as those associated with Conrad Grebel (c.1498-1526), Jacob Hutter (c.1500-1536) or Menno Simons (1496-1561).

In 1552, the Church of England produced its first articles. Of these, Article Thirty-Six, "De civilibus Magistratibus", read, *Christianis licet, ex mandato Magistratus, arma portare, et justa bella administrare*; "It is lawful for Christians, at the commandment of the Magistrate, to wear weapons and to serve in lawful wars". The purpose of the article was to assert the source and limits of power in the new order. In the magistrate's job description, this clause was the last of the issues considered, following the claim, *Leges civiles possunt Christianos propter capitalia et gravia crimina morte punier*; "The civil laws may punish Christian men with death, for heinous and grievous offences".[7] The articles were approved in Latin in 1562, and the text was further amended by a convocation called in 1571. Royal authority was given the same year to the English text, which was not intended to be dominant, but equally authoritative. Although a clause on capital punishment failed to survive later drafts of the articles, that on the serving in lawful wars remained, albeit subject to variation and interpretation. In 1615, Article Sixty-Two of the Articles of the Church of Ireland read, "It is lawful for Christian men, at the commandment of the Magistrate, to bear arms, and to serve in just wars". The form that found its way, as Article Thirty-Seven, into the Thirty-Nine Articles of the 1662 Book of Common Prayer read, "It is lawful for Christian men, at the commandment of the Magistrate, to wear weapons, and serve in the wars". Thus the Latin, *justa bella*, was translated in three different ways: "lawful wars" (1553); "just wars" (1615); and "the wars" (1662). The text, commented on in 1607 by Thomas Rogers (d.1616), chaplain to Archbishop Bancroft, referred to "the wars". Rogers seemed to struggle to justify the item, only managing to cite Ecclesiastes 3.8, "a time for war", and Luke 3.14 and Acts 10 where soldiers were not rebuked for their profession, a double negative that is not particularly persuasive, to suggest that war was permissible. By way of contrast he was able to cite contrary views at length, including those of Lactantius, the early Christian author, Vives, the Spanish humanist and the general stance of Anabaptists and Familists.[8]

The precise meaning of *justa bella* was open to debate. It could be argued that the word *justus* carried no moral associations and applied simply to the declaration of war by the legal authorities; this argument pointed to the definite article in the phrase "the wars" as indicating war involving the government. From this point of view, it was lawful to serve in any war the state waged, whether or not that war was "just". However, that approach would make the use of the word *justa* superfluous, merely repeating what had been noted earlier in the article. More significantly, it ignored twelve centuries of discourse behind the phrase *bellum justum*, in which moral factors were highly significant.[9] The word *justa* was not to be ignored, or passed over as if it was not there.

The interpretation of the phrase *bellum justum* historically belonged more to the sphere of moral theology than to jurisprudence. A late-seventeenth century commentary on Article Thirty-Seven by Bishop Beveridge limited its application to "lawful war"; i.e. "nothing less but the just defence of the Magistrate's person, kingdom and prerogatives".[10] A war could not be deemed "just" merely by virtue of being called so by a government; the cause and conduct of the conflict had to be considered as well.

The second feature of Article Thirty-Seven of significance to future pacifists was the opening word *licet*, "it is lawful". Some of the other articles were forceful in expressing the duty of Christians, for example *obiendum est* – "we must obey" the civil magistrate, and *debet* – every person "ought" to give liberally to the poor. This firm tone was not evident in Article Thirty-Seven, which rather reflected the usage of *liceat* in Article Thirty-Nine – a person "may" swear, and in Article Thirty-Two, "it is lawful" for clergy to marry. Thus the wearing of weapons and the serving in (just) wars was deemed "lawful", but it was not at all suggested that it was a Christian duty. Indeed, the fact that it needed stating at all indicates a realisation that many would have assumed the contrary. It could almost be seen as the exception that proved the rule, namely that a normative Christian attitude would have been pacifist and that exceptional permission has had to be given to those who might be asked by magistrates to serve in a "just" war.

Not all future generations of Anglican pacifists were discouraged by Article Thirty-Seven. In the ordinal, clergy were required only to give general assent to the articles, not detailed assent, and in any case they themselves would not be eligible to bear arms.[11] No Anglican was under any doctrinal obligation to bear arms and serve in "the wars", and even for those who would, such service would only be lawful insofar as "the wars" were *bella justa,* with all the conditions and caveats that implied.

Article Thirty-Seven was hardly a statement of Christian pacifism; indeed it was designed to counter the same. A superficial reading of it was often used as a stick with which to beat later Anglican pacifists, particularly conscientious objectors in 1916-1918, but a deeper reading shows that it tolerated the position of Anglican pacifists and, at best, could be seen to make the pacifist position the norm from which non-pacifists would have to depart. Paul Gliddon, a conscientious objector in the First World War, summed it up as "an extraordinarily unenthusiastic way of summoning us to the colours . . . paralleled by the lukewarm assent parents sometimes give to the marriage of their daughters, 'If she wants to marry him, we won't stop her' ".[12]

The Roots of the Peace Movement

Foundations

Opposition to war in western culture has a long history, and can be traced back to classical and biblical times, both New Testament and Old. There is a strong undercurrent of nonviolence in Patristic writings in the first four centuries of the Christian era. This was summed up by the dictum of Martin of Tours (316-397), "I am the soldier of Christ: it is not lawful for me to fight".[13] Stories of opposition to war are found throughout the Middle Ages; from groups deemed heretical (Bogomils and Cathars), church reformers (Francis of Assisi, b. c.1181), and pioneers of the Reformation (Pierre Valdès, d.c.1206; John Wyclif, c.1330-1384; Jan Hus, burnt at the stake at Constance in 1415; Petr Chelčický, c.1390-c.1460).

A lasting consequence of the social, spiritual and political turbulence of the seventeenth century in England was the formation of the Religious Society of Friends ("Quakers"), with its developing tradition of non-aggression. Even the Church of England had its outspoken voices for peace, the most eloquent being that of the mystic William Law, whose 1761 letter, *An Humble, Earnest and Affectionate address to the Clergy,* was one of the most powerful condemnations of war in the eighteenth century.[14] Law hoped that his letter would inspire the generations of the clergy who would come after him. Its impact was far-reaching: reprints were published by John Wesley and, with England at war with both France and Spain, the anti-war sections were reprinted by the dissenter Benjamin Flower of Cambridge in 1796 (and again in 1799) .[15] Law wrote that, in the context of nonviolence, as with all else, there was to be no distinction between individual and corporate behaviour: "Look at that which the private Christian is to do to his Neighbour, or his Enemy, and you see that very thing, which one Christian Kingdom is to do to another".[16]

Thomas Clarkson and the Early Peace Society

By the end of the eighteenth century, one in six adult Englishmen were involved in the wars of the French Revolution and the Napoleonic Wars, conflicts with France and her allies that lasted for most of the period up to 1815.[17]

Even in the midst of this atmosphere of social tension, voices of dissent could be heard. Vicesimus Knox (1752-1821), Master of Tonbridge School, translated and reprinted works of Erasmus on peace. Annual fast days, instituted to encourage preaching and prayer on the wars, led some to question their validity. In a 1795 fast-day sermon, John H. Williams (c.1747-1829), Vicar of Wellsbourne, Warwickshire, denounced the concept of "a MILITARY CHRIST" in *War, the Stumbling-block of a Christian; OR, The Absurdity of Defending Religion by the Sword*.[18]

Knox and Williams did not, however, rule out defensive war, unlike J. Scott of Islington (1757-1832), whose 1796 tract, *War Inconsistent with the Doctrine and Example of Jesus Christ*, was historically significant for its title as much as its content.[19] Scott's proposition was simply "That War in every shape, is incompatible with the nature of christianity; and that no persons professing that religion, and under the full and proper influence of the temper and mind of Christ, can adopt, pursue, or plead for it".[20]

Amongst other anti-war sermon preachers and tract writers, the most influential figure to emerge in this era was Thomas Clarkson (1760-1846), a non-practising deacon of Playford Hall, Suffolk. He was publicly known, on both sides of the Channel,[21] for his leadership in the campaign against slavery, and was instrumental in the formation of the Society for Effecting the Abolition of the Slave Trade. This brought him into close contact not only with William Wilberforce (1759-1833)[22] but also, more significantly in this context, with a number of Quakers. In 1806 he published a study on the Quakers and their beliefs, including a sympathetic critique of the Quaker peace testimony, followed by a survey of Patristic pacifism, *An essay on the doctrines and practice of the early Christians, as they relate to war*. His own description of war was "bloodshed *not unawares*, which is the scriptural definition of murder" and he asked "how can his kingdom ever come, while wars are tolerated"?[23] Clarkson's experience of single-issue campaigning against slavery led him and others to consider launching a campaigning society for peace.

One of those influenced by Clarkson's work on the Church Fathers was David Low Dodge (1774-1852), an opponent of the slave trade in the United States. He cited Clarkson in his 1812 volume, *War Inconsistent with the Religion of Jesus Christ*. Three years later, Dodge became the founder of the New York Peace Society. At last, learning lessons from campaigners against the slave trade on both sides of the Atlantic, those who would resist war would discover the benefits of co-ordination and organisation. The modern peace movement was born. With the end of the war in Europe, the pacifist and cross-denominational Society for the Promotion of Permanent and Universal Peace (the "Peace Society") was formed in London in 1816, a year after Dodge's organisation in the United States. Membership of the Peace Society was open to persons of every denomination (which factor alone would have been challenging for many in the Church of England) "who are desirous of uniting in the promotion of Peace on earth, and good-will towards men". The object of the society was to produce and distribute tracts and other information showing that "War is inconsistent with the spirit of Christianity, and the true interests of mankind; and to point out the means best calculated to maintain a permanent and universal Peace, upon the basis of Christian principles".[24] Their first publications included reprints of works by Vicesimus Knox, J. Scott and Thomas Clarkson. Another early publication was a pacifist tract by Thomas Clarkson's brother, John (1764-1828), *The Substance of a Letter, addressed to a Clergyman of the Established Church, on the Subject of War*. In the first ten years of the Society's existence, membership rose to a peak of slightly under fifteen hundred.[25]

There were various branches of the Peace Society ("auxiliaries") around the country, including, by 1823, women's groups in Lymington, Leeds and Guisborough.[26] On occasion the auxiliaries were more radical and active in campaigning than the centre. The Huddersfield auxiliary was the first to hold public meetings, starting in 1826. One chair of the London committee of the Peace Society, John Lee (1783-1866), spoke in 1840 of a petition to change Article Thirty-Seven, and urged other Anglicans to join the society.[27]

From 1846, the peace movement in Britain gathered momentum, staging revolts against a proposed reintroduction of the militia and the revoking of the Corn Laws. There was an increased confidence that public campaigns could change Government policy. An invasion scare and the presence in Britain of the American Congregationalist, Elihu Burritt (1810-1879) added to public concern and awareness. In its first year alone, Burritt's League of Universal Brotherhood achieved around 6,000 signatories to its pacifist pledge, or 10,000 when both sides of the Atlantic were taken into account. Burritt also established Olive Leaf Circles, to enable genteel women to discuss peace issues, correspond with similar groups across Britain and other countries, and write pacific stories for children. He reported that such societies included a number of socially well-connected Anglican women.[28]

Burritt was also responsible for promoting an international peace congress in Brussels in 1848. 130 people travelled across the Channel from Britain to attend. The success of the venture was hailed by Burritt, who called it "the inauguration of the 'Peace Movement' ", a decisive turn towards international co-operation and negotiation upon which hopes for peace would be built for the next 65 years. Soon, the

Manchester industrialist and parliamentarian Richard Cobden (1804-1865), described as the "Champion of Peace", risked his political prestige, hard-won from a successful anti-Corn Law campaign, to become the movement's de facto figurehead and spokesman. The period 1846-1851 was to be a high point for British peace campaigning, with a momentum not seen again for 80 years, when Dick Sheppard (1880-1937) revisited Burritt's concept of peace pledge. There were key parliamentary debates on disarmament in both 1849 and 1851, and a series of international peace congresses in Paris (1849), Frankfurt (1850) and London (1851).[29]

Richard Cobden

A consistent advocate of adult (male) suffrage and Corn Law repeal, Richard Cobden's primary motivation for campaigning for peace was to ensure stable conditions for free trade. At the same time, he argued that free trade produced the mutual dependence between nations that itself promoted peace. In 1835 and 1836 he suggested that Britain should cease from all political intervention in international affairs, so that free trade could become the sole means by which nations would work for peace. Of war, he asked,

> How shall a profession which withdraws from productive industry the ablest of the human race, and teaches them systematically the best modes of destroying mankind, which awards honours only in proportion to the number of victims offered at its sanguinary altar, which overturns cities, ravages farms and vineyards, uproots forests, burns the ripened harvest, which, in a word, exists but in the absence of law, order, and security – how can such a profession be favourable to commerce, which increases only with the increase of human life, whose parent is agriculture, and which perishes or flies at the approach of lawless rapine?[30]

At a protest against the First Anglo-Afghan War (1839-1842), held at the 1842 re-launch of the Manchester auxiliary of the Peace Society, much was made of war's negative effect on trade. Cobden was convinced that peace was a necessary pre-condition for any sustained increase in commerce.

Following the 1848 peace congress, Cobden committed himself more completely to the cause of peace. Having a petition of 200,000 signatures in support, he proposed, unsuccessfully, a parliamentary motion on disarmament and arbitration. He so immersed himself in subsequent peace congresses and Parliamentary campaigning, including a second disarmament debate in 1851, that the term "Cobdenism" entered the language in 1852/3.[31]

Despite tensions with France, the next British imperial war was with

Russia in the Crimea in 1854. Cobden's Quaker Parliamentary ally, John Bright, spoke movingly of "the Angel of Death" being abroad. Peace Society campaigning took place across the country; in Leeds, 300 people stood in the yard outside the packed hall where Cobden was speaking, unable to get in.[32]

The conclusion of the war was marked by the 1856 Treaty of Paris. Protocol 23 of the treaty recommended that all future international disputes should be settled by mediation. The prospects of being able to work through legal channels for peace clearly resonated with many Anglicans. It was claimed soon afterwards that there were "more clergymen of the Church of England who sympathized with peace principles" than Dissenters.[33] The movement towards seeking international agreements was strengthened with the 1864 adoption of the Geneva Convention on the conduct of war.

The Late Nineteenth Century

At the same time as the parliamentary electoral franchise widened,[34] the Peace Society found it was no longer the sole channel for expression of anti-war sentiment. In the aftermath of the Franco-Prussian war of 1870, a Workman's Peace Association – later the International Arbitration League – was formed by W. Randal Cremer, a Liberal MP.[35] Both working class and middle class campaigners agreed that there was a need for a High Court of Nations for the resolution of international disputes. Cremer's organisation mocked the archbishops for their uncritical support of British imperial military actions in North Africa. "The Mahdi and the Archbishop are both supplicating the same deity for success, and both alike are violating reason and religion".[36]

Realising that for some "arbitration" was a less loaded word than "peace", the Peace Society formed local International Arbitration Associations in the latter half of the nineteenth century. The move seemed to work; both William Thomson, Archbishop of York and the Dean of Ripon consented to be patrons of the first association, for Yorkshire, founded in Leeds in 1872.[37]

Independent of the Peace Society, an International Arbitration and Peace Association for Great Britain and Ireland was founded in 1880 and drew a number of prominent Anglicans into membership, including Canon Henry Scott Holland (1847-1918), John Percival, Bishop of Hereford (1834-1918),[38] and Brooke Foss Westcott (1825-1901), who were all active in preaching international peace. Percival, one of the more prominent and consistent episcopal figures in peace circles, became a vice-president of the Peace Society in 1895,[39] and spoke at the 1896 Church Congress, decrying jingoism as "bastard patriotism".[40] He also addressed those assembled for the 1899 Hague Conference. Westcott's initiatives led to various ecclesiastical bodies passing resolutions in support of arbitration,[41] and the *Arbitrator* (International Arbitration League) spoke warmly of "the anti-war movement which has been lately started by some leading Anglicans and other divines".[42] Westcott wrote to the outstanding Austrian author of *Die Waffen Nieder!* (*Lay Down Your Arms!*), Bertha von Suttner, looking forward to the time when "natural works of peace will be found able to furnish nations with the invigorating discipline, wrought through self-sacrifice, which is now supplied by the preparation for war".[43] As Bishop of Durham, Westcott was a reconciling figure in industrial disputes but not such a fervent advocate of arbitration as had been hoped; in 1894 he only agreed to sign a petition on arbitration "on the understanding that the Government does not think it inopportune".[44] To the disappointment of many, Westcott supported the Boer War, with the sole concession being that he did insist on prayers for both sides.[45]

In 1889, the movement to develop international structures to prevent war was gathering momentum. That year, not only was the Inter-Parliamentary Union formed, but also a Universal Peace Congress was held in Paris, the first of what became an almost annual tradition of peace congresses previously seen in the middle of the century. The second Universal Peace Congress was held in London in 1890, when one of the joint secretaries was Joseph Frederick Green (1855-1932), an Anglican priest who had left his clerical ministry to become Secretary of the International Arbitration and Peace Association.[46]

The Peace Society instituted the fourth Sunday in Advent as an annual "Peace Sunday", to promote peace preaching in churches across the land. Take-up was slower among Anglicans than members of the free churches, but among the most powerful preachers was Canon William Benham (1830/31-1910), who was to become an active vice-president of the Peace Society and who argued that a Europe with eight million men under arms could not be considered truly Christian.[47] Septimus Buss preached in Shoreditch on his vision of weapons being consigned to museums.[48] Despite many episcopal reservations, by 1896 Peace Sunday was marked by 277 Anglican clergy across eight dioceses.[49]

The bishops, however, possibly influenced by Westcott, were slowly becoming more tolerant of moves toward international war-prevention. The July 1897 Lambeth Conference caught something of the contemporary mood.[50] It was in favour of finding a method of international arbitration to resolve disputes that might otherwise lead to war. In their encyclical, the 9 archbishops and 185 bishops claimed, in somewhat patronising tone, that "Arbitration leaves behind it a generous sense of passions restrained and justice sought for".[51] Hence they resolved to welcome more enlightened public conscience with regard to arbitration.[52]

Pro-Boer or Anti-War?

Implicit in much early thinking about arbitration was an expectation that that model of resolving conflict would be applied to disputes within Europe, to build closer relations between European states. It was not anticipated that it would be needed for disputes between those states and their colonies, nor to settle competing claims for such colonies. William Moore Ede, Rector of Gateshead, flagged up the danger ahead when, mindful of the debacle of the Jameson Raid in South Africa, he proposed a resolution at the 1897 annual meeting of the Peace Society in Newcastle, condemning "the annexation of territory" as being the "cause of cruel and unnecessary wars . . . frequently associated with injustice to the rightful proprietors of the soil".[53]

Simmering disputes in South Africa came to a head at the end of 1899, with the outbreak of war between British and Dutch settlers. There had been attempts to dissuade the British Government from military action. Several bishops in the Province of South Africa had made it known that they were worried about the suffering that would result from an internal war in that country. Archbishop West Jones of Cape Town lobbied the high commissioner in an attempt to achieve a negotiated settlement. In Britain, a national memorial against the threatened war was signed by four prominent Anglican clergymen. 200 anti-war resolutions were delivered to the Colonial Office in the lead up to the war, most from Nonconformist sources.[54] Bishop Percival also wrote to the Prime Minister, Lord Salisbury, urging that, "In the published dispatches & the known facts of the case we can see nothing that wd justify us in going to war, or wd make a war anything but a hideous blunder and a crime."[55]

Percival's arguments were not heeded, and the Government embarked upon a war. In its popularity and in its sidelining of opposition, it indicated a foretaste of what was to come in 1914. A long-standing opponent of British imperial policy, Wilfrid Lawson, bemoaned in Parliament the fact that the war marked a turning away from the Prince of Peace towards "the heathen Deity Mars", a sign that Christianity was losing its influence on the people of Britain.[56] The Church of England, in particular, lost its attraction for some young people as a result of its militancy: the teenage Harry Hodgson, later to serve two years in prison as a First World War conscientious objector, left the church over its stance on the war in South Africa.[57]

Members of the establishment pulled together in support of the war. One commentator remarked that "Critics of the war were a tiny, unpopular minority of the Anglican clergy in England", and an even smaller one in South Africa, with another describing Anglican protest as an "aberration".[58] A number of children of Anglican clergymen did oppose the war, from John Xavier Merriman, Treasurer General of the Cape, who travelled to London in an attempt to dissuade the Government from military action, to the Irish historian Alice Stopforth Green. Emily Hobhouse (1860-1926) was Secretary of the South Africa Conciliation Committee, a group founded by Catherine (1847-1929) and Leonard Courtney (1832-1918) to press for a negotiated settlement to the conflict. The Dean of Winchester, William Stephens, who noted how "the boastful confidence not unmingled with the spirit of revenge" with which the troops embarked "met with due chastisement" in early defeats, was a member of the Conciliation Committee.[59] Stephens regarded the Jameson Raid which led to the war as "a crime and a blunder", and felt that pre-war negotiations should have been conducted "with the utmost patience and forebearance", instead of in the arrogant tone that led to their breakdown.[60] The vehemence of the patriotic protests that these comments provoked, exacerbated by public reaction to the high-profile, anti-war stance of his predecessor, shook Stephens, who had quickly to apologise and backtrack publicly. Only one anonymous "Hampshire Rector" dared to suggests that those who wielded such hateful epithets as " 'pro-Boer', 'unpatriotic', 'treacherous' &c". were themselves being "unloving, unchristian, un-English".[61] Within a year, even rumours that he was opposed to war were enough for a local Primitive Methodist preacher to get his windows smashed.[62]

Any opponent of the war, for whatever political, moral or religious reason, was given the traitorous moniker, "Pro-Boer", a term that encompassed a range of anti-war opinions and motivations. Some argued that the war was the consequence of the wrong kind of imperialism, driven by lust for power and possessions rather than by any desire for human progress. Certain opponents of the war considered that it was driven solely by the demands of capitalist exploitation, hence Keir Hardie's response to the Anglican support for the war, that "Nowhere is Mammon more firmly seated than in the church".[63] An outspoken Baptist minister, John Clifford, complained, with disgust, "John Bull will annex . . . and the churches will bless his theft!"[64] Hardie, with Lloyd George and more politically-minded Nonconformists, came together in a Stop the War Committee, which distributed millions of somewhat moralistic pamphlets at the time of the 1900 "khaki election", demanding an immediate end to the war. Clifford, President of the National Council of (Evangelical) Free Churches (N.C.F.C.), was Stop the War President and prominent in the South Africa Conciliation Committee. Opponents of the war did try to find expression through the N.C.F.C., but theirs was a minority voice even in that forum, and once the war commenced it dwindled further. One observer commented, "It was in 1899 that the nonconformist conscience came to grief".[65]

At the end of 1900, on New Year's Eve, Canon William Barker of Marylebone addressed five hundred people in Acton, calling the recourse to force, "a reversion to savagery and barbarism".[66] Barker was to become a regular figure on peace platforms in the months ahead.

In September 1901, at a meeting called by the Quakers in Glasgow, Barker reported that he had never met a Christian who could say that war was sanctioned either by the teaching or the example of Christ. The saying "They that take the sword shall perish by the sword" was proven by the downfall of the empires of Babylon, Assyria, Greece and Rome, and these events were a warning for the British people to "think twice before they launched thoughtlessly into another war".[67] On the following Peace Sunday, he claimed that, "The man who was at peace with himself and at peace with God was a strong man, a valuable man, a hero", whereas the untempered were the ones who caused wars. "If a peaceful temper and a humble and gentle and manly desire for Peace were to be manifested", said Barker, "Peace would ensue".[68] Others who opposed the war included Canon William Benham and William Henry Fremantle, Dean of Ripon, who, with Charles W. Stubbs, Dean of Ely, preached in The Hague at the time of the Peace Conference of 1899,[69] principally objecting to the Boer War because it had not been offered for arbitration.[70] Fremantle was frustrated that the success of The Hague conference had been so quickly eclipsed by the development of militarism in society. He moved a Peace Society resolution deploring "the existence of the present unhappy war in South Africa". Prebendary H.W. Webb-Peploe told the Peace Society that it was the duty of the church militant to seek peace and pursue it.[71] The episode was a painful reminder to the Peace Society that they were much further from influencing public affairs than they had sometimes liked to hope.

Canon Edward Lee Hicks (1843-1919), Rector of St Philip's, Salford, who was dubbed "Pro-Boer", told the Manchester Women's Peace Association that he was "prepared to question" the view that war was a necessary condition of civilisation.[72] His anti-war sermon in Manchester Cathedral in January 1900 was published by the Manchester Transvaal Peace Committee under the title, *The Mistakes of Militarism*.[73] Late in the war, Hicks told the Oldham Peace Society that "people were beginning to doubt the expediency" of the conflict, and if they had known the cost at the beginning they might have tried harder to avoid it.[74]

George William Kitchin (1827-1912), Dean of Durham, had been Stephens's predecessor as Dean of Winchester. In both roles he gained a reputation as an opponent of the war. Writing to the *Hampshire Chronicle*, supporting his successor's short-lived stand against the war, he asked readers what they understood by "Love your enemies". "For centuries", he said, "the Church met the hostility of a pagan and unscrupulous world and never flinched. . . . It was not till later on, when dross had mixed in, that the Church took to bad and aggressive ways". Kitchin's attention was fixed on the enthusiastic lies of those who would make war.

With what spirit do we send out our fighting men? The drunken revels which form the music hall ideals of good fellowship – the excitement of the gin palace and the London streets ... the cries to the poor lads to avenge this or that; the greedy newspapers spreading unfounded slanders against our opponents, the insistence by which prejudice and angry ignorance have persuaded us that the enemy was but a horde of savages, who would run away at once. The whole temper of our times is so utterly anti-Christian that it appals me, when from the quietude of this home I look out upon it all, and note the intolerance with which men hate opinions opposed to the momentary enthusiasm. We know that these noisy people who let no voice but theirs be heard on platform, in pulpit, in the newspaper and will never themselves bear the brunt and pains of it, are far from being the sane mind of our English people.[75]

Kitchin was duly denounced as an unpatriotic pro-Boer by a judge from the bench.[76] His anti-war reputation was cemented further in May 1900. In a Sunday sermon he rebuked the drunken celebrations of the people of Durham after receiving the news of the Relief of Mafeking. His rebuke was primarily related to the drunkenness and its manifestation on that particular day of the week, but many took it as proof of his opposition to the war.[77] Kitchin told the Darlington Peace Association that the way the pulpits of the land had gone in favour of the war was a blasphemy, and that the people of Britain would pay for what the satirist Horace had called the "follies and madnesses the rulers of your people are guilty of".[78] The National Peace Council later described Kitchin, at that time the President of the Tyneside branch of the International Arbitration and Peace Association, as "A Liberal who speaks his mind boldly and has no fear of temporary unpopularity".[79] Kitchin, together with Canon Samuel Augustus Barnett (1844-1913), the warden of Toynbee Hall, were amongst a group of "influential and well-known leaders of thought" who signed a statement claiming there was "a special duty laid on those who disapprove of the war to express their disapproval . . . "[80]

Barnett was described by Scott Holland as having "something of the Quakers' craving for the soul's rest in secret peace".[81] He certainly possessed their desire for peace and justice, and was probably the most outspoken of all senior Anglican clergy. Toynbee Hall was one of several university settlements set up in the nineteenth century to enable Oxford and Cambridge graduates to undertake charitable work in areas of poverty in East London.[82] Local socialists like George Lansbury (1859-1940), were unsympathetic to the scheme, believing that the settlements did more for educated upper classes than they did for the poor.[83] Even accepting Lansbury's criticism, the settlement experience often meant that the decision-makers of the future were more sympathetic to and more easily able to communicate with those in need. Dick Sheppard was a prime example. However, in the paternalistic days of 1899, it was left to educated liberals to speak for the masses in such middle class gatherings as the annual meeting of the Peace Society which, unusually, that year included a substantial Anglican presence. William Benham, from the chair, described Christ's methods of conquering as "Not by the sword, not by fighting, but by love, by Calvary, by self-sacrifice . . . and by teaching".[84] In a speech that brought together many strands of the meaning of peace, Samuel Barnett admitted to being an unwilling spokesman for the people among whom he worked. "Would that I could claim to be the voice of East London", he said, "Would that I could claim to interpret the minds of those thousands and thousands of people who live a somewhat mysterious life east of the Bank. They have a mind, but they have not a voice to express it . . . " In this powerful and prophetic address, Barnett commended Tsar Nicholas II for calling a Universal Peace Conference at The Hague, and linked military spending with the deprivation, squalor and the brutal attitudes found in the East End of London. He had a vision of the wholeness of peace and he connected international violence with the domestic and community violence that he saw on a daily basis. There was an economic dimension to his philosophy, as he saw the people of East London impoverished and without amenities. Yet the resources to help them were withheld. Why was that, he asked?

> There is no principle involved in not providing them with the means of a healthy and happy life. Why is it withheld? The expenditure, we are told, is too great. . . . The taxes could not endure it; but the taxes are used in keeping up the war instruments. Well, sires, the money that is being spent yearly in the instruments of death might be spent in keeping thousands and thousands of children alive, and in making more healthy and strong the men and women who are alive. . . . It is, therefore, sir, on the part of these people who starve and die that I protest against this great expenditure on war material, and claim that a far wiser expenditure would be in making the conditions such that the children should grow up to be men and women, and that when they do grow up they shall be healthy in body, happy in mind, home lovers, real patriots; fond of England, for England's care of them.

Barnett's most shrewd observations concerned human behaviour. He spoke of how the spirit of war in society led the rich and strong to develop excessive "masterfulness". Landlords and employers would become more contemptuous of the poor, less charitable, and demand greater subservience as a result. Barnett spoke too of his poorer neighbours in East London who were "brutalised" by national belligerency, who enjoyed tales of horror, whose "conduct is often coarse and their manners are rough". These people could be extremely cruel and were prone to thinking that force could right wrongs.

> These people then are "brutalised", and war, as I understand it, has always thrown a sort of halo over a character, and war has enabled people to be brutal by making them believe that they are heroes. The consequence is that whenever there is a talk about war, and when men are worshipping the heroes of war, and when they are thinking about what war is going to do, they themselves are more easily inclined to brutal pleasures, and are themselves more proud of being brutal.

In other words, implied Barnett, even the threat of violence abroad can breed violence at home.

> In the name, therefore, of the people, of my neighbours, who are capable of being tender, who are capable of being considerate for the weak, who are capable of the highest pleasures of thought and feeling, who are capable, at any rate, of following the Prince of Peace, and of admiring Him, I protest against this light talk about war, which allow them to live a more degraded life than they ever meant to live.[85]

Barnett continued to be an outspoken critic of war after his appointment as a Canon of Bristol. Was the spirit that drove England to war the Christian spirit, he asked? Christians had been misled before:

> The spirits, for example, which roused Christians in the name of Christ to persecute the Jews, or Royalists to force their neighbours to own the divine right of Kings, or Englishmen to break the independence and compel the loyalty of Colonists.
>
> Is, then, the present war directed by the Christian spirit? When many Christian leaders and teachers – learned and highly reverenced – approve the war, Christians who think differently are bound to examine their grounds and modestly offer the result for others' consideration.

Barnett argued that belief in Christ as the Son of the Almighty must mean that "His way of meekness or forebearance is above the way of self-assertion and force". He held that Christians "are to see something worthy of respect in every human being, because they see in every one the likeness of Christ". Barnett argued that,"If the English people who are now approving the war were meek and charitable . . . it would be more possible to believe that a Christian spirit directs the present war. But the people are not so, and the war is their war, and the war is not Christian. Statesmen might have blundered in their diplomacy", said

Barnett, and "conspirators might have conspired and set race against race, capitalists might have corrupted the Press; but, if the people had been Christian, there would have been no war". The fault for the war, therefore, was with Christian teachers, "who, being commissioned to teach the unity of power and love, have let the minds of the people worship the power without love".[86]

The unity of power and love was far from the minds of those who ran Britain's vicious concentration camps in South Africa. Following revelations by Emily Hobhouse, Percival was shocked to discover that nearly 2,000 children had died in the brutal British-run camps. He was appalled by such a "holocaust of child life".[87] Canon Charles Gore (1853-1932), about to become Bishop of Worcester, wrote angrily to the *Times* in October 1901 to denounce concentration camp policy.

In 1904, Percival, along with W. Boyd Carpenter, Bishop of Ripon,[88] attended the Thirteenth Universal Peace Congress in Boston, U.S.A.. Percival, doubtless reflecting on the South African War, criticised Christian nations for "squandering their wealth and their manhood on armies and navies". He told the Congress, "We have to learn to feel that the jingo spirit which swaggers in its pride and delights in warfare and aggression is in the main a survival of those brutal instincts that should be eliminated from every civilised and Christian life".[89] He spoke during the "scramble for Africa", a period of European imperial expansion in the continent. When the land-grab of overseas territories was exhausted, the next bloody scramble would be over Europe itself.

The End of the Beginning

Although the story of the organised peace movement in Britain and the United States is post-Napoleonic, the history of western war resistance can be traced further back to ancient, classical and biblical times. The beliefs and attitudes of those who would be caught up in opposition to the First World War were not idiosyncratic, outrageous, or unheard of, but rooted in a tradition that dates from the beginning of the Christian story. When society is caught up in the nationalistic fervour of war, the lone voice upholding the ancient rule, "You shall not follow a majority in wrongdoing", is very vulnerable.[90] The story of war resistance so far indicates the existence of an extended historical community within which subsequent opponents of mass violence could find solidarity and solace. Echoes of the voices raised against war can be heard through the ages: the voices of 1914-1918 are but one part of this narrative. It is to their more immediate context of Edwardian England that we now turn.

2.
An Era Ends and a New Pacifism Emerges

An Etymological Digression

At the Tenth Universal Peace Congress in Glasgow in 1901, the French President of the International League of Peace and Liberty, Emile Arnaud, coined the term "pacifiste".[1] The more etymologically accurate term for peace-makers, "pacificist" was the word favoured by some Britons. The two terms, however, did not have separate meanings and they were often used interchangeably. The more dominant word was "pacifist", used, for example, in *Concord* in April 1905 with a familiarity that implied it was already common parlance in peace circles.[2] Together, over time, the two words underwent changes of meaning. Arnaud's use, which remained the commonest use of the word until 1914, described an anti-militarist working to create or perpetuate peace. Thus, the *Arbitrator*, noted that "A pacifist is not necessarily a non-resistant, but the name rightly belongs to every man who is against any unjust war, and who holds that international disputes should be settled by the arbitrament of reason rather than by that of the sword".[3] At the outbreak of war in 1914, the meanings changed. When so many of those internationalists who had previously wanted to perpetuate peace came, instead, to justify war, "pacifist" (and, more rarely, "pacificist") soon came exclusively to mean those who refused to take part in any war. After this period, whenever "pacificist" was used, it was for the purpose of etymological correctness, not to indicate any distinct earlier meaning. Dick Sheppard, who became a pacifist after the period of this study, still used both words interchangeably in 1935 and 1936.[4]

Whether in the pre-war usage, or in the more common usage of total war-refusal, the meanings of "pacifist" and "pacificist" were always the same, at any one time. In recent years Taylor, Ceadel *et al.* have described liberal internationalists, anti-militarists and those who speak peace enthusiastically when there is peace but less so when there is war as "pacificists". That may reclaim the word's original meaning, but for the first time makes it distinct from the contemporary meaning of "pacifist".[5] It is appropriate to have distinct words for distinct groups of people, but the historic interchangeability of "pacifist" and "pacificist" can at times lead to a lack of clarity, especially when related to the period I am here considering. I will use "pacifist" exclusively to indicate total war resistance, even during times of war.

Where Does Responsibility Lie?

In amongst the news and the noise of the latter stages of the Boer War the Curate of St Luke Camberwell found space for some original thinking. Arthur J. Waldron delivered a lecture on the ethics of war at the Earl's Court Military Exhibition in May 1901. In an address crowded with references to the anti-war writings of Carlyle, Tennyson and Longfellow, Waldron asked rhetorically whether a soldier could sit light to his conscience.

You may remember Hosea Biglow's saying:

> "Ef you take a sword and dror it,
>   An' go stick a feller thru',
> Guv'ment ain't to answer for it,
>   God'll send the bill to you."[6]

Personally, I believe that the ethics of the question ought to be applied to the individual soldier. I know what will be said – that it is impossible to allow the soldier the right to the exercise of his individual conscience; that whatever the Government decides the soldier is bound to do. If the Government makes war, the soldier is not to ask any question; and if the Government murders, the soldier is to be exonerated. Personally, I hurl that from me. I believe – and, I think, the feeling is growing in this country – that no Government in the world, no tribunal in the world, can answer for the individual conscience, that every man is responsible, to himself if not to some higher power, for the right of the faculties which he possesses. . . . I know the argument adduced is, that, if he did, he would leave the Army. Then so much the worse for the system. It is condemned on the face of it. . . .

But the question is: Is the soldier responsible for the acts of the Government? I hold that no man has any right, by any system, legalised or not, to hand over his personal responsibility to any Government, or to any other power. And therefore, he, the man, intelligent and moral, should be allowed to be the judge of what is right for him to do in any war. . . .[7]

As with so many other Anglicans at that time, Waldron himself believed in the theoretical acceptability of some defensive war.

However his assertion that each individual was a responsible being, and that ethical issues concerning war were not confined to the morality of arbitration and other matters of international politics, was unusual for an Anglican. According to Waldron, opponents of war must do more than complain about the government that engaged in a war; they themselves must refuse to participate in it. This would prove to be a step too far for many proponents of internationalism, and would become the defining issue for pacifism in 1914-1918.

Waldron's scenario would be prophetic, but it was not in tune with the spirit of his own age and quickly disappeared. After all, the principal hopes for peace were concentrated on progress in matters and structures of international law. With the main peace societies emphasising arbitration, and preferring to seek the support of the Anglican establishment than engage in controversy, there was no requirement to consider a strict pacifism. Few saw any reason for engaging with the alternative and absolute approach of, say, the Russian novelist Leo Tolstoy (1828-1910).

In the second half of his life, Tolstoy undertook a spiritual journey which brought him into contact with various pacifist groups, including Quakers, Shakers, Mennonites and the New England Non-Resistance Society of William Lloyd Garrison. He became particularly close to such indigenous Russian pacifist sects as the Doukhobors and Molokans. He supported their imprisoned conscientious objectors and used royalties from his novel *Resurrection* to finance a mass emigration of Doukhobors to Canada in 1898-9.

Tolstoy argued that mainstream religion was one of the principal causes of war when its ideologies legitimised national self-defence. The emphasis of his approach to the Sermon on the Mount was on unconditional obedience to "Do not resist evil". Absolute love of enemies, he said, regardless of any subsequent suffering, was essential, for individuals and for nations. Many of his ideas were summed up in his 1893 book, *The Kingdom of God is Within You*.

For all his literary fame, however, his spiritual and ethical writing had little direct influence on the British peace movement in the early twentieth century, which gave minimal consideration to the concepts of individual or collective non-resistance.[8] If international agreement and arbitration were going to prevent wars occurring, there was little need for individuals to think through their own attitudes in response to war. Nearly all the most prominent Anglicans involved with the Peace Society would have held open the possibility of a legitimate war, approaching issues of war and peace with an attitude akin to that of supporters of the "just" war concept who demanded such meticulous adherence to its conditions that few, if any, wars could be deemed acceptable.

The Logic of Internationalism

Edwardian hopes for improvements in international relations continued to build on an increasingly heady legacy of fin de siècle internationalism. Except for several brief interludes, the largest of which occurred between 1914 and 1921, Universal Peace Congresses were held annually from 1889 until 1939.[9] The Inter-Parliamentary Union was founded in 1889 by Frédéric Passy and Randal Cremer. The ground-breaking Hague Conference of 1899 established a Permanent Court of Arbitration in the city, with the Court's first decision being made in 1902.[10] The first museum of war and peace, inspired by Jan Bloch, opened in Luzern the same year. Nobel Peace Prizes were awarded from 1901, with von Suttner, Passy and Cremer among the first Laureates.

In Britain, the first National Peace Congress, for which J.F. Green was honorary secretary of the organising committee, was held in Manchester in 1904. 250 delegates gathered from 92 diverse organisations: churches and Quaker meetings, political and co-operative societies, peace society auxiliaries, local arbitration groups, women's and student representatives, trade unions and temperance associations.[11] The committee continued organising annual National Peace Congresses, including the successful Universal Peace Congress in London of 1908, in its guise as the National Council of Peace Societies,[12] after which it became known as the National Peace Council (N.P.C.)[13]

From 1910 the secretary of the National Peace Council was Carl Heath, who had been "tempted" by Anglicanism whilst spending time at Toynbee Hall. There was also a huge Inter-Parliamentary Union assembly in London in 1906 and a Second Hague Conference in 1907. The 1908 Lambeth Conference recorded its "deep appreciation of the practical work achieved" at The Hague, and urged "earnestly upon all Christian peoples the duty of allaying race-prejudice, and of promoting among all races the spirit of brotherly co-operation for the good of all mankind".[14]

The Peace Society also flourished at this time. The cause of international law and arbitration became sufficiently fashionable within liberal-minded middle-class circles for a number of senior Anglican clerics to consent to become its Vice-Presidents. Alongside John Percival (Bishop of Hereford) in that role were Edward Lee Hicks (who became Bishop of Lincoln in 1910) and the deans of Ripon (William Fremantle), Bristol (Francis Pigou), Carlisle (William Barker), Hereford (Wentworth Leigh) and Worcester (Moore Ede), along with Canons William Benham, Henry Bodley Bromby, Leighton Grane and John Howard Bertram Masterman.[15] Masterman and Arthur J. Waldron, now the vicar of Brixton, became members of the Peace Society Executive and Canon George Head of Bristol and Caroline Playne were amongst two hundred names on the Society's Council.[16] This was all part of an expansion of activity which reached a peak in 1909-10 with the Peace Society sending out over forty thousand invitations to ministers of religion to take part in the 1909 Peace Sunday, resulting in over 5,000 sermons being given and the distribution of more than 500,000 papers, pamphlets and other forms of literature.[17]

With all the activity of a strengthening, largely middle-class peace movement, nationally and internationally, and with concrete progress towards international law coming from the Hague Congresses, it was tempting to mistake the channels of peace for peace itself, to cry peace where there was no peace. After all, in an inter-connected world, there could surely be no logic in going to war? Norman Angell, in 1909, echoing Jan Bloch a decade earlier, extended Cobden's argument that, pragmatically and economically, war was an *Optical Illusion* or (later) a *Great Illusion*.[18] It led one gullible commentator to suggest that the issue was logically concluded:

> It is the achievement of Bloch and Norman Angell to have shown that even a successful conflict between modern states can bring no material gain. We can now look forward with something like confidence to the time when war between civilised nations will be considered as antiquated as the duel, and when the peacemakers shall be called the children of God.[19]

Just because peace might be logical, doesn't make it a reality.

William Leighton Grane, Prebendary of Chichester, whilst not refuting Angell, stated that "history holds no record of selfish motives ever having compassed any great reform in the whole story of the world's progress".[20] However, in a book of the same title, Grane himself argued in 1912 for *The Passing of War* on moral and religious grounds, rather than economic ones. "In War itself, in war *quâ* war", said Grane, "there is not, nor can be, any good. War is nothing but a barbarous anachronism, of which the civilised world ought to be utterly ashamed".[21] Thus, "since the essence of war is Hate, and the essence of religion is Love, no sophistry can atone these antinomies. . . . Here ambiguity spells treachery, and compromise is absurd. For War is not crime only: it is sacrilege. If it be true that 'God is Love,' war violates the very shrine of the eternal".[22] Noting Clausewitz's dictum that "War is an Act of Violence which in its application knows no bounds",[23] Grane cited, with approval, a contrasting comment from R.W. Church, sometime Dean of St Paul's:

> It was a great reversal of all accepted moral judgment, and of all popular traditions, when the teaching of the Gospel put in the forefront of its message God's value for Peace, and His blessing

upon it; when it placed Peace as a divine and magnificent object, to be aimed at with the earnestness with which men aimed at glory. . . . However in practice Christians have fallen short of it, this standard of what is true and right never has been and never can be lowered.

Do not let any one cheat us out of our inheritance of Peace by saying that God means it for Heaven, not for earth. He means it for Time as well as for Eternity.[24]

Grane lamented that war was often thought of as a lesser evil, with its wrongs regarded as being outweighed by some justifying benefit. Although "the Call of Religion in regard to War's passing is imperative and clear", such a call "has been habitually made to sound indefinite and doubtful, by being qualified unduly".[25] He particularly urged the clergy to preach peace faithfully and frequently. Grane's thesis was that a universal appreciation of the laws of right and wrong would bring about a moral resistance to war, far more powerful than economic logic. The seeds of the passing of war were already liberally sown. Properly educated, people would not want to make war, and nations, even in times of conflict, would seek justice by peaceful methods and would not choose to fight.[26] Grane, though, despite refusing to admit the inevitability that there could be worse evils than war,[27] was by no means a pacifist. For all his recognition of the ruinous cost, danger and evil of European armament competition, he argued that only internationally arranged and concurrently effective reduction of armaments was acceptable. Grane was an internationalist, an advocate of arbitration, of international law and such internationally agreed structures that would prevent war. His advocacy of the passing of war was not, despite his book's title, a claim that war had indeed passed, but an attempt to show a moral case for people to choose to make it pass.

Altogether, the combined effect of the efforts of Angell and Grane encouraged the belief that international disputes could – which for some readers became "would" – henceforth be settled by saner, more peaceful methods. Angell's book sold around two millions copies from 1910 to 1913.[28] Many people would have regarded themselves as pacifists, simply because they supported some – any – movement for peace, for arbitration, for international goodwill. Bishops, favouring goodwill, could participate in peace societies without risk of controversy.

There were setbacks, which should have rung alarm bells; in 1912 Italy did not go to The Hague before going to war with Turkey, and in 1913, when Churchill announced a large increase in military expenditure despite resolutions of concern about the "ever-worsening burden of armaments" from the Independent Labour Party (I.L.P.) and the various peace societies.[29] The British Government's actions were not unilateral, but formed part of a frantic arms race which saw the aggregate military spending of the major European powers increase threefold in four years.

Despite the illusion of peace and stability, Edwardian Britons were living in an increasingly militaristic society. 1910 to 14 were years of "great unrest" in industrial relations, and in 1911 the Government called on the army to keep the trains running and on the navy to send warships to the Mersey during a seaman's strike. Large numbers of growing boys uncritically absorbed the paramilitary values of the Boys' Brigade and other similar organisations.[30] The strong state was exalted above the righteous state. Caroline Playne later remarked that "[t]he Churches, the teaching profession, the Press had bad records in the pre-war years. The clerics failed. . . . Clerics no longer lead the masses, they are led by them".[31] When, in 1914, the whole world-view of the Edwardians fell apart, the institutions in which they had trusted were not able to prevent the catastrophe to come.

1914: Representatives of the Old Order

The Peace Society

Peace advocates, socialists, feminists, and Christians all found that within their number were those who supported the Government's call to war, and those who opposed involvement in any war.[32] The peace structures of the past were sunk almost without trace as the Titanic had been two years before. Only the National Peace Council was to exist in any recognisable form after 1918 largely because it was more of a co-ordinating body than an independent voice, which concentrated more on looking to a future peace than on commenting meaningfully about the war.[33]

The Peace Society in particular lacked authority of commitment. Pre-war rhetoric was not enough to prevent many members from supporting war in 1914. In the presence of Percival, Grane and other dignitaries, the Society President, J.A. Pease, addressed the 1912 Annual Meeting. "In the whole history of the Society", he said, "no year has been so full of encouragement". This was because "nations were vying with one another in expressions of friendship." There were improved methods of transit and communication, and more straightforward diplomacy. Which might indeed have been encouraging, had it not been that "the resources of civilization were being more and more directed to preparations of an unprecedented magnitude in connection with provision for war".[34] When it came to war, the Peace Society had no answer. Its members were not willing to countenance "Peace at any price". Indeed the Society's own journal, the *Herald of Peace*, bemoaned that some members seemed unable to accept peace at any price at all.[35]

The Society was certainly in no condition to respond with unanimity to the challenge of August 1914. Worse than that, Pease was and remained a member of the war cabinet, thereby compromising every value that the Society's founder members had held dear a century earlier. It was ironic that the centenary Annual Meeting of the society on 22 May 1916 had to be cancelled because the owners of the meeting hall feared that the presence of any peace organisation could provoke mob violence. Peace Sunday did, however, continue to be observed in December each year, and in May 1917 a perceptive Dr Darby told the annual meeting of the remnant that "You cannot enforce peace . . . and for a League of Nations to come into existence with military force at its back, however you may conceal the fact, is simply a repetition of what has already convulsed the world".[36] In 1916, Herbert Dunnico took over as Secretary of the Peace Society and although in the inter-war years he maintained the Society as a forum for Labour and Liberal M.P.s to discuss disarmament and related issues, it never regained its earlier prominence.[37]

The Church of England Peace League

The Church of England Peace League was formed in October 1910, the founder members agreeing that "the Church should take a definite part in promoting unity and concord among nations by encouraging the growth of international friendship, and by working for arbitration in the place of war as a means of settling international disputes".[38] The objects of the League included encouraging members of the Church of England to recognise the duty of "combating the war-spirit as inconsistent with the spirit of Christianity, and of working actively for peace as part of the divine ideal of human society". They also aimed to promote universal and permanent peace, to encourage the growth of international friendship and to work for the adoption of arbitration and conciliation in place of war. The President, from 1910 until his death in 1919, was Edward Lee Hicks, Bishop of Lincoln, who was aware of how armament manufacturers would benefit from war, yet felt the fate of Belgium and the pledges made by the British Government were still sufficient causes for Britain to take part. Unusually, the posts of honorary treasurer and secretary were taken by two sisters, F.S. and M.H. Huntsman.[39] The League was chaired by J.W. Horsley (b.1845), Rector of Detling, Kent, and was based, like the International Arbitration League, at St Stephen's House, Westminster.

Although membership of the League was only around 100, there were over 20 vice-presidents, including Lansbury.[40] In 1911 Hicks lobbied 823 Rural Deans, requesting clergy support for arbitration. The 1911 Church Congress, in Stoke, asked T.J. Lawrence to speak on "The Church's Duty in Furthering International Peace". Lawrence was the author of two more of the League's early publications, one on arbitration and one on the ideal of universal peace. Horsley wrote one tract, *The Prayer Book and Peace*, as well as editing William Ellery Channing's *Wise Words on War* from 1839. Playne similarly edited the writings of Westcott, and together with a sermon by Hicks there were other tracts produced by A.J. Waldron, Frank Lascelles and Hewlett Johnson (*Why Wars Must Cease*).[41] In April 1913 Grane preached for the League, regretting the way that the church had neglected the teaching of Jesus and upheld the military.

> *"Lovest thou Me?"*. . . . Forsake this barbaric doctrine and these false ideals, which you have allowed to impoverish and enslave mankind. How can you love Me if you twist My teaching? How is it you believe the opposite of what I taught? Even the Press and the Pulpits of your Church now proclaim that they who take the sword shall *flourish* by the sword! . . . What has befallen My beatitudes? What is this new sort of benediction? Blessed are the violent, for they shall inherit the earth! Blessed are the proud in spirit, for theirs is the Kingdom of Heaven! Blessed are the war-makers, for they shall be accounted sons of God![42]

The League was always going to be a more respectable than radical organisation, as was shown by aspects of its 1913 circular to diocesan bishops, protesting against the advocacy of compulsory military service. The appeal allowed that in certain circumstances "a State might be justified in summoning to arms its whole manhood".[43] Lansbury and Playne were included in the membership of the League, but it was clearly not a pacifist organisation and it made little impact once war was declared.[44] The League was one of the constituent groups on the National Peace Council and played an active role in it. Playne and Charles Warlow, Rector of Bloomsbury, were at one time charged with considering the nature of the relationship between the N.P.C. and its constituent societies.[45] The League's representatives on the N.P.C. for 1918 were F.A. Evelyn, J.W. Horsley (on the Executive), William Corbett Roberts (1873-1953), and a Miss Strachan.[46] Hubert Burge, Bishop of Oxford, became the President in 1921,[47] but by then the days of the League were numbered.

The Student Christian Movement and the World Alliance

Two other organisations existing in 1914, both ecumenical (the roots of the ecumenical movement were laid at an Edinburgh conference of missionary societies in 1910) and of some influence, included the Student Christian Movement (S.C.M.), and the World Alliance for Promoting International Friendship through the Churches.

The S.C.M., part of the World Student Christian Federation (1895), started as the Student Volunteer Missionary Union in Cambridge in 1892.[48] It had increasingly addressed social issues since they were first raised at a Versailles conference in 1900 (at which the Quaker, Henry

Hodgkin, 1877-1933, was present). Particularly influential was the S.C.M. conference at Matlock in 1909, chaired by William Temple (1881-1944): the theme was social concern.[49] During a period of international tension in 1912, leaders of S.C.M. exchanged letters of friendship with German students.[50] S.C.M. was the principal focal point for many educated young Christians and a considerable number of future Anglican leaders were influenced by S.C.M. concerns. Although only about five per cent of S.C.M. members were pacifists – a reflection of the dearth of consideration given to issues of peace and war prior to 1914 – the Movement later risked disapproval by defending its right to employ pacifists.[51] Maude Royden, and the Marquis of Tavistock were two of many S.C.M. figures involved later in the Fellowship of Reconciliation.[52]

The World Alliance for Promoting International Friendship through the Churches (later to be incorporated into the World Council of Churches) had its roots in 1907, when various denominations prepared to make presentations to the Second Hague Conference. It marked increasing international ecclesiastical concern for issues of peace. In the following two years there was a substantial exchange programme between Christians in England and Germany, including the 130 or so German Church dignitaries – Lutheran, Roman Catholic and Nonconformist – who attended the Seventeenth Universal Congress for Peace, in London in the summer of 1908.[53] The return visit the following year, warmly received by the Kaiser, included four Anglican bishops in a party of over 100. One of their guides was the secretary of the German Committee, Dr. Friedrich Siegmund-Schültze.[54] It was recorded that at the end of the meeting the two groups sang "Now thank we all our God".[55] From this continuing programme evolved the Associated Councils of Churches in the British and German Empires for Fostering Friendly Relations between Two Peoples, launched in London in February 1911.[56] 7,000 people joined in the first year.[57] Norman Angell was definitely not one of them, deriding "Anglo-German junketings, dinner-parties, exchange visits of clergymen, and what not".[58] On one of the visits to Berlin at this time, Edward Stuart Talbot (1844-1934), Bishop of Winchester, spoke of greater ideals than patriotism:

> The Christendom of Europe is one; the Human Race is yet another; and the Kingdom of God upon earth, that is a third. Loyalty to the country is splendid; but there are other loyalties. Patriotism is a noble ideal; let us not make of it an idol. . . . What we need to cherish is the spiritual force which binds man to man, and nation to nation, by an inner bond, stronger than selfishness, or ambition, or any material thing.[59]

Two Liberal M.P.s, the Quaker J. Allen Baker and the Anglican Willoughby H. Dickinson, were in the forefront of this movement with Dickinson raising funds for a journal, the *Peacemaker*, the circulation of which was to grow to 67,000 by 1914.[60] With financial backing from Andrew Carnegie, who endowed £400,000 to generate income for "uniting the Churches of Christendom for Peace, and in promoting Conferences of their representatives",[61] the vision grew beyond Europe and provisional committees were formed to organise a conference for protestants at Constance on 2-4 August, 1914 and for Catholics at Liège the following week. The outbreak of war meant that the second conference never took place, but around 90 delegates,[62] including Hodgkin and Moore Ede, the Dean of Worcester, did gather briefly in Constance on 2 August at the former Dominican monastery where, 500 years earlier, the Council of Constance ended in the tragedy of the condemnation of Hus. This conference ended in the tragedy of war. Ede noted hopefully that:

> Huss appeared to fail, but the principles he advocated eventually prevailed. Our Conference appeared to militarists a failure. . . . But the ideas and principles which we met to advocate will eventually prevail, and perhaps sooner than many expect. . . .
>   A Conference for Promoting Friendly Relations between the Nations held at the moment when the nations were entering on the greatest and most disastrous war in history may seem to some a ridiculous fiasco.[63] That is a mistake. The horrors of the war prove the sanity of the ideals of those who met at Constance, and show the necessity for action by the Churches when the war comes to an end. Had the Churches exercised the influence they can and ought to exercise sooner, the war-makers would have found it more difficult to make war. The Churches have been too slow in taking action. They must never be too late again.[64]

Prayers in many languages were said on the Sunday morning, with the noise of troops movements audible outside. Before the delegates hurried home on the Monday they passed four resolutions which later influenced the direction taken by the Fellowship of Reconciliation. The first two resolutions were:

> I. That, inasmuch as the work of conciliation and the promotion of amity is essentially a Christian task, it is expedient that the Churches in all lands should use their influence with the peoples, parliaments, and governments of the world to bring about good and friendly relationships between the nations, so that, along the path of peaceful civilization, they may reach that universal goodwill which Christianity has taught mankind to aspire after.
> II. That, inasmuch as all sections of the Church of Christ are equally concerned in the maintenance of peace and the promotion of good feeling among all the races of the world, it is advisable for them to act in concert in their efforts to carry the foregoing resolution into effect.[65]

The third resolution called for appropriate councils to be set up by the churches in each country, with an international bureau to co-ordinate the work of the Alliance. The fourth set up an interim committee, including Baker and Dickinson (who was the Honorary Secretary to the Constance Conference), with Moore Ede, Siegmund-Schültze and others. Siegmund-Schültze was the young Pastor of the Lutheran Church at Potsdam, Chaplain to the Kaiser, and Conference organiser and chairman.[66] On 5 September Hodgkin was invited to join this group and he immediately became the treasurer.

A British committee, including Moore Ede, Dickinson, Hodgkin, Ruth Rouse (travelling secretary for women students in the World Student Christian Federation), William Temple, William Boyd Carpenter (retired Bishop of Ripon) and others met in November 1914. Their declared objects included, "To aid the development of the national Christian conscience and to promote all measures that will lead the nations to realize that the progress of humanity demands that the reign of law and the principles of love shall prevail in international affairs".[67] The approach of the British Committee was reflected by J.H. Rushbrooke, the editor of its journal, *Goodwill*. Rushbrooke was prepared to carry letters from Christians of opposing nations, acknowledging that hostility, however prolonged, would be temporary and that "[T]he two great Teutonic peoples of Europe have to live together". He also reported that "[We] shall set ourselves resolutely against any stimulation of passion and hatred, and especially of indiscriminate hatred directed against an entire people" and rejoiced that "various committees in this country [Great Britain], with the encouragement of the Archbishop of Canterbury and other leaders, have assisted peaceful men and women, many of them long resident in our land, who are technically 'alien enemies' ".[68]

Yet despite this condemnation of irrational hatred and prejudice, Rushbrooke acknowledged that Great Britain was "engaged in a strife from which there was offered to the nation no honourable way of escape".[69] He also announced that the British group would publish papers in accordance with various principles, including, "[T]hat Great Britain was in August morally bound to declare war and is no less bound to carry the war to a decisive issue".[70] He later tried to reconcile the two sets of sentiments by stating that "[C]hristian men who hold it a first duty of the British nation at the present moment to concentrate all its energy upon the war have not departed from their conviction that military force can of itself settle nothing, although it may, and it is hoped will, prepare the way for the dominance of a reasonable attitude".[71]

Such an attitude appealed to the episcopal supporters of the World Alliance, namely the bishops of Winchester (Talbot), Kensington (John Maud) and Southwark (Hubert Burge). Clearly, for all the fine words at Constance, the World Alliance would not be a happy home for pacifists, though some, like Marian Ellis, Stephen Hobhouse, Henry Hodgkin, William E. Orchard, and Richard Roberts tried to be of influence. Despite the war the international committee continued to function, and Moore Ede, Hodgkin, Siegmund-Schültze, John Augustine Kempthorne (1864-1946; the Bishop of Lichfield), and others met again in Berne in August 1915. Together they supported *"Inter arma caritas"*, the International Committee of the Red Cross, in its provision of aid to interned civilians and prisoners of war.[72] The failure of the World Alliance to oppose the war, however, meant that it lost the respect of many Christian pacifists, who in time would look to form their own international organisation. By the end of the war the World Alliance had become, if it had not always been, a highly respectable organisation, with its journal reporting the well-meaning speeches of well-heeled leaders of church and state. There was no sense of incongruity in the juxtaposition of articles on "Famine in Europe" and "King George and President Wilson at Buckingham Palace: Speeches at State Banquet".[73]

Beyond Constance: Seeds of a New Order

Siegmund-Schültze had been chairman and organiser of the Constance conference of 1914. The meeting between him and Hodgkin, or, more accurately, their departure, became part of Christian pacifist mythology. They travelled back from Constance to Köln in the same train and, as they shook hands in Köln, Siegmund-Schültze stated that the war would make no difference to their work.[74] "Whatever happens", he was reported as saying, "nothing is changed between us. We are one in Christ and can never be at war".[75] Their vale-dictum is regarded as the start of the process which would eventually lead to the creation of the International Fellowship of Reconciliation (I.F.O.R.).

In the interchange of various subsequent committee papers and personal letters, Hodgkin affirmed to Siegmund-Schültze that their friendship could not be broken by the war.[76] The content of a personal letter to that effect was similar to a public "Message to Men and Women of Goodwill", largely written by Hodgkin and published on 7 August 1914 by the Friends' Meeting for Suffering. This stated that the "war spells the bankruptcy of much that we too lightly call Christian. . . . If we apportion blame, let us not fail first to blame ourselves and to seek forgiveness of Almighty God". It continued with calls to faith, to love all people, to make preparations for life after the war, to avoid a spirit of vindictiveness, and to daily prayer.[77] This "Message" anticipated much of the thinking that was later promoted by the Fellowship of Reconciliation (F.O.R.).

3.
1914:
A New Peace Movement

The Peace Movement Re-aligned

In the socialist newspaper the *Daily Herald*, the dominant stories in the first half of 1914 concerned Ireland and industrial disputes. It was not until 25 July of that monumental year that a small paragraph reported the possibility of trouble in the Balkans. Two days later that story had reached the front page, and by the twenty-eighth, the implicitly anti-imperial headline was "Every European Power Stirring The Stew".[1] The following day came news of the mobilisation of troops in various countries, countered by optimistic accounts of workers' protests across Europe, and especially in Paris. The editorial stressed the responsibility of organised labour in a time of international crisis: "It is the duty of the Trade Unions to declare that this thing shall not be".[2] There were reports of strikes across Russia and, with news of an anti-war demonstration 100,000 strong in Berlin on 28 July (and up to seven times that number in other demonstrations across Germany), the hope of those on the political left was that Germany and Russia might stand aside from any conflict.[3] The Second International Congress of socialists in Basel in 1912 had declared war on war, and had urged members to "exert every effort in order to prevent the outbreak of war", using the opportunity of industrial action during a political crisis to hasten the downfall of capitalist class rule. The leading French anti-militarist, Jean Jaurès, following a meeting with Keir Hardie, Rosa Luxemburg and other European socialists, called for general strikes across France and Germany. Jaurès was assassinated on 31 July by a nationalist who wanted revenge over Germany for the French defeat of 1870-71, not collaboration with Germans to prevent war .[4] There had been social and industrial unrest in all the major European countries in the years before 1914, but it could not be sustained or coordinated in a way that would prevent war.

WAR against WAR

Under the auspices of the International Labour and Socialist Bureau,

A TRAFALGAR SQUARE DEMONSTRATION

WILL BE HELD

To-morrow (Sunday) Aug. 2.
AT 4 p.m.

Chairmen : J. KEIR HARDIE, M.P.,
GEORGE LANSBURY H. M. HYNDMAN.

A newspaper cutting from the Herald *announcing an anti-war demonstration.*

The *Daily Herald*'s socialist analysis was that the crisis was fuelled by capitalism. A cover cartoon portrayed a theme that would be revisited many times in the months ahead, with a wealthy armaments exporter saying, "Don't I stimulate the Nation to protect itself from national danger by providing the national danger?"[5] An editorial argued, "this war is a sordid commercial business. Financiers pull the strings, and foreign ministers are the puppets".[6] Within a week of the first news item, the front page headings were, "WORKERS MUST STOP THE WAR!", "THE GREATEST CRIME OF THE CENTURY", and "NEXT SUNDAY'S GREAT PROTEST".[7] That protest, promoted and partly organised by the *Daily Herald*, and taken up by the Labour Party, took the form of a Trafalgar Square demonstration on 2 August 1914, jointly chaired by Keir Hardie, H.M. Hyndman (1842-1921) and George Lansbury.[8] The latter had tried to persuade people to attend by writing of the fact "that war means murder pure and simple; that it means the destruction of human life in a wholesale manner; that it is the great working class who will pay the heaviest toll".[9] From the platform Lansbury praised the influence and example of the recently assassinated Jean Jaurès, then urged everyone who loved England to avoid the "abominable crime" of war. He called for the miners, transport workers and railwaymen to refuse to produce coal, run trains or transport materials of war, arguing that wars only favoured the "possessing classes", whereas the workers of every country "are all sweated, robbed, exploited, in times of peace, and sent out to be massacred in times of war". He predicted starvation, and came close to urging civil disobedience by saying that the hungry should "go into the streets and get what you require". In metaphorical language that brought loud cheers, he urged workers to "fight to the death against this atrocity".[10] In the event, 20,000 people braved the rain, shouted "down with war", and passed a resolution calling upon the Government to secure peace, and on "the workers of the world to use their industrial and political power in order that the nations of the world shall not be involved in the war".[11] It was a commendable turnout for a rally called at such short notice, but far short of the numbers required to have any chance of influencing Government policy. There were similar gatherings across the country. Labour M.P. Fred Jowett (1864-1944) closed the Bradford demonstration in a resigned rather than a rallying tone, urging those present to "keep our minds clean, our hearts free from hate, and one purpose always before us – to bring peace as soon as possible on a basis that will endure".[12]

Despite an appeal for neutrality from unnamed leading members of Cambridge University, and the refusal of South Wales miners to put in extra work for the war effort, the European scenario was described as the "arrival of Armageddon".[13]

Something similar was predicted in a number of sermons preached on Sunday 2 August 1914. Most opposition to the war was voiced from Nonconformist pulpits, but at Cleethorpes, Bishop Hicks of Lincoln urged prayer to God "to keep our people from war", arguing that "a continental war could be nothing short of disastrous when one thought of the militarism of Europe, of the hell of battlefields, of the miseries of the wounded, of ruined peasants". He said that Britain had no quarrel with Germany and going to war without a reason was tempting providence; "moreover it would inflict upon our industrial community one of the most terrible curses possible to inflict".[14] The Rector of St Mary, Newmarket, Henry Brook Young, recognised the consequences of developments in arms technology, in effect anticipating the naval bombardment of Scarborough, Whitby and Hartlepool of 1914, and the Zeppelin raids on London in 1915:

All the horrors of war in ancient times would be nothing to the horrors of war today. . . . All the resources of science had been called upon to perfect weapons of destruction for mankind . . . no town in England was now safe. At night it might be turned into a smouldering ruin and its inhabitants into blackened corpses.[15]

The cheers that had greeted the Trafalgar Square speeches quickly faded. Within a few days, following the invasion of Belgium, even some of those present, together with the majority of the population, became convinced by the power of the press that one's duty to the state was greater than one's loyalty to humanity and that the "honour" of the state compelled one's participation in the forthcoming war. Any hope of international socialist solidarity was shattered. Even members of the Church Socialist League were divided: Lansbury, who had become chairman in 1912, and Lewis Donaldson were opposed to the war, yet Conrad Noel was in full support.[16]

Edward Collett, a high church priest at Bower Chalke, Wiltshire, produced a regular village newspaper from his vicarage. He echoed the bewilderment of Hicks as to the cause of the crisis, and he was surely not alone in wondering whether war was the only way to preserve national honour;

> THE CONTINENTAL WAR – which has unfortunately broken out and may possibly affect our country is very greatly to be deplored. Whatever the cause of it may be, the inevitable consequence cannot fail to be bloodshed and misery for many. It is true that a nation's honour must be upheld but surely that might be accomplished without loss of life.[17]

The fact of the outbreak of war took a few weeks to seep into the nation's consciousness. Once established, enthusiasm for the cause set in, and within a month recruitment was running at up to 174,000 per week. Even football matches were targeted by the recruitment campaigners, with 200 signed up at half time at Elland Road, Leeds. A similar number enlisted at a Liverpool vs Everton fixture.[18] For the pacifists it became increasingly uncomfortable to maintain a counter-cultural opposition to the war in the face of such widespread support. The peace organisations existing in July 1914 would certainly not be up to the task.

Britain's entry into the war on 4 August 1914 caused a regrouping of the peace movement in England, with a tranche of new agencies coming into being. Within a few days the Quakers convened an Emergency Committee for the Assistance of Germans, Austrians and Hungarians in Distress. Like the Church of England Peace League, it was based in St Stephen's House, Westminster Embankment, ironically a building also used for recruiting purposes. This assistance for "enemy aliens" had the support of several bishops including Randall Davidson, Edward Lee Hicks, John Kempthorne and Edward Stuart Talbot, along with parliamentarians Lord Parmoor (Charles Alfred Cripps), Willoughby H. Dickinson and others.[19] Even their opponents could recognise the importance of Quakers in wartime, with Hensley Henson, Dean of Durham, acknowledging that they had "a priceless value as a protest against Christian acquiescence in a lower level of practice than the Christian conscience".[20] Other societies were formed with the aim of stopping the conflict and preparing for the peace. A League to Abolish War, emphasising the value of the Hague Conferences, was founded by the Revd F. Herbert Stead, Warden of the Robert Browning Settlement. The League had the support of the Brotherhood Movement, and its President was George Nicoll Barnes, M.P.[21] Of greater future significance, a League of Nations Society was formed in May 1915.[22] Once it had been separated in people's consciousness from efforts to obtain a negotiated peace, the issue of enforcement was raised. As early as autumn 1916 prophetic pacifists were expressing concern over a "League to Enforce Peace".[23]

Two of the most significant new organisations, both more overtly political than many of the peace organisations that had gone before, were the Union of Democratic Control (U.D.C.) and the more grass-roots No-Conscription Fellowship (N.C.F.), both of which were formed in the closing months of 1914.[24]

The U.D.C. was a cross-party alliance favouring international links between democracies and a negotiated end to the war. Charles Trevelyan, Edmund Dene Morel, Ramsay MacDonald (who, in a declaration of his opposition to the war, resigned as Chairman of the Labour Party in August 1914) and Norman Angell were amongst the leaders.[25] They were not a united group by any means with the radical Morel of a rather different character to the cautious, neutralist Angell. Carl Heath, the secretary of the National Peace Council, was a member of the General Committee.[26] The U.D.C. was a relatively respectable umbrella for soft opposition to the war. It did not become the mass-movement successor to the pre-war peace groups, as some of its leaders had hoped, but it did provide valuable support for those who would express their reservations in parliament. Maude Royden was amongst its many supporters.[27]

For most committed opponents of the war, the more important organisation was the N.C.F., founded by Labour activist Fenner Brockway at his wife Lilla Brockway's instigation.[28] He published announcements on 12 and 19 November in the Independent Labour Party journal *Labour Leader*, of which he was the editor.[29] The N.C.F. was to become the principal body campaigning first against the introduction of conscription, then later against its application and continuation. Perhaps reflecting Brockway's upbringing as the son of a clergyman, and his having been sub-editor of the *Christian Commonwealth*,[30] even such a non-religious body as the N.C.F. was still prepared in its Statement of Faith to refer to the sanctity of human life:

The No-Conscription Fellowship is an organization of men likely to be called upon to undertake military service in the event of conscription, who will refuse from conscientious motives to bear arms, because they consider human life to be sacred, and cannot, therefore, assume the responsibility of inflicting death. They deny the right of Governments to say, "You shall bear arms," and will oppose every effort to introduce compulsory military service into Great Britain. Should such efforts be successful, they will, whatever the consequences may be, obey their conscientious convictions rather than the commands of Governments.[31]

Clifford Allen described the religious tone of the statement as a reflection of a previous general assumption that conscientious objection to conscription or war "arose from a definite religious belief in a supernatural authority. Conscience related man to God". It soon became clear, however, that for most N.C.F. members the motivation came from "fundamental beliefs either about the value of human personality, or about the relationship of human beings to each other. Each precluded them from engaging in war. Conscience related man to man".[32] With Allen as its chairman, and Fenner Brockway as its honorary secretary, the N.C.F. was largely, but not exclusively, a socialist organisation, with many Christian members. According to Bertrand Russell, the socialist philosopher, Allen showed "admirable impartiality" in the difficult task of "keeping harmonious relations between Christian and Socialist pacifists".[33]

Those who were inspired by their religious convictions were certainly not restrained from expressing their opposition to war in terms of their faith. One example, early in the war, came when the Bermondsey medic Alfred Salter explained in the *Labour Leader* why he could not answer the call to arms

Look! Christ in khaki, out in France thrusting His bayonet into the body of a German workman. See! The Son of God with a machine gun, ambushing a column of German infantry, catching them unawares in a lane and mowing them down in their helplessness. Hark! The Man of Sorrows in a cavalry charge, cutting, hacking, thrusting, crushing, cheering. No! No! That picture is an impossible one, and we all know it.[34]

Salter listed world empires that had ruled by force but were long forgotten, "but the word of the Lord endureth for ever". His plea was that his readers would "Do [God's] will and take the consequences". Holding that "Thou shalt not kill" applied both to individuals and to the state, he realised that such an approach could lead to him being shot, either by an enemy in war or by his own state, for treason. "Very well", he said, "I say deliberately that I am prepared to be shot rather than kill a German peasant with whom I have no conceivable quarrel". In leaflet form, a million and a half copies of Salter's article were distributed in Britain, not to mention translations made into European languages. At least eighty people received prison sentences (in one U.S. case for ten years) for distributing Salter's call in Australia, New Zealand and South Africa.[35]

In the light of parliamentary moves towards conscription in 1915, the N.C.F's Statement of Faith was extended:

> The members of the Fellowship refuse to engage in any employment which necessitates taking the military oath. Whilst leaving the decision open to the individual judgment of each member, the Fellowship will support members who conscientiously resist compulsory alternatives to military service involving a change of occupation.[36]

By the time conscription was introduced in 1916, there were probably around 15,000 members of the N.C.F. who were committed to resisting any call to bear arms. A weekly paper, the *Tribunal*, was published giving details of the struggle against conscription, and the *C.O. Hansard* monitored parliamentary steps to keep the plights of conscientious objectors in the political domain. Joan Beauchamp, editor of the *Tribunal*, was twice imprisoned; once for printing a controversial article by Bertrand Russell, and once for refusing to reveal the identity of the journal's printer. Violet Tillard was imprisoned for two months for refusing to identify the printer of the N.C.F. News Sheet. Edith Ellis was sentenced to six months in prison for not submitting a leaflet to the censors. By the end of the war, the N.C.F. had produced over a million copies of its leaflets and pamphlets.[37]

Excursus: a "Just" War?

Although, a century on, it has become commonplace to analyse conflicts according to the criteria of the "Just War" tradition, there is little evidence that such a mode of analysis held any contemporaneous influence upon those who argued for the war, or those who would protest against it. As David Fisher has observed, "at the beginning of the twentieth century just war thinking had fallen out of fashion".[38] There had been a peak of interest in the theory in the seventeenth and eighteenth centuries, but thereafter only sporadic reference until debates on the morality, or otherwise, of nuclear weapons in the 1960s. In any case, the nature of the concept, supposedly humanitarian and altruistic in the context of twentieth-century capitalist intervention, would have been very different to that devised by the philosophers of earlier centuries.[39]

In 1914, "just" war theories were simply not part of the philosophical or political landscape. As far as the Christian opponents of war were concerned, the overwhelming majority were from protestant denominations, whereas the "just" war tradition is rooted in Catholicism. The immediacy of political developments meant there was little time for that tradition to be recovered and explored in depth by those who were already heading for war, even in the unlikely event that they were minded so to do. Any attempt, therefore, to consider the war of 1914-1918 in terms of "just" war criteria is anachronistic, and an exercise in hindsight.

Insofar as the war was regarded by its proponents as just it was because it was perceived to have a just cause. Although that would have been highly debatable before 3 August 1914, war, inevitably, soon provides its own justification, and within twenty-four hours the British people were being stirred to counter the German invasion of Belgium. The shelling of towns on the North Sea Coast of England, an action that would not have happened without the declaration of war, was regarded as providing justification after the event.

Popular and political understanding of "just" war is, largely because of its name, inevitably reduced to just cause, yet the tradition within Christian thought regards just cause as only one criterion among many, and that the one most open to abuse. In theory, "just" war is about the limitation of armed conflict, providing conditions that need to be fulfilled in order for the conflict to be morally tolerable.

Cicero (106-46BCE), for example, was convinced that only the Roman Empire had the authority to engage in war. So as well as being for a just cause, war must be called by a legitimate authority. The concept of Christian "just" war was developed by Augustine (354-430) in order to justify certain kinds of war (contrary to the pacifism of the first centuries of the Christian era) subject to strict moral conditions. Augustine added the need for right intent, that the motivation is for good, consistent with love for the enemy. Given the 1914 context of rival imperial nations jostling for political and economic dominance, driven by pride and nationalism, it is hard to argue for purity of intent. Giving the proponents of war the benefit of the doubt, however, leads to the disturbing conclusion that the carnage that followed was unleashed by those who simply meant well.

Alongside these *jus ad bellum* conditions, Augustine followed Cicero and before him Plato (427-327BCE) in arguing for *jus in bello*, for a right conduct of the war. These were refined and developed further by Thomas Aquinas (1225-1274) and later by Francisco de Vitoria (c.1492-1546), Francisco Suarez (1548-1617) and Hugo Grotius (1583-1645). In the process, more requirements were added: first, the need for military action to be the last resort when peaceful means had been exhausted;

secondly, the need for near certainty that the war would have a successful outcome; and, finally, the need for the harm done to be proportional to the injustice being addressed, for the level of good to be achieved exceeding the level of wrong that would be caused. Proportion is also a *jus in bello* criterion, applying to individual actions within war, as does the principle of discrimination which protects civilians, the innocent and non-combatants.[40]

Which of these principles were satisfied by the decision to go to war in August 1914, and which were over-ridden? All the criteria need to be satisfied for a military conflict to satisfy "just" war conditions, but one after another they fell short.

Simply because politicians and diplomats were floundering did not mean that the declaration of war was a last resort; the sheer pace of the descent into war meant that no party was standing back, with patience, reflecting on alternatives.

It was well known beforehand that the costs of any war would be disproportionate to any benefit; Bloch and Angell had already warned that technology had advanced so much that the scale of any war would be colossal, far greater than any good that might be wished for, and could not be proportionate. That had long been apparent before the most extreme consequences of using modern weaponry became apparent at the Somme. Combining the loss of human life on both sides, there were over a million casualties in the transfer of six miles of mud.

Neither was the war discriminate; as swathes of Europe became battlefields, civilians were uprooted, populations enfeebled, immune systems weakened with disease rampant, and countless families bereaved through direct or indirect death of loved ones. Some *in bello* actions deliberately targeted civilians, such as the British naval blockade of Germany, intended to induce starvation, or the retaliatory bombing of Freiburg in April 1917.[41]

The slogans about the war being over by Christmas, when there was no substantial reason to believe that it would be so, were simply wishful-thinking propaganda. As for believing in a net benefit at the final outcome, what constitutes finality? It's a question that leads into recent attempts, not universally accepted, to formulate and add *jus post bellum* conditions.[42] From an "eternal" perspective, the consequences of a war must include the future wars that are generated, and the global culture of "might is right" that results. There can be no defence in claiming that these were unintended consequences; responsibility lies with those who contributed to the causes. So the First World War and its flawed settlement sowed the seeds of the Second World War, which in turn provided the seed-bed for the development of atomic weapons, which are still targeted on hundreds of cities around the world. This was not the war to end war, for war begets war begets war, and many of the war resisters, without the benefits of "just" war theories, held that only the rejection of the whole concept of war could break the cycle of slaughter.

Re-forming Christians, Autumn 1914

Christian pacifists, like most of the rest of the British population were taken completely by surprise by the outbreak of war. The *Herald of Peace* lamented that, "Even the foremost pacifist leaders of the Churches have surrendered. . . . Up to a certain point they were firm. At that point their Christianity failed them, and they had to leave it, as unworkable".[43] Church and state would stand "shoulder to shoulder", to use a phrase of the Foreign Secretary, Edward Grey.[44] Chapel was little better than church, given that it was a Liberal Government that was going to war.

Maude Royden was one of those who waited in vain for some Christian body or newspaper or person to speak out and condemn "not only war in general but *this* war". Arthur Winnington-Ingram, Bishop of London wrote to her, describing the war as "the last Armageddon" after which "the great sun of Love. . . . will shine out in its permanent strength".[45] Later he told her "Even God can only get out of each age the morality of which the age is capable. . . . Your 'ideal morality' is not possible yet".[46] Not having any sons himself, he had been advocating conscription even before the war had started.[47] He would soon revel in the crudest, most bloodthirsty and gospel-denying recruiting sermons, openly urging his listeners to kill good Germans along with the bad.[48] In the third week of the war Royden wrote to the *Challenge* journal, "We are all agreed . . . that war is an evil; but to what purpose, if we justify each war as it arises? . . . I hear of no Christians who refuse to shoot down Christians". Yet, in disarming Peter, Christ disarmed every soldier.[49] The response was universally hostile, with her views described as traitorous and unfit reading for loyal English people. Royden replied by asking:

> Is it not clear that we cannot end war except by refusing to make war? It is useless to wait till we find a war we can condemn, for we justify each as it arises. . . . Even now it is contended that the present conflict is a "war to end war" and those who hate war most persuade themselves that *this* time at least war is justified for the sake of peace. So do we perpetually assume that Satan can be induced to cast out Satan. No illusion is more common, no hope more undying.[50]

She was disturbed to discover that even Gilbert Murray, an opponent of the Boer War, had contributed to a pamphlet supporting this war. Under the weight of such opposition, Royden began to wonder if she was the one who was mistaken. But, as she wrote to Murray, she was only interested in knowing what the teaching of Christ was. "Your difficulty is 'Is war ever right? Is this war right? Were we bound in honour to make war?' Mine is, 'What is the teaching of Christ about war?' "[51]

The roots of the organised Christian pacifist response to the outbreak of war, and the Churches' support for it, can be traced to an initiative by Richard Roberts (1874-1945), Presbyterian minister at Hornsey. He was taken aback on the first Sunday of the war by the absence of young German businessmen, normally regulars in his congregation. Distressed, he telephoned a number of his friends and S.C.M. colleagues, including Hodgkin and George Bell, then Chaplain to the Archbishop of Canterbury, and invited them to his home to discuss a response to the war. It was a "bewildered" gathering that could agree on little else other than war was unchristian and that they should meet again. They did appeal to the Archbishop to bring together leading Anglicans, or to hold an emergency Lambeth Conference, to consider the church's duty in wartime.[52] Their own subsequent attempts to clarify thinking led to the publication of a series of position papers published as *Papers for War Time*, edited by the young Rector of St James's, Piccadilly, William Temple. He wrote the first tract, *Christianity and War* (published in November 1914) arguing both that "all war is contrary to the mind and spirit of Christ" and that Britain was right to declare war because it defended a just cause. He stated both that pacifists were necessary, because "the nation could ill do without them", and that "it was not possible for England on 4 August, nor for any Englishman then or now, to act in full accord with the mind of Christ".[53] Temple was to become an infuriating but friendly adversary of pacifists for the next thirty years. Given the sentiments he expressed, and the fact that he rejected a pacifist article by Hodgkin, it was hardly surprising that the *Papers for War Time* group soon split into two, with a pacifist section breaking away from those, like Temple, prepared initially to tolerate, and subsequently to promote, the war.[54]

The break was brought closer by two events occurring in September. First, a group of Free Church pastors issued a statement that "the Passion and Cross of Jesus Christ seem to us the utter repudiation of the method of violence. . . . Christian men should feel themselves forbidden to take part in war; the only legitimate and practical way of the Church is the way of love".[55] Then, a Quaker gathering at Llandudno, originally planned as a time of renewal for the Society of Friends, developed into a debate on the relationship of war to other social ills. Involving Henry Hodgkin, Lucy Gardner and other Friends, as well as some non-Quakers like Richard Roberts, they concluded there was more work to be done. A series of follow-up meetings ensued, including non-Quakers uncomfortable with the *Papers for War Time* group.

Late in November, Roberts wrote to Hodgkin advocating "foundations for a deliberate and forthright propaganda of the Kingdom of God outside the ordinary ecclesiastical channels". In other words a new organisation which he suggested should make use of touring caravans, taking preachers to street corners around the country who would preach a reconciliation that was not only personal but social and international as well.[56]

The follow-up to the Llandudno gathering took place in early December at the Collegium, the Pimlico base of the Swanwick Free Church Fellowship.[57] Anglicans Maude Royden and Mary E. Phillips were among those present. Royden was uncomfortable with calls for the reconstruction of the whole fabric of society. Her pacifism was always to be more pragmatic than principled; she stated that she had no interest in seeking martyrdom. Phillips and Basil Yeaxlee called for a "peace army", an idea that Royden, despite her reluctance to seek martyrdom, was later to take up with vigour. The practical conclusion of the Pimlico conference was a call for:

> the holding of a school of study and prayer during the Christmas vacation at which all who are prepared to take part in the campaign to follow should come together in order to discuss the lines of their message, how to meet the arguments which will be brought forward, and the message of approach to others. An important feature should be ample time spent in prayer and waiting upon God.[58]

Royden was one of the initial members of the planning group for the study school, along with Hodgkin and Roberts. In turn these invited Lucy Gardner, McEwan Lawson, J. St G. Heath (Warden of Toynbee Hall), William Fearon Halliday (1874-1932, Presbyterian) and (later) Roderick K. Clark to join them.[59] On their behalf, pacifist student Rendel Wyatt (later a conscientious objector sent to France) asked Ebenezer Cunningham (1881-1977, a deacon of Emmanuel Congregational Church and a mathematics fellow at St John's College) to find an appropriate venue for the study school in Cambridge. Correspondence with the Vice-Chancellor, Montague R. James, led to the offer of the Arts Theatre as a meeting place.[60]

Silent Night, Stille Nacht

Whilst Christian opponents of the war were preparing for a momentous gathering in Cambridge, British and German soldiers were engaged in their own commentary on the insanity of war, climbing out of their trenches, exchanging gifts and even, in isolated pockets, playing football in No-Man's Land on Christmas Day. The situation varied along the hundreds of miles of Western Front, but the letters and diaries of those involved leave no doubt as to the extraordinary nature of the occasion. While struggling to articulate the deeper meaning of their experiences, the soldiers concerned were cautiously acknowledging that common humanity, and the Christian narrative of Incarnation and peace on earth for all people, went beyond the national call to war.

Private Walter Mockett wrote to Master Charlie Miller on 28 December 1914:

> Xmas Day was spent by us in a most remarkable way, the Germans and our fellows got out of their trenches and shook hands with each other, the Germans said "you no shoot, we no shoot", so we agreed, and all day long we walked about on top of the trenches, where in the ordinary course of events it would have been instant death for us. I went over and talked to some of them, they said they were fed up with the war and were ready to go home.[61]

Sergeant Spence Sanders, whose trench was separated from the German lines by a mere fifty yards of frozen mud and bodies, wrote to Miss Noel Sanders on the same day:

> Christmas Day in the trenches! And of all extraordinary days, it took the biscuit.
>
> An order passed along the line not to shoot. A few minutes after, I saw the Germans getting up out of their trenches. I was with the Capt. & the Colonel. We rushed along to see that the men didn't shoot – found our men getting out of the trench as well. I'm dashed if they didn't walk out, meet the Germans & start shaking hands and chatting to them like old friends! Lots of the Germans could talk English – I went out, of course. In a few minutes we were ordered back to the trenches, but shortly after a proper truce was arranged to bury the dead. There were lots of dead between the trenches – English who had fallen in a charge a week or so before & Germans who had been there for ages. They were not a pretty sight.
>
> We all went out & chatted to the Germans – they were nice fellows & quite decent clean looking men – not the dirty ruffians I had expected. When the dead were buried, the Padre, who, by a stroke of luck had come down with the Col. that morning for a look round, read a short service, the Germans standing at one side & we at the other. The truce was to continue till 5.30 in the evening but we found the Germans did not want to do any firing & agreed that we would not if they didn't & so there had been no firing when we came away last night. . . . [62]

That padre was a Church of Scotland minister, J. Esslemont Adams, who, according to Sanders, read "just a prayer and a bit of the Gospel or something – it was a queer scene".[63] Unattributed press cuttings refer to an impromptu game of football between the opposing armies elsewhere along the Front, using a hare as a ball. Other articles include an account by Lance-Corporal George Dyce, who said of the Germans, "They don't want to fight any more than we do; they are as fed up of this game as we are fit to be. They told us that they would not shoot if we did not, so we have had a holiday for the last two days we were in the trenches. . . . I thought peace was proclaimed, but no such luck."[64]

Sanders's diaries go into more detail about his experience and indicate that, in his part of the Front, the truce lasted well into the New Year. On the 27th he reported that there had still been no shooting, and on the 30th, "practically no firing", adding, "The Germans fired on a ration party one night but apologised the next day – said they thought it was reinforcements". Writing from No. 2 subsection Chartreux Trenches on New Year's Day 1915, Sanders noted once again:

> Of all extraordinary warfare this takes the biscuit. There was no firing until midnight or thereabouts when a few volleys were fired into the air to welcome in the new year. We got a crowd together and sang Auld Lang Syne and God Save the King. The Germans sang some songs and played God Save the King on the mouth organ and everyone shouted "Happy New Year". Then the Pipe major came along and played; he had come down specially. We fortunately were able to give him a drop of rum. This morning the men are wandering about all over getting brown bread and other things from the Germans. Our artillery is going to start shooting soon. I believe the Germans have been warned.[65]

In fact even on 3 January, Sanders noted, the truce continued, with the Germans shouting to him at one point to get back into the trench to avoid some artillery fire. It was not war resistance as such, and the participants would soon become combatants once more, but the spontaneous seasonal truce was a powerful critique of the deadly exercise in which they were engaged.

December 1914: "More Than We Have Yet Seen"

On the evening of Monday 28 December 1914 over 120 people (only half of whom were Quakers) assembled at Trinity Hall, Cambridge to consider their personal and corporate response to the war. It was a diverse inter-denominational gathering, at a time when the ecumenical movement was in its youth. Anglicans present included Lansbury, Mary Phillips, William Corbett Roberts, Royden and Temple. The dominant figure was Richard Roberts, who presided over the conference and who presented a draft "Basis" for the new organisation on that first evening to allow participants to consider it in good time, "waiting upon God".

The following morning Royden spoke on "The Nature of Christian Obedience", an obedience that must be greater than one's obedience to the nation, and an obedience that could not be deferred until some later date when humanity, somehow, might be more receptive. The limit of Christian obedience to the state would prove to be less of a concern in England than it would be elsewhere, particularly for Lutheran churches. It would be an issue that greatly exercised the new peace-making Archbishop of Uppsala, Nathan Söderblom, and his Scandinavian colleagues.

It was clear to Royden that Jesus himself rejected the nation's claim to absolute obedience.

> His refusal to take the "national" position, and become the leader of a national revolt against oppression, is the more significant that – by our own standards – it was not an unjust cause that He was desired to lead. . . . It was His refusal that turned the people against Him. When they cried "Crucify Him!" they expressed their hatred of the man who might have helped his people, and who would not.
>
> The impression left upon His disciples was that they must follow His example. They offered no resistance to persecution. Their women and their children suffered, and themselves; but it did not occur to them that they had a right to resist, or that the example given to them by their Master could be for any reason set aside. They seemed to have felt, with Tertullian, that when He disarmed St Peter, Christ disarmed them all. . . .
>
> Christ came to a world not ready for Him – so unready that it crucified Him. He taught His disciples that they must not be overcome with evil, but must overcome it with good; and by 'good' He does not seem to have meant swords and other arms but love and patience and kindness and meekness. He rebuked a disciple who imagined that he might defend his Master with the sword, and those others who desired to punish a village which rejected Him. He did not wait to come until the world was sufficiently advanced at least not to crucify Him and torture His disciples. He did not tell them that some day, when good was stronger and men better than now, it would be their duty to rely wholly on love and put aside earthly weapons of defence. He told them to overcome evil with good *now*, and in this command there was surely contained a promise – the promise that good is really stronger than evil; not to be stronger some day, but stronger *now*. They were, they believed, to stake everything on this promise, and to go on believing it, even if it resulted in their death. For Christ, believing in the triumph of love, was crucified, and so they knew that the most frightful risks and the most abject (apparent) failure were to be accepted with

unshaken confidence in His promise. They were to "be perfect" not at some future time when other people also were better, and they no longer tied and bound with the chain of their own sins; but *now*.[66]

In his refusal to lead a national revolt, Jesus was true to his own ideal, said Royden:

If we had followed Him without compromise, as did His first disciples, we should have been accused, as they were, of being "bad citizens", disloyal to the State; but we should by now have made war impossible, and saved the world from evils unspeakable, and hatred and disunity. If we had accepted in August, 1914, His teaching in its glorious idealism, we should even then perhaps have saved Belgium and the world from a devastating conflict. If now we did so, not because the sacrifices of war are too great, but because we see that peace is better, and love a greater force than war – what then would happen?[67]

Royden had heard church representatives claiming, as they would in future wars of the twentieth century, that the Sermon on the Mount was a picture of God's future Kingdom, and not a manual for present behaviour in a sinful world. She disagreed, arguing for greater loyalty to the one who had said, "I am the Way":

There is no time at which our Saviour ceases to be the Way. There is no time at which good is less strong or evil stronger than before. We plead that *now* is not the time, and point to our own sins as ground and excuse for putting off the hour of the ideal. We "make a god of our own weakness and bow down to it". And it is true that every succeeding sin has made it harder to turn to Christ, but it is not true that any sin has absolved us from doing so. It is true that in putting off so long our attempt to make the will of God prevail "in earth as it is in heaven", we have made a world very unlike heaven; but it is not true that at any time we are justified in putting it off a little longer, until it is a little easier. It will never be easier. If we do not believe in the Sermon on the Mount in such sense that we consent to live by it when it is dangerous, we shall not find the world ready to listen to it when it is safe.[68]

In other addresses the Conference not only considered the relation between war and the Cross, but the diversity of themes that were to be the strengths and weaknesses of the body that was about to be formed. These included piety (the group was nearly called the Order of Reconciliation, which would have reinforced the thinking of those who saw pacifism as a vocation for a few) and politics, including diverse social issues of a sort that were often to prove distractions. They would always be at their most effective when they focussed on the specific issue of war and peace, rather than on the ills of society in general.

Not all were content with the socially unthreatening direction the gathering was taking. Lansbury, who had written earlier in the month that the world was plunged into war because it refused to literally accept the teachings of Christ, wanted more commitment to political action.[69] He had reservations about the "indefiniteness" of the conference: "We were rather nebulous in our conclusions and did not, as an organised body, do very much against the war. William Temple, when I met him later, seemed to have given up any idea of being able to put an end to the slaughter till it reached its appropriate high-water mark. . . . We talked a lot about Christian witness, but few among us were willing to say war was murder".[70]

On 31 December 1914, the final day of the conference, it was agreed that a new organisation be formed to enable Christian pacifists to face up to what was already threatening to become a lengthy war.[71] The Fellowship of Reconciliation was born, and its "Basis" became one of the formative statements of Christian pacifism.

1. That Love, as revealed and interpreted in the life and death of Jesus Christ, involves more than we have yet seen, that it is the only power by which evil can be overcome, and the only sufficient basis of human society.
2. That, in order to establish a world-order based on Love, it is incumbent upon those who believe in this principle to accept it fully, both for themselves and in their relation to others, and to take the risks involved in doing so in a world which does not as yet accept it.
3. That, therefore, as Christians, we are forbidden to wage war, and that our loyalty to our country, to humanity, to the Church Universal, and to Jesus Christ, our Lord and Master, calls us instead to a life of service for the enthronement of Love in personal, social, commercial and national life.
4. That the Power, Wisdom and Love of God stretch far beyond the limits of our present experience, and that He is ever waiting to break forth into human life in new and larger ways.
5. That since God manifests Himself in the world through men and women, we offer ourselves to Him for His redemptive purpose, to be used by Him in whatever way He may reveal to us.[72]

It was held to be a matter of principle that the Fellowship would state its message of reconciliation "positively and constructively", and "not spend itself in mere protest".[73] Political action, therefore, would be more likely to be taken up by the Union of Democratic Control and

the No-Conscription Fellowship. For some, the F.O.R. was essentially a
political pressure-group, but most members of the F.O.R. desired rather
"to proclaim their conviction in a spirit of humility, honour and love,
to exercise forbearance in argument, and to guard against the danger of
controversial methods, believing that they are but a few out of many,
both in this land and others, who are seeking to know and act upon the
truth at this time".[74]

With a basis that emphasised the love of God and the service of
humanity, it was inevitable that the new organisation would, at times,
be tempted to branch out into attempting to tackle a variety of social
ills. Nothing less than "a new order of life" was desired, though the
immediate task was "the call to make clear the Christian witness in
relation to war".[75] The formation of the F.O.R. was welcomed by the
Peace Society, though the feeling was not always reciprocal, as F.O.R.
members like C.J. Cadoux felt that the Peace Society was irrelevant and
insufficiently pacifist.[76] The key concern for the F.O.R. would be the
pacifist commitment of its members to the refusal to wage war, albeit
as part of an all-encompassing world-view. Unlike other campaigning
groups F.O.R. members rejected all war and hatred, rather than merely
the specific conflict of the moment. The F.O.R. would be less concerned
with immediate political action than with the (eschatological) theology of
the Kingdom of God.[77] The most active of the early F.O.R. subcommittees
were a Children's Committee, considering how practically to educate
the younger generation in F.O.R. values, and a group responsible for
the production of Christian pacifist literature – pamphlets and leaflets
abounded. In the first month of its existence the F.O.R. issued a call "To
Christ's Disciples Everywhere", taking up the eschatological theme of
waiting for the revelation of God. The glory of war was definitely not
the glory of God. It was a powerful and moving call:

> Listen to the tread of the armies in all countries! With what glorious
> self-abandon are men to-day offering their lives in the service of
> their nation! Surely the heart of Him Who gave His life for men is
> rejoicing in this heroism. "Greater love hath no man than this that
> a man lay down his life for his friends".
>
> Listen again, and you shall hear another sound! It is the deep
> sorrow of a world in anguish. Men stricken, women bereaved,
> children fatherless. In that cry of pain we hear the tones of the Son
> of man. In our affliction he is afflicted. Yes, more – He is cast out;
> for we have not followed Him whose name we profess to honour.
> We have builded our city on the wrong foundation, and now it is
> falling upon us. We have denied our lord; we have betrayed Him;
> we have crucified Him again. Yet in the day of His rejection we
> still hear Him say, "Father, forgive them, for they know not what

they do". We have thought to please Him when we slew the men for whom he died and pierced to the heart the women whom He loves. Our prayers have been mingled with bitter thoughts of our enemies. When we have risen to the height of self-sacrifice, we have found no better way of expressing it than by going forth to kill our brethren.

This is not the way in which our Master overcame the world. He opposed evil with good, hate with love, violence with meekness. On the Cross He accepted the full consequences of this choice of weapons. Forsaken Himself, leaving His dearest friends outwardly unprotected, and with His cause apparently shattered, He there and then established a kingdom which has continued to grow until this day.

We, in our wisdom, have chosen other methods for the establishment of truth and goodness in the world. Our choice is seen to-day to be fraught with infinite pain and disaster to mankind. Let us turn from this great folly and sin. Let us learn again at the feet of Him whose name we take. His way is best.

We cannot wait until the world is converted. Our Master did not wait. It is high time that we were ourselves converted to a genuine following of Jesus. For His disciples there is no call to anything less than a life-service. It is one of never-ceasing resistance to every form of evil. No quarter can be given to this enemy, whether we find him in our hearts or in the world in which we live. This resistance calls forth the very best that is in us, and, as we give it, is reinforced by the unfailing power of the Love of God. We may be forsaken and apparently defeated. But at no point can we resist evil with evil, hate with hate, violence with violence. In this resolve we pray to God to strengthen us. . . .

We wage war against all breeds of war. We believe in and seek with all our strength to build a new order in which war shall be done away, and all peoples may unite in a fellowship of mutual service. For the development of all that is best in human life, and for the sake of the generations that follow us in all nations, we determine to press forward to this goal in the firm conviction that God has called us, and that He will defend the right.[78]

4.
The Pen is Mightier Than the Sword:
George Lansbury

Background of a Revolutionary

Following the death of his father, and under the influence of the then Rector of Whitechapel, George Lansbury was confirmed, aged sixteen, in 1875.[1] Even as a schoolboy he was politically active, organising a petition demanding a playtime, signed by the pupils of his Whitechapel school and handed to its headmaster. There were early speaking engagements, in favour of toleration of minorities in Ireland, and on the subject of peace and war; there were meetings and demonstrations against Disraeli and imperialism. Influenced by William Morris, Tolstoy and Francis of Assisi, Lansbury was later to describe himself as an "inconsistently consistent" pacifist all his life, opposing all wars and violent upheavals, whilst having a "pugnacious disposition" and sheltering all manner of revolutionaries and freedom-fighters.[2] After a failed attempt to emigrate to Australia, Lansbury and his wife Bessie – who was also politically active – settled in Bow, East London. From an early age Lansbury was not averse to direct action: during a period away from the church, he attended a meeting where a vicar attempted to impose his own choice for trustee of a local charity before promptly closing the meeting. Lansbury urged everyone to remain in their place; he was then elected chair and other trustees chosen, a decision that was later upheld by the Charity Commissioners.[3] He joined the Social Democratic Federation (S.D.F.) in 1892, becoming a leading socialist campaigner. Within three years he was organising secretary, chair of the party conference and a parliamentary candidate. Standing again at the general election of 1900, he found his campaign meetings were disrupted by patriots complaining that he was a "Pro-Boer" traitor.[4] Lansbury chaired one "Stop the War" meeting of 1,500 people in the East End, where speakers had to overcome thuggish renderings of "Rule Britannia". At another meeting in Trafalgar Square, knives and missiles were thrown. S.D.F. opposition was not necessarily against all war, but was consistent in its condemnation of the speculators and capitalists on whose behalf, they argued, the war was fought. Lansbury's views were expressed in one of his election campaign leaflets: "the war in South Africa was an unjust war, got up, like the Jameson Raid, in the interests solely of diamond mine owners and millionaires".[5]

When a wealthy Liberal M.P. tried to influence Lansbury by telling him that he gave away one tenth of his income to the poor, Lansbury replied that "we Socialists want to prevent you getting the nine-tenths". He was quite prepared to speak on a platform alongside prominent Liberals, however, when he considered the cause just, as for example as when campaigning against the Boer War. Indeed his opposition to any imperialism can be traced to the influence of Gladstone. In an article sympathetic to the Liberal leader in 1892, Lansbury had written, "Let us refuse (either as individuals or as a nation) to sanction the increase of wealth at the expense of others, be they white, yellow, red or black men".[6]

In 1902, two years after Lansbury had been the Social Democratic Federation candidate for Bow and Bromley at the General Election, he was called upon by the local curate, William Corbett Roberts.[7] Roberts wanted Lansbury's political support for a victimised elderly woman in the area. It was the start of a long friendship between the two men. Lansbury had moved away from the church in the final decade of the nineteenth century and was only just beginning to make his way back.[8] Roberts influenced Lansbury's attendance at Bow Church one Sunday, when Bishop Lang of Stepney came to preach, and the two men met at supper afterwards in the rectory.[9] Roberts was largely responsible for Lansbury's permanent return to active Christian faith.[10] To the astonishment and concern of many of his socialist colleagues, Lansbury committed himself to the Church of England, and to Bow Church in particular, where his family became active and where his children joined the Sunday School. It was to be a love-hate relationship for nearly forty years, with the articulate, socialist, pacifist, working-class Lansbury a thorn in the flesh of those who might otherwise have been complacent in the comfortable higher echelons of the church.[11]

In the general election of 1910, Lansbury was elected Labour M.P. for Bow and Bromley. He was soon arguing for workers' rights (the Liberal Government was unsympathetic to his demand for an annual holiday entitlement), and he nearly succeeded in steering through legislation to allow Church of England clergy to become M.P.s. At an I.L.P. conference in 1910, he called for international action by workers to preserve peace in the event of national leaders declaring war (attempting the same, with negligible success four, years later).[12] In a controversial court case Tom Mann, co-founder of the Transport Workers' Federation, was one of several activists convicted of publishing a "Don't Shoot" pamphlet during the seamen's strike of 1910. The treatise incited soldiers to lay down their arms during labour disputes and not fire on their fellow workers. Inside parliament, Lansbury and his colleagues argued that the case should be dropped; outside Parliament, they supported a "Free Speech" campaign and raised funds for the defendants. The convictions were upheld, but the prison sentences slightly reduced.[13] The defining moment of his first, brief, period in the House of Commons came after only two years when he was suspended following an altercation with Prime Minister Asquith concerning the mistreatment of imprisoned women suffrage campaigners. Demanding that women's suffrage be added to a Government bill on universal male suffrage, Lansbury resigned his seat with the intention of having his stand endorsed by the electorate at the subsequent by-election. To his horror, he lost, and did not return to Parliament until 1922. In the interim he continued to support calls for women's suffrage, being imprisoned himself for such campaigning in 1913, whilst also being active on Poplar Council and editing the *Herald*.

A New Herald *for Peace*

Lansbury regarded the time of his association with the *Herald*, from its inception in 1912 until 1925, as one of the most worrying, yet happiest, episodes of his life. Initially it was the *Daily Herald*, attempting to address a socialist, working class readership that other newspapers did not reach. Amongst the early benefactors of the paper was Harold Jocelyn Buxton, at that time the curate of Thaxted.[14] Lansbury was editor throughout the traumatic years of world war. Within days of the outbreak of war he was forced by economic pressures to increase the price, and, by the end of September 1914, the frequency of publication was reduced to a weekly edition, the *Herald*. It was a credit not only to Lansbury and his supporters, but also to the much-criticised Government, that such an anti-establishment, anti-war publication was able to survive during the emotionally charged years of 1914-1918. Yet survive it did and found new strength, reverting to printing daily editions again by the end of March 1919. Regular contributors with diverse views included G.K. Chesterton (1874-1936), Gerald Gould (1885-1936) and John Scurr (1876-1932).[15] Occasional articles were published from figures across the Labour movement, keeping alive debate about such issues as Ireland, trade unions, and the hopes and aspirations for a transformed social order when the fighting should eventually cease.[16]

Attitudes expressed towards the war were many and varied. A consistent line was that illustrated in the cartoons of Will Dyson. The beneficiaries of the war, the armaments manufacturers whose sales increased and the mill owners whose prices were raised, were ruthlessly portrayed as exploiters of those who would lose their lives or limbs and

of the poverty-stricken families left without a breadwinner, not only
during the war but afterwards. But Dyson was no pacifist, and neither
were many others on the left.[17] If there was opposition to the war (and
not all contributors were opposed) it came from a sense of socialist
solidarity, and contempt for the abuses of international diplomacy
which had resulted in the war.[18] For many it was acceptable to participate
in the war, despite being critical of it. Despite catching the national
mood of "To Berlin in Three Weeks", there was in the *Herald* none of
the jingoism of the mainstream press.[19], Readers were also cautioned
about the sensationalist stories of German atrocities appearing in many
newspapers.[20] As the war progressed though, there was a tendency
for some commentators to single out the special nature of Prussian
militarism. Yet there remained a sense of international solidarity with
the German people. An early editorial, noting that militarism was the
enemy of German and British workers alike, stated, "We cannot draw
up an indictment against the German people. We have no quarrel
with them. Many of their ideals are our ideals. The struggle of their
workers is our struggle. Their foes are our foes".[21] The Kaiser's Day of
Prayer at the start of the war prompted A. St John Adcock to express,
in verse, his observations on Christians killing Christians, with one
stanza ending, "Thou wert their God no less than ours".[22] A report that
German Catholic bishops had issued a pastoral statement calling for a
spirit of penance ("We do not wish to busy ourselves with the account-
book of other nations, but with our own; we do not want to examine
the conscience of our enemies, but our own") indicated the humanity
of German people, and countered the popular tendency for demonising
them.[23] The *Herald* also printed accounts of German peace movement
activity that would not have reached the pages of other newspapers.[24]

The intense feeling of solidarity that Lansbury had towards working
people did not lessen because of his isolation on the issue of war. During
the first autumn of the war, he spent a number of weeks touring the
country, "With Kitchener's Army", in solidarity with working people who
had volunteered to join the armed forces.[25] He confessed to admiring the
spirit of the men: "I hate and detest the war with all its hideous massacre
and waste of human life, and even now wish to cry aloud "Give peace
in our time, O Lord!" but in the spirit of it all, my heart goes out to my
fellow-men here at home and abroad. . . ."[26] His pacifist commitment,
however, was increased by the war; even anger at social injustice could
no longer be used as an excuse for violence, as he told his readers in 1915:

A few short years ago in East London I took part with many of you
in a struggle where the weapon used by the governing class was
that of starvation. In and out of the homes of East London I went
day by day in that terrible year of 1913, and saw with my own eyes

the starvation of women and children. Over and over again I wished to kill, and when, one day in Liverpool and another in London, I saw police and soldiers, horse and foot, charging and bâtoning my unarmed brothers and sisters my whole being rose in rebellion, and for a moment I hated both police and soldiers. Now I hate no longer. Soldiers and police in these struggles are the agents of governments, who in turn are the agents of monopolist possessing classes. I know now as I never knew before that force and violence are not the weapons we must use for securing our happiness and well-being; that these can only come to us when brotherhood, love, and co-operation are the guiding principles of our life. We of the working-class and labour movements have again and again proclaimed our belief that all human life is sacred. It is easy to do this when days are bright and the sky clear. Let us, in these days of murder and rapine, of brutal, unashamed slaughter, still preserve our faith, and under all circumstances and conditions proclaim our undying faith that the object and mission of life is to establish here in our midst the kingdom of love and brotherhood which we have been taught by the Churches to believe is the kingdom of God on earth.[27]

Later, he wrote that, "Nothing which comes to us by inflicting injustice, suffering and wrong on others can ever be of the least worth to anyone".[28] Still, he remained totally committed to social revolution, but conducted nonviolently, and he resisted any attempt to draw the Labour movement into violence: "We must have not only a pure faith but pure methods".[29]

In January 1915 Lansbury was permitted to visit France, from where he produced four articles on the front.[30] He was well aware of the human suffering the war was producing. Before and after his journey there were impassioned pleas, in the *Herald*, for war to stop. At Christmas in 1914 Francis Meynell called the war a "ghastly crime". He believed that this and every war was seen by God when issuing the command, "Thou shalt not kill", and by Christ when rebuking those who took up the sword in Gethsemane. "Evidently", argued Meynell, "the Bishop of London thinks we are now fighting for something far more sacred than the life and freedom of Christ, his God!"[31] It was a poignant time, not least for those soldiers of opposing armies who fraternised in No Man's Land. The *Herald* editorial carried Lansbury's distinctive tone:

The little Child whose birthday we celebrate this week grew to be a man, and was slain as a pestilential agitator because He taught the greatest thing in life was service. . . . Today, even with the guns' boom in our ears, let us all renew our faith in the ultimate triumph of the Gospel of the Prince of Peace, and proclaim with an ever-insistent voice that the only enemies worth fighting are those which engender envy, hatred, malice, and all uncharitableness, and the only thing worth dying for is the sacred truth that we are each our brother's keeper, and that an injury to any one of the children of men is an injury to us all. . . . If we Englishmen loved our German fellow-men as we love ourselves we should not be slaughtering each other in France.[32]

First-week predictions of air warfare came to pass three years later, when air raids on London were recorded.[33] Anti-war protests were regularly reported, including an initial statement from the N.P.C.[34] It was noted that Madame Lucy Thoumaiam, the founder and president of the Women's Swiss Union of Peace, had urged a London meeting of women to pray, to nurse (the opposite of fighting) and to call for arbitration.[35] It was regarded as a sufficiently compatible publication for the Women's Peace Crusade to advertise a gathering in Hyde Park on the eve of All Souls' Day 1914 to remember those who had died in the first three months of the war.[36] There were supportive accounts before and after the International Congress of Women at The Hague in 1915.[37] When, in response to German peace moves in December 1916, U.S. President Wilson asked both sides to state their peace terms the following month, the *Evening News* ran the headline, "NO!", to which the *Herald* responded with a special edition bearing the headline, "YES!"[38]

Wilson's was not the only American initiative to stop the war. The previous December a boat, *Oscar II*, had left New Jersey for a tour of neutral European nations, hoping to persuade them to broker a peace deal. The sponsor of this venture, persuaded by such noted radicals as Jane Addams, was the capitalist Henry Ford, manufacturer of motor cars. As an American businessman, Ford realised that if Europeans stopped fighting and made tractors and motor cars instead, everyone would be better off, including him. He took over a transatlantic vessel and filled it with diverse peace activists and celebrities in an unsuccessful attempt to start independent diplomacy between the belligerents through the mediation of neutral countries. One of the celebrities on board was a singer, Alfred Bryan, the composer of a popular 1915 song, which the dockside band was playing as the ship set sail. The song was called, "I didn't raise my boy to be a soldier", which sold 650,000 copies in its first three months (see illustration on p. 73).[39]

The *Herald* was more at home with socialist action. As well as the campaign against conscription, the newspaper publicised various peace demonstrations, such as that by an alliance of left groups in London on 15 April 1917, and the parade of peace banners in front of Westminster Abbey in September that year by the Workers Suffrage Federation. The banner, "England Arise! Start Negotiations and Save the World", provoked strong debate on the streets.[40]

As the war ended the *Herald* led a clamour for Labour to be represented at any peace conference, in order to establish what earlier manifestos had called a "people's peace". Originally two Albert Hall rallies were planned, but the second was banned for fear of a demonstration of revolutionary character. Under strong pressure the management of the Albert Hall relented and allowed two further rallies to replace the one that had been repressed, thus permitting more than had originally been planned.[41]

Journalists, Christians and Communists

Attitudes towards Christianity in the columns of the *Herald* were complex. When prelates stepped out of line they received their come-uppance. Pre-war advocacy by Edward Talbot, the Bishop of Winchester, of the use of the cat against young offenders, for example, was mercilessly lampooned.[42] On the other hand, a number of clergy, sympathetic to the *Herald's* aims, would contribute articles. W.J. Piggott urged people to join trade unions and hold protest meetings to get the war stopped.[43] John M. Maillard used graphic language to describe "the lass and the mother whose love lies mangled by the war-engines of the insatiable and callous lust-monger", before calling on people to resist "every attempt to profane life by an ignominious sale of our sacred humanity".[44] There were statements published by the Society of Friends and the Fellowship of Reconciliation, an item on the "Social Influence of Good Friday" by Scott Holland, and a debate on religion between H.G. Wells and Conrad Noel.[45] The pioneering and inclusive ministry of the socialist priest Percy Dearmer at Primrose Hill was commended, including a reported tribute from Maude Royden.[46] The Christian Left's contempt for the peripheral National Mission of 1916 was well documented.[47] It was noted that Russell Wakefield, the pro-war Bishop of Birmingham, had admitted "if the religion of Christ were the prevailing moral force, war would not be".[48] The founding of the Baptist Peace Fellowship with one hundred members agreeing that "all war is contrary to Christianity", was commented upon, as was the founding of a Roman Catholic group, the Guild of the Pope's Peace.[49] The *Herald* applauded papal initiatives for peace, including an appeal issued by the new Pope, Benedict XV, on 28 July 1915 as the anniversary of the outbreak of war approached. Describing himself as "sharing the troubled trepidation of numberless families, and conscious of the imperious duties imposed upon us in days so sorrowful by the sublime mission of peace and love to us entrusted", Benedict said he "quickly conceived the firm intention of consecrating our every activity and all our power to the reconciliation of the belligerent peoples".[50] Benedict cried out, "Let the mutual will to destroy be laid aside!", adding, "Blessed be he who shall first raise the olive branch and shall extend his right hand to the foe, offering reasonable condition of peace!"[51] The new Guild of the Pope's Peace circulated Benedict XV's Easter message of 1916:

'Peace be with you.' These sweet words, spoken by the risen Saviour to the Apostles, the Holy Father readdresses to all men. May those nations now at peace preserve it, thanking God for so great a blessing! May those at war soon lay down the sword and so end the slaughter that is dishonouring Europe and humanity![52]

The *Herald* also reported that the Roman Catholic Bishop of Middlesbrough, Richard Lacy (1841-1929), had told Middlesbrough Peace by Negotiation Society that "if the present inhuman war is ever to be brought to an end, it will only be brought about by negotiation. . . . Meanwhile, rivers of blood are flowing, and countless hearts are made desolate".[53]

Alongside such articles were others indicating that the working class regarded as irrelevant or harmful that which passed for Christianity.[54] Yet Lansbury's Christmas message for 1915 was simply 1 Corinthians 13,[55] and the following February he gave over half a page to describing in positive terms the regular village church service he had been to the previous Sunday, and the hope it had engendered.[56] As the war was entering its third year, he wrote:

We shall not get over the difficulties of today, we shall not transfer the evils of militarism from our own backs or destroy the causes which make for war, until we have destroyed the spirit which is prevalent everywhere – that spirit which sends men and women out into the world merely to get something rather than to give. . . . The only thing that can save us is the practice of true religion – Cooperation, Brotherhood, Love and Care for one another. . . . [We must] fight against Mammon and greed, selfishness and lust of power, whether of individuals or nations. . . . The world will have peace when men and women are good enough to accept all the implications of the Gospel of Christ.[57]

Lansbury, who spoke at Kingsley Hall on "The Future of Religion", dearly wanted the church to be a force for peace, and would support or criticise it accordingly.[58] His language became increasingly religious as the war dragged on, with an article at Christmas 1917 being a powerful evangelical sermon. By then he had come to see pacifism, socialism and Christianity as inseparable, or, perhaps more accurately, as a trinity in unity. He argued that Jesus, "was, and still is, the greatest Social Revolutionist", and all the Labour movement should heed him.

To my comrades and friends who cannot accept any religion based on the supernatural, may I say "Christmas has the same message of life, and life more abundantly, for you as well as for all mankind"? What better law of life can there be than His great law "Be not overcome by evil, but overcome evil by good"? All wars, all revolutions have so far failed to accomplish the salvation of the world. They have all failed because those who organise war and physical force revolution rest their faith on the assumption that it is possible by brute force and the domination of material power to compel humanity to order its method of life and conduct in a particular way. History proves that all such policies ultimately fail, that empires built on force – whether such empires are created and kept going by Roman, German, or British rulers – are bound to fail, certain to perish. . . . From what quarter shall hope come? Comrades, from the hearts and consciences of ourselves, from the ranks of those men and women of every class, of every race, and every colour and creed by whom Christ's words "The Kingdom of God is within you" are understood.[59]

The major Christian festivals were opportunities for Lansbury to reflect on days "when false prophets call us to worship the god of war in the guise of the Prince of Peace, when bishops and others bless the banners of opposing armies, and call upon Christians of all the warring nations to rend each other". Such days gave him and others the chance to extol a faith of peace, whilst being highly critical of a religion that enabled war. "A Carol" was a seasonal poem by John Scurr:

> Lay aside your wars and fighting,
> Let your foolish quarrels cease;
> Thrust out envy, banish hatred,
> Hail the lowly Prince of Peace.
>
> Tell again the simple story
> Told to shepherds in the night,
> Christ is born in manger lowly,
> Lord of all and King of Light.
>
> While around the oxen kneeling,
> Symbols of the trusting weak,
> He has come, to them revealing
> Triumph for the faithful meek.
>
> Love shall conquer. It was promised
> In that lowly manger bed;
> Wars shall cease, and passions vanish,
> Malice number with the dead.
>
> See the Star of Love ascending
> Making rosy all the dawn;
> Love is her on earth appealing,
> Sing with joy, 'tis Christmas morn.[60]

Ben Turner's "Christmas 1916" carried a similar theme:

> Glory to God in the highest,
> Peace and Goodwill towards men;
> Thus sang the angels in Christland,
> When shall they sing it again?
>
> When shall the guns become silent?
> When shall the slaughtering cease?
> When may the people find wisdom?
> When shall the people have peace?
>
> Glory to God in the highest,
> Peace and Goodwill towards men;
> Sighing we speak the old message.
> Softly we sing it again.
>
> Heart throbs go out to the trenches,
> Out to our lads on our ships,
> Out to our lads in death's quarters,
> Wishes for Peace cross our lips.
>
> Glory to God in the highest,
> Peace and Goodwill towards men;
> Sing it aloud, oh ye angels,
> Speed it abroad once again.
>
> Tell us that God's great commandment
> Bids us to love – not to slay;
> Call all the nations together,
> Bid them His precepts obey.[61]

Although the *Herald* attracted Christians who were opposed to the war, or who were on the political left, most of its readers would have been from the secular Left, who would have agreed with Lansbury that, "organised Christianity has in the matter of this, as in every other modern war, ranged itself on the side of guns and explosives".[62] Yet it was that majority non-Christian readership whom Lansbury addressed on Good Friday 1918, giving his own distinctive analysis of Christian history:

> People may disbelieve the doctrine of the divinity of Christ; may treat as legendary the story of His death and resurrection; but no one can refuse, at least, consideration of the fact that He gave to the world the greatest example of strict logical adherence to the principle of passive resistance. He was not concerned to save Himself, neither was he willing to sacrifice others for His own safety, and though this course of conduct was sure to bring

apparent ruin, He held by it to the end. After His death, for a few short centuries, His followers strove to live as He lived, and the story of their glorious struggle with the militarism of Rome is to be found in the history books dealing with the first three centuries after Christ. Nowadays this has all changed, and priests in khaki, bishops in khaki, are loudly calling to us to fight in a material sense for the "Prince of Peace." No wonder the chaplains at the front tell us with an almost unanimous voice that the Churches have practically lost all influence with the mass of mankind. . . . [63]

His was a revolutionary appeal to evangelical faith; "The call of Christ is to each individual man and woman", he said, unapologetically adding verses from the Sermon on the Mount.[64] For the final All Saints Day meditation of the war, he remembered the casualties on all sides, not only who perished on the battlefield but also the conscientious objectors who died in prison. His conclusion was that "The greatest, grandest, most lasting memorial we can set up to our 'Immortal Dead' will be the abolition of brute force and the establishment of the law of love".[65]

But that is to jump ahead. Of the preceding years, 1916 had been dominated by the issue of conscription (of which more will be said later) and 1917 by the extraordinary news from Russia – the fall of the Tsar. The left held major rallies in London and Leeds to celebrate the end of tyranny. At the end of March, in front of twelve thousand people at the Albert Hall, Lansbury said of the Russian Revolution, "This triumph has come, friends, because for the first time that I know of in history – at least in modern history – soldiers, working class soldiers, have refused to fire on the workers". He added that "when the working classes of all nations refuse to shoot down the working-classes of other countries, governments won't be able to make wars any more. . . . This war would end tomorrow if the troops on all sides march out in No Man's Land and refused to fight any longer".[66] In Leeds, Lansbury commended the Russian people and called for "Liberty, Equality and Fraternity the world over". The *Herald* report of the meeting boldly asked, "Leeds Leads: Who Follows?"[67]

It was an optimistic time for printing manifestos for a post-war peace. One such manifesto stated, "Armies and Navies Must Cease To Be".[68] A subsequent scoop was being able to print in full "the treacherous, sordid, thieving Secret Treaties" revealed by the new regime in Russia, showing the deceit of diplomats intent on carving up the post-war map of Europe for economic gain.[69] For such opinions and articles, and for being the editor of the most widely circulated anti-war journal, Lansbury gained a national notoriety that he had not known before. The jingoist Horatio Bottomley even produced a poster, "To the Tower with Lansbury".[70]

5.
Women for Peace

Anglican Pacifist Women

For all that the Peace Society had been reporting women's peace auxiliaries as far back as the early 1820s, the profile of women peacemakers was lower than that of their male contemporaries. There were occasionally female authors of Peace Society publications, though they sometimes felt obliged to hide behind a cloak of anonymity. The nineteenth-century Olive Leaf Circles sounded more genteel than the Quakeresses reported at the 1849 Peace Congress, who apparently reduced French soldiers to shamed timidity. By the end of that century the women's peace movement had become more visible. The activities of political, social and religious women's groups, typified by the campaigning of Catherine Courtney and the revelations of Emily Hobhouse, reached an apotheosis with the writing of Bertha von Suttner. Above all, there was the over-riding issue of suffrage (of which more below) which galvanised increasing numbers of women.

Mary Phillips, who worked for many years with the Y.W.C.A. and "was an authority on industrial problems especially in relation to girls", was one of the women on the F.O.R. General Committee.[1] She found the consensual decision-making "peaceful and uplifting".[2] When F.O.R. debated materialism, she condemned poor labour conditions and argued that the Christian concern should be not with wealth but "well-th", by which she meant a right sharing of the resources God had given to humankind: "the rich need to learn how to live efficiently on less, and the poor how to live wisely on more".[3] She served on F.O.R.'s Conscription Committee, set up following the introduction of compulsory military service in 1916, and also the New Commonwealth Group. This group attempted to define political principles which would be consistent with the values of the F.O.R. Their proposals were described as being

Bradford Women's Peace Crusade !

GREAT DEMONSTRATION

IN CARLTON STREET (SCHOOL YARD),

Sunday next at 3-0 p.m.

SPEAKERS :

Mrs. Philip Snowden,   Miss I. O. Ford,   Mrs. Muir,
Mrs. Pickard,   Mrs. Sandiforth.

PROCESSION, headed by Band, leaves Westgate at 2-30 p.m.

A ticket advertising a Women's Peace Crusade demonstration in Bradford.
Ethel Snowdon was a travelling speaker for the WPC in the north of England. Isabella
Ford, a Leeds Quaker, was a leading figure in the suffrage movement and the ILP.
Fanny Muir was imprisoned for speaking out against the war, with Ethel Sandiforth,
in Shipley Market Place (see p. 167).

of a very far-reaching, if not revolutionary, character. . . bringing
into the minds of people the idea of such changes as would be
needed to bring about a society in accordance with the mind of
Christ. This . . . seems a very large programme, and almost more
than the F.O.R. ought to think of; but yet we feel that there is an
urgent need for men and women to face these questions from the
fundamentally Christian standpoint.[4]

Any recommendations – moderate, left-wing proposals that would
not have been out of place expressed in the U.D.C. or the Independent
Labour Party (I.L.P.) – were never developed into F.O.R. policy, and
remained the work of a handful of selected members.[5] The Group
appears to have disbanded soon after a New Year's conference at the
Quaker centre at Jordans, Beaconsfield, at the start of 1918, to which
Lansbury, Royden and Hewlett Johnson had been invited.[6]

The number of women on the original General Committee was an
indication that the new organisation intended to take a responsible
approach to issues of gender. In 1915, for example, F.O.R. published
a document, *To All Women*. This consisted of appeals from women
in Austria, Britain, France, Germany, Hungary, Russia, Sweden and
Switzerland – including one article from *Jus Suffragi* – and indicated
friendly relations with the newly formed Women's International League
(W.I.L.), hardly surprising given that both Royden and Theodora
Wilson-Wilson held prominent positions in both organisations.[7]
Royden's concerns included "the inconspicuous deaths of those who
never come near the field of battle. It is children unborn, and babies
who die because their mothers are pressed to death with anxiety and

fear and overwork". She had noted that the infant mortality rate in Great Britain rose dramatically in the early months of the war and she suspected the same would be true in Germany. "It makes our rules for the protection of non-combatants seem farcical when we face the fact that the desired exhaustion of Germany means – and must inevitably mean – the deaths of women and children".[8]

Maude Royden is such a significant individual in the story of early twentieth-century Christian war resistance, that I will consider her story in more depth.

Maude Royden, from Wirral to War

Finding Friendship and Faith

In the late nineteenth-century the port of Liverpool was known the world over for its passenger liners, in particular its transatlantic fleet. In the age before air traffic the seas were the dominant medium for long distance travel, bringing wealth to Merseyside and to those who owned the shipping lines. Much of the shipping wealth of Liverpool went to the Royden family. Maude was born in 1876, the sixth daughter and eighth child of Thomas Royden, of Frankby Hall, Birkenhead, a Tory councillor (later M.P), baronet and millionaire. Born with both hips dislocated she was permanently lame, a characteristic which would always cause her to stand out in any gathering.

Reading history at Lady Margaret Hall, Oxford from 1896, she developed a college friendship with Kathleen Courtney (1878-1974). Their correspondence reflected the concerns of affluent, carefree, upper-middle-class youth. There was little indication – barring an aside on the Dreyfus Affair – that both young women would spend their lives at the forefront of the politically aware and active world of social and international issues.

A High Anglican, and describing herself as a Ritualist,[9] the twenty-three year old Royden travelled in Italy. The journey, made her consider – and reject – either becoming Roman Catholic, or even joining a religious order.[10] She was coming to terms with her own religious faith.[11] In Rome she was deeply moved by a painting of the crucifixion by Guido Reni, staring at it for half an hour. This, she felt, was the truth. No one could go to that church every week and not come out a Christian. Struggling with the meaning of this experience on her return home, she concluded prophetically, "I should like to be a philanthropic radical! Doubtless the young and foolish always start with this idea!"[12]

True to her word, she started undertaking social work at the Victoria Women's Settlement, amongst the residents of the slum dwellings around Liverpool's Scotland Road.[13] As she wrote at the time, "This horrible life that is led in the slums must corrupt a nation which cannot at least, solve the problems of pauperism".[14] Her real education had begun. At the end of 1900 she reflected on the interaction of social conditions and moral and spiritual expectations, realising the absurdity of preaching obedience to the seventh commandment on adultery, whether to the letter or in the spirit, in a house where decency was impossible. She added that keeping it to the letter only was not enough, as one was required not merely to be good but to be holy, to engage in a "holy" war, a striving for holiness. She added, hopefully, "Just imagine a whole new century to do something with!"[15]

Royden and the Suffrage Movement

By the time Royden moved back to Oxford as a University Extension lecturer in 1905 she was politically aware and deeply committed to the suffrage movement, soon becoming a formidable speaker in its cause. In 1908, she joined the National Union of Women's Suffrage Societies (N.U.W.S.S), the non-militant suffragists, led by Millicent Garrett Fawcett, who were to number around 100,000 by 1914.[16] Royden became editor of its journal, *Common Cause*, in 1913 but, together with Kathleen Courtney and others, she resigned from the N.U.W.S.S. Executive early in 1915, when Fawcett led it into a pro-war position.[17] Royden continued to write occasionally for *Common Cause*, as when, during the slaughter of war, slips were widely distributed urging men to "forgo no opportunity of paternity", implying that the principal task of women was to replenish the supply of British fighting men for the next generation.

> The nations have gone to war. They have . . . jeered at the work of pacifists . . . and . . . given nothing to . . . less frightful methods of deciding international disputes. Now . . . we have what we have worked for – destruction. Let us bear the anguish with what fortitude we may: but let us not consent to the reckless lowering of the moral standard involved in the advice "forgo no opportunity of paternity"; in the brutal disregard of the rights of the unborn; in the reduction of women to the status of mere breeders of the race.[18]

There was no lasting animosity between Fawcett and Royden, for, in January 1918, when "votes for women" at last reached the statute book, Maude Royden spoke passionately at a major celebratory rally in Queen's Hall – at Fawcett's request. Her speech was followed by the first rendering, in suffrage circles, of the musical setting of Blake's *Jerusalem*, specially composed by Hubert Parry.[19]

In such circumstances it was hardly surprising that, when she compared the generally positive relations and co-operative nature of the suffrage movement with the cumbersome organisation and squabbling of the church, she would be highly critical of the latter. Even in 1917 an Archbishop's Committee on church and state declined to endorse women's suffrage, inciting Royden to rue,

Anyone who has cared about any reform has the same experience. The Church does not ask if it is good or bad; she inquires into the state of public opinion.[20]

Is God dead, or has His promise failed, that we, instead of confidently expecting to be led by His Holy Spirit, must be led by the public opinion of the world instead?[21]

It had been the chosen people of God who had crucified Christ, she said,

And we? If we refuse to preach the revolutionary Gospel of Christ, if we lag always in the rear, if we leave to others the difficult and dangerous work of the pioneer, if we must depend on the State to preserve a little decency, a little respect for freedom, a little toleration in our borders, may we expect a more favourable judgment than the chosen people?[22]

She pleaded for the church to have the courage of faith: "Let us try out our Christianity, and the world will see and believe. Let us, in God's name, be a little reckless – a little faithful".[23] Yet she had found some allies in Anglican high places. It was in 1913 that Royden was invited by Bishop Talbot of Winchester to become the first woman to address the Church Congress, a significant occasion given that women, at that time, were not even allowed to sit on Parochial Church Councils. She duly spoke about sex to a gathering of 2,000 males, including the Archbishop of Canterbury and numerous other ecclesiastical dignitaries.[24] By that time she was also involved in the Church League for Women's Suffrage (she had been its first chairman when it was founded in 1909) a group whose supporters included several of the mildly socialist Anglo-Catholic members of the Christian Social Union.[25] She had also responded positively to an enquiry by Ursula Roberts about the possibility of the ordination of women to the priesthood, and planned to speak to a 1914 conference exploring the issue.[26] That conference had to be postponed as by then international affairs had taken centre stage.

Women's International League: the Founding

"Labour has failed. Christianity has worse than failed: it has denied itself".[27] With that dismissive comment, from the anonymous author of *Militarism Versus Feminism*, published early in 1915, it was clear that a women's peace movement would head in a different direction from that chosen by male church leaders. Maude Royden played a significant part in the formation of that movement.

The Women's International League was built upon the suffrage campaigns that preceded it. Various suggestions as to how they might proceed were made in the early months of the war. One early idea came from a Hungarian feminist journalist, Rosika Schwimmer. In her mid-thirties, she was the international press secretary of the International Women's Suffrage Alliance, and based in London. Soon after the start of the war she wrote to the *Pall Mall Gazette* commenting on previous correspondence that had invited foreign men, resident in England, to form a voluntary Foreign Legion of soldiers: "I wish to appeal to all foreign *women* living in England to form a Foreign Legion, which shall support any serious effort organised to urge mediation on the part of the States not yet involved in war".[28] Her Women's Foreign Legion would urge an immediate negotiated political settlement. Soon afterwards, Schwimmer went to see President Wilson of the United States, to urge him to take the initiative of mediating between the warring European nations.[29]

A somewhat different approach was advocated in October by Dorothea Hollins of the Women's Labour League. Writing to the *Women's Dreadnought*, the journal of the East London Federation of Suffragettes, (founded by the pacifist Sylvia Pankhurst in 1912), Hollins suggested that a thousand women could interpose themselves between the warring trenches. The idea came to nothing, but, given later events, it may have influenced Maude Royden to some extent.

Jus Suffragi, the journal of the International Women's Suffrage Alliance, reported the next move in January 1915. Royden was one of many women (including Mrs M.K. Gandhi) who had signed an open Christmas letter to the women of Germany and Austria.

> Sisters, – Some of us wish to send you a word at this sad Christmas tide, though we can but speak through the Press. . . . Do not let us forget that our very anguish unites us. . . .
>
> As we saw in the South African and the Balkan States, the brunt of modern war falls upon the non-combatants, and the conscience of the world cannot bear the sight.
>
> Is it not our mission to preserve life? Do not humanity and common sense alike prompt us to join hands with the women of neutral countries . . . ?
>
> We must all urge that peace be made . . . to save the womanhood and childhood as well as the manhood of Europe.
>
> We are yours in this sisterhood of sorrow.[30]

The initiative that had most substance, however, came from a meeting convened by Aletta Jacobs of the Dutch branch of the International Suffrage Alliance.[31] Four Belgian, four German and five British women (including Kathleen Courtney, Chrystal Macmillan and Catherine Marshall) came together in Amsterdam in February 1915. They decided to hold an International Congress of Women at the end of April in The Hague, and they invited Jane Addams, one of the founders in January of the Women's Peace Party in the United States, to chair the Congress. Addams, a future Nobel Laureate, had been much influenced by Henrietta and Samuel Barnett's Toynbee Hall, and had set up Hull House, a similar and influential venture in Chicago. After the Amsterdam meeting Courtney and Macmillan remained on the continent, but Marshall and the other two, on their return, organised a British committee. It consisted of well-known radical women, including Royden, Sylvia Pankhurst, Olive Schreiner, Helena Swanwick, Margaret Ashton, Isabella Ford (a Quaker suffragist from Leeds) and many others.[32] In their manifesto they justified the proposed Congress:

> Women cannot disregard the appeal sometimes expressed, as in letters from . . . soldiers, who from the battlefield call upon them to save civilisation; but more moving and more terrible is the silent appeal from the daily growing cemeteries, from the devastated villages and ruined homes, the orphans, the outraged, and the starving.
>
> It is much more difficult for men to meet in conference; they are in the silent armies. Women as non-combatants have this right, and as guardians of the race they have this duty.[33]

Maude Royden spoke at a meeting called to approve the programme for the Congress. With her historical awareness she had no doubt that women had an important part to play in the peace process:

> the vast mass of the women of the country were only waiting for a lead to perceive that peace and the women's movement went together. War was the women's worst enemy, and it affected the whole position of women as a sex. The advance of civilisation depended on their realisation of the fact that men and women were not, and could not be, governed by violence, but only by spiritual force. Everywhere, where there was pacifism the women's movement advanced; everywhere where there was militarism it went back.[34]

That the Government regarded the women's action as a serious threat was shown by the fact that out of 180 enthusiastic respondents, Courtney and Macmillan (already in situ) and Emmeline Pethick-Lawrence (who, having been campaigning with Schwimmer in the U.S.A. travelled across the Atlantic with the American delegation) were the only British women able to attend. Passports had been introduced at the outbreak of the war, making international travel impossible without Government permission. The Government demanded dossiers on each woman before being prepared to consider issuing passports. One week before the Congress the Home Office wrote, "His Majesty's Government is of opinion that at the present moment there is much inconvenience in holding a large meeting of a political character so close to the seat of the war".[35]

After much discussion Marshall persuaded Reginald McKenna, the Home Secretary, to issue a token twenty-four passports to selected women. McKenna claimed in the House of Commons that he "selected women who represented organisations and well-known sections of thought".[36] One of the selected women was Maude Royden. However, the Government intended to take with one hand as it gave with the other. At the same time as it conceded the principle of the passports, the authorities were preparing to close the North Sea to all shipping. Despite this Admiralty Order, the British Organising Committee learnt that there was to be one more boat allowed to go to the Netherlands, and they arranged a train for Tilbury to catch it. The Home Office then said it could not process the passports in time. When a delegation of women returned to the Home Secretary the following day (Wednesday 21 April), they were told that he had consulted with the Prime Minister and the Lord of the Admiralty and there would be another boat, and a set of passports ready by Thursday 22. Telegrams were sent out immediately and those hoping to travel to The Hague made their way expectantly to London. Maude Royden arrived at dawn.[37] When the women went to the Home Office on the Thursday, a cynically gleeful McKenna handed over their travel documents at the same time as informing them that the shipping ban would be complete, immediate and indefinite. Their passports were useless. Furious, but ever hopeful, the twenty four decided to make their way to Tilbury in any case, and wait in a hotel, as the Congress did not start until 28 April. At their expense, the right-wing press had a field day.

> All Tilbury is laughing at the Peacettes, the misguided Englishwomen who, baggage in hand, are waiting at Tilbury for a boat to take them to Holland, where they are anxious to talk peace with German fraus over the teapot.[38]

Ten days later, the historic Congress having happened without them, the women trudged home.

The Hague Congress was indeed an historic occasion. More than 1,100 women participated, representatives of 12 countries and over 150 organisations. Its purpose, said Jacobs, was to be "an International Congress of Women assembled to protest against war and to suggest steps which may lead to warfare becoming an impossibility".[39] Amongst the resolutions passed were a request for neutral countries to offer mediation to the belligerent nations and the setting up of a delegation to meet with a number of prominent heads of state, in order to press for such a mediation service to be established.[40] The immediate effect of the Congress was to energise and empower women on both sides of the Atlantic. In Britain, Marshall chaired a follow-up meeting in

Central Hall on 11 May, and two days later, with Swanwick in the chair, Kathleen Courtney and Addams spoke to a crowded meeting about the Congress resolutions. The British Committee, 155 strong, rushed out a Congress report and held their first general meeting in Westminster from 30 September to 1 October, adopting the title of the Women's International League. Theirs was an urgent mission:

> linking together two movements felt to be vitally connected: the Women's Movement and the Pacifist Movement. The first has been recognised as one of the greatest of world movements towards liberation: it is time the second should be recognised as another. Only free women can build up the peace which is to be, themselves understanding the eternal strife engendered by domination.[41]

Helena Swanwick was to chair the new movement, and Maude Royden was to be the first vice-chair, supported by Ashton and Kathleen Courtney.

Women's International League: The Practice

Royden was not the only link between the W.I.L. and the F.O.R. Both Marian E. Ellis and Theodora Wilson-Wilson were also on the first W.I.L. executive committee.[42] It was Royden, though, who was the most active, chairing and speaking at countless meetings throughout the war. She held to the opinion expressed by Olive Schreiner, that "No woman who is a woman says of a human body, 'It is nothing' ".[43] In December 1915 she spoke at the Portman Rooms, Baker Street, "To Present the Women's Case Against Conscription". Those present agreed that "the introduction of any form of industrial or military conscription in Great Britain would be a grave blow to liberty and social progress", and "far from contributing to the successful prosecution of the War, it would constitute the greatest victory of German militarism".[44]

The methods and debates of parts of the peace movement were not dissimilar to those of parts of the suffrage movement, and for similar reasons. For all her complete commitment to both causes, Royden was firmly on the side of constitutional and legal action wherever possible, and regretted the actions of those who deliberately broke the law. She disapproved of the W.I.L. lending its secretary, Catherine Marshall (who co-ordinated the N.C.F.'s impressive parliamentary activities), to the N.C.F., in order to make the latter's campaigning more efficient, because, as she told Marshall, she disapproved of the N.C.F.'s tolerance of law-breaking.

> I have for it much more respect, yet rather the same *kind* of respect, that I had for the best kind of Militant. I think it wrong, though not

nearly so wrong, in much the same kind of way. The more I see, both of Militants and political Pacifists, the more I realise that their mistakes are only possible to very fine people. But I still think them mistakes.[45]

A few months earlier she had told Marshall that she was uneasy about campaigns that focussed on the suffering of imprisoned conscientious objectors. Royden said she was,

horribly uneasy about your whole method of campaign. It seems to me . . . just like the old militant [suffragette] plan of creating impossible situations and forcing persecution, and then making a fearful uproar about it. And this plan, in our case, has the enormous disadvantage of being compared with the sacrifices made by the soldiers. . . . I do most deeply disagree with the line that the NCF has taken. It seems to me that if anything *can* destroy the effect of persecution and suffering of the C.O.s, it is advertising and demonstrating about it. [46]

She had expressed a similar concern earlier in the war, when she stated the essential discrepancy between feminism and militarism:

The Woman's Movement in all its aspects, but especially, of course, in its political one, is an assertion of moral force as the supreme governing force in the world. . . . Militarism and the Woman's Movement cannot exist together. Take a militarist religion like that of Islam, and you see women reduced to the lowest level of degradation. As militarism waxes or wanes so, in inverse ratio, does the Woman's Movement. . . . The victory of one is the defeat of the other. Women, whatever other claim may be made for them, are not equal to men in their capacity to use force or their willingness to believe in it. For them, therefore, to ask for equal rights with men in a world governed by such force is frivolous. Their claim would not be granted, and if granted would not be valid. Like the negro vote in America, it would be a cheat and a delusion. But if moral power be the true basis of human relationship, then the Woman's Movement is on a sure foundation and moves to its inevitable triumph. Its victory will be an element in the making of permanent peace, not because women are less liable to "war fever" than men, or more reluctant to pay the great price of war, but because their claim and its fulfilment involves the assertion of that which war perpetually denies.[47]

The principal role of W.I.L. at that time was educational, and Royden played her full part in this. Her addresses in the first six months of 1916, at the Fabian Rooms, Westminster, show the breadth of her concerns: "What has Investment of Money to do with War and Peace?"; "Is it

Unpatriotic to be a Pacifist?"; "What has the Woman's Movement to do with Foreign Policy?"; "Patriotism"; "Nationalism, Internationalism and the Churches", and "The Declining British Birthrate".[48] In the second half of the year she spoke on "Women and the Sovereign State". George Lansbury also gave two of the talks in these series, on "War and the Journalist" and, at Christmas, on "Peace to Men of Goodwill".[49] Lansbury was also one of the signatories, with Royden, Lewis Donaldson (Rector of St Mark's, Leicester), the Bishops of Hereford (John Percival) and Lincoln (Edward Hicks), and others in supporting a suffrage letter to Prime Minister Herbert Asquith in June 1916.[50]

Throughout 1917 Royden's skill in chairing W.I.L. meetings was in high demand. She presided over a conference on teaching history and scripture (the purpose of which was "the adaptation of education to the higher ideals that are necessary for successful reconstruction after the War"); there was a meeting on "Married Women after the War – their Work in Industry and the Home"; in July there was a conference of representatives of different suffrage societies to consider long-term co-operation. Royden also made further speeches – on Mothers' Pensions, Prostitution, and in support of the Reform Bill.[51] The speeches continued into 1918: "What are Women For?", "The Great Adventure" and "The Science of Power".[52]

That, for Royden, the themes of peace and women's liberation were inseparable, is clear from her writings of the period. On one occasion she considered the morality of those men who deprived women of "honour". In the fields of both commerce and warfare, the concept of honour appeared a sham, inseparable from lying and deceit. The conduct of war would be impossible without deceit, she said, as would the (male-determined) forms of commercial and political morality.

> The assumption that lies are permissible not only between the sexes but between the nations creates an atmosphere of suspicion and hostility which make the solution of international problems impossible except by war – if war may indeed be a solution. Honour becomes a term as arbitrary in the masculine as in the feminine sense. And from this disastrous contempt for truth flows a poison which destroys the life of the State.[53]

Maude Royden: The Great Adventure of Peace

The Great Adventure

Immediately following the Cambridge founding of the F.O.R., Royden set about making her mark on the new society's early thinking. *The Great Adventure* was published in January 1915. It was a powerful presentation of Christian pacifism and its thesis – that pacifists and disarmed nations should take a risk for peace, should embark on the

The sheet-music cover for the anti-war song, I Didn't Raise
My Boy to be a Soldier, *artist unknown, 1914 (see p. 56).*

adventure of peace even at risk to themselves – was one that stayed with Royden for the next twenty-five years. For Royden, those who sought peace must necessarily put their peace-making ideals into action: "Those who in Christ's parable are found fit for the Kingdom are not those who believed rightly or prayed well, or kept themselves without blame, but those who, in corporal works of mercy, served their fellow-men".[54] That applied to the nation as it did to individuals. She cited the words of Alexander Mackennal, written in 1900:

> If England, in the plenitude of her power, should lay down every weapon of carnal warfare, disband her armies, call her fleets from the sea, throw open her ports, and trust for her continual existence only to the service she would render to the world, and the testimony she would bear to Christ, what would happen? .... It might be that Christ, Whose "finished work" is the trust of His people, would declare that the purpose of such a sacrifice is sufficient, and that the example would be enough, and that the nation would continue to be, living and strong in the gratitude of all peoples.[55]

Unlike many other campaigners, Royden acknowledged that the German invasion of Belgium, a country the Britain had pledged to defend, meant that Britain had a Christian duty to defend both Belgium and France. Her distinctive approach was not to call for neutrality, but sacrifice:

> War was better than neutrality, if these were the only alternatives. But is it not tragic that, nineteen hundred years after the Crucifixion, we Christians should still conceive of peace in terms of *neutrality*? Was Christ the "neutral" on the Cross? Or was His life one long act of "non-resistance" ? Was it not rather a perpetual resistance to evil, and in spite of apparent failure, a triumphant resistance? Christ was not neutral between God and man, but neither did He make war. He chose another alternative – He made peace.[56]

To Royden, Britain would have been better placed to make peace without the British record of exploiting other nations, most recently Egypt and South Africa, which had been so blood-stained and shown little regard to treaty obligations. Furthermore, high levels of British armaments had encouraged German fears of a British attack, and the belief of many German people that they were fighting a defensive war. Without such fears, Royden suggested, socialists in the Reichstag would not have supported the war votes, and a high proportion of the German army would have refused to march. Neutral nations could have been called upon to refuse aid to the aggressor, who would be left with "the appalling responsibility of marching against an absolutely non-resistant people".

She imagined men and women peace-lovers the world over flinging themselves in front of troop trains and being ready to show as much courage as those who marched to war – dying if necessary – in the cause of peace. "And had they been organised and ready, there would have been no war".[57] Some years after the war Royden would start a national recruitment campaign for a Peace Army, for people "ready to die for peace". In 1915, she was aware that her proposal to disarm, and to appeal to the love and pity of humanity, would have sounded strange:

> Yet no stranger surely than the Sermon on the Mount, still read aloud in our churches, by apparently serious priests, to seemingly receptive congregations. And as certainly as I believe that if we lived after the pattern there set forth, we should realise the kingdom of Heaven on earth, so certain am I that if we had disarmed in the first week of last August – not by an arbitrary decision of the Foreign Office, but on a demand from the people – there would have been no war. So great a moral miracle would have had its effect. The world would have been changed. No nation would have rushed into war "in self-defence". There would have been no war.[58]

In that way alone, she argued, Belgium – people, cities, industry – would have been saved. Disarmament would have been a risk, but she pointed out that war was not only an adventure but a risk too.

> Those who go to war risk defeat, and they rightly glory in their willingness to take that risk in a good cause. When people advocate neutrality, they are met with the boast that England was prepared to risk something in defence of her word, and surely they are answered? I, too, would have risked something – everything, indeed – to win, not a devastated and a ruined Belgium, but Belgium unscathed. . . . Had we been willing, for the peace of the world, to risk all, and had we suffered for it, our suffering would, like the Crucifixion, have been redemptive, and outward failure truest victory. For such a nation could not die, though for nations as for individuals, it is true that they must sometimes lose their lives to save them.[59]

Behind the pledge to Belgium was the threat of German militarism. Royden acknowledged the ends but not the means.

> Is it not time that we abandoned the hope of exterminating heresies by killing heretics? The history of the Christian Church is stained with blood shed in this belief. And it is true that, though very rarely, "heresies" have sometimes been for a time crushed out in blood. But to do this is to fall into a worse heresy – it is to believe that such cruelty is justifiable. We no longer torture those who disagree with us theologically; but we seek to put a nation to the torture still.[60]

If, in the end, Germany was beaten, what would that prove, Royden asked? "That we have larger armies and more powerful navies, and greater financial resources!" But that would be all, and at the risk of establishing the heresy of militarism at home.

> Once more we seek to destroy a heresy by violence, and we enthrone that very heresy in our own hearts. The desire to "avenge Scarborough", the determination to crush the enemy altogether, the hatred of individual "alien enemies", the belief that war is after all a good thing, as well as an inevitable thing – all this, which is the very opposite of Christianity, is openly professed by people who are quite unaware that they are not Christians.[61] We seek to convert the Prussian from his heresy, but we ourselves know not what spirit we are of.
>
> There is only one way to kill a wrong idea. It is to set forth a right idea. You cannot kill hatred and violence by violence and hatred. You cannot make men out of love with war by making more effective war. Satan will not cast out Satan, though he will certainly seek to persuade us that he will, since of all his devices this has been throughout the ages the most successful. To make war in order to make peace! How beguiling an idea! To make Germans peaceable by killing them with torpedoes and machine-guns – that does not sound quite so well. Yet this is what we set out to do when we "fight German militarism" with the weapons of militarism.
>
> You cannot kill a wrong idea except with a right idea. This warfare is the most heroic of all, and heroism will always move mankind. . . . Well, I tell you that there is a mightier heroism still – the heroism not of the sword, but the cross; the adventure not of war, but of peace. For which is the braver man when all is said – the man who believes in armaments, or the man who stakes everything on an idea? Who is the great adventurer – he who goes against the enemy with swords and guns, or he who goes with naked hands? Who is the mighty hunter – he who seeks the quarry with stones and slings, or he who, with St Francis, goes to tame a wolf with nothing but the gospel? We peace people have made of peace a dull, drab, sordid, selfish thing. We have made it that ambiguous, dreary thing – "neutrality". But Peace is the great adventure, the glorious romance. And only when the world conceives it so, will the world be drawn after it again. "I, when I am lifted up, will draw all men unto Me".[62]

Those who sought peace must give no less than their best, she said.

> For the truth, as they see it, men are laying down their lives to-day in Belgium and in France. And we who see another truth –

shall we be less true to it than they? Not so does the world go forward. "We are all trying to see", said one to me the other day; "if you think you see something we do not, tell it us. *Truth is more to us than Victory*". Let us, also, believe this. We cannot sacrifice the Christian ideal even to a national necessity. Truth is more than victory. Christ indeed consecrated patriotism, as He consecrated every earthly love. He taught us that love is all one, and all divine, because it is love. But in spite of His own love for the Jewish race, His anguish as He foresaw the destruction of Jerusalem, He would not sanction war. He might have led a revolt against the cruel tyranny of Roman rule in Palestine, and – whether in success or failure – have added another name to the long list of patriot-heroes who shed their blood for their country. Yet He refused. Was He more or less true to humanity by that refusal?

Truth is more than victory. We cannot tell whether defeat or triumph is best for a nation, or whose success upon the battle-field is better for the world. But we know that only he who is ready to die for an ideal can truly be said to be loyal to that ideal, and this hard saying is true of nations as of men. What is the Christian ideal? Submission to evil? Resignation to the sufferings of others? No. "Be not overcome with evil – *but overcome evil with good*".[63]

Victims of Violence

Maude Royden's own adventure came in the summer of 1915, following the F.O.R. Summer Conference at the S.C.M. centre at Swanwick.[64] Various women there asked her what they could do whilst their brothers were fighting. Royden at once replied, "There is the country! Go! Convert England to Christian pacifism!"[65] One group of young people agreed to attempt precisely that. Royden, prospective travelling secretary for the F.O.R., was the leading figure in the group of nine women and eight men who took part in the Caravan Campaign, or "Pilgrimage of Peace".[66] They took with them a horse-drawn caravan to hold literature and stores, and to provide sleeping quarters for the women, whilst other young men and women cycled or walked alongside. Royden was the principal preacher, but a number of the F.O.R. party attempted open-air preaching, in the counties of the east Midlands, en route for London. Other speakers were expected to join the party as it passed through their area. Each day began with prayers around the caravan, reports back of the various meetings of the previous evening, and planning for the day ahead.

Those taking part knew there was a risk attached to such an exercise. The sinking of the *Lusitania* in May had provoked riots in Liverpool; London had also experienced aerial bombing. W.E. Orchard had earlier abandoned a public meeting in Beaconsfield because of the disturbance it provoked. Yet the F.O.R. caravan prompted little more than curiosity, as it made its way through Derbyshire. At other meetings there was latent hostility, but the missioners still felt satisfied with their efforts. More serious was their reception in Mansfield. The town was close to a substantial military camp, and a crowd of soldiers and civilians jeered and scoffed at one young woman in the group who was attempting to pray from the town's market cross.[67] The caravan party moved on, first to Nottingham, where a number of successful meetings were held, then into Leicestershire. At Loughborough, the mayor's sister-in-law, a supporter of Royden's suffrage work, offered her hospitality, even though the mayor was in charge of recruiting.[68]

On 30 July, unaware that a local battalion had recently been destroyed during an attack in the Dardanelles, fifteen Pilgrims visited Hinckley. On their second day there, an indoor meeting addressed by the women missioners created uproar. Two of the men had a similar experience at their meeting, and were afterwards attacked in a street, finding refuge eventually in a chemist's shop. Two missioners, who had been to a nearby town, returned to find Hinckley in uproar. One went to investigate, only to need rescuing by the police. The other went to warn those in the tents and the caravan. A hostile crowd, many of whom were drunk (it was payday) had decided – following the line promoted by certain national newspapers – that the preachers were pro-German, either spies or funded by Germany.[69] Royden's response was to gather the missioners together in a circle, sitting on the ground in silent prayer, waiting for any attack. Several hundred people, with the local recruiting sergeant to the fore, headed towards the field where they were camping.[70] The mob "quite beside itself with rage and hatred" overturned the caravan, before setting it on fire, destroying it completely, and singing "Tipperary" as the roof fell in.[71] Tents were pillaged and destroyed. The horror lasted for two or three hours, as the shouting and the flames attracted more and more people, between two and three thousand in all. The circle of prayer did at least protect some of the missioners, disconcerting and disarming some of their attackers:

> We remained in their hands and at their mercy . . . saved from physical attack that night by our sheer pacifism. Not one of us – there were about a dozen, including Ebenezer Cunningham, later Chairman of the Congregational Union of England and Wales, and Reginald Sorensen, later a Member of Parliament – made the slightest resistance or protest . . . and not one of us received a blow. Many times some of the crowd would threateningly approach us . . . with raised fists and with violent reproaches threaten what they were going to do to us, but they always stopped at the last moment. One man seized Maude Royden by the throat, but was the worse for drink and, looking foolish when no one interfered,

released her. Several of the men in khaki dragged two Church of England young curates to the burning caravan, now a big bonfire, to throw them on it, but refrained at the edge of the fire.[72]

As the flames died down so the crowd began to disperse, and eventually members of the party were able to creep away to the police station for safety. Sorensen later said that, at first, even the police thought they were Germans because of a "strange Bible sort of book" found in the ashes of the caravan. It turned out to be a copy of the Apocrypha![73] Reassured, the authorities stopped a passing night train to move them on from the scene of the disturbance. To the surprise and delight of the missioners, the Hinckley stationmaster told them, "Keep on with it! I share your beliefs".

The F.O.R. missioners had seen hatred at close range, in the faces of those whose "husbands, fathers, sweethearts and sons had been mown down in Suvla Bay". Royden later commented, "They could not hear or see us without hated, convinced as they were we were betraying the cause sealed with that blood". She added, "If I must be killed by an enemy, may I be killed at long range!"[74]

Despite their horrific experience, five of the group spent another day in the town attempting to set "powerful reconciling influences at work". Such influences notwithstanding, the first caravan venture was something of a tactical failure, leading as it did to the first large-scale violence in Britain against pacifists. To the Government and the press it provided useful propaganda that the F.O.R. consisted of troublemakers. Nonetheless there were those within the F.O.R. who wanted the caravan campaign to be continued, addressing open-air gatherings and Adult Schools.[75] Royden realised now that "the military situation was making people more incapable of listening to talk", and considered that "to go on preaching peace to people in such straits . . . seemed intolerable".[76] But, however much she was shaken, she remained undaunted by her Hinckley experience. Her appointment as travelling-secretary was confirmed in September.[77] Campaigning lessons had been learnt at Hinckley, and subsequent speaking engagements were less confrontational. When Royden addressed an audience of almost two thousand in Birmingham Town Hall, the event passed peacefully and her message was well received.[78] Later, small groups of members across the country tried to promote Christian pacifism on "peace tramps" or cycle tours.[79] From the end of 1917, by which time Stanley James had become travelling secretary, the mood of the country had changed and large indoor and open-air meetings were successfully held – sometimes jointly with the I.L.P. – in Bristol, Leeds, London and across the country. It was even possible for local groups to set up shops for the sale of pacifist literature.[80] By the end of the war F.O.R. membership had grown from an initial membership of 120 to around 8,000.[81]

6.
Clergy in the Front Line of Resistance

There were a few Anglican clergy who stood out for peace. One, Philip Carrington (1892-1975), later Archbishop of Quebec, was an ordinand at Selwyn College, Cambridge. He became pacifist having read such literature as George Bernard Shaw's 1914 publication *Common Sense About the War*, which argued that both sides were equally to blame for the war. Carrington knew a pacifist priest "who travelled around defending pacifists when they came into conflict with the law".[1] Generally, such clergy were individuals who found themselves in a very lonely, isolated place and vulnerable to repression if they refused to conform to the increasingly militarist norms of society.

An Army Chaplain

Edward Gordon Bulstrode (1885-1953) had served his curacy in East London, after which he tested his vocation with the Society of St John the Evangelist, Cowley (S.S.J.E.). The difficulty for him there was that, in the vow of obedience to a Superior, he could foresee possible conflict with the higher authority of God. With the door closed on conventional monasticism, the be-cassocked Brother Edward became assistant curate at Temple Balsall, near Coventry, where a community resembling *Little Gidding* existed, living in simplicity and devotion. In December 1914, at the suggestion of Father Maxwell, S.S.J.E., Brother Edward became an unofficial chaplain to the troops awaiting embarkation for France, at Roffey Camp, Horsham, Sussex. He felt ambivalent about such a role; on the one hand, he understood the war effort and appreciated the sacrifice it called for, and was keen to get involved. Yet, on the other, he himself held pacifist views: "the more I meditated on Christ's life and example and on his teaching, the less did I find it possible to reconcile it with fighting and intentional slaughter".[2] The local vicar told him not to express pacifist opinions in sermons to the troops, advice which was hardly likely to be heeded by a man who had left S.S.J.E. in order to say and to do as the Holy

Spirit guided. In any case, Brother Edward's position was, after all, independent and unofficial. Relations with the military command soon reached breaking point and he left after a confrontation in May 1915. As he wrote to his mother:

> I am now not allowed to speak any more to the troops in Horsham. . . . The officers of the Artillery complained to the vicar that what I said to the men the Sunday before last had had a depressing effect and they did not like what I had said about being men of peace. So the vicar asked me to take a certain line with them which I could not in faithfulness do. I *cannot* tell beforehand what the Lord shall put into my mouth. I try to ask the Holy Spirit to speak through me and I cannot limit His operation. So I offered to cease my ministrations and the offer was accepted.[3]

Brother Edward returned to Temple Balsall.[4]

Lansbury's Converter

The clergyman whose influence had led to the conversion of Lansbury remained close to the *Herald* editor. William Corbett Roberts urged Lansbury to become more actively involved with the Fellowship of Reconciliation, and Lansbury reproduced in full Roberts's 1916 address to the Church Socialist League, in which he referred to "the demand of the Christian conscience that wars shall cease".[5] Roberts began the war as Vicar of Crick. Writing in the *Peterborough Diocesan Magazine*, he stated that:

> I cannot think of any war as coming within the Will of God for which we pray. War is the denial of that Will. The "incredible good" that our faith holds out before us is not going to be helped by War. Its presence in men's hearts is indeed displayed in many deeds of self-sacrifice shown on the battlefield, but the spirit which inspires these deeds is not a spirit that war implants in men; it has been there long before, and was learnt in a different school. Is it not true that all the heroism and self-sacrifice of the war will be wasted unless, when the war is done, the same fine spirit, so freely devoted to the cause of the fatherland, is devoted to the cause of the Kingdom of God?
> People say that the war was inevitable. It is only true if sin is inevitable. There are no "necessary" evils. God always leaves the ideal way open, open that is to repentance and faith. The trouble is that we have not got faith, and do not really believe the Gospel. As long as this is so, war will remain "inevitable", like other sins of individuals and people which we frankly profess ourselves "helpless" about. . . .[6]

He left Crick for six months near the end of 1915 to lecture at St Stephen's College, Delhi, where C.F. Andrews (of whom, more later) had recently been vice-principal, and in May 1917 he was instituted as Rector of the parish of St George, Bloomsbury, which became something of a pacifist stronghold between the wars.

There is also a suggestion that, whilst at Crick, W.C. Roberts may have been persecuted for his pacifist views. His wife Ursula – a feminist poet and novelist writing under the pseudonym Susan Miles – produced an epic novel, *Blind Men Crossing a Bridge* (1934). It was a substantial work of fiction centred on a woman, Mazod, one of a pair of twins conceived in an ill-fated relationship between a squire's son and a woman from a farm-labouring family. The setting was the village of Dill, quite possibly based on Crick. In the novel, not long after the outbreak of war in 1914, a group of drunkards attacked the vicarage because there were pacifists inside. A bedroom window was smashed and the family inside the vicarage were threatened with a ducking in pigwash. Soon afterwards the family needed to hire a pony and trap in order to seek help for a sick girl. The owner of the pony and trap refused, in dialect, "Not for hire, I told y', to pashfists and Fritzes".[7] Such scenes may well have been autobiographical.[8]

Rebel in a New Cathedral

As a young man Henry Cecil (1882-1954) came across many early Labour leaders, including Lansbury, Philip Snowden, Arthur Henderson and Ramsay MacDonald, at Stepney Working Men's College. A socialist and pacifist himself, Cecil was ordained and in 1913 accepted a position at what was about to become Sheffield Cathedral. With the outbreak of war, local recruiting campaign meetings were held in the Cathedral churchyard, with the blessing of the senior clergy and the Bishop, Leonard Burrows. Cecil's response each time was to set up a rival meeting denouncing the war and the Church's collusion in it. The Cathedral congregation were horrified and on several occasions Cecil was physically assaulted by hostile crowds. On his appointment in 1917 to the parish of St Philip, Sheffield, Cecil continued his campaigning, finding some support among his steelworker parishioners. The Bishop of Sheffield was not enamoured with Cecil's message, but he refused many demands for his suspension, removal or unfrocking, accepting Cecil's right to express a pacifist view, however unpopular or (in the bishop's eyes) wrong that view might be.[9]

A similar case arose in Durham in 1918, when one unnamed vicar was reported to have declared to the patriotic Bishop Handley Moule that he was a pacifist. The bishop reluctantly advised the vicar to express his views cautiously in his parish magazine of June that year. The article exalted "Love your enemies" over the old way of "an eye for an eye", with the author proclaiming, "I cannot square the way of war with the way of Christ".[10]

An Embryonic Brotherhood

Also in Sheffield was Thomas Pickering, who ran a hostel for local youth in the parish of St Mary.[11] The parish curate, Charles Casson Stimson (1889-1964) was five years younger than Pickering. Stimson had grown up in what he described as a "cautiously liberal" household, with the writings of Tolstoy and the nineteenth-century Christian socialists on the bookshelves. After training at Ridley Hall Stimson was made deacon in 1912 and ordained priest the following year. The ordaining bishop in 1912 was Archbishop Cosmo Gordon Lang, with whom Stimson had several discussions concerning his considerable objections to the Thirty-Nine Articles, some of which he thought were "seriously in error".[12] Far from being shocked at possible heterodoxy, Lang was impressed by Stimson's thoughtfulness, and assured him that assent to the Articles was but a "general assent", and did not imply complete agreement. Some in the parish were suspicious of the effect that the radical Pickering was having on the local youth, and they hoped that the new curate would draw the young people away from his influence.[13] Instead, Stimson soon warmed to Pickering's ideas himself, and the two became lifelong friends.

Initially, Leonard Burrows, Bishop of Sheffield, was so impressed by the youth club's work that he asked the local Church of England Men's Society (C.E.M.S.) to support it. Pickering's team of workers called themselves the St Paul's Brotherhood, and Stimson drew up a simple rule of life, based on the Sermon on the Mount.[14] The rule was placed above the fireplace in the youth club, unnoticed until the outbreak of the war, when a visiting C.E.M.S. steward objected to the pacifist slant and the clause about loving one's enemies and complained to the Bishop. Pickering was sent for by Burrows, and when he refused to remove the offending clauses and bring the rule into line with the war effort, the support of both the Bishop and the C.E.M.S. was withdrawn. The hostel was closed down quickly to avoid bankruptcy, with Pickering losing all his money in the process. Stimson managed to persuade Bishop Hicks of Lincoln to fund Pickering's ordination training at Lincoln, but when Hicks died Pickering was transferred to Burgh Missionary College. The Principal there was not impressed by Pickering's pacifism, and his ordination was held up indefinitely, with few bishops or parishes willing to tolerate a pacifist priest. Eventually Pickering consented, against Stimson's advice, to be ordained by Bishop Vernon Herford of the Evangelical Catholic Church.[15]

Stimson, too, aggrieved the middle-class congregation, including employers (whose workers were involved in an industrial dispute) who did not take kindly to Stimson's support for striking grinders; there was also a mothers' meeting whose members disapproved of hearing readings from Tolstoy. With the outbreak of war in 1914, Stimson's employment lasted but one sermon. The congregation who were already antagonised by his social attitudes could not tolerate his pacifism under any circumstances. Stimson was immediately told to move on.[16] In a number of parishes he met with the same response.

Stimson came, in 1915, to the parish of St Andrew, Clifton and St Luke, Bristol. Although Rashley, the vicar, was a pacifist, it was the outspoken pacifist curate who soon alienated those parishioners whose money was required for his stipend.[17] Stimson decided to ask Bishop George Nickson for permission to fund his own ministry by combining factory work with being an unpaid curate. The request was refused until Archbishops Davidson and Lang appealed to younger clergy to help in munitions factories.[18] Stimson would not do this, but the precedent enabled him to get the Bishop's consent for him to earn his living as a labourer in a soap factory whilst assisting the local vicar. Years before French Catholics tried experimenting with worker-priests, and before Geoffrey Studdert Kennedy's Industrial Christian Fellowship took off, Stimson was acting, in effect, as an unofficial chaplain, working anonymously alongside the unskilled labourers whilst exercising his more open priestly ministry, without pay, in different parishes.

Although, as a priest, Stimson was exempt from being called up, he worked on behalf of his conscientious objector colleagues. In Bristol, he reported on the proceedings of tribunals to local pacifist societies. When possible, he followed up the treatment undergone by those whose appeals were unsuccessful. Working in a factory alongside those facing call up into the military, he was embarrassed at the prospect of hiding behind his clerical collar. Attracted by the itinerant ministry of Francis of Assisi, he handed in his notice, and after some time of prayer in Malmesbury Abbey and Cirencester Parish Church, he took to the road in his cassock and collar, "penniless, and completely dependent on God".[19] Preaching Christian socialist pacifism, he journeyed from the south-west to the north Midlands, with overnight stays either in workhouses or with sympathetic listeners to his message (often Plymouth Brethren). That his 1918 Franciscan experiment only lasted a fortnight was due to Stimson receiving an invitation to accept a curacy in County Durham.[20] It would not, however, be the last time that Stimson and Pickering would preach peace to those who were near and those who were far off, as they were to be founder members of a radical pacifist order, the Brotherhood of the Way, spending most of the next quarter century as tramp-preachers for peace across the country.

A Tractarian Radical

One prominent figure in the Fellowship of Reconciliation was as far removed as could be imagined from the Nonconformist majority of that organisation. Bernard Walke, who from 1913 was the parish priest in the village of St Hilary, Cornwall, just inland from St Michael's Mount, followed in the tradition of his Tractarian father and grandfather, combining the ministry of an idiosyncratic, unwavering Anglo-Catholic priest with a commitment to ecumenism and a determination to promote a distinctive Christian and pacifist lifestyle. Walke was a radical pacifist with a great appreciation of nature, who spoke of his awareness of "the increased friendliness among all living things".[21] He dedicated two chapels in church to St Francis and to St Joan (whom, even though she was a warrior, Walke upheld for placing conscience before the authority of the state). He described his feelings when war was approaching in August 1914:

> When I stood in the pulpit, looking down on the people whose faces were now so familiar to me, I had the sensation of being in the centre of a cataclysm which was approaching as inevitably as a thunderstorm against the wind. It was contrary to reason, yet no ingenuity of man could prevent it. The noblest motives would be exploited and the most generous natures would offer themselves willingly to this monster that was about to destroy them.
>
> I felt strangely alone standing there in the pulpit before all these people, with nothing to say, with no word of comfort or assurance to offer them. I was certain only that I could have no part in what was coming.[22]

Recalling the answer of George Fox to an enquiry about the wearing of swords, "Wear it as long as thou canst", Walke resolved to follow Fox's advice.

> "Wear it as long as thou canst." I could wear it no longer. As I stood looking down on the people on that Sunday night in August 1914, I saw no way of reconciliation between the way of the Gospel that I had been called to preach and the war that was approaching. I was not, as far as I know, carried away by my emotions; I was empty of all feeling but an awareness that this rejection of war as an altogether evil thing, was at one with whatever intelligence I possessed.[23]

There was a loneliness in this stand, and some accused Walke of being a German spy ("Half your pay do come from the Pope and the other half from the Kaiser").[24] He constantly feared arrest for his peace activities. Support came from local Quakers, and Walke attended many of their meetings. In both sermons and liturgy, Walke addressed the evils of war.

> It had been my custom to say daily, after Mass, the prayer for the ending of the war composed by the saintly Pius X, who when

asked to bless the armies of Austria replied, "I bless peace and not war." I had also instituted the service of Benediction on Sunday evenings, as an act of reparation to the Sacred Heart for the wrongs of war, and as a means of uniting ourselves with our enemies in that Sacrament that knows no frontiers.[25]

In the spring of 1917, Walke joined the F.O.R., an ecumenical pacifist but still an Anglo-Catholic. He raised some Nonconformist eyebrows at the 1918 F.O.R. conference when he arrived in his cassock and with little luggage save a portable altar.[26] His peace witness, for him the living out of his priestly vocation, was by then going far beyond his parish boundary. He wrote almost daily articles and letters to the press, and spoke at meetings in London, Liverpool, Bristol and in many of the towns and villages of Cornwall.

> The message that I had to deliver was the one I had been charged to preach on the day of my Ordination. I could not regard that commission as having come to an end because the world was at war. It was still a message of "Peace and good will"; an affirmation that peace did not depend on the armies in the field; that there was no other way to peace for nations or individuals but the way of Jesus who had met and overcome the forces of evil on the cross, and offered to those, who could receive it, a share in His victory. If that message of peace was ever to be effective among the nations, there must be some to witness to this power at a time when men had ceased to believe in it. To keep silence now was to seal our lips for ever. The world would rightly distrust a message of peace that could not stand the test of war.[27]

One meeting, in the Labour Hall in Penzance, was broken up violently by a gang of one hundred and fifty men from the Naval Reserve, a "howling mob" with faces "changed by hate". Walke received a blow which laid him out. Eventually he, his wife Annie, and a Quaker woman who was also on the platform at the meeting, were escorted to safety by two soldiers home on leave from France, who were appalled by the tactics of the mob.[28] Together with George Hodgkin, a Quaker, Walke travelled around Cornwall on foot, talking to those they met about seeking peace within themselves and avoiding occasions of war. Walke reported that cobblers, basket-makers and other tradesmen were among the most attentive listeners.

Hodgkin also suggested to Walke that he try to get Home Office permission to visit the conscientious objectors (C.O.s) at Princetown. The bleak Dartmoor prison was a "work centre" for C.O.s, not that local clergy felt that the work was hard enough, passing a resolution complaining about the "ridiculously lenient treatment" afforded C.O.s there.[29] William Gascoigne Cecil, Bishop of Exeter, described his own attitudes towards the interred members of his diocese in a letter to the *Times* in October 1917, headed "Anarchic Dartmoor – a Hotbed of Malcontents".[30] Walke was naturally far more sympathetic to the C.O.s, though he had little more awareness of the true nature of the work centre and its inmates than did the hostile bishop. He naively looked forward to being able to stay with the C.O.s for one week in February 1918, little realising the diversity of the group and the destructive individualism of so many within it. A meeting Walke held with 600 of the men was a depressing experience.

> Was there ever gathered together so strange a collection of individuals? – quiet Quakers who sat unmoved while men stood up and shouted around them, wild-looking men from the Clyde and Rhondda Valley whose hopes for the regeneration of society lay in a class war, strange melancholy men whose message was the immediate coming of the Messiah and the end of the world, men of all trades and professions, mathematicians, scholars, musicians, actors, miners and farm labourers, with nothing to unite them but a refusal to bear arms in the present war.
>
> I was distressed and dismayed by the clash and conflict of theories and personalities with which I was confronted. Some brandished Bibles, accusing me of not knowing the Word of God as revealed in the Book of Daniel, others with red flags proclaimed me as a traitor for not accepting class war and the dictatorship of the proletariat.
>
> I had come, expecting to find, in this assembly of youth, some hope for the future, but failed to discover among these men who talked ceaselessly, waving flags and Bibles, the kind of material out of which a new world might be constructed.[31]

Yet there was still work to be done there. Rising early, Walke would wait for the prison gates to open at 6 a.m., so that he would be available to hear confession and to say Mass at a time when those men who wished to could attend. Being unable to obtain permission to use the Anglican chapel, he set up an altar in the Wesleyan meeting-house, and the daily service was attended by a few young men of "the Catholic Faith" and a number of silent Quakers. His visit was not in vain.

Walking alone on the evening of Armistice Day, "to enjoy the peace that had at last come to the world", Walke looked over lights in a valley, from cottages no longer blacked out, and rejoiced.[32] In this new context, Walke turned his mind to issues of living: "As pacifists we had rejected war as altogether evil and yet we were content to live in a society which was built largely on fear and distrust of our neighbour".[33] He was to commit the rest of his life to experimental Christian communities attempting to build sharing, openness and trust.[34]

A Cambridge Academic

In 1914, Trinity College Cambridge boasted two gifted mathematicians on its staff who seemed, at a cursory glance, to be similar, but who were actually poles apart. Bertrand Russell (1872-1970), aristocratic, atheist lecturer, and Ernest William Barnes (1874-1953), bourgeois, Christian Fellow, were both pacifists and both members of the U.D.C. Barnes's pacifism had been newly arrived at, but was to be more consistent than Russell's. In the first few days of the war, Barnes thought that Britain was right to have taken that course of action. It did not take long for him to change his mind.

> My conversion to extreme pacifism dates to the latter part of August 1914. The war had broken out, men had flocked to the colours, and a camp had been established in Cambridge, where I was then a don. I was asked to speak to some of these men on a Sunday morning. I accepted without hesitation and then began to write out my address. I wrote it once, then I went back to Christ's teaching and tore it up. I did the same a second and a third time, and then I ventured an address which seemed to me ludicrously inadequate.

"I still have that address", he admitted to the Church Assembly in February 1937, "but I have never since spoken in favour of war"[35].

His subsequent addresses in Trinity Chapel must have taken his congregation by surprise. He preached on loving enemies and on war being contrary to the mind of Christ. He argued that any concept of a Christian God of battles was a pagan illusion, and that Christians were only bearing arms because "a chain of evil circumstances . . . forced them to ignore Christ's teaching". He believed that all governments – including the British (supported by the Church) – bore responsibility for the war, and how "only at the foot of the Cross can a permanent treaty of peace be signed".[36] Such teaching was hardly calculated to win him friends. Not only was Trinity College far from sympathetic to pacifism, there was a concern among other dons that any residual taint of pacifism might persuade patriotic parents after the war to send their offspring to other colleges. Within the college Barnes spoke up for Russell, both in urging that Russell be appointed a Fellow and for Russell to be granted leave of absence (for which the atheist philosopher had unsuccessfully applied) in order to engage in political activity. In March 1915 Barnes chaired the first public meeting of

Cambridge U.D.C., at which Russell spoke. However, the possibility of escaping the tensions of college to become Master of the Temple was tempting for Barnes and he moved on soon afterwards. As he remarked as late as 1942, "The bitterness of college feeling in 1915 against those of us who were pacifists was such that even now I do not like to recall it".[37] That bitterness came to a head soon afterwards, with the College banning U.D.C. meetings in its premises, the politically active Russell failing to achieve his Fellowship despite the support from Barnes, and, a year later, being stripped of his lectureship after a conviction for prejudicing the recruitment of the armed forces. Barnes wrote Russell a letter of support. Barnes's own position suffered in all this as his own Fellowship was not renewed and he lost the chance to become a Life Fellow.[38]

In contrast to Trinity, the Temple had a reputation for liberal opinion. Those who heard Barnes preach there may not have agreed with his pacifism, but they tolerated it. In a Good Friday sermon Barnes drew attention to the fact that "Today another crucifixion is taking place. Europe is crucifying her young men", and he asked his congregation what they were doing about it. Any nation, including Germany, that shared the system of material greed and national rivalry bore responsibility for the war. He was critical of the deadly games of diplomats, a criticism reinforced when the Bolsheviks published treaties showing how the allies planned to carve up Europe in their own interests. The Left, with the "essentially Christian" element of their aspirations, were also preferable to some of the clergy:

> When the war began, some of the most virulent abuse of Germany came from those who professed to follow Him who said, "Love your enemies". . . . Those who have done most to preach peace and love among the belligerents are not the Christian Churches but workmen and their leaders. . . . If you wish to inflame the passions of war, do not imply that you do so as a follower of the Prince of Peace.[39]

After the war Barnes reflected that, in his protests, he repeatedly found himself working alongside agnostics. He had no time for Christians who cited "an eye for an eye" – a "detestably evil maxim" – as a basis for demanding reprisals against German people. Far from purifying a nation, as some claimed, war brought out the worst in people: drunkenness, intolerance, sexual licence, and fortunes for war profiteers. It also had a detrimental effect on the civil liberties of conscientious objectors. He supported some C.O.s by letter, others by appearing at their tribunals, and all by his public pronouncements.

His own growing unpopularity as a result led to the Lord Chancellor muttering that Barnes himself ought to be in prison.[40] Yet Barnes's criticisms sprang largely from his patriotism. He worried about what the war was doing to Britain. He could see traditions dating back to the Magna Carta being swept aside. He looked forward to the ideals of the Kingdom of Heaven being reclaimed with England helping "to give such a pure ideal of righteousness to mankind that never again will the present conflict of the nations be renewed".[41] He became vice-president of the (non-pacifist) League of Nations Society, arguing that disarmament and the inclusion of Germany in a League of Nations was essential for future peace. "If we impose [on the Germans] conditions of peace which they think unjust, if we exclude them from the League of Nations, they will await an opportunity to strike again. . . . Disarmament all round is a fundamental idea of the League. No nation must retain more troops than will suffice for police work".[42] Eventually becoming Bishop of Birmingham, he spoke strongly for pacifism in the Church Assembly.

7.
World War, Worldwide War Resistance

The focus of the war, the central battleground, was Continental Europe, but the reach of the conflict spread to all corners of the globe. As societies became increasingly affected by world war, opposition also increased. In this chapter I begin by looking at two very different aspects of that opposition. To do this I will contrast the exploits of a little known peace hero, who made a contribution to peace in India far beyond his modest reputation, with the political and ecclesiastical confrontations in the United States resulting from opposition to war. I conclude with an overview of parts of the British Empire, specifically Canada, Australia and New Zealand, as they faced up to the possibility of conscription into the armed forces.

First, to India, and a spiritual journey.

India and C.F. Andrews

From Absolutes to Relatives, and Friendship

Gandhi later professed to having no closer friend than Charles Freer Andrews (1871-1940). Andrews, in turn, regarded Gandhi as a twentieth-century Francis of Assisi: "St Francis also went weaponless and ready to suffer into the armed ranks of the Saracens in order to bring peace to the warring armies by his message of suffering love. The same *ideas*, therefore, were in the heart of St Francis which Mahatma Gandhi cherishes. They were thus kindred spirits".[1]

As one of fourteen children of a tub-thumping millennial preacher in an independent sect, Andrews's start in life was an unlikely basis for a liberal Christian pacifist. A conversion experience on the eve of going up to Cambridge in 1890 led Andrews to see a Christ who was a destroyer of barriers, who overcame religious conventions and narrow dogmas.

> There is no more now the impossibility of worshipping an unknown God who can only be described by negatives, but a human God whose very nature and name is love; who is so close to us that He

suffers with every pang we feel, and bears the wound of every sin we commit. . . . He suffers shame unspeakable, is mocked and scourged and crucified for love's sake. . . . It was this love of Christ within the heart which now began to constrain my life and mould my whole character.[2]

Accordingly, he rejected the eternal torment of the damned he heard preached by the University Christian Union, together with his father's biblical fundamentalism. Rather, he warmed to the perspective of his friend Basil Westcott, High Church son of the Bishop of Durham. Andrews was confirmed, became first secretary of the Cambridge Christian Social Union, and went as a lay worker to the ancient Celtic parish of Monkwearmouth in Sunderland, where both his vocation and his socialism were fostered. He consented to be ordained, his commitment to Christ overcoming his reservations about giving general assent to the Articles, the Athanasian Creed and the psalms of vengeance. "It seemed to me impossible to use such blasphemous sentences in a church whose ideal was the Sermon on the Mount, and whose golden precept was to love our neighbours as we would love ourselves".[3]

After a curacy in the East End of London, he returned to Cambridge in 1899 as Fellow of Pembroke College and vice-principal of the Clergy Training School (later Westcott House). He had long been fascinated by India, and on hearing of Basil Westcott's death from cholera in Delhi, resolved to take the place of his late friend. In March 1904, Andrews arrived in India, to teach at St Stephen's College, Delhi.[4]

The Influence of Tagore

Arriving in India, the direction of his faith moved yet further toward an inward and spiritual realisation of God. He saw this emphasis all around him. "There was no less awe than in the West", he wrote, "but it was of a more inward character". The more he became aware of the insights of Eastern religions, the less he could tolerate "the desire to capture converts from Hinduism".[5] He was increasingly disinclined to defend the West in its treatment of the East, whether by church or state. Recognising the qualities of every race combined in Christ, Andrews became a fierce opponent of prejudice, and a keen supporter of Indian independence. In his desire to reconcile people who were divided, Andrews attended Presbyterian Communion service, and took a service for a sick Baptist minister and friend.[6] He even lived for a time with the Arya Samaj, a group of fanatical Hindu revivalists, listening, serving, and attempting to break down barriers.

In 1912 Andrews met the Indian poet Rabindranath Tagore, finding in him, "a depth of stillness and quiet calm which I had never personally witnessed with such intensity before".[7] He visited Tagore's

Ashram at Santiniketan (translated as "the Abode of Peace"), in March 1913.[8] Returning four months later he resolved "to give myself wholly into the hands of God, to go where He leads and to take up whatever work He gives me to do".[9] The following November, soon after Tagore had been awarded the Nobel Prize for Literature, they met again at Santiniketan. As they embraced, Andrews resolved to break his links with the Cambridge Mission, to be a "foreign" missionary no more, but to stay instead at Santiniketan.[10] "I longed to be bound up with the life of India in every respect", he said. "If I were to find Christ truly in India as the Son of Man, then I must live and move among the people of India as one of themselves, and not as an alien and a foreigner".[11] There he could meditate on Christ's restfulness of soul with Tagore as his spiritual "Master" and Santiniketan as his spiritual home, his place for meditation and inner peace, as a necessary complement to action.

With Gandhi in South Africa

Barely had he so resolved, than Andrews was called to South Africa. In Transvaal in 1913, Mohandas Gandhi had led a march of exploited Indian labourers into an area where their entry was restricted. He, and the other leaders of the protest, were arrested and imprisoned. In India, G.K. Gokhale gathered support for the resisters.[12] Andrews threw himself wholeheartedly into this campaign, giving his life savings over to the cause, acutely aware of the pain caused by white racism.[13] Gokhale told him, "We need you in South Africa. When do you start?"[14]

Andrews arrived at Durban on New Year's Day 1914, and was surprised to see Gandhi waiting for him at the quayside, to escort him to his ashram. The Indian leader had been released from prison twelve days earlier.[15] Europeans at the quayside were horrified when Andrews stooped down to touch the feet of Gandhi.[16] "They boil with indignation that I – an *Englishman* mind you! – should have touched the feet of an Asiatic", Andrews wrote to Tagore. "When I remind them that Christ and St Paul and St John were Asiatics they grow restive and say that things were altogether different then".[17]

Although there were a few allies like Emily Hobhouse, Andrews was shocked by the levels of racial prejudice he saw in South Africa, describing racism as "an evil . . . like a poisonous infection. . . . The Christian Church, in some of its branches, was itself infected".[18] One Sunday morning in St George's Cathedral, Cape Town, Andrews preached passionately against such attitudes. On another occasion Gandhi, wishing to hear Andrews preach, was refused admission to a church by a churchwarden. Andrews later said that given the treatment that Gandhi had received from Christians, it was no surprise that he remained a Hindu.[19]

During his couple of months in South Africa, Andrews threw himself into campaigning alongside Gandhi. With each understanding the inseparability of the search for truth and the nonviolent struggle for justice, they were drawn increasingly together. Andrews commented thus on Gandhi's influence upon him:

[T]his sovereign power of winning victories through suffering was apparent in every aspect of his hard life of pain. Our hearts met from the first moment we saw one another, and they have remained united by the strongest ties of love ever since. To be with him was an inspiration which awakened all that was best in me, and gave me a high courage, enkindled and enlightened by his own. His tenderness towards every slightest thing that suffered pain was only a part of his tireless search for truth, whose other name was God.

In him, from the very first, I felt instinctively that there had come into the world, not only a new religious personality of the highest order, moving the hearts of men and women to incredible sacrifice, but also a new religious truth, which yet was not new, but old as the stars and the everlasting hills. His one message was that long-suffering and redeeming love is alone invincible.[20]

The admiration was mutual, with Gandhi commenting of Andrews:

Nobody probably knew Charlie Andrews as well as I did. When we met in South Africa we simply met as brothers and remained such to the end. There was no distance between us. It was not a friendship between an Englishman and an Indian. It was an unbreakable bond between two seekers and servants.[21]

It seemed obvious to Andrews that Gandhi and his followers were instinctively taking the true Christian position, with their persecution and common life reminding Andrews of the early Church. They suffered wrongdoing patiently and overcame evil with good, whilst still being true to their Hindu origins. By way of contrast, there were many aspects of the life of the Christian Church which seemed to be far from Christian. He was aware that "Christ had no words strong enough to condemn religion, however hallowed by antiquity, which relied merely on profession apart from practice".[22] He was aware, too, of how Jesus had overcome the racial barriers of his day, confronting his followers with radical new attitudes to the Samaritan, the Roman centurion and the Syrophoenician woman – people supposedly outside God's grace. Similarly, Paul had rebuked Peter for refusing to eat with Gentiles. Such reflection demanded action:

Like Paul, I might have to withstand to their faces those who would bring racialism inside the Christian Church.

Also I must recognise, without any reserve whatever, the Spirit of Christ present in those who did not call themselves Christian. I had to stand on their side, and not with those who were keeping alive the spirit of racial and religious exclusion. There must be not a single vestige of the caste spirit left in my own heart. I must be wholly on the side of God, who is no respecter of persons.[23]

The Temptation of a War Far Away

Returning to Santiniketan, Andrews struggled to take Sunday services at the nearby village of Burdwan. The exclusiveness of credal and doctrinal pronouncements continued to give him difficulties of intellectual integrity and his Bishop agreed that, although he need not renounce his orders, Andrews might refrain from exercising them for a while. He continued to be an active Anglican and would, some years later, resume his priestly ministry.[24]

Santiniketan was the place where Andrews found peace. In July and August 1914, as Europe was preparing for war, and despite his own crisis of ministry, he was enthusing about his "dream of endless peace":

Peace in the deep mid-air surrounding,
  Peace in the sky from pole to pole,
Peace to the far horizon bounding,
  Peace in the universal soul.

And peace at last to the restless longing
  Which swept my life with tumult vain,
And stirred each gust of memory thronging
  Avenues drear of by-gone pain.

Tossed to and fro I had sorely striven
  Seeking, and finding no release:
Here, by the palm-trees, came God-given
  Utter, ineffable, boundless peace.[25]

With the outbreak of war, however, the utter peace was shaken. Andrews could even feel something of the war spirit move within him. Should he return to Europe? Realising what was happening to him, he turned to the three most meaningful influences in his life: Christ, Tagore and Gandhi.

The scales at last fell from my eyes, and I went back sobered and alarmed to the New Testament in order to study more carefully and thoroughly the words of Christ. With Him as guide, I saw that there could be no halting between two opinions, no serving of God and Mammon. He was unmistakeably clear in His utterance: 'Love your enemies, do good to them that hate you, pray for them that despitefully use you, that ye may be the children of your Father which is in heaven'.

Clearly the whole character of God was at stake in this very issue. Either I must choose the tribal idea of God from the Old Testament, or Christ's idea of God from the New. In the end, I saw that I had very nearly betrayed Christ, my Master, when I had allowed the war fever to get possession of me. Now Christ Himself had cleansed me by His word, and I was back in my right mind.[26]

The quiet wisdom of Tagore was a great help too. He had soon realised that a new, better order would not emerge from the brutality and the cruelty of this war. Tagore had studied the Sermon on the Mount, and he asked Andrews what Christians were doing at war: "You have the clearest moral precepts. Why do you not follow them?"[27]

Accompanying Tagore on a visit to Japan, Andrews acknowledged the peacefulness of Buddhism, which he felt had assimilated the Indian concept of *ahimsa* (harmlessness, the refusal to take life), whilst being simultaneously repelled both by the overt militarism of tiny, uniformed school-children doing military drill, and by the popular opposition to Tagore's anti-war, anti-nationalist message.[28] Andrews knew which model was the way of Christ.

The third influence on Andrews was the memory of Gandhi in South Africa. If Tagore was the master who led him to solitude and peaceableness, Gandhi was the friend who helped him to fulfil his vocation to act for justice and against suffering, but in a way that had to be right. To Andrews, Gandhi lived out the Sermon on the Mount, putting Christians to shame. Andrews commented, "What he called Satyagraha, or Truth Force, was obviously Christian; while the savage brutality of war was the reverse".[29] The implication for a potential European combatant was clear.

As the three influences converged, Andrews resolved that, if necessary, he would refuse any order to military service, even if such refusal led to imprisonment. It was a spiritual decision, as he found daily strength in Christ more than at any time since his mission days in Sunderland and London. It convinced him that Christ himself was suffering amidst all the human misery of war. Alongside which, the war was caused by the same evils of exploitation and commercial rivalry that had produced the racist treatment of the African and Indian people in South Africa. "Now Christ was with the oppressed", wrote Andrews, "and was saying to them with pity, 'Come unto Me, all ye that are weary and heavy laden, and I will give you rest'".[30]

Tagore agreed with his critique of the war, calling it a "bitter harvest of death". When Andrews wondered hopefully that it might be a purge, he heard Tagore speak prophetically: "if the root of the evil, which is greed, is not removed, then after the war there may be a still more feverish haste to recover economic losses by further exploitation of the weak. It is this inward disease of greed which needs remedy, not merely the outward symptoms".[31]

Andrews was called not to the war being fought in the trenches of Europe but to "Christ's own war on behalf of the down-trodden peoples all over the world". He wanted to do more than take up a negative attitude towards conscription and military service. "There was a positive duty to perform, and I had to fight the good fight of faith on a wider battlefield".[32] He later wrote:

> By this time, I had become a Christian pacifist without any reservations. Ways must be found of showing a loving spirit even to those who were bitterly hostile to the things I held most dear and of keeping my thoughts quite clean from hate. However lacking in what the world calls 'realism' such an attitude might seem to be, I had to grasp firmly its supreme inward strength which came from God alone. It might mean suffering beyond anything I had ever known before; but in the end it would bring nearer the victory, not of my own country, or of any other country, but of the Kingdom of God and His righteousness.[33]

The war was a turning point for Andrews as it was for India. Tagore expressed something of the change in attitude it brought to many Indians towards the values of their English rulers. He said that the sight of "Western mentality in its unscrupulous aspect of exploitation" revolted him more and more. No longer could England, or the rest of Europe, expect to be regarded as a champion of fairness and principle, but as the upholder of race supremacy and the exploiter of those outside her own borders. "For Europe it is, in actual fact, a great moral defeat that has happened".[34] Given the closeness between Tagore and Andrews, it is more than likely that the "Master" was speaking for them both.

Untainted by that moral defeat, Andrews committed himself to the welfare of Indian people wherever in the world they lived, not least in Fiji. He visited the islands and campaigned strongly for the abolition of the "indenture" system, by which Indian labourers were recruited for Fiji and elsewhere.[35] Indian workers in Fiji were the first to give Andrews the nickname *Deenabandhu*, friend of the poor.[36] By the end of 1919, the last indentured labourer was free.[37]

The U.S. Experience of Opposing War: Three Case Studies

Bishop Paul Jones

The U.S. branch of the Fellowship of Reconciliation was founded in November 1915, when Henry Hodgkin met sixty-eight American citizens at Garden City, New York. One of the founding members, and one of the first to chair the F.O.R., was an Episcopalian priest, John Nevin Sayre. In due course he would be a campaigner for the rights of conscientious objectors, including those who were mistreated in Leavenworth Penitentiary. He went directly to President Wilson to protest against their inhumane treatment and torture. Sentences could be as long as twenty-five years or even life imprisonment. Other active Episcopalians included former classmates at Bryn Mawr, Tracy Mygatt and Frances Witherspoon. They lobbied Congress in 1917 against the U.S. declaration of war and founded various peace groups during the conflict, with Mygatt concentrating on writing anti-war articles and Witherspoon specialising in draft counselling. They visited the camp commander at Camp Upton to protest at the mistreatment of conscientious objectors held there. In one spectacular demonstration they rode a papier-mâché dinosaur down Wall Street to remind onlookers that armour-plated monsters court extinction. It was apparent to them that there was a distinct shortage of Episcopalians amongst those resisting the draft. Mygatt later reflected that "we waited in vain for the young Episcopalian whose conscience would send him to jail rather than the trenches. None such came. There had been neither preaching nor teaching to prepare him".[38] The one Episcopalian figure for whom there was a sacrificial element to war resistance was, perhaps surprisingly, a bishop. The protest of Bishop Paul Jones (1880-1941) of Utah cost him his job.

Of Welsh ancestry, and following a family line of clergy, Jones was educated at Yale and the Episcopal Theological School at Cambridge, Massachusetts. With one other colleague he agreed to be an Episcopalian presence in a hostel at Logan University, Utah, an appointment with negligible income. He was recruited by the socialist and pacifist Bishop of Utah, Frank Spenser Spalding, who promoted Jones to Archdeacon in Salt Lake City in 1913. Spalding's influence encouraged Jones's pacifism. The following year Spalding was killed by a speeding motorist, and the House of Bishops appointed Jones, only thirty-four years old, as his successor. He immediately set about becoming a well-travelled, missionary bishop, visiting mines and reservations. As war raged across the Atlantic, Jones's ministry became less welcome. There was patriotic, anti-German feeling in Salt Lake City, where German Avenue was renamed West Kensington Street and sauerkraut became known as "liberty cabbage". Mormons were eager to publicise their loyalty: "It was difficult for pacifists to stem the patriotic tide in any American city, but in Salt Lake, the religious situation made it impossible".[39]

Such was the context in which Jones had to exercise his Episcopal ministry. He preached against war in 1915, and spoke at a public rally, denouncing "hot-headed pseudo-patriots", whom, he said, "put democracy, loyalty, and truth in terms of guns, fighting and bloodshed, terms that this world, if not the old, has grown beyond".

He wrote a pamphlet in which he explained his views:

After thus studying again [Jesus'] life and teaching, I find it quite impossible to believe that people can be true to the things which he taught and the example which He gave and at the same time take part in war; for war is the organized destruction of our enemies and it is always accompanied by hatred and bitterness, thus necessitating an attitude of mind and course of conduct the opposite of that enjoined by Christ. . . .

It is unthinkable that [Paul, James, Peter or John] would have taken part in a war or in preparation for one. And I need only to refer to the example of the Christians of the early centuries who preferred to die rather than go into the army and cause some-one else's death, to show that they all interpreted our Lord's teaching in the same way. . . . [40]

I have gone in search to the sources of our Christian standards, and in the light of what I find there, as I love my country, I must protest against her doing what I would not do myself, because it is contrary to our Lord's teaching. To prosecute war means to kill men, bringing sorrow and suffering upon women and children, and to instil suspicion, fear and hatred into the hearts of the people on both sides. No matter what principles may appear to be at stake, to deliberately engage in such a course of action that evidently is un-Christian is repugnant to the whole spirit of the Gospel.[41]

The day will come when, like slavery which was once held in good repute, war will be looked upon as thoroughly un-Christian. At present it is recognized as an evil which nobody honestly wants, but not yet has it received its final sentence at the bar of Christian morality. Only when Christian men and women and churches will be brave enough to stand openly for the full truth that their consciences are beginning to recognize, will the terrible anachronism of war . . . be done away.[42]

Despite support for Jones in much of the diocese, members of two parishes, including the Cathedral parish, took exception to his stand. In October 1917, whilst visiting Los Angeles, Jones addressed a meeting of Christian pacifists and then left: shortly afterwards the meeting was raided by the police, with the leaders arrested. The press in Salt Lake City had a field day: "Swarms of Police Chase Bishop Jones" and "Paul Jones Flees Deck of Burning Peace Ship" were amongst the headlines.[43] Jones's adversaries acted. They were prominently represented on his Council of Advice, a body which, as its name suggested, had a purely advisory role. However, the Council wrote to the national House of Bishops in October 1917 expressing concern over Jones's "pacifist attitude in relation to the present war", arguing that his usefulness was "at a complete and permanent end" and asking for a new bishop in whom they could have more confidence. An initial committee of bishops recommended to the House of Bishops that Jones remain in his post, but their report was then referred to a second committee that was less tolerant. These bishops – Daniel S. Tuttle of Missouri (the Presiding Bishop, and himself a former Bishop of Utah), George Herbert Kinsolving of Texas and Harry S. Longley of Iowa – decided to reconsider the concerns of the Utah diocese. They recommended that Jones take leave of absence pending a more thorough investigation.

Bishop Jones made a statement to these committees explaining his position. He was a patriot, he said, and would be prepared to give his life for the extension of democracy, a sound peace and an end to German aggression. "But the question is that of method. It is not enough to say that the majority have decided on war as the only means of attaining those things and that therefore we must all co-operate". The problem went deeper. He recognised (incorrectly, as it turned out) that everyone felt that war was "wrong, evil and undesirable", yet many felt that the way the world was constituted left no option but to use it.

> In spite of my respect for the integrity of those who feel bound to take that course, and in spite of the knowledge that I am occupying an unpopular and decidedly minority point of view, I have been led to feel that war is entirely incompatible with the Christian profession. It is not on the basis of certain texts or a blind following of certain isolated words of Christ that I have been led to this, for I am not a literalist in any sense of the term; but because the deeper I study into it the more firmly I am convinced that the whole spirit of the Gospel is not only opposed to all that is commonly understood by the word 'war,' but offers another method capable of transforming the world and applicable to every situation which the individual or the nation is called to face.
>
> If we are to reconcile men to God, to build up the brotherhood of the kingdom, preach love, forbearance and forgiveness, teach that ideals are worth more than all else, rebuke evil, and stand for the good even unto death, then I do not see how it can be the duty of the Church or its representatives to aid or encourage the way of war, which so obviously breaks down brotherhood, replaces love and forbearance by bitterness and wrath, sacrifices ideals to expediency, and take the way of fear instead of that of faith. I believe that it is always the Church's duty to hold up before men the way of the cross; the one way our Lord has given us for overcoming the world.

The nation, said Jones, could not argue that participating in war was following the way of the cross. It would be a false analogy to compare the allied sacrifices with the sacrifice of Christ. He did not die to save his loved ones, or to punish evildoers, but he died for the unjust. Besides, "because Germany has ignored her solemn obligations, Christians are not justified in treating the sermon on the mount as a scrap of paper". Prayer, he said, was the best test of the matter.

> If it is right and our highest duty to fight the war to a finish, then we should use the Church's great weapons of prayer to that end; but the most ardent Christian supporter of the war, though he may use general terms, revolts against praying that our every bullet my find its mark, or that our embargoes may bring starvation to every German home. We know that those things would bring the war to a speedy, triumphant close, but the Church cannot pray that way. And a purpose that you cannot pray for is a poor one for Christians to be engaged in.

Germany was faulted for exalting the supremacy of the state over religion and morals; it had become the supreme cause for its people, reliant on its own might. Yet for people of the United States there was also a danger in exalting obedience to the state "without regard to whether Christianity seems to stand in the way".

> I would appeal to my own Church on the larger ground of our claims to catholicity. How can we ever say again that we are the Church for men of all nations and ages, if we so abandon the world ideal and become the willing instrument of a national government?. . . . If the method is wrong, I believe that the Church should have nothing to do with it; for back of the things that may be possibly achieved by the war, stands the terrible indictment that will be made that the Church abandoned the way of the cross that she was teaching. . . . It is often necessary for citizens who love their country, because they love their country, to oppose the policy of the government. . . . History has not always vindicated the opinions of the majority.

He ended by expressing to his inquisitors a determination to continue preaching opposition to the war.

> As I believe, then, that the adoption of the way of Christ would be the best thing possible for this land we love and through it for all the world, I must, with all the wisdom God has given me, and with all the earnestness which I possess, try to reach men with that message in the terms which I can express it. If you believe that the Church and the nation are better off without my message, I am

quite ready to accede to your judgment, but as long as I represent the Church as I do now, it seems to me that I would be apostate to my high commission did I take any other course. And if I have misinterpreted the meaning of the Gospel, I shall be glad to be set right.[44]

The investigating commission reported two months later, at a "time of an excited condition of public opinion". In the tones in which they damned Bishop Jones, the church authorities damned themselves more:

The underlying contention of the Bishop of Utah seems to be that war is unchristian. With this general statement the Commission cannot agree, and, specifically, it thinks that the present war with Germany in which our country is involved, being, as it is, for liberty and justice and righteousness and humanity among nations and individuals, is not an unchristian thing. This Church in the United States is practically a unit in holding that it is not an unchristian thing. In the face of this unanimity, it is neither right or wise for a trusted bishop to declare and maintain that it is an unchristian thing. If the compelling force of conscientious conviction requires such utterances, fairness demands that it not be made by a bishop of this Church. The making of such an Episcopal proclamation should be preceded by the withdrawal of the maker from his position of Episcopal leadership. . . . It seems abundantly manifest that an end has come to the usefulness of the Bishop in his present field, and that no earnestness of effort on his part would suffice to regain it.[45]

Put simply, Jones was out of a job, not for opposing the Gospel, but for opposing Government policy. After receiving that report, Jones wrote his first letter of resignation in the week before Christmas 1917, effective from April 1918.

The commission, speaking, I take it, for the House of Bishops, maintains, first that war is not an unchristian thing and that no Bishop may preach that this war is unchristian; and second that a Bishop should not express the opinion that peace can be secured otherwise than by the prosecution of the war when the Government and the preponderance of the membership of the Church believe otherwise.

Those conclusions I cannot accept, for I believe that the methods of modern international war are quite incompatible with the Christian principle of reconciliation and brotherhood, and that it is the duty of a Bishop of the Church, from his study of the Word of God, to express himself on questions of righteousness, no matter what opinion may stand in the way.[46]

Bishop Jones said farewell to the Diocese of Utah in January 1918. He acknowledged that the diocesan Council of Advice had acted according to its best judgement, and only time would show the folly or wisdom of that judgement. His greatest concern was with the remarkable conclusions expressed by the Commission of the House of Bishops. "Expediency may make necessary the resignation of a bishop at this time, but no expediency can ever justify the degradation of the ideals of the episcopate which these conclusions seem to involve".[47]

In his uncompromising witness for peace, Jones was regarded as an embarrassment by comfortable Episcopalians. There was even a request from the Executive Committee of the Alumni Association of the Episcopal Theological School in Cambridge, Massachusetts, that he should withdraw from a preaching engagement there. He continued to witness for peace, and worked as secretary for the Fellowship of Reconciliation, into the 1920s. He was the leading American F.O.R. representative at the 1920 follow-up meeting in Holland, after the 1919 launching of the International Fellowship of Reconciliation. By 1929 he was defining pacifism as "an attitude to life arising from a belief in human capacity for social action, which stresses the importance of the reaction of person upon person and group upon group, and which consequently uses only methods calculated to evoke co-operative action in seeking to achieve a progressive integration of life in every field of human relations".[48]

He emphasised the role of co-operation in the field of evolution and human survival, saying that, for the pacifist, "the means and the end are so intimately related that it is impossible to get a co-ordinated and co-operative world by destructive methods that violate personality and increase antagonism and distrust".[49] Jones held that an awareness of God as Father was the foundation of moral human society and relationships. War and exploitation were a direct denial of this common fatherhood of God, whereas those who were absorbed in expressing that essential unity had all the spiritual resources of the universe working with them.

> It is not to be wondered at that the conscientious objector, or anyone else, who has taken a stand against activities or practices which are a denial of that spiritual unity, has a power and influence out of all proportion to his individual importance. . . . With the example of Jesus giving himself without stint or limit to express his sense of his solidarity with both men and God, the pacifist feels that in endeavoring to use the same methods he is on sure ground.[50]

There is a postscript to this story. In the 1930s Jones was a chaplain at Antioch College, Ohio. Although he led reconciliation trips and collected directorships at the League for Industrial Democracy and the National Consumers' League, he never again served as a diocesan bishop nor attended the House of Bishops. He was active in helping refugees from Nazi Germany to settle in the U.S., and a founding member of the Episcopal Pacifist Fellowship in 1939, serving on its National Executive until his death in 1941. The wheel turned full circle in 1998, when representations to the General Convention of the Episcop Church led to Jones being added to the Calendar of Saints, with a feast day of 4 September, the anniversary of his death.[51]

Vida Dutton Scudder

Also in the U.S., in the years before women's ordination, was the Episcopalian socialist and academic Vida Dutton Scudder (1861-1954), whose radicalising post-graduate years had been spent at Oxford, including attendance of lectures by John Ruskin. She visited the Toynbee Hall initiative of Samuel and Henrietta Barnett, and channelled her own activism through college and the Society of Christian Socialists. Her spirituality was rooted in the Society of the Companions of the Holy Cross. She was involved in women's trade union campaigning and was a co-founder, in 1911, of the Episcopal Church Socialist League. Her thinking about social justice – though hardly her social background – in many ways mirrored that of Lansbury in England. She edited a volume of writings by the itinerant American Quaker, John Woolman, and had a developing awareness of the Franciscan tradition. This, together with the results of future Communist cruelties, would lead her to discard her attachment to violent revolution. Calling herself, in 1917, a "doubting pacifist", she later acknowledged that she was slow to speak out against the U.S. participation in the violence in Europe. She had found it hard to identify with those whose motivations were a refusal to kill or simply a recoiling from suffering. Yet, when she considered the sum total of the pain induced by war, her clear conclusion was that "War must go", and that "the hope of ending it rests on educating the race to perceive the degradation and demoralization of life which it involves". She looked to address the causes of war, the conflicts which she regarded as being at the heart of "a system that drives peoples, classes, and individuals alike, into a defensive and potentially hostile attitude towards one another". It was a process of building peace that would engage the whole of society in "the emancipation and reconstruction of human relationships on a basis of harmony".[52]

Although she did not join the Fellowship of Reconciliation until 1923, her study of the early English Church had led her to conclude that Christianity "must displace the Fighter from the heart of the world, and must put the Sufferer there".[53] Her 1917 volume, *The Church and the Hour*, a manifesto for social justice, included a lament at the failure of the church. Having condemned the sentimental Christianity that preceded 1914, she continued:

Then came the war, with its appeal for devotion to the uttermost; and the peoples of Europe responded with a sort of sacred joy. They obey the call of governments to destroy fellow-men at any personal cost in the name of patriotism. . . . In the hideous glare of the firing, it is possible to see Mars and Mammon, twin supporters of the old Capitalistic order, rushing on their own destruction.[54]

She rued the fact that people would always defend ancient sanctities, when it required courage and imagination to live in uncertainty and to find new ways for love to enter.

The world has never been so conscious of Christ as in these days of horror. Cartoons show Him everywhere. The hand of the dead soldier rests on His wounded Feet; the sorrowing wife feels His consoling Presence. Kaiser and King turn their backs on Him or pierce Him with the bayonet. To His gray figure on the Cross . . . climb bowed processions of phantom mourners, chanting in all the tongues of the warring nations to Him Who is their Peace. Meantime, those actual Calvaries that stand so grave and still, watching the battle-fields, bring a message of hope rather than despair. . . . [55]

It was a hope she expressed in verse:

Beyond our fierce confusions,
Our strife of speech and sword,
Our wars of class and nation,
We wait Thy certain Word.
The Church and the Hour
The meek and poor in spirit
Who in Thy presence trust
The Kingdom shall inherit,
The blessing of the Just.[56]

Irwin St John Tucker

One of the most outspoken clergy, who did not hesitate to condemn the war, was Irwin St John Tucker (1886-1982). A priest of some notoriety, Tucker was described by a judge in the U.S. Supreme Court as "an Episcopal clergyman and a man of sufficient prominence to have been included in the 1916-1917 edition of *Who's Who in America*".[57] This outspoken Chicago priest was one of the more colourful U.S. opponents of the war from the outset, describing it as "a struggle between Germany's Berlin-to-Baghdad railroad and England's Suez Canal, with no more of idealism in it than a battle of cash registers".[58] A leading figure in the Socialist Party, Tucker was briefly head of the Party's Literature Department, and editor of the *Christian Socialist*. One of his more graphic pieces of writing, in opposition to the war and conscription in particular, was described in court as "highly colored and sensational".[59] It was published by a Californian journal, *The World*, in 1917, and distributed widely as a separate leaflet. Entitled *The Price We Pay*, Tucker's article described how recruiting officers would teach his readers' sons not to think, only to obey without questioning, before being shipped to the "bloody quagmire" of Europe:

> Into that seething, heaving swamp of torn flesh and floating entrails they will be plunged, in regiments, divisions, and armies, screaming as they go.
>
> Agonies of torture will rend their flesh from their sinews, will crack their bones and dissolve their lungs; and every pang will be multiplied in its passage to you.
>
> Black death will be a guest at every American fireside; mothers and fathers and sisters, wives and sweethearts will know the weight of that awful vacancy left by the bullet which finds its mark.
>
> And still the recruiting officers will come. . . .
>
> And still the toll of death will grow. . . .
>
> Then perhaps you will believe what we have been telling you! For war is the price of your stupidity, you who have rejected Socialism!

Tucker recalled watching a film showing laughing soldiers preparing for the Battle of the Somme. The commentary said that fewer than twenty per cent of those soldiers were alive at the end of the day.

> All the horror and agony of war were exhibited; and at the end a flag was thrown on the screen, and a proclamation said:
>
> "Enlist for your country!" The applause was very thin and scattering; and as we went out, most of the men shook their heads and said:
>
> "That's a hell of a poor recruiting scheme!"

Tucker mocked the capitalists' denunciation that socialism would "destroy the home". For Tucker it was the capitalists' war that had led to the ravages of venereal disease, to families being deprived of husbands and fathers; to the return to twenty million women of "ruined wrecks of men; mentally deranged, physically broken, morally rotten". And the reason for all this suffering was nothing to do with democracy:

> War has been universal; and the cause of war is always the same. Somebody wanted something somebody else possessed, and they fought over the ownership of it.
>
> This war began over commercial routes and ports and rights; and underneath all the talk about democracy versus autocracy, you hear a continual note, an undercurrent, a subdued refrain – 'Get ready for the commercial war that will follow this war.'

Commercial war preceded this war; it gave rise to this war; it now gives point and meaning to this war;

And as soon as the guns are stilled and the dead are buried, commercial forces will prepare for the next bloody struggle over routes and ports and rights, coal mines and railroads;

For these are the essence of this, as of all other wars!. . . .

We are beholding the spectacle of whole nations working as one person for the accomplishment of a single end – namely, killing.

Every man, every woman, every child, must 'do his bit' in the service of destruction.

We have been telling you all for, lo! these many years that the whole nation could be mobilized and every man, woman, and child induced to do his bit for the service of humanity; but you laughed at us.

Now you call every person traitor, slacker, pro-enemy, who will not go crazy on the subject of killing; and you have turned the whole energy of all the nations of the world into the service of their kings for the purpose of killing – killing – killing. . . .

For this war – as everyone who thinks or knows anything will say, whenever truth-telling becomes safe and possible again – this war is to determine the question whether the Chambers of Commerce of the allied nations or of the central empires have the superior right to exploit undeveloped countries.

It is to determine whether interest, dividends and profits shall be paid to investors speaking German or to those speaking English and French. . . .

In a final flourish for his readers, Tucker wrote:

Until human life refuses to sacrifice itself for private gain;

Until by the explosion of millions of tons of Dynamite, the stupidity of the human race is blown away, and Socialism is known for what it is, the salvation of the human race;

Until then – *You will keep on paying the price !*[60]

This extraordinary outburst of anti-militarist anger made Tucker a marked man in the eyes of the authorities, and, alongside four other members of the Socialist Party, he was prosecuted for treason and sentenced to twenty years imprisonment, a sentence later overturned by the Supreme Court. Even distributing Tucker's pamphlet was enough to bring other Party members to court. A court in Baltimore decided that the leaflet should not be distributed, and members of the Socialist Party in Albany were prosecuted for the house-to-house delivery of hundreds of copies of Tucker's work. They were charged with:

The offense of unlawfully, feloniously and wilfully attempting to cause insubordination, disloyalty and refusal of duty in the military and naval forces of the United States when the United States was at war and to the injury of the United States in, through, and by personal solicitations, public speeches and distributing and publicly circulating throughout the United States certain articles printed in pamphlets called *The Price We Pay*, which said pamphlets were to be distributed publicly throughout the Northern district of New York. . . .

Although convicted at the time, the defendants were later acquitted by the Supreme Court.[61]

The British Empire's Struggle with Conscription

Having considered those personal stories from India and the United States, I briefly give an overview of opposition to the war in some other nations of the British Empire, particularly in relation to compulsory conscription to military service.

Canada

A Military Service Act, preparing the way for conscription, was introduced by the Conservative Government in Canada in August 1917. With what was, in effect, the re-election of the Union Government the following December, the terms of the Act were enforced in the New Year. The country was divided largely on ethnic lines, with strong Francophone opposition to conscription, leading to the violent Easter 1918 riots in Quebec. Ethnicity was a factor in other ways, as a diverse population included communities from both sides of the European war. In particular, there were some rather insular communities, descendents of Mennonite, Doukhobor, Tunker or Hutterite settlers, with their own anti-war traditions who, along with the Quakers, were regarded as being the historic peace churches. Enemy aliens, Mennonites, Doukhobors, and conscientious objectors were disenfranchised under a Wartime Elections Act. More than that, anyone who did cast a vote became unable to claim C.O. status.[62] Unlike in Britain, no campaigning or support organisation was formed for conscientious objectors, who were especially vulnerable as a result. One group of twenty-five Canadian C.O.s was sent to England, some being beaten into unconsciousness, then sent to Wandsworth Military Prison for further maltreatment, before being returned to Canada.[63]

The Church of England in the Dominion of Canada, as the Anglican Church was then known, had no doubts about the war, and its Synod passed a resolution in support of the aims and actions of the British Empire. "Spectator", a pseudonymous columnist for the Anglican journal *Canadian Churchman*, did however recognise that such a stand was at odds with the fact that "The Gospel of Christ is generally interpreted as a Gospel of peace and good will among men" and he questioned "How are these things to be permanently and logically harmonized?" Although "Spectator" himself strongly supported the Synod's attitude to the war, he did recognise that, up until 1914, the Church had opposed armament, but "When the blow fell we at once threw ourselves into the promotion of war. Were we right or wrong before the war?" Does the Church speak peace when there is peace? Though no supporter of C.O.s himself, he did ask, "We have been sending conscientious objectors to prison, but are they not carrying to a logical conclusion the doctrines we taught them in time of peace?"[64]

One such Anglican C.O. was Frederick Benson, from Norwood, Manitoba. Benson, a streetcar motorman, testified to his tribunal "I am personally opposed to fighting. I conscientiously believe that it is wrong to take up weapons. I have been brought up to think so". It was acknowledged that he had a family history of opposition to war (including a C.O. relative in England), but he was still sentenced to almost two years in prison.[65] Other Anglican C.O.s included: Mitchell Burrows, a bookbinder from Brampton, Ontario; Charles Darlington, a machinist; Cornelius Friesen, a teamster from Gull Lake, Saskatchewan; and Clifford Greenfield and John Moore, both carpenters from Toronto.[66]

Australia

Almost one in twenty-four Australians were wounded or killed in the First World War, mostly men between eighteen and thirty-five: men from a Dominion of the British Empire, fighting for an Empire of which they were, or were told they were, a part. Although they were involved in many war zones (some of which, like Passchendaele, were far more costly) the conflict that remains most etched upon the national psyche was the defeat of the Gallipoli invasion forces by Turkish resistance in 1915. As the casualties began to mount, more and more Australians began to ask what exactly it was that they were fighting and dying for.

Opposition to the war came from the political left and from a section of the women's movement. Vida Goldstein, of the Women's Political Association, opposed the war, supported by Jenny Baines and Adela Pankhurst, the youngest of the Pankhurst sisters, who had emigrated to Australia. Goldstein formed a new organisation, the Women's Peace Army, as a vehicle for her anti-war campaigning.[67]

The Labor Government, under Billy Hughes, decided to hold a referendum on conscription in 1916. There was already compulsory military training for teenage boys so, in law, any referendum would be purely "advisory", reflecting the Government's need to have the visible backing of the population for such a contentious issue.[68] Military losses, however, were so great that the first stages of compulsory recruitment were introduced whilst an increasingly tumultuous, and at times violent, referendum campaign was still under way, thereby fuelling the anti-conscription cause. In the end, the country was divided, with the "No" vote gaining a slim, 2.2 per cent majority. The result fractured the governing party, but Hughes continued with a new party, the National Labor Party, introducing a second referendum the following year. With some infamous exceptions, there were generally fewer disrupted meetings on each side, leading up to the second vote. With the Catholic Archbishop of Melbourne, Daniel Mannix, drawing large crowds, and the Labour Premier of Queensland also prominent, the "No" campaign was once again victorious, increasing its majority to 7.6 per cent.

Archbishop Mannix had initially supported the war and, like most of the other Catholic bishops, he condemned the violence of the 1916 Dublin rising. However, his solidarity with the Irish cause, against a British Empire in whose name Australians were being asked to fight and die, led him to oppose conscription in the 1916 referendum. In January 1917 he described the war as "an ordinary, sordid trade war".[69] His was a rare voice against the war from within church leadership. His opposition to conscription in 1917 was only supported late in the day by the Catholic Archbishop of Sydney.[70] Mannix's protests clearly struck a chord with the mainly working-class Irish Catholic community who made up one in five of all Australians.[71] The more he protested against the war, the larger were the crowds – tens of thousands – who turned out to hear him. It was not a pacifist cause, and it certainly was not Anglican, but it was democratic, and it did show that the Australia born between 1914 and 1918 was not to be defined exclusively by its commitment to the Empire, but must also be defined by its repeated, democratic rejection of military conscription.

New Zealand

Initial opposition to the war from New Zealand's British population appeared minimal, with thousands of men coming forward as recruits at the start of the war, perhaps a result of a policy of compulsory military cadet training for teenage boys since 1909.[72] Recruitment levels were not sustained, however, despite intensive campaigning, and conscription was introduced in 1916. Only four M.P.s registered their opposition. There was an anti-conscription conference, involving 200 organisations, in January 1916, but to no avail.[73] Subsequent public speakers against conscription found themselves at risk of arrest and imprisonment. Parents and others who harboured or employed C.O.s were liable to a sentence of up to three years hard labour.

At the outset, only single men of European descent (*pakeha*) were eligible for conscription.[74] Many of the Maori population retained memories of violence and injustice shown towards them by British settlers of previous generations. Representing "hostility to the Empire by conquered races" they were hardly minded to fight for a British cause.[75] Not surprisingly, the extension of recruitment to "native people" was a controversial development, and the Native Contingent Committee struggled to meet its recruitment targets, not least in the Taranaki and the Tainui-Waikato regions:

> Kingitanga leader Te Puea Herangi maintained that her grandfather, King Tawhiao, had forbidden Waikato to take up arms again when he made peace with the Crown in 1881. She was determined to uphold his call to Waikato to 'lie down' and 'not allow blood to flow from this time on'.[76]

When conscription was extended to include Maori men in June 1917, there was an element of malice in the focus of the regulations on regions that had responded least to recruitment campaigns. Te Puea (1883-1952), mindful of the nonviolent heritage of her people, offered refuge and support to any who resisted conscription, and attempted to visit in prison those she had sheltered who were subsequently arrested.

As with Australia, there was also an Irish dimension to war resistance, particularly on the west coast. Influential trade union leaders were involved: a miners' strike in early 1917 called for the repeal of the Military Service Act.[77] A number of socialists, including future Prime Minister Peter Fraser, were imprisoned for their opposition to conscription and any war against German workers. For daring to call for the repeal of the Military Service Act, Fraser received a twelve-month sentence for sedition. The socialist M.P. Paddy Webb was first imprisoned for supporting the miners; then, when called up himself, he resigned his seat and stood again – unopposed – on an anti-conscription platform, albeit to no avail. A court-martial sentenced him to two years hard labour; he was stripped of his seat and his civil rights for ten years.

With the Prime Minister, William Massey, arguing that there would be "no escape for the shirker", exemption was limited to those who, since the outbreak of the war, had "continuously been a member of a religious body the tenets and doctrines of which declare the bearing of arms and the performance of any combatant service to be contrary to divine revelation".[78] That included long-standing Quakers and Christadelphians, but few others.[79] When an attempt was made to conscript priests and those in orders, Thomas O'Shea, Catholic Archbishop of Wellington, said "to put a rifle in his [a priest's] hand and to expect him to take the life of another would be an outrage on the sanctity of his profession and an outrage on the Catholic conscience".[80] Even then, those exempted were expected to undertake alternative service, and 170 objectors were sent overseas in non-combatant roles in the 13 months from September 1917. A New Zealand Government website reports:

> By the end of the war only 73 objectors had been offered exemption, and 273 were in prison in New Zealand for refusing to serve. As a consequence of their actions, 2,600 conscientious objectors lost their civil rights, including being denied voting rights for 10 years and being barred from working for government or local bodies.[81]

The level of brutality shown towards one group of New Zealand C.O.s was as harsh as that in any nation in the British Empire. The worst example came when a group of fourteen men were forcibly taken from Trentham Military Camp prison on board the *Waitemata*, via Cape Town and Sling camp on Salisbury Plain, to France.[82] One of those men was Archibald Baxter, who held that "passive resistance to evil is the power that will yet conquer the world".[83] Baxter was one of a long line of brothers (two of whom were also on board) who were imprisoned for resistance to the war. Another was Mark Briggs, brought up a Wesleyan near Market Weighton, who had emigrated to New Zealand when he was twenty; Briggs exercised passive resistance from the moment of his arrest and had to be dragged aboard the *Waitemata*.[84] After maltreatment on the boat and solitary confinement in England, ten of the men, still refusing to wear khaki, were taken to Étaples. Three men were told they had a sentence of five years hard labour (the legal maximum was two years). Three others, imprisoned and tortured, together, responded to news that no more New Zealand C.O.s would be sent forcibly to Europe by consenting to become stretcher bearers in the Royal Army Medical Corps (R.A.M.C.).[85] Archibald, Briggs, Lawrence Kirwen and Henry Patton were subjected to the vicious treatment called "Field Punishment No. 1", after which Archibald, Briggs and Kirwen were sent, beaten and hungry, into a heavily shelled section of the front line. Briggs, still refusing to walk, was tied with cable wire then dragged through water and across rough planks, eventually being classed as medically unfit for active service.[86] At the Front at Ypres, and upon hearing a sermon by a military chaplain, Baxter wondered, "Was there a parson at the Front who dared to preach: 'Thou shall not kill?' "[87] Baxter was eventually diagnosed insane and taken to a British hospital for mentally ill soldiers, before being returned to New Zealand. His story has become part of the foundation of a subsequent New Zealand anti-war tradition.

8.
Conscience versus the Military State

Conscription and Objection

The most serious demand that the State could make on an individual was to force that person to fight in the army. In some countries, that was generally perceived as a given requirement. With the British people's history of hard-won liberties and traditions of dissent, the fact that such freedoms and rights were now threatened by conscription was a sign of the moral slippage provoked by war.

The slaughter of the early months of the war had taken its toll of the early volunteers and "wastage" was running at around 15 per cent a month. Early recruitment rates of 100,000 per month could not be sustained, even by raising the upper age to 40. Ironically, the human cost increased popular and political support for the war and any methods that might be used to win it; those who had already died must not have perished in vain. A coalition Government announced at the end of May 1915 included several right-wingers in the cabinet, all of whom favoured conscription. The national register of 15 July, intended to determine how many men were available, was the next logical step. The retreat from Gallipoli indicated that the state would require every possible body in order to sustain the war to the bitter end. There was one last recruiting drive by Lord Derby, in which a mere 200,000 "volunteered" for immediate enlistment, although ten times that number agreed to "attest", to become part of the reserve for future enlistment. The drive was regarded as a failure as over half of eligible married men, and over one third of eligible single men, still refused to come forward as cannon-fodder, despite what the F.O.R. described as the "intimidation" of such campaigns.[1]

The path, then, was clear for the introduction of compulsory conscription. Two men from Leeds, Thomas Ferris and Sydney Overbury, were sentenced to six months hard labour for daring to produce a leaflet opposing conscription and war.[2]

Asquith duly saw the Military Service Bill through Parliament in January 1916. Only thirty eight M.P.s objected, mainly U.D.C., I.L.P. or Quaker members; in the upper chamber Leonard Courtney spoke on the history of conscientious objection from the Dutch Mennonites of the sixteenth century, but his attempt to permit objections to any actions that supported the war and not merely to military service was rebuffed by one of the Government's principal recruitment officers, the Bishop of London.[3]

Legislation of this kind had been feared by the N.C.F. since the earliest weeks of the war, and such fears were proved to be justified, at great sacrificial cost to its members. Three years later the N.C.F. President, Clifford Allen, looked back on the mental and physical struggles of those who chose to resist the predominant national mood of:

> bitterness, hatred, and terror . . . men were afraid to be isolated from the life of the nation. . . . Above all things, men were held by a world spell, and that was the spell of the military machine. Fearless men, keen-minded men, gentle men, believed it their duty to bow before that machine. Others held it to be infallible and irresistible. We, like others of our generation, were called upon to become part of this world adventure; we were challenged by the community to bow before the military power; we were expected to engage in war and acquiesce in conscription.[4]

For all the intense social pressures, that was something they would not do. Indeed, from a campaigning perspective, opposition to conscription was actually an issue that those with diverse anti-war views could unite around. There was also slightly more popular sympathy for the anti-conscription cause, not least from a subset of the House of Bishops and other establishment figures, who could appreciate the human rights issues involved. As the prospect of conscription came closer, therefore, resistance to it was even greater than resistance to the war. The socialist poet W.N. Ewer (1885-1976), launched a cynical attack on the Dean of Exeter (Alfred Earle, Bishop of Marlborough) for suggesting that "Conscription will lead the way to the higher life":

> When, hark! There comes a voice from Devon!
> The Dean has found the keys of heaven,
> Has found the path that none could find,
> Has seen where all the saints were blind.
> Marlborough is come to bring salvation
> And Higher Life to all the nation.
> Sure and simple his prescription:
> All mankind needs is – Conscription![5]

Lansbury used the *Herald* to mount a vigorous campaign on what he called an "Outrage", writing numerous articles on such themes as " 'Labour Can Yet Kill Conscription' ", arguing that "while Parliament is to be asked to conscript flesh and blood and thus provide cheap soldiers for the defence of the rich man's land and wealth", the Trades Union Congress should take direct action to stop it.[6] He believed that, "If the Government Bill is carried it will mean that Britain has joined the nations that believe in militarism".[7] He put forward an economic case against the military conscription of working people, calling instead for the Government to "Conscript Lord Derby's Land!"[8] There were reports of a newly formed National Council Against Conscription, with Lansbury as one of the executive members.[9] More disturbingly, there were reports of an anti-conscription meeting on 16 January at the Brotherhood Church in north London being disrupted by pro-war outsiders who caused "uproar and physical violence".[10] Amongst a host of actions opposing conscription was news of an F.O.R. letter to the Prime Minister stating that, "We are compelled to resist compulsory military service not by any desire to embarrass the Government, nor by any thought of merely saving our souls, but by the firm conviction that in making such a witness to the supreme demand of the love of God upon our lives we should be offering the national service which is called for at our hands to-day".[11] The F.O.R. Group in Bristol protested "against the threatened violation of the religious and moral liberties of the people".[12] Labour parliamentarians received a mixed press; Lansbury called on Arthur Henderson to resign from the cabinet, whilst Philip Snowden was commended for producing an explanatory booklet on the Military Service Act, and for speaking out in favour of negotiated peace terms.[13] A powerful, full-page cartoon by Frederick Carter in the *Herald* showed Mary at the foot of the cross, with the caption, "The Mother of the 1st C.O."[14] (illustrated on p. 153). The *Herald* launched its own anti-conscription campaign fund, and there were letter-writing campaigns to Prime Minister Asquith.[15] A published poem by "J.S." was entitled, "To a Conscientious Objector":

> O! you stand in the pathway alone
> With your dream for a shield and a sword,
>   Caring naught for the might
>   Of a world that is strong.
> Bearing witness, in faith, for your Lord.
>
> But your dream is an armour divine
> Beaten out on the anvils of love –
>   So you stand, with your smile,
>   And the arrows of scorn
> Are destroyed by the strength of the dove.[16]

Despite all this activity, the attempts by the *Herald* and the N.C.F. to prevent the introduction of conscription were both unpopular and unsuccessful. Lansbury addressed some 1,500 members of the N.C.F. at a rally in Devonshire House, the Friends' Headquarters in London in April 1916.[17] His speech was full of Holy Week and Easter imagery:

> We believe that you are standing in line with that man who was God and who in Gethsemane stood alone and who, forsaken by everyone, even then loved his enemies. There must be no hatred in us. There is something that follows Gethsemane, and that is Easter – the resurrection of this old world from the damnable conditions of today.[18]

That was at a gathering of sympathisers preparing for future imprisonment. At public meetings, though, he would struggle to finish his speech because of the hostility his opinions aroused. As he explained later, the only conscription he could tolerate was the conscription of wealth: "Nobody should be allowed to make a penny out of the ruin and bloodshed a war inevitably creates". On the other hand, "There must always be a conscience clause for those who will have no hand in the work of legalized murder"[19] The Military Service Act took effect from 10 February 1916. From a military perspective it could not come soon enough, with replacements soon to be required for local "Pals" battalions of volunteers who would be decimated at the start of the Somme offensive on 1 July.[20] Unmarried men between eighteen and forty-one were regarded as having been "duly enlisted in His Majesty's regular forces . . . for the period of the war". The Liberal Prime Minister could conceive that particular individuals or communities might have specific practical skills or needs that required certain men to continue in their present employment, and that members of historic peace churches could have religious objection to combatant service, so he was prepared to tolerate some exemptions to the Act. Members of Parliament, whose support his coalition Government required, extended the possibility of exemption through conscientious objection to three categories: temporary, conditional or absolute.[21] The first to be tested were young single men, but the Bill was soon extended to include married men, and, in 1918, those aged up to fifty-one.

The Statistics of Conscience

The precise working of the act was to be determined by 1,800 local tribunals across the country with few guidelines to help them, though many would have concurred with the Prime Minister's sentiments. In any case there was always an armed forces' representative to guide the Tribunals appropriately. The vast majority of cases coming before the tribunals had no element of opposition to the war, but were made on employment or domestic grounds. They concerned the safe keeping of businesses, ailing relatives and essential services. Among the larger operations, the Birmingham Local Tribunal gave 90,721 decisions between 1916 and 1918, sending 34,760 men into the army. In Leeds, the Tribunal processed 27,000 applicants in over 55,000 hearings.[22] The local worthies, cognisant in local trade, businesses and society, struggled to keep up with the huge workload, and applications on grounds of conscience were an annoyance and a frustration, emotions often seen in the quality of their judgements. Those whose task it was to rate the conscience of appellants did not gain a reputation for knowledge, wisdom or impartiality. They were charged with arguing with the applicant, and then themselves deciding who had the best of the argument. One sympathetic commentator has described tribunal proceedings as "a strange mixture of a *viva voce* in scriptural knowledge and the Spanish Inquisition".[23] Within weeks of the Act coming into force, the *Herald* was complaining that "some of these tribunals do not know what the human conscience is".[24] One of the worst examples was in Sutton, where the military representative was the local vicar who opposed every argument based on conscience.[25] Lansbury, who vainly expected the churches to be in the forefront of the campaign for conscience, especially as almost every denomination's existence or survival came out of struggle, was moved to comment:

> It seems impossible to make these local potentates understand that men and women have been endowed by God with a sense of right and wrong, that Christianity for 2,000 years has been telling us that the still small voice of conscience was God's method of speaking to each individual soul, and that the sin against the Holy Ghost was to deny the truth as revealed by one's own conscience.[26]

There were examples of one tribunal member who believed Tolstoy to be a place-name and another who was astounded that the New Testament was written in Greek because he held that Jesus "was British to the backbone!"[27] A piano-tuner was turned down for having an inconsistent conscientious objection, because he must have known that his pianos could be used for playing military marches and patriotic tunes. Similarly, a baker's application for exemption was rejected because he could not prove that his bread was never eaten by soldiers.[28] As one commentator observed, most of the tribunals were "revealing a total inability to understand either a conscience or an Act of Parliament".[29] Another said later that "not since Lord Jeffrey's Bloody Assize have judicial bodies left to posterity a reputation so closely identified with bias and injustice".[30]

Unconditional exemption was very rarely granted, only to three hundred and fifty men in total, largely because tribunals were faced with a far more bewildering range of conscientious objections than the Government had anticipated, not all of which were religious or pacifist.[31] There were those whose religious principles had more to do with the refusal to recognise external authority, for example, the Plymouth Brethren, and those who objected that the state coercion of individuals constituted a breach of personal freedom and civil liberty (anarchists, for example). However the largest single group of objectors, the Christadelphians (more than ten per cent of the total number of C.O.s) were prepared to make munitions, provided they were not placed under military discipline.[32] In these cases the objections were as much about conscription itself as about the war. Some political objectors (for example, some socialists or revolutionary communists) opposed this war in particular but not necessarily all wars or violent revolutions – this objection was rarely recognised by tribunals. Other objectors (for example, Christians taking a "just" war perspective, or Christians who objected specifically to war against fellow Christians) argued on religious grounds against this war in particular. There were some who would accept the secondary violence of sanctions or blockades, but not the direct violence of warfare. Others would tolerate specific smaller scale violence – assassination or capital punishment, perhaps – but were opposed to the wholesale violence of war. There were also humanitarian or political pacifists who objected to all war in all its forms.

Although Christian objectors were accused of hiding cowardice behind their Christianity, non-religious pacifists received much harsher treatment from tribunals than those who could argue from religious conviction; secular socialists were often told they could not have a conscience.[33] Those religious pacifists (for example, members of F.O.R.) who objected to all war presented a variety of underlying reasons, arguments and theologies behind their decision. There were also a few who objected to all acts of violence against any living creature. It was not unknown for cynical tribunals, unsympathetic to the liberal exemptions within the act, to assume that, unless an objection could be proven in this final, most extreme category, then it was invalid. In practice, however, applicants would base their objections on a mélange of religious and political arguments.

Not only were there different types of objection for bewilderingly diverse reasons, there were also a variety of approaches to alternative occupations. Some of the objectors described above would obviously not tolerate any state-imposed activity of any kind.[34] Others refused all alternative occupations because any work would, in some way or another, assist the war effort, perhaps by releasing another person for the army. Such objectors were termed "Absolutists". Many objectors only objected to working with the military, and were prepared to consider civilian "Work of National Importance", such as agricultural, educational, shipbuilding or Red Cross work, or working for the Friends' Ambulance Unit, which bravely provided medical aid on the battlefields. Other objectors were content to be freed from the demand to kill, and were prepared even to don military uniform to contribute to the needs of the nation, even a nation at war. Some joined the Royal Army Medical Corps (R.A.M.C.), and others the Non-Combatant Corps (N.C.C.), formed in March 1916 amid suspicions that its task of "field engineering" was, to all intents and purposes, still combatant work.[35]

Those who resented tribunal decisions and refused to co-operate with them, were not all necessarily Absolutists; their resistance was often wrongly assessed. Thus an objector who might have been prepared to undertake agricultural work would refuse to wear a military uniform and be placed unwillingly in the N.C.C.. Rebelling, he would then be imprisoned alongside Absolutists and others whose objections had been misdiagnosed. The *Herald* dubbed the N.C.C. the "No-Cowards" Corps, but complained that, possibly through good but misguided motives, the Government "erred in not understanding what the conscience of the conscientious objector was, and they erred still more in not attempting to find out".[36] All told, the mosaic of reasons for objection, together with the varying attitudes towards military and civilian work were sufficiently complex as to be beyond the comprehension not only of most of the local worthies sitting on the tribunals, but also of the Government and its officials.

Extraordinary situations arose, such as at Richmond Castle, Yorkshire, where a Non-Combatant Corps of objectors was based alongside an imprisoned group of Christian, sectarian and socialist Absolutists.[37] Despite the generally helpful advice from the Government's own Pelham Committee (which processed 3,964 objectors, of whom only 51 were known Anglicans), the nature of objections continued to be misunderstood, and consequently inappropriate alternatives offered, because a valid objection was not recognised in the first place.[38] The overall effect was that many conscientious objectors, of thoroughly diverse backgrounds, faced a series of tribunals and court-martials, and found themselves brutally treated in prisons throughout the country.[39]

Socialist objectors to all war would often have much in common with Christian (F.O.R.) objectors to all war, whereas members of more exclusive Christian sects, like the Plymouth Brethren, would steer clear of political debate. On the other hand there were communists and other, sometimes violent, political extremists who could well despise their pacifist neighbours as much as the authorities did. One conscientious objector would not necessarily have any more in common with another than he would with men in the armed forces, a situation which reinforced the popular feeling that conscientious objectors were all troublemakers. Charles Raven later commented that "In the First World War ... pacifism was apt to be the creed of uncompromising individualists, men or women inheriting the fine tradition of independence which its critics were apt to stigmatize as the "Nonconformist Conscience" '.[40] Such was the range of objection that one can almost speak of diverse *pacifisms*.

Approximate figures for conscientious objectors during 1916-19 suggested that 6,261 were arrested (of whom some 1,350 were Absolutists), a further 3,964 were found alternative work by the Pelham Committee. A further 3,300 joined the Non-Combatant Corps, 1,200 joined the Friends' Ambulance Unit, and 900 worked directly under the tribunals. Around 200 were allowed to undertake alternative service by working for the Friends' War Victims' Relief Committee, perhaps restoring French villages, providing a pure water supply, or serving in maternity hospitals.[41] 100 C.O.s joined the Royal Army Medical Corps and around 175 managed to evade the Military Service Act altogether, making a total of 16,100 objectors.[42] This group, and especially the much smaller number of Absolutists, were to exert a long-term moral influence across the nation.

The poet S. Gertrude Ford compared the sufferings of the C.O. with that of Christ:

> His crime was that he loved Peace; followed her
>   For Christ's sake, in His name, even to the death
>   Faithful; and felt in war red murder's breath,
> Volleying the flames of hell, the blasts that stir
> Bedrock of world-foundations. Messenger
>   Of Truth, and hearing what the Spirit saith,
>   How should he fear the Fear that palsieth,
> That can the light of all things blot and blur?
>
>   They bound him, mocked, maltreated; wounded sore
>   They left him, crying 'Coward.' So once the rude
> Cries of the crowd rang round the Tree that bore
>   Leaves for the healing of the nations strewed.
> Few then His followers; now, the wide world o'er,
>   Behold them as the stars for multitude.[43]

Certainly, there was a religious motivation for many of those imprisoned. Eric Chappelow wrote "Evening thoughts in prison" whilst incarcerated in Wandsworth prison in June 1916:

> O what to me my narrow room,
> O what to me my straitened ways,
> If through it all, to give God praise,
> My heart can bud and burst and bloom?

Richmond Castle today.
The cell block is to the right of the twelfth-century keep.

O what, before the sun doth rise,
Through dreams that grow 'neath memory's spell
The pang when, on the same drear cell,
Open the disillusioned eyes?

O what the heart that sickens of
Mean toil, monotonous, soulless ways,
The lack of the Belovèd's face,
The heart that starves for lack of love?

O what the vista without end,
O what the sense of things sans hope,
The persecution lacking scope
To kill the thought of the Heart's Friend,

My spirit rights itself and sees,
When at the last the evening falls,
Through vanishing and widening walls,
The Angels of the Prince of Peace![44]

The Working, or Otherwise, of Tribunals

The stand of a conscientious objector was inevitably a personal, individual commitment, even when supported by a political campaign group, or by a sympathetic faith community. It is hardly surprising that the majority of Christian conscientious objectors came from Free Churches with a long history of upholding the conscience of the individual, the dissenter. It has been estimated that only around 7 per cent of conscientious objectors were Anglicans, a lower figure than for almost any other church, and fewer than the 12 per cent who were atheists, but even that figure could be generous.[45] The most reliable database has identified 350 men who were "C of E", out of nearly 17,000 C.O.s. However, as the religious affiliation of many of the others is not known (or at least they did not indicate that it was the motivation for their objection) it is difficult to assess the true figure.

The lack of a rebellious tradition and, with a few exceptions, the bellicosity of the church leaders – not only Arthur Winnington-Ingram, Bishop of London, but also Bishop Francis Chavasse of Liverpool, who suggested that conscientious objectors should leave the country – meant that Anglicans had a particularly hard time in front of tribunals.[46] In the words of one commentator:

In religious terms the unpredictable source of conscientious objection was a Christian pacifism that was unsupported by a specific teaching of the applicant's Church. . . . In this the Anglican pacifists were particularly vulnerable. In the past the

Anglican Communion had not accepted a pacifist interpretation of scripture and showed no inclination to do so in 1914. . . . It is hardly surprising that the tribunal members tended to regard the Bishop of London as the authentic voice of Anglicanism. In this context, the Anglican pacifist seldom found it easy to establish the merits of his case.[47]

It was not uncommon for a tribunal to ask an applicant if he had actively protested to the bishops about their attitude to the war. A negative response would contribute to the grounds for turning down his application for exemption.[48] A journalist present at a number of tribunals reported one thus:

Mr C. was a letter sorter at the G.P.O. and he claimed total exemption. He had been a member of the Church of England since infancy and had held his opinions since the South African war. He said that he conscientiously objected to taking life, though he would not object to Red Cross Work if it were voluntary.

Question: Do you believe in the Bishops?
Answer: Yes.
Question: In the Bishop of London?
Answer: I do not agree with his going to the front.
Question: We are defending ourselves and Christianity, what would you do to help us?
Answer: Trust in God.
Question: Do you Trust Him in everything?
Answer: Yes. He always does what I ask Him.
Question: Do you simply ask God and do nothing yourself?
Answer: I spread the Gospel.
Question: Do you make an effort yourself?
Answer: Yes.
Question: What are you doing now?
Answer: I am preaching Christianity.
Question: How can that stop war?
Answer: Are not all the men fighting, Christians?

[A member of the Tribunal interjected:]
Faith without works is dead – what will you do?
Answer: I am leading the life of a Christian.

[Another member of the Tribunal:]
If you pray, should you not make some effort to get what you want?
Answer: I believe I must make some effort.

Question: What do you do to stop war?

Answer: I preach the Gospel to others.

Question: Do you think that sufficient?

Answer: I do think it sufficient. If people believed the Gospel it would stop war.

Question: Do you try to get hold of the responsible people?

Answer: I can't say I go as far as that.

Question: Have you taken action with regard to the Bishop of London? Did you protest?

Answer: I did nothing.

Question: You are employed by the Postmaster-General, do you object to serving the Government?

Answer: No. I have already tried also to do Red Cross work but was refused as of military age.

The application was refused.[49]

Chris Massie was one who did protest publicly to Winnington-Ingram. Writing from the French front, where he was engaged in medical service in the R.A.M.C., he suggested to the Bishop that "when these young men who believe in Christ stand before the tribunals they are only doing what Christ did when He stood before the tribunals".[50] Similarly, when the socialist Ben Tillett attacked the clergy's exemption from military duty, Lansbury admitted that his defence of the clergy was not helped when they urged others to go out to fight. The Bishop of London came in for the strongest criticism.[51]

Another young man whose tribunal wilfully misunderstood his situation was a theological student from Jesus College, Oxford, Herbert F. Runacres, who claimed exemption from military duties. He would have expected to have been exempt anyway, because he was preparing for the ordained ministry, itself an exempt occupation, but he still wished to register as a conscientious objector. Unbeknownst to him, a member of the college who disagreed with his politics had written a secret letter to the military representative on the tribunal, a letter which, in contravention of legal principles, Runacres was not permitted to see. His difficulties began when the Town Clerk failed to state the reasons Runacres had submitted to justify his exemption, or that the church had supported and funded his ministerial training. The interview continued:

Town clerk: You are also at Pusey House [an Anglican theological institute]?

Applicant: Yes, sir.

[Town Clerk reads letter from Dr Stone, Principal of Pusey House:]

I have known Mr H.F. Runacres for some years and believe that his objections to military service are conscientious and of long standing.

Applicant: May I make a statement in support and explanation of my claim?

President of Tribunal: Yes.

Applicant: I have applied for exemption on ground F., *i.e.*, on conscientious grounds. I ask the Tribunal to grant me an absolute exemption on these grounds. I beg to state that I would equally object to the R.A.M.C. or any form of military service and combatant service. It is only reasonable that the Tribunal should require to know that I am engaged on work of national importance. My present work is recognised by the Government as of national importance.

The Clerk: What is it?

Applicant: I am preparing for ordination, but I have applied for exemption on conscientious grounds, and it is in the power of the Tribunal to grant absolute exemption under Clause 2, Sub-Section 3, of the Military Service Act, which states that 'any certificate of exemption may be absolute, conditional or temporary.'

Lieutenant Baldny: Have you ever had any trouble with your College?

Applicant: Not to my recollection.

[Here a further question was asked by the Lieutenant as to whether the College had prevented the applicant from holding meetings. Answer in the negative. Applicant made a statement with regard to an enquiry which had been made of him by a College official with regard to meetings which he had addressed.]

"A conscientious objector of the most objectionable type. A man who, till he was stopped by his College, addressed Socialist and working-men's meetings to discourage recruiting. Should be given no quarter for his proselytising work, but if granted exemption from combatant duties, should be put to do work of an unpleasant nature."

Lieutenant: Do you know who this letter is from?

Applicant: I can guess.

Town clerk: How long have you been at Pusey House?

Applicant: Since last October. I repeat that I have applied as a conscientious objector.

Lieutenant: I submit that this man has not produced evidence that he is in immediate preparation for ordination.

Applicant: That evidence is on my form under head of occupation.

[This had not been read out by the Town Clerk. It was a statement that applicant was in receipt of a grant from the diocese of Southwell.]

Town clerk: Mr Stone does not say that you are a candidate for ordination.

Applicant: I appealed on conscientious grounds. Dr Stone therefore only testifies to that.

A Member of the Tribunal: When are you going to be ordained?

Applicant: I have no fixed date. I shall be ordained at the time which seems to me fitting. That is not a matter for the jurisdiction of a Tribunal.

[In reply to a question from Mr Frimley, Labour representative on the Tribunal:]

Applicant: I only once to my recollection addressed a meeting of working-men. That was in the Central Labour Club some time last term. The subject was, so far as I recollect, 'Socialism and the War.' I dealt with it as an industrial question. It had nothing to do with recruiting.

[Lieutenant again read portions of the letter.]

Applicant: I still dispute the statements in that letter.

[Tribunal retired.
On returning,]

Chairman of the Tribunal: The claim is disallowed.
Applicant: Then I give notice that I shall appeal.[52]

The case was subsequently raised in Parliament on 15 March by the Labour M.P. for West Bradford, Fred Jowett, whose own anti-war record stretched back to the Boer War. He asked the President of the Local Government Board, William Hayes Fisher, what action he proposed to take regarding the conduct of the Oxford Local Tribunal. Unhelpfully, but unsurprisingly, Hayes Fisher refused to interfere. The following day, Bishop Gore of Oxford had a letter published in the *Times* asking tribunals to be more respectful of those seeking exemption where there is good evidence of conscientious conviction. He referred in particular to two men whom he knew personally, who were "not shirkers, men whom you might accuse of fanaticism but never of cowardice or stupidity. I think these men have not been treated by the tribunals with sufficient respect. I feel sure that they will be driven to passive resistance, and that, whatever punishment is finally meted out to them, they will take it gladly".[53] The outcome of Runacres's appeal was that he was indeed registered as a conscientious objector, and sent to perform alternative service at a Work Camp at Dyce, near Aberdeen, under the Home Office Scheme. Runacres also spent time imprisoned at Brockenhurst.[54]

The Church of England's Response to Conscription

The attitude of ecclesiastical authorities to the introduction of conscription was mixed. The Bishop of London did not accept that any conscience, sufficiently educated, could but agree with his own. He was too busy recruiting and informing congregations that it was their Christian duty to be prepared if necessary to "Kill Germans". However, other, less vocal proponents of the war, were uneasy, both about the assessment of conscience and also the treatment of objectors. Bishops Gore and Hicks both wrote letters to the *Times* advising tribunals to be "more respectful" of conscientious conviction. Gore, Temple and Free Church leaders collectively published another letter expressing the same concerns.[55]

In May 1916 concern was growing about the initial workings of the Military Service Act. Twenty-one people, including such prominent church leaders as Scott Holland and Hicks, together with members of the F.O.R. and the N.C.F., made "An Appeal to Christians", expressing that concern.

> At such a time as this we are reluctant to add anything to public controversy, but we are constrained to do so under a deep sense of the danger which at present threatens us of losing the very treasure for which we are assured our country has gone to war – the priceless treasure of freedom. We cannot, even in such an hour of danger as this, see the rights of conscience ignored without immediate protest, whether we ourselves agree with the 'conscientious objector' or not.
>
> Many – indeed, most of us – do not agree with him. But we hold that respect for conscience is of the very stuff of which freedom is made. It is bound up with the whole history of our country. It is the provident and the best of the traditions our fathers fought for and left to us, their descendants, to hold in trust. So truly has it become a part of our national being, that, at perhaps the greatest crisis in our history, it has been preserved and embodied in the Military Service Act. We are proud to know that the rights of conscience were admitted and safeguarded at such a time.
>
> But on this point both the letter and the spirit of the Act have been repeatedly violated by those who administer it. In spite of the terms of the Act itself, in spite of instructions, issued from headquarters, some tribunals have denied their right to grant absolute exemption on conscientious grounds; others have derided the claim of the objector to a conscience at all; and yet others have refused to recognise a genuine conviction because it was based on moral rather than purely religious grounds. In all these things the tribunals have actually defined the law which it was their duty to administer in an impartial spirit. . . .
>
> We contend that in violating the Military Service Act the tribunals have violated the finest traditions of our race. . . .

The signatories urged an enquiry into the methods of the tribunals, some of which had been known to state that they could not deal with questions of conscience but rather intended to "stop this rot". Pending an enquiry, the signatories felt that C.O.s should be treated under civilian, rather than military, authority.

> And we appeal to all Christian people, however convinced in their minds of the necessity or the duty of war, to reflect upon their own religious history, to remember by what great sacrifices in the past their present liberties have been won, and what grievous harm has been done to the cause of religion by persecution and intolerance. Let us who call ourselves Christians, to whatever communion we belong, continually urge upon our friends, our churches, the Press, the public, and above all those in authority, the great fact that, while we have a right at all times to seek to convince those who disagree with us, we cannot persecute them for opinions conscientiously held, without cheapening our own conscience, coarsening public morality, destroying the foundations of all freedom.[56]

When a conscientious objector had had his case turned down by two tribunals, or even accepted by one, but with an inappropriate form of exemption, he would be handed over to the military and placed under military authority. At the first refusal to salute or to don military uniform he would be confined to a cell, to await court martial. Even in detention, refusal to participate in drill, or to obey other orders, was regarded as further disobedience leading to further punishment. Physical and psychological torture, for example, beatings, enforced nakedness for those unwilling to wear military khaki, and the most minimal of diets, were commonplace. Across the country threats were made that the punishment would be execution. In the most extreme case, the punishment the Army intended for a group of objectors taken forcibly to France was exactly that.

The French Connection – a Death Sentence

Government Distrust of the Military

The Government had good reason to distrust the military since there had been recent reports of captured Irish rebels being shot without trial, including the arbitrary execution, by order of a British army captain, of the Irish pacifist Francis Sheehy Skeffington (1878-1916) in Dublin on 25 April. Skeffington had previously stated that, "If I lived in England I should still deem it my duty to join such a [Stop the War] society and to insist on the propaganda to stop the war in the only way in which the people can stop the war, namely by stopping recruiting, by ceasing to provide the food for powder".[57]

Writing in the *Herald* on 6 May 1916, Bertrand Russell asked the question regarding conscientious objectors, "Will They Be Shot?" He indicated the possibility that conscientious objectors could be forced against their will into the N.C.C. or other military units, sent to France where they would refuse a military order, and then be sentenced to death by the military. Although the Military Service Act forbade execution as a punishment for conscientious objection itself, it made no reference to the appropriate punishment for subsequent offences. The Army definitely wanted to set an example. Asquith, though, not wanting a public scandal, assured Arnold Rowntree on 9 May 1916 that no executions would take place. Yet, having been tipped off by a letter from A.W. Evans successfully smuggled out of a train passing through London en route to Southampton, the watchful N.C.F. and Friends' Service Committee knew that seventeen men, who had refused non-combatant service, had already been taken two days earlier from Landguard Fort, near Felixstowe, via Southampton-Havre, to France.[58]

On 10 May those men refused an order to march on a parade ground; physical ill-treatment, bullying and threats ensued.[59] The group included two Anglicans, Harold Brewster from Merton Park, South London, and Geoffrey Hicks from Burgess Hill.[60]

The Harwich C.O.s

Brewster had first met the Quaker C.O., Harry Stanton, at Landguard. According to Stanton, Brewster had been forced into uniform, and was awaiting developments in his case. The Landguard Fort contained both Absolutists and N.C.C., the latter "mainly composed of men who were C.O's on religious grounds, such as Plymouth Brethren, who objected to taking human life, but did not feel able to refuse other forms of military service".[61] One morning, Brewster and Stanton refused to parade.

> [We] strolled round the camp watching the N.C.C. perform duties of picking up scraps of paper and burnt matches. Apparently this misdemeanour was overlooked, for nothing was said until after breakfast, when we again refused to parade. The Non-Combatant Corps formed up in double rank, while we walked up and down with our hands in our pockets, inspecting them. After a time one of the corporals came up and said in a resigned tone 'Well! I expect you'll have to go to the guard-room. Just wait a minute while I get an escort!'[62]

The consequence was that up to a dozen of the C.O.s were sent to the prison block, Harwich Redoubt. "We spent most of our time in reading our small stock of books, and in discussion. We were confined in the small cells – rather less than half the size of the usual prison cell, and two of us occupied each apartment. Our letters, both in and out, were subject to censorship, but were not limited as to number".[63] The protestors were left without food or water in cells that were completely dark and overrun with rats.[64] It was a taste of things to come.

On Saturday 6 May, the first group of absolutist C.O.s was told they would be sent from Harwich to France, under military discipline as army members of the 2nd Company of the Eastern Non-Combatant Corps. Two days later, seventeen men left for Southampton and Le Havre.[65] They had contemplated but declined undertaking a hunger strike, believing that they would need their strength for challenges ahead. Quakers in the group, recalling those who had drawn up the Peace Testimony of the Society of Friends, prayed that they might have the strength to follow worthily in the footsteps of their seventeenth century predecessors.[66]

Around 9 May, having been tipped off in a letter from Stanton, the parents of one of the other Harwich C.O.s, Rendel Wyatt, sent a telegram to Gilbert Murray. He, via the services of his brother-in-law Geoffrey Howard, managed to arrange informal interviews first with Lord Derby, who seemed content that the men in France could be shot, and then with Asquith who wrote to the Commander-in-Chief forbidding the executions without the knowledge of the Cabinet. That may have caused the decisive stay of execution. It is likely that the Government did not intend death sentences to be carried out – at the end of the month the Cabinet accepted in principle a proposal to transfer court-martialled C.O.s into civilian jurisdiction – but the closing date for applications for exemption was 24 June, and it served the Government's purposes to uphold the threat of death as a deterrent to claims for exemption.[67] Certainly, the Army continued to transfer other men across the Channel, despite the half-hearted opposition of the Government. On 22 May, the family of Norman Gaudie sent telegrams to W.J. Chamberlain at the N.C.F., and to supportive M.P.s Fred Jowett and Philip Snowden, reporting that a military captain at Richmond Castle, Swaledale had let slip that a group of C.O.s imprisoned there was about to be sent to France.[68] One week later sixteen men were indeed sent to France from Richmond Castle, and eight men from Kinmel Park, Abergele. A further nine, handcuffed, left Seaford, Sussex, the following day, 30 May, with more from Kinmel Park to follow.[69] Not all of these groups were conscientious objectors, but forty-one men known to be C.O.s were sent to France at that time. A further five from Manchester and fourteen barbarically-treated New Zealanders, were to follow later.

Meeting other "out & outers" on the *S.S. Viper* from Southampton boosted the morale of the Richmond sixteen. As one of them recorded: "We soon were at one with each other & the spirit manifest now was beyond description, & we, although being a very mixed gathering Agnostics – Artists – Christians of different sects, joined in our hymn singing with great fervour".[70]

The Richmond C.O.s

The Richmond group had resisted various attempts to persuade them to join up, including talks to assure them that "God is on our side". Those C.O.s, from diverse backgrounds, held firm and left a record of their stand in the graffiti on their cell walls in Richmond Castle. They pencilled on biblical verses, sectarian hymns, quotations from the poems of James Lowell, and political slogans. As they began their journey to France, they formed an ad hoc choir and performed a number of hymns on the platform of Darlington station.[71]

One of the group was John W. Routledge, from Hunslet, Leeds, thought to have been a lay-reader in the Church of England.[72] Routledge underwent a period on hunger strike in Richmond which left him hospitalised. When Norman Gaudie first met him he described Routledge as having a face he felt he had known for years.[73] The camaraderie in adversity provided strong encouragement for the men in the torturous days ahead. Their plight became known to the N.C.F. thanks to a carefully doctored official postcard sent by Bert Brocklesby soon after arriving in France. Such cards had options to cross out, but, to ease the work of the censor, could not be added to. Brocklesby, en route to Boulogne, took the original message, "I am being sent down to the base. I have received no letter from you for a long time" and selectively crossed out letters to produce the message, "I am being sent to ... b ... ou ... long".[74]

The French Experience

The Harwich seventeen arrived in a military camp at Harfleur.[75] Here further parade-ground non-compliance led to the bizarre punishment of the forfeit of five days' pay, which the C.O.s had no intention of receiving in any case. Stanton and Brewster discussed their beliefs with numerous soldiers who all assured them that the only options were giving in or being shot.[76] Brewster and Hicks were among those sentenced by the Commandant to twenty-eight days Field Punishment No. 1.[77] For this dehumanising torture, a man was "attached to a fixed object", in practice a wheel, gun carriage or horizontal rope. The practice, also known as "crucifixion", could last for two hours per day, three days in four, over a period of four weeks. One of the victims recalled that:

> Each of us was placed with our backs to the framework, consisting of uprights at intervals of four or five yards, and cross-beams at a height of about five feet from the ground. Our ankles were tied together and our arms then tied tightly at the wrists to the cross-beams; and we prepared to remain in this position for the next two hours.[78]

Stanton described one vicious variation of this:

> Brewster and I found ourselves being taken off to quite another part of the camp. The prison was surrounded, not by a wall, but by a double barbed-wire fence, through which one could see, and be seen by everyone passing. We two were on this occasion placed with our faces to the wire of the inner fence, and tied in the usual manner at the wrists and ankles. As the ropes with which we were fastened were tied around barbed wire instead of the usual thick wooden posts, it was possible to tie them much more tightly, and I found myself drawn so closely into the fence that when I wished to turn my head I had to do so very slowly and cautiously to avoid my face being torn by the barbs. To make matters worse it came on to rain, and a cold wind blew straight across the top of the hill. Some soldiers who were passing by stopped to look at us for a minute or so, but the sight was evidently no new one to them and they soon walked. . . .
>
> I did not feel however that we had any special grounds for complaint – we were exceptional cases, and militarism was making an effort to break down our resistance. What did seem to me shameful was that any voluntary soldier, who was offering his life in what he believed to be his country's service, was liable to such a punishment for quite a trivial offence, or at the instance of a prejudiced superior.[79]

For the rest of the time the punishment was imprisonment in cramped conditions, with hard labour. After one night-time discussion on conscientious objection with a hostile Canadian soldier in Harfleur, Brewster and Stanton refused to carry out quarrying work and were handcuffed to a tentpole. Discovering their plight, the previously aggressive Canadian soldier became supportive and comforting.[80]

The next stop for the C.O.s was Rouen, where more torturous punishments were administered, and then on to Boulogne, intended to be the last stop before leaving for the front line of the fighting where disobedience would automatically result in execution. A smuggled letter from Stuart Beavis to his mother read:

> We have been warned to-day that we are now within the war zone, and the military authorities have absolute power, and disobedience may be followed by very severe penalties, and very possibly the death penalty. . . . Do not be downhearted if the worst comes to the worst; many have died cheerfully before for a worse cause. . . . [81]

The prisoners' spirits were boosted by a Quaker visitor, Hubert Peet (soon, himself, to receive a sentence of hard labour), together with

Some of the Conscientious Objectors sent to France
This has been annotated by one of the men in the picture, Norman Gaudie, who included a faint pencil arrow pointing to himself (he is on the back row, second from the right). The annotations not only identify the men in the photo, but make it a personal and unique image.

the Revd F.B. Meyer, who arrived as a direct result of Brocklesby's surreptitious postcard. They could confirm that the C.O.s' plight was known and that pressure was being applied at the highest levels of Government. Brocklesby's brother, an army officer who was in the area, also arranged a visit.[82] The meeting up of the Harwich and Richmond contingents further lifted morale, but events were building to a crisis.

On Saturday 10 June, Brewster was the first to be tried at a Field General Court-martial in a Y.M.C.A. hut in the barracks near Boulogne. The trial lasted half an hour, though for many of the men who followed him this was reduced to fifteen minutes as the authorities tried to limit the duration of the speeches some of the C.O.s made in their defence. The charge was that each had refused, while undergoing Field Punishment, to obey a lawful command given by a superior officer. The defendants would have agreed, with Stanton, who was the last tried that day, that irrespective of the legality of the order, they were not soldiers and did not recognise the right of any court-martial to try them.[83] At the start of the following week, a further twenty-two C.O.s who had not originally passed through Harwich were court-martialled.

For four of the men, Howard Marten, Harry Scullard, Jack Foister and John Ring, the sentence, that they would "suffer death by being shot", was read out in front of the regiment at Henriville Camp, Boulogne, on Thursday 15 June.[84] After a pause for effect came the notice that the sentence would be commuted to ten years' penal servitude. Over the next ten days, thirty-four of the forty-one (including Brewster, Hicks and Routledge) were sentenced to death.[85] On 26 June, the Government admitted that all thirty-four sentences had been so commuted.[86] There were five C.O.s in France sentenced to imprisonment, another whose court-martial was delayed due to his hospitalisation, and another whose sentence was late in being delivered. Of the forty-three men sent to France, only two capitulated and transferred to the N.C.C.[87] One of those sentenced to death gave an account of his experience:

We turned into the midst of a huge military camp and many curious eyes, evidently puzzled by our cheerful demeanour under such circumstances, followed us as we made our way to a large open space in the middle, 150 yards or more square, and evidently used as a parade ground. . . . After a wait of perhaps three quarters of an hour, the various groups of soldiers began to form themselves into three sides of a huge square until several thousands were present. . . . When an appropriate hush had been arranged, the Adjutant, who was to read out the sentence, took charge. . . . "Private, No., of the 2nd Eastern Company Non-Combatant Corps, tried by Field General Court-Martial for disobedience whilst undergoing field punishment. Sentenced to death by being shot." – (Here a pause). "Confirmed by General Sir Douglas Haig" – (a longer pause) – "and commuted to ten years' penal servitude." . . . I was number three on the list, and as I stepped forward I caught a glimpse of my paper as it was handed to the Adjutant. Printed at the top in large red letters, and doubly underlined, was the word "Death."

I can hardly analyse the feelings that flashed through my mind as I caught sight of the word. They could certainly not be described as an emotion. I had faced the possibility of a death sentence before, and now accepted the fact almost without concern, whilst my mind was occupied mechanically and dispassionately with considering the immediate practical effects . . . "And commuted to ten years' penal servitude." So it was not so after all!

But as I stood listening to the sentences of the rest of our party, the feeling of joy and triumph surged up within me, and I felt proud to have the privilege of being one of that small company of C.O.s testifying to a truth which the world as yet had not grasped, but which it would one day treasure as a most precious inheritance.[88]

THE HERALD

THE NATIONAL LABOUR WEEKLY

New Series, No. 850. [Registered at G.P.O. as a newspaper. Postage U.K. newspaper rate. Canada and Newfoundland magazine rate.]   SATURDAY, JULY 1, 1916.   [PUBLISHED EVERY SATURDAY]   ONE PENNY.

THE PRICE OF CONSCIENCE.

34 CONSCIENTIOUS OBJECTORS SENTENCED TO DEATH

NOW COMMUTED TO PENAL SERVITUDE (Four now, in Winchester Civil Prison).

A newspaper cutting from the Herald *announcing the fate of the conscientious objectors in France*

Examples of Graffiti in the Cells of Richmond Castle

Christian Graffiti

"Jesus Hominum Salvator/ 'Every cross grows light beneath/ The shadow Lord of Thine.'/ (J.A. Brocklesby fecit – 22nd May 1916".
Brocklesby is quoting the poet Jane Fox Crewdson.

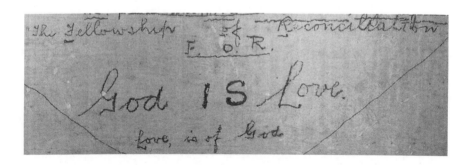

"The Fellowship of Reconciliation/ F.O.R./ God IS Love/ Love, is of God".

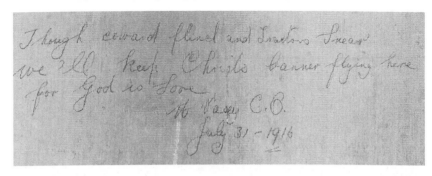

A Christian version of the Red Flag: "Though coward flinch and traitors sneer/ we'll keep Christ's banner flying here/ for God is Love./ H. Vasey C.O./ July 31 – 1916".

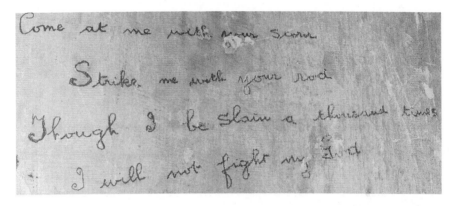

"Come at me with your scorn/ Strike me with your rod/ Though I be slain a thousand times/ I will not fight my God." A wartime verse by Wittner Brynner.

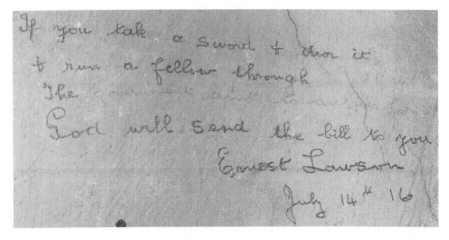

"If you take a sword and dror it/ To run another fellow through/ The government aint to answer for it/ God will send the bill to you/ Ernest Lawson/ July 14th 16".
Lawson is quoting the American poet James Russell Lowell.

General Graffiti

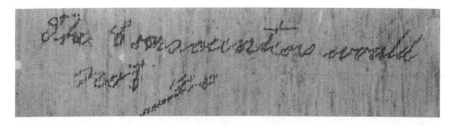

"The conscientious would not go".

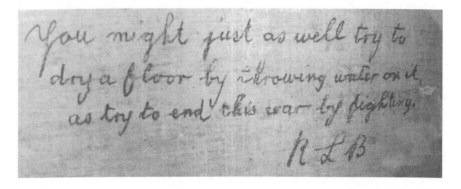

"You might just as well try to dry a floor by throwing water on it as try to end this war by fighting. RLB".

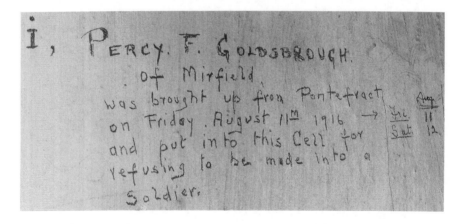

"I, Percy F. Goldsbrough of Mirfield, was brought up from Pontefract on Friday August 11th 1916 and put into this Cell for refusing to be made into a soldier".

Socialist Graffiti

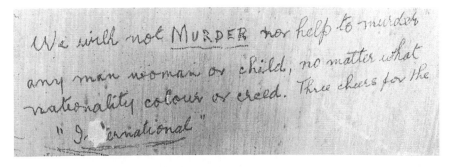

"We will not MURDER nor help to murder any man woman or child, no matter what nationality colour or creed. Three cheers for the 'International'."

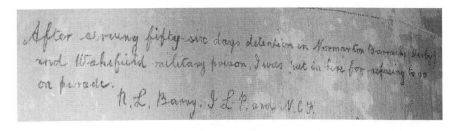

"After spending fifty-six days detention in Normanton Barracks (Derby) and Wakefield military prison, I was put in here for refusing to go on parade. N.L. Barry. ILP and NCF."

"I.L.P and N.C.F."

9.
The Cost of Resistance

The Origins and Fates of Conscientious Objectors
England

The most comprehensive information on the diverse stories of conscientious objectors has recently been painstakingly collected from multiple sources by the Huddersfield historian, Cyril Pearce.[1] He has identified over 16,800 men, of whom 357 are identified as being in some way "Church of England". Less than a dozen are obviously nominal, being regarded as "atheist / C of E" or "no religion / C of E" or similar. There are also a handful whose religious affiliation is in flux, perhaps because they were in the process of becoming International Bible Students (Jehovah's Witnesses) or because of growing appreciation of the Quakers, both of which were supportive of conscientious objection.[2] Inevitably the net will have caught a few rogues, but it is clear that the overwhelming majority had genuine conscientious reasons for opposing participation in the war. Because of the breadth of the backgrounds of Anglican conscientious objectors, consideration of this particular sample of around 350 stories, less than one fortieth of the total, gives a glimpse into the experiences of the wider population of C.O.s.

The first point to note in this sample is that as many were motivated by political considerations as by religious. Thirty-nine of the men were connected to the N.C.F., and twenty men had socialist or trade union backgrounds. Despite the assumptions of hostile tribunals, few men stated they were vegetarian.[3] Twenty-five men across England and Wales were involved in some form of religious training, including a group of theological students from St David's College, Lampeter, who joined the R.A.M.C. *en bloc* (see below). London theology students A.L. Jones and T.R. Jones also joined the R.A.M.C.[4] John Yarrow, a theology student in Leeds, joined the Non-Combatant Corps.[5] One ordinand, Basil Atkinson, appealed for absolute exemption and refused to join the N.C.C., being sentenced to hard labour in Maidstone prison followed by a work centre at Dyce.[6] Brother Paul Beresford (previously W.H. Muller), a lay brother of the Society of Divine Compassion, Plaistow, was ordered to do Work of National Importance, but was permitted to undertake parochial work for St Paul's, Covent Garden.[7] Fifteen of the Anglican C.O.s were known members of the Fellowship of Reconciliation, eleven of whom were later to belong to the Dartmoor branch, where they were brought together with other C.O.s at the Princetown Work Centre.[8]

For some would-be C.O.s, the practice of non-co-operation began early, with refusal to give details, sign papers, have a medical, attend a tribunal or pay a fine. Half of the cohort refused to join the N.C.C. Others refused to accept Work of National Importance, or to work on the Home Office Scheme.[9] Of Anglican C.O.s who did accept constructive engagement with the conscription authorities, around fifteen per cent are known to have joined the R.A.M.C., a figure likely to increase as more data becomes available.[10] Attempts at co-operation were not always successful, however: Edgar Watson was offered a post at Ackworth School, but that was not recognised as being suitable for Work of National Importance; Robert Derbyshire accepted Work of National Importance but was still called up, his subsequent refusal of conscription resulting in a sentence of hard labour.[11] Norman Wild gained exemption from combatant service only, and was drafted into the N.C.C., where he was ordered to dig a bombing trench; his refusal led to a court martial and a sentence of hard labour in Wormwood Scrubs.[12] Walter South, with the N.C.C. in France, refused to load cases of rifles on to a truck and was sentenced to 56 days Field Punishment No. 1.[13] Cyril Coleman, a schoolteacher from Hucknall, refused to handle ammunition and was court-martialled at Rouen.[14] Cuthbert Morson, a schoolmaster from East Stanley, was with the R.A.M.C. in Egypt when he refused an order to take up a weapon; his sentence of five years penal servitude, even though commuted to two years, meant he was still in prison in the second half of 1919, with his case being raised in parliament.[15] Ernest Turner had originally volunteered for the R.A.M.C. He, too, refused to take up a weapon in Egypt, and suffered the same sentence as Morson, at great cost to his mental health.[16] Half a dozen Anglican C.O.s were accepted into the Friends' Ambulance Unit (F.A.U.), but John Baker, who had voluntarily served with the F.A.U. earlier in the war, had his application to become a C.O. rejected and was sentenced to hard labour at Canterbury prison, followed by a series of work-camps.[17]

For two-thirds of the sample, conscientious objection led to imprisonment with hard labour, in almost every case involving at least some time in Wormwood Scrubs. 125 men engaged with the Home Office Scheme, with over 50 based at Dartmoor alone, and a contingent at Dyce. 38 men experienced the Knutsford work centre, and 25 the one at Wakefield. 30 faced multiple sentences amounting to over two years in prison. There were a number of recorded examples of brutality: James Atherton was beaten up in Preston prison, Henry Alty's treatment at Oswestry led to questions in the House of Commons, as did Wilhelm Thiel's experiences in detention.[18] Albert Lake was brutally treated at the barracks in Pontefract and James Brierley at Ashton-under-Lyne barracks.[19] Seven Anglican C.O.s went on hunger strike, including Harry Derbyshire, Robert Wilkinson, Robert Jones and William Angrave. Willie Jermy was part of a concerted hunger strike at Walton Prison, Liverpool, in July 1918. Albert Roberts, a Putney musician, was drafted into a Labour Battalion and faced a court martial "in the field" in France. Undergoing hard labour back in Pentonville prison, he went on hunger strike and was force fed seven times, before eventually being released under the Ill Health Act. Alin Saunders was also force fed during a Pentonville hunger strike.[20]

Ill health was a major concern for all C.O.s, given the circumstances of their incarceration. Of the sample, it was particularly serious for twenty of the men. Harold Hoad, a stonemason from Hollingbourne and an N.C.F. member, was first arrested in July 1916. He received a number of sentences of hard labour, to be served in Wormwood Scrubs and Maidstone, during which he contracted tuberculosis. He was released on health grounds in May 1917 and died shortly afterwards.[21] If it appeared that an illness could prove fatal, the authorities were likely to order an early release to avoid the political embarrassment of C.O.s dying in prison. Among those who were released from at least one period of imprisonment, on grounds of ill health, were: Percy Whitehouse, E.M. Mandale, Robert Jones, Willie Jermy, Frederick Colman, William Hamlyn, Norman Elliott, Frederick Cox (mental health), Percy Williams, George Wells, William Thiel, Charles Gooding, Edmund Jones, David Farrington, Horace Herbert, Thomas Edmonds, Cyril Butler (mental health) and Edward Mason.[22]

For a variety of reasons, a number of C.O.s were taken to France. The saga of those sentenced to death in 1916 did not stop other C.O.s being sent across the Channel later in the war. Charles Keeley was one of five men from Manchester who were sentenced to hard labour by a court martial at Étaples in 1917.[23] Charles Allen and Albert Roberts were forced into Labour Battalions against their will, and both faced a court martial "in the field".[24] Some C.O.s were stationed with the N.C.C. or the R.A.M.C. in France. A handful relented under pressure and became soldiers. Yet others attempted the difficulties of that journey in reverse, developing a conscientious objection to the war once they had become soldiers and experienced the unjustifiable reality of war, and trying to convince the authorities that they were not cowards or seeking to desert.

Second Lieutenant Arthur Hunter from Belper, who had originally enlisted into the Sherwood Foresters, resigned his commission whilst serving in France, on grounds of conscience, and protested against the war. For his action he was court-martialled in France, cashiered and stripped of his status, before being transferred to face a sentence of hard labour in Wormwood Scrubs. After the conflict was over, he worked with the Friends' War Victims Relief Service in Poland.[25]

Wales

Welsh Anglicans were in transition. As with legislation on Irish Home Rule, implementation of the Welsh Church Act of 1914 was suspended for the duration of the war. In due course it would lead to the disestablishment of most of that part of the Church of England that was in Wales, which in 1920 became the Church in Wales, an independent Anglican province.

There were over 800 conscientious objectors from Wales, around 0.035% of the total population of 2.4 million. Preliminary analysis of the data available suggests that those expressing religious affiliation came from a variety of traditions: Methodist (91, of whom 60 were Calvinistic), Christadelphian (72), Congregationalist (70), Baptist (57), Quaker (26, including some associated with other denominations) and Brethren/ Plymouth Brethren (21). These figures indicate the relative strengths of Nonconformity in Wales. What is more surprising is the relatively high figure of 29 known Anglicans in the sample. This includes a group of fifteen theology students at St David's College, Lampeter, who all joined the R.A.M.C. (Welsh Company) with a non-combatant agreement.[26] Others, like Frank Pugh, a grocer's assistant from Ferndale, Rhondda, agreed to join the Non Combatant Corps and spent three and a half years in France, not being demobilised until the end of 1919.[27]

Of those Anglicans from Wales who refused any association with the military, there is a common pattern of men being taken against their will to military units, almost immediately being court-martialled and receiving a sentence of hard labour, a pattern that could be repeated throughout the war unless the conscripts agreed to go to a Work Centre or to join the Home Office Scheme (see below). Oliver Jenkins, a collier at Aberfan, and the nineteen-year-old Arthur Gibbs, both followed that route from Wormwood Scrubs to Knutsford Work Centre.[28]

Wallace Cartwright from Ystradgynlais, and Daniel Harris, a tin plate worker from Swansea, were put on the Home Office Scheme at Princetown Work Centre, Dartmoor.[29] The same experience broke the health of Stanley Hughes, from Pant, Dowlais, Merthyr Tydfil, who was taken from Dartmoor to Pantawel Sanitorium.[30] William Thomas, also born in Dowlais, was transferred from hard labour in Wormwood Scrubs to the Home Office Scheme in Wakefield.[31] The health of Thomas

Edmonds, a plasterer and socialist from Gwaun-Cae-Gurwen, was so badly broken by his second spell of hard labour, at Walton prison, Liverpool, that he was released on medical grounds in the summer of 1918.[32]

Arthur Lawrence, a Cardiff plumber, refused to join the 3rd Welch regiment, was court-martialled at Kinmel Park and sent to Wormwood Scrubs. There followed an equally futile attempt to get him to join the Non Combatant Corps at Ripon, where he was court-martialled once more, but after a short stay in Armley prison, Leeds, he did agree to take part in the Home Office Scheme of labour camps instead. It was a compromise, as he was entered into the army Class W Reserve, a category devised in June 1916 "for all those soldiers whose services are deemed to be more valuable to the country in civil rather than military employment".[33] Technically he was subject to military discipline, without army pay, and theoretically subject to being recalled to the colours, but allowed to wear civilian clothes. William Lees, a pawnbroker's manager from Cardiff refused to sign his call up papers and also ended up on the Home Office Scheme and in Army Reserve Class W.[34]

The attempt to get a Dolgelly butler, William Harris, into the army failed spectacularly. His court-martial charges included desertion, loss of kit, escaping from his escort and disobedience. He was not regarded as a genuine conscientious objector and was sentenced to one year's hard labour. What was particularly notable about his case was that the court-martial took place after the end of the war, 29 November 1918. He was not released until June 1919.

Ireland

Attitudes to the war were not identical across the whole of the United Kingdom of Great Britain and Ireland. For many in Ireland there was hostility to what was seen as a British war. The immediate impact on Ireland of the outbreak of war had been the suspension of the highly controversial Government of Ireland Act 1914, which would have brought an element of Home Rule to Ireland, though not initially to the Ulster counties in the north east of the island, where resistance to the Act was strongest. Although suspension of the introduction of devolved powers was intended to be temporary, it lasted until beyond the end of the war, by which time Irish politics had moved on considerably.

In such a context, it was clear to the Government in London that any legislation regarding conscription – and hence, conscientious objection – could not and should not apply to Ireland. The Easter 1916 rising in Dublin, occurring within a few days of the full introduction of compulsory military service in Britain, reinforced the correctness of that political assessment. For the British Government to try to enforce conscription in Ireland, even if it had had the will to do so, would have been impossible. One outcome of the different Irish legal status on conscription was that a significant number of British men, fleeing from call up on conscientious grounds or otherwise, headed to Ireland in the hope of being able to lie low for the duration of the war. The police and army were still keen, however, to apprehend as many of these "deserters" as possible.

There is little or no discernible evidence of opposition to the war coming from the (Anglican) Church of Ireland. Although the second largest Church in Ireland, it had never made significant inroads into the majority population, even in the age of Henry VIII or when formally merged with the Church of England at the inception of the United Kingdom in 1801. For many it was seen as an agent of the English state. Its disestablishment in 1871 changed its legal status, but did not substantially change the historical and cultural affinity of the Church. Members of the Church of Ireland were hardly likely to be in the forefront of criticism of the British Government's foreign and war policies, especially when there were more than enough issues of concern for them nearer to home.

Some of the Irish story had ripples in the rest of the United Kingdom, where many Irishmen were resident and eligible for conscription. A small number of Catholic conscientious objectors gave support for Sinn Fein as their reason for refusing to join the British army. John and Ernest Nunan, a London window-cleaner and clerk respectively, were described as "Irish rebels" and each underwent six months hard labour before the War Office conceded that their services were "no longer required".[35] Paul Gillan, another similarly-motivated Irishman living in London, was also sentenced to hard labour; he died in Winchester prison before the end of the war.[36]

There were also Irish-born Anglican conscientious objectors. Harry Pemberton, born in Dublin, underwent hard labour in Wormwood Scrubs before being transferred to Wakefield prison.[37] Richard Lowe, an Irish socialist Anglican living in Wales, was sentenced to hard labour in Wormwood Scrubs and then taken to Princetown Work Centre, Dartmoor, where he joined the prison branch of the Fellowship of Reconciliation.[38] Frederick and Arthur Woods, Cork-born brothers living in Newcastle, described themselves as "evangelists" but still had to serve 112 days hard labour in Wormwood Scrubs.[39] 36-year-old, Belfast-born John Burns was refused non-military service, taken into the Scots Fusiliers, and court-martialled at Ayr in April 1917; after his Wormwood Scrubs sentence he was sent to a Work Centre in Knutsford.[40] There was no let-up: Alfred Mills, originally from Dublin, was court-martialled at Shrewsbury in the final month of the war.[41]

Scotland

Undoubtedly, some of the Roman Catholic C.O.s in Scotland would also have had Sinn Fein loyalties, but this would have been a tiny percentage of objectors north of Hadrian's Wall. Around 1,300 C.O.s came from Scotland, though many other Scottish objectors to the war would have been resident in England. Per capita, this was the lowest percentage of population in Britain, around 0.027% of a 4.8 million pre-war population. Had an independent heritage lost its radical edge, or were there more complex reasons for the relatively low level of opposition to war?

131 C.O.s were known to be members of the N.C.F., including Stephen Kelly from Dumbarton, Secretary of the Glasgow branch, and one of 14 known Scottish Roman Catholic C.O.s.[42] As with the rest of Britain, religious affiliation – if any – is only known for a portion of C.O.s. Within that, there are significant populations of Quaker members or attenders (103), Plymouth Brethren (78), Christadelphians (37), International Bible Students (Jehovah's Witnesses) (32) and, not surprisingly, Presbyterians (95 – a handful of whom would also claim Quaker association). The religious establishment in Scotland was Presbyterian, and whereas in England any nominal Christian affiliation would probably have been "C of E", in Scotland it would probably have been (Presbyterian) Church of Scotland.

Apart from some seventeenth century attempts at establishment, from which it was "ejected", the Scottish Episcopal Church has a more independent tradition than the Anglican Church elsewhere in Britain. Indeed, in the eighteenth century the Episcopal Church, with its Jacobite sympathies, was on the receiving end of the kind of persecution its Anglican neighbours were prone to handing out in England to Nonconformist or Roman Catholic minorities. This period saw the church reduced from representing possibly the majority of the population to around only 5 per cent. By the time of the First World War, this proportion had halved again.

Scottish Anglican conscientious objectors included: William Edmond, a sewing-machine mechanic, from Dennistown, Glasgow, who was court-martialled three times at Nigg, serving three sentences amounting to more than two years in prison before his final release in April 1919; both Hugh McColl from Bridgeton, Lanarkshire and George Morton, originally from Darvell, each of whom underwent three months hard labour in Wormwood Scrubs before transfer to Knutsford Work Centre; Donald McDonald from Aberdeen who faced two court-martials in Hamilton, each time receiving hard-labour sentences, for one of which he was at Wormwood Scrubs and the other at Barlinnie prison; William McCaig, from the village of Law, near Carluke in Lanarkshire, who was sentenced to hard labour by a court-martial at Invergordon in the summer of 1918, being transferred from Wormwood Scrubs to Wandsworth prison before his release early in 1919.[43] Edmond, McDonald and McCaig were categorised as "Class D", indicating that they had failed to convince their tribunals that their claim to C.O. status was genuine.

The F.O.R. and Conscription

On 7 January 1916, two days after the Military Service Bill had been presented before Parliament, the F.O.R. wrote to Prime Minister Asquith and other M.P.s in an attempt to make the position of the objector, particularly the Christian objector, better known. The following week the F.O.R. News Sheet brought the Fellowship openly, if reluctantly, into the political arena: "We refuse to participate in war, whether voluntarily or under compulsion, because our submission to Jesus Christ and our salvation through Him commit us to an endeavour to bring in His Kingdom in His way".[44]

It was now clear that there would be a cost to being a pacifist that many would have to pay. Furthermore, the F.O.R. would have to become a source of strength, support and inspiration for those who would come before a tribunal. More positively, the F.O.R., which started the year with a membership of around 4,000, experienced its highest ever rate of membership applications in January 1916. An F.O.R. Conscription Committee was set up, including the Anglicans Mary Phillips and Thomas Attlee, which continued to meet for the next three years.[45] It worked closely together with the N.C.F. and the Friends' Service Committee in a Joint Advisory Council, an umbrella body formed at the time of the national register in July 1915.

Before arrest, conscientious objectors were given legal assistance by the National Council Against Conscription, a responsibility assumed by the N.C.F. after arrest. [46] So when J.H. Brocklesby sent his "I am being sent to b . . . ou . . . long" postcard, it was prompt action by the N.C.F. and the Friends' Service Committee that led to some of the men taken to France receiving a brief visit by the Revd F.B. Meyer and the Quaker journalist Hubert Peet. Such action helped to convince the authorities that no executions could be undertaken without causing a public outcry, and it may well have contributed to the C.O.s' ultimate survival.[47]

Although it joined the N.C.F., and the Men's Service Committee of the Society of Friends, in a joint statement to Asquith in July 1916, the F.O.R. was better suited to pastoral, rather than political, action.[48] For all the activity surrounding the Military Service Act, the F.O.R. remained primarily a spiritual body, promoting a spirituality of peaceableness and a Kingdom theology, rather than being an organisation of political activists. The second annual conference of the F.O.R., at Swanwick, was "largely of a devotional character", with such themes as "Seek

First the Kingdom of God", "The Meaning of the Cross", and "The Memory of the Church and our relation to it"; only on the fifth day did the conference move on to consider "International Problems".[49] Mary Phillips summed up the position as "first to BE before to DO".[50] Yet such an approach did still allow for secondary actions, and there were activist members, notably Walter Ayles and Theodora Wilson-Wilson. It remained generally true, however, that F.O.R. members were less politically active than those in the N.C.F.[51]

The F.O.R. Conscription Committee retained close contact with conscientious objectors, and set up an emergency fund to provide relief for them and their families. There were frequent calls for clothing to be donated. In due course this led directly into hospitality and convalescent work for recently released C.O.s, with medical assistance, holidays and light training.[52] An F.O.R. Employment Bureau was set up to assist C.O.s who had lost their jobs, and, later, to find employment for men who had been granted conditional exemption.

The Home Office Scheme

That such a Bureau was necessary was an indication of the failure of the Government's own Home Office Scheme, set up in the summer of 1916, with the theoretical aim of securing release from prison and giving civilian work of national importance to those whose principal objection was to military call-up. William Hirst, an Anglican conscientious objector from Huddersfield, was one who was offered Work of National Importance on appeal in 1916.[53] One of the main groups accepting the scheme were religious objectors whose initial willingness to undertake Work of National Importance had not been recognised by tribunals. There were also socialist or moral objectors who, having made their stand against the army, felt there was little difference between work in prison and work under the Home Office. The hidden political agenda behind the introduction of the Scheme was the Government's attempt to sow division within the ranks of conscientious objectors by separating the "alternativist" from the "absolutist". Lloyd George's admitted aim was to break the absolutists and to persuade them to accept alternative occupations. Referring to the absolutists, he told Parliament on 26 July, "With that kind of man I, personally, have absolutely no sympathy whatsoever. I do not think that they deserve the slightest consideration. . . . I shall only consider the best means of making the path of that class a very hard one".[54]

Remembering the Prime Minister's own opposition to the Boer War, Bertrand Russell's response to Lloyd George was scathing.

> Our politicians may, for aught I know, have made a careful study of [conscience] in dictionaries and histories, but have evidently

been denied by nature the opportunity to learn about it by looking within. Does Mr George think St Paul would have been satisfied with a certificate excusing him from preaching Paganism? Does he think that Luther would have acquiesced in a dispensation from maintaining the doctrine of indulgences, on condition that he should preserve silence as to his objections to the doctrine? Does he think that Joan of Arc would have accepted civil alternative service? Would he himself have been willing to spend all his time during the Boer War in growing cabbages?[55]

The potential for division was seen in a conscientious objectors' newsletter produced at the short-lived Dyce work-camp settlement near Aberdeen. Herbert Runacres wrote an article in which he acknowledged the motivations of the absolutist, whilst advocating the stance of the alternativist.

> There are two possible lines of action in the face of evil. There is the spirit of rigid moral rectitude – an attitude which has one overmastering motive, that of avoiding every action which might involve a compromise with evil. The other line of action is that of meeting evil with well-doing in the sense of doing good to the evil man even while he is engaged in evil actions. While the former excels in logic the latter may be said to display more human qualities. It cannot be said that Christianity sanctions the one more than the other. Sternness in the face of evil was as much a part of the original Christian teaching as was the command to 'overcome evil with good.' To the Socialist ruthless opposition to the evils of Capitalist society is a necessary method of revolution, while, on the other hand, service is the motive without which there can be no Socialist State.[56]

However, the absolutist, according to Runacres, presented one of two arguments. In the first of these, it is accepted that the economic and military powers are working to the same end in war; in which case, "to place oneself at the disposal of any Government department is to become part of an organisation for the carrying on of war". The second absolutist argument is that any service "which is accepted as a condition of exemption from military service is an alternative to military service and constitutes a compromise with conscription". Both views represented "the rigid negative avoidance of evil". Yet, to Runacres, they both required a psychology of warfare, with the Government as the enemy. But to expect an ideal Government was unrealistic: "All the principles which govern men in their relations with each other must be based on a recognition that men and society are not ideal". Runacres had no objection to a society organising its resources, even pursuing a Conscription Act with a properly administered conscience clause, but he did oppose the vindictive way the Home Office Scheme had been administered:

Roughly it may be said that the right of the State to demand a particular service of the individual when the performance of that service does not directly involve a moral principle, and even when the demand might appear unwise, is the basis of the Home Office scheme for the employment of conscientious objectors. For this reason it was by many accepted. But the scheme contained one fatal error. More serious than the economic waste of employing skilled or professional men on the most unskilled kind of labour was the mistake of making the conditions and regulations of that labour vexatious to the point of penalisation. It was, in effect, a denial of the principle contained in the Military Service Acts, that conscience is consistent with citizenship. It is a denial of the whole philosophy of alternative service for service is a duty performed in return for the rights of a citizen and prisoners and slaves have neither duties nor rights.

Runacres summed up his commitment to an alternativist philosophy:

> The triumph of the C.O. will not consist in his having stopped the war or smashed conscription. The Pacifist supports principles which are only true if they can be practiced in the face of evil. He must, therefore, stretch to the uttermost his willingness as a citizen to serve an imperfect State. By this habit of mind he can best act as a corrective to the mind which is full of war and thinks only of humiliation, pride and power.[57]

The Joint Advisory Council recognised that many conscientious objectors, if not most, would want to take up the chance of leaving their prison cell in order to undertake civilian work, but it was not impressed with the Home Office Scheme. Amongst other objections they recognised: that men would continue to languish in prison until undergoing a new test of conscience; that those outside the churches could not have their testimony supported by a minister of religion; that those who "failed" the test would be regarded as not genuine and their conditions would become even more severe; that those transferred to an Army Reserve would still be deemed to be in the Army and liable to recall; and that the genuine absolutists would refuse to make the bargain the Government wanted.[58] There was also concern that the Scheme would extend the tribunals' practice of requiring civilian work in terms of "equality of sacrifice", a punishment for the individual rather than as a genuine service to the community. Furthermore, the Government's demand that there should be no peace propaganda was regarded as an intolerable restriction on freedom of speech.

The N.C.F. National Committee wrote to Asquith demanding that absolute exemption be granted to those who could not accept any service imposed by a Military Service Act.

It is not killing only to which they object; it is war, and therefore Militarism. They believe it wrong to accept conditional exemption because they hold it to be a bargain with a *Military Service* Act, which to them is the most complete expression of Militarism yet admitted in this country. They welcome the obligation of every man to serve the community, but believe that their refusal to be a party to this Act is the highest form of service they can render.[59]

Given such attitudes, it was hardly surprising that the Home Office Scheme was a failure, despite attracting 3,750 men. The penal spirit was indeed retained and, far from the Scheme being bait to tempt absolutists, by making alternative service so repellent it confirmed to many absolutists the veracity of their stand. Some C.O.s – around 20 per week – voluntarily returned to prison, rather than continue to work in the atrocious conditions of some of the prototype concentration camps.[60] The first settlement, at Dyce, which involved living outdoors in damp conditions and working in granite quarries, was abandoned within weeks, by which time the first of many C.O.s had already died.[61] The transition of Dartmoor prison to a Work Centre involved little more than the removal of the locks, with the only concession being increased opportunity for the eight hundred conscientious objectors to mingle and recognise their own diversity.[62]

The work of the camp, the prolonged hard labour, was almost as physically and psychologically destroying as a prison regime. There were a variety of such camps across the country. In a minority of cases there was an attempt to make them as tolerable as possible: Harold Brewster, for example, was sent to Warwick under the supervision of a local Quaker, Edwin Gilbert.[63] In most of the camps, however, the work imposed took its toll of the health of the objectors. In general, conditions were far worse than for those who had originally been allowed to find work through the Pelham Committee, although the conscientious opinions held by the two groups would have been almost indistinguishable. Later, it became possible for work to be undertaken with private employers, provided conditions were no less harsh than in the camps. After the war, this approach was relaxed to enable outside agencies – C.O. support groups – to find more appropriate work.[64]

Conditions were further impaired by a vitriolic press campaign against the men, which succeeded in provoking a number of violent attacks upon them. C.O.s were the victims of assaults or riots in Knutsford, Lyme Regis, Lyndhurst, and Wakefield.[65]

Imprisonment

To say that the treatment of conscientious objectors in the prisons was harsh would be an understatement. They ate a minimal diet, becoming weaker by the day. Conversation was forbidden at all times. Even writing was prohibited. (On occasions, ingenuity was able to overcome such restrictions.) Apart from forty-five minutes of exercise, each day would be spent alone in a small dark cell, with the opportunity to sew mailbags for the reward of an extra piece of bread and a drink in the evening. Visits and letters were kept to a minimum and refused entirely to those, like Fenner Brockway and Stephen Hobhouse, who infringed any rules (further punished by being kept in solitary confinement and being fed for weeks on bread and water).[66] The question of whether to co-operate as much as possible with the authorities or whether to be deliberately awkward, to strike, or even to hunger-strike, was a constant dilemma. All approaches were tried at different times. Release as a reward for co-operation was invariably a short-lived blessing, as a cat-and-mouse policy of immediate re-arrest led to instant re-imprisonment. One F.O.R. member, Paul Gliddon, regarding himself as belonging to the "completely casual, impromptu and inexperienced movement" of conscientious objectors, described his experience:

I was fortunate in having a good Army Chaplain when I was a prisoner at Morn Hill Camp, Winchester, and a friendly enough sergeant. My second sentence to two years' imprisonment was announced at a parade, I suppose with the idea of impressing the men. It did, though, I think, not quite in the way intended. I know that the officer who prosecuted me at one court-martial was good enough to send a message through the Chaplain to say how much he disliked having to do so.

Of course in those days no talking was allowed in prisons and some of us got into punishment cells for breaking this rule. . . . A cell is a very small place in which to live for more than a year, yet many were there for twice that time or longer! Shortage of staff made it difficult to allow men much time out of their cells, and at week-ends, except for chapel times, we were locked in from noon on Saturday until Monday morning. Not to keep one's mind fully occupied would have been pretty fatal, and prison must have been hard to endure for those to whom constant human companionship seems essential. Perhaps the most trying times were those when, from a higher landing of the prison, one caught sight of a bit of the country beyond the walls: those were dangerous moments: better far to forget the unreachable world outside. Visiting days, too, were trying, and not only because your visitor was kept on the other side of the grille.

On the whole I do not think we grew too sorry for ourselves. I had myself two younger brothers, both officers. The married one was killed while I was in prison; the other was dug out of a trench where he had been temporarily buried and was in hospital for a

year. Prison might not be much fun and, especially for those of us who were vegetarians, the food was very thin; but they were years in which all the others were suffering too, and even such food as was brought to us came through other men facing all the dangers of the high seas in time of war.

I did not get half through my second sentence of two years because something went wrong with my health just at a time when, as I heard afterwards, one or two of our men had died in other prisons, leading to questions in Parliament. I was sent over to the prison hospital, and there conditions were less rigid. As Clifford Allen, afterwards Lord Allen of Hurtwood, was one of the other patients, those last days in prison were among the most interesting. I was discharged on the Feast of the Annunciation, 1918, during the final great push made by the Germans; though it meant freedom for me, for so many others those were weeks of naked horror.

Of course it might be said that 'doing time' is a waste of time; even if that were wholly true it would only put the imprisoned conscientious objectors on much the same level as the service men, for surely there is no wastrel like war. Between the lot of us, C.O.s must have spent a total of

Frederick Carter, The Mother of the First Conscientious Objector, *the* Herald, *25 March (Feast of the Annunciation), 1916.*

some 2,000 years in prison, and it may not be very clear what we purchased with all that time. But in that 1914 war 2,000 men would die in a single day and it was not always clear what good was gained by all that sacrifice of life. We did at least say a blunt NO to war just when most of the world was saying YES.[67]

Gliddon was unusual in having a positive experience of an Anglican prison chaplain. In most cases the chaplain was an extra burden, a figure of smug criticism rather than a source of comfort. Some – but by no means all – prison doctors did respond to their patients as if they were human beings. The physical and mental health of the prisoners deteriorated rapidly, especially under extended periods of forced labour (the severest punishment short of hanging) and there were a number of deaths. Far more would have died inside prison if, following an announcement by Lord Curzon in December 1917, the authorities had not frequently concluded that a last-minute release would be more politic and, as in the cases of Clifford Allen and Stephen Hobhouse, less likely to cause public unease. Those two men, considerably weakened, did eventually recover, but a number did not, dying soon after their release. The physical and mental health of many more was irreparably harmed. Altogether ten men died in custody, whilst a further sixty-three died as a direct result of their imprisonment, mostly within weeks of their release.[68] As a result of the conditions which they themselves had experienced, a number of C.O.s later worked for prison reform.

Hobhouse's uncle was Charles Alfred Cripps (subsequently Lord Parmoor), Vicar-General of York from 1902 to 1914, and a Tory M.P. from 1914 until 1924, the last four years of which he was the first chairman of the House of Laity. Cripps, with links to the World Alliance, was an opponent of the war, and especially the treatment of conscientious objectors. It was noted that he, "all through the long Parliamentary struggle, represented fearlessly and with all the weight of his great ability and legal standing, the cause of the oppressed in the house of Lords".[69] In May 1917, the Archbishop of Canterbury harshly criticised the conscientious objectors, whilst backing Parmoor's attempt, in the House of Lords, to improve the conditions of those imprisoned.[70] Parmoor's case, as he told Margaret Hobhouse, was that

It is a fundamental principle that punishment should be imposed in reference to the nature of the offence. Judged by this standard there is no justification for the terms of successive imprisonment inflicted on Conscientious Objectors who are recognised to be straightforward and sincere. This punishment is, moreover, contrary to the express declarations of responsible Ministers when the Military Service Act was under debate in Parliament.

The severity of the punishment, inflicted by successive terms of imprisonment, is in sinister contrast with the national appeal for a higher standard of right and justice, and negatives any claim we may make to maintain the supreme test of civil liberty, viz. the determination to give full protection to an unpopular minority at a time of national excitement. It is forgotten that obedience to conscience is a primary duty in Christian ethics, and there is a curious confusion of thought in stigmatising a deep sense of religious duty, as though it were a mean attempt to evade the claims of a national obligation.[71]

In the House of Lords, Archbishop Davidson argued that "nobody can doubt that there are at this moment men undergoing terms of imprisonment whose character is high, whose motives are unimpeachable, however extraordinary and illogical we may deem them to be; and you are not going to shake them by the adding of month after month or year after year of penal infliction upon them".[72]

Davidson also made special pleadings for individual conscientious objectors on various occasions during and after the war.[73] Bishop Gore also spoke on three occasions on behalf of C.O.s, and William Temple regarded the "contemptuous approach" of many of the tribunals as "a reproach to our civilization".[74]

In November 1917 a petition from the Committee of the (non-pacifist) Howard Association, which included the signatures of Edward Hicks (Bishop of Lincoln), Moore Ede and Scott Holland (Regius Professor of Divinity, Oxford), called the Government's attention to:

> . . . a grave contravention of justice that men should be subjected to repeated sentences of imprisonment for what is in reality the single 'offence' of refusing on conscientious grounds, obedience to military orders. . . . The Committee therefore earnestly requests the Government at once to release from prison, and to discharge from the Army, all men who have proved the genuineness of their conscientious objection to any form of military service.[75]

At the end of April 1918 Parmoor moved a resolution in the House of Lords which would not only put an end to the practice of re-arrest on release (so called "cat-and-mouse") by fixing a limit for the total term of imprisonment, but would also guarantee that the non-combatant work of conscientious objectors would be of value to the community rather than merely of a penal nature. He cited an instance in Dartmoor where adjacent courts of men were taking up stones and laying them down, before being changed from the one court to the next.

By September 1918 there was sufficient public unease about the conditions of those who had undergone two years or more imprisonment with hard labour, for the Home Office to try a charm offensive, bringing the most long-standing absolutists together in Wakefield in more humane conditions. Men from Durham and Dorchester were the first of 120 C.O.s to arrive. Within the prison there was effective freedom of association and the prisoners had more control over their lives. In return, the Government hoped that the prisoners would undertake work, principally on mailbags, to which many had previously been resistant. One of those involved said "they were offered very comfortable quarters if they would only be quiet and obedient".[76] It was one more example of the Government's inability to comprehend the struggle in which those men had taken part for the past two years and which they were now unable even to consider compromising. "They did not want easy conditions, but liberty to serve the community".[77] One of those who had been in France, admitted to "doubts as to whether 'work of national importance', at Wakefield or elsewhere, was really the right thing for me. It held the prospect, not of an easy conscience, but of a series of compromises".[78] On 14 September, Walter Ayles, who chaired the prisoners' committee, signed a collective statement:

> (1) Our vital principle as Absolutists is not a refusal to serve the community. It is that we cannot accept either military service or any compulsory work organized to facilitate the prosecution of the war.
> (2) Therefore we cannot accept any scheme of work involving our actual or implied consent to the carrying out of any such purpose.
> (3) We are faced with a situation, submission to which may involve the complete denial of our principles, by implicitly introducing an element of voluntary or semi-voluntary co-operation on our part.
> (4) It appears that the Government still misunderstand our principles, in that they take for granted that any safe or easy conditions can meet the imperative demands of our conscience. No offer of schemes or concessions can do this. We stand for the inviolable rights of conscience in the affairs of life. We ask for liberty to serve, and if necessary to suffer, for the community and its well-being. As long as the Government deny us this right, we can only take with cheerfulness and unmistakeable determination whatever penalties are imposed upon us. We want no concessions. We desire only the liberty to serve.[79]

The Wakefield experiment failed, and the Government, its prestige deeply wounded, drafted in large numbers of prison officers and three days later dispersed the uncompromising absolutists to various other prisons around the country, where they stayed until their release in the summer of 1919.

Thomas and Kathleen Attlee

Standing up as a conscientious objector was not a soft or cowardly option. For many, it was a life-changing, health-destroying experience. The case of Thomas ('Tom') Simons Attlee (1880-1960) is not untypical.

The sixth child of eight, Attlee had a Victorian middle class upbringing, including spells in the rifle corps at private school, and the Volunteer Corps at Oxford University. Samuel Barnett made a deep impression on him when, as an undergraduate, Attlee heard him lecture on university settlements. Attlee later showed some Toynbee Hall boys the sights of Oxford. Together with his reading of Morris and Ruskin, this experience contributed to his developing political awareness and drew him towards socialism. His reading also fuelled his fascination with social architecture. After university he joined the Christian Social Union (C.S.U). and helped out at Maurice Hostel, run by the C.S.U. in London.[80] His younger brother Clement was not attracted to Thomas's Christianity, but he was by his social awareness.[81] Together they attended Fabian meetings, hearing such notable thinkers as Beatrice and Sidney Webb, George Bernard Shaw and H.G. Wells, and they both joined the Independent Labour Party, where the elder brother's Christianity was a minority adherence. In 1910, Thomas Attlee worked hard for the election of George Lansbury in Bow and Bromley. That December he attended possibly his first I.L.P. anti-war meeting.[82] In 1912, his fiancée, Kathleen Medley, was elected the first woman on Poplar Council, joining a Labour group led by Lansbury.[83]

With the outbreak of war, and the realignment of peace groups, Attlee joined both the F.O.R. and the N.C.F. and, by October 1915, he was already serving on both the F.O.R. General Committee and its Social Services Committee. With the introduction of conscription, he applied to Poplar Military Service Tribunal for exemption. Four months later he was offered, but refused and appealed, non-combatant service.[84]

Addressing the F.O.R. Summer Conference in 1916, Attlee stressed the need for reconciliation to take place at all levels of society:

> We don't love our neighbours: we exploit them. We were at war long before the Great War began. I say "we" advisedly, for we in the FOR are predominantly well-to-do; we belong to the classes which seem to profit, materially, by the existing systems: we are part of that system. We are interested parties, not impartial arbitrators.[85]

He cited his own situation of possessing shares in a South American railway without any idea about the conditions of the railway workers. His uncomfortable conclusion was that "Reconciliation means Revolution".[86]

The same month he read a similar paper to the London branch of the C.S.U., an organisation with mixed views on the war. He showed how some classes had actually profited by the war. The whole economic system needed changing. "Let us then preach Reconciliation and with exactly the same emphasis no more and no less – let us preach Revolution".[87] Also that summer he wrote to his sister, Margaret, explaining his, and the F.O.R.'s stand against the war:

> We don't think you must take just one text and interpret it literally all by itself, but you must, as you say, amplify it and explain it by others. Thus the *negative* command "Resist not evil" is completed by the *positive* command "Love your enemies" and the two combined in a third – "Be not overcome by evil but overcome evil with good".
>
> We think that the prohibition of resisting evil by physical force is not just one of the many instructions of Our Lord's, but the central fact of his life and teaching. . . .[88] The Jews who acclaimed him as a deliverer on Palm Sunday called for his Crucifixion on Good Friday because he would not by force deliver his country from Roman domination, as they expected. He declined what was a patriotic thing to do – to fight for a just cause against oppression – because his whole teaching was that that is not the way.

Attlee rejected suggestions that Jesus's teaching merely reflected the ideal practice of the future Kingdom of Heaven and had no relevance to present behaviour.

> If you've a dispute with a man and honestly believe that you have the right on your side, you can either kill him (which we all rule out) or you can somehow so call out what is reasonable and just and honest in him that he will see the justice of your cause. If you really love him you will have enough insight into his point of view, enough *sympathy* with him, to manage it; really saintly people do.
>
> On the other hand if you fight him you weld all his qualities together into one vigorous force of opposition, you submerge for the time being all that is reasonable and righteous (in the literal sense) in him under his pugnacious, violent, self-regarding, self-protecting instincts – and, when it is all over, you will have to start afresh just where you left off – trying to be reasonable, trying to call out his decent qualities, his better self. . . .
>
> Now apply that to Europe today. In every country there is a minority of aggressive, greedy and violent persons who believe in aggrandizing their nation by force, who want war, who believe in it as an instrument of progress. In every country too there is a great mass of ordinary people – peaceable, reasonable decent souls who

are normally opposed to the militarists. Normally they are, but let the militarists be able to say 'our country is in danger, we are not attackers but attacked, we stand for defence not defiance' – and the whole mass of peaceable people will be driven to rally to their support and will support them through any atrocities as long as that danger exists.

Attlee held that Britain's threat of retaliation on Germany actually contributed to the German decision to invade Belgium, as it could be used to justify the military action to the German people by saying it had been taken under external threat.

Now you may say that it would have been the better way, but as we didn't choose it then, we must now go ahead with the worse. But war is not a *worse* way – *it is no way at all*. Our Lord was talking hard common sense – his way is the only chance of success: there is no other. When has war ever 'settled' anything? How has the present war succeeded? We have not saved Belgium – she has been devastated from end to end. . . .

And suppose we win, suppose we do thoroughly beat Germany. There are only two courses to pursue – either to kill off all the Germans en masse or to live with them as neighbours. And (as in a private quarrel) we're faced with exactly the same problem as we had to solve at first – how to get the 'better self' of Germany on top. . . . War doesn't work: to kill one devil you call up seven new ones. Every day it lasts puts the triumph of justice further off. . . . I think the growth of envy, hatred, malice, pride, vainglory, hypocrisy and certainly all uncharitableness is enough to drive me crazy. . . .[89]

At the turn of the year, Attlee's confident statements were to be put to the test. He attempted to speak at a Suffragettes' "Peace" Meeting at East India Dock Gates. When he stood on his chair, he was asked why he was not in military uniform, and a hostile crowd pushed him off. In the disturbance that followed, some of the women clung to railings. Sylvia Pankhurst, whom some in the crowd had wanted to throw in the dock, was charged with obstructing the highway.

In January 1917, Attlee himself was arrested, handed over to the military, court-martialled, sentenced to three months' imprisonment and sent to Wormwood Scrubs, home to several hundred conscientious objectors on hard labour. For the first fortnight he faced a diet of bread and water, sleeping on a plank with no mattress. For the first month he was in solitary confinement.

Upon his release in May, Attlee was briefly sent to barracks at Frimley, Surrey, before facing another court-martial and a second spell of imprisonment in Wandsworth prison, another centre for the detention of conscientious objectors, with yet another introductory month in solitary confinement, which did nothing for his health. There were a few Anglicans there, but most C.O.s asked for a Quaker chaplain. After a year in prison, Attlee became eligible for some modest "concessions": his own clothes, more exercise "with conversation", more letters. Unrepentant, he was released again in March 1918, telling his sister Margaret that "The gigantic experiment in justifying the means by the end is ending in the hopeless degradation of the end through the means".[90] Soon afterwards he was sentenced to a third term in Wandsworth, slightly less severe than before, as inmates were by now beginning to send messages by Morse Code, and supporters sang hymns and songs outside the windows to cheer up the conscientious objectors inside.

A suggestion that all C.O.s might be moved to Wakefield made Kathleen Attlee distraught. Her own health, and that of one of her children, was poor, and money was tight, with no income from her husband. She was spending more and more time at a family home in Seaton, Devon, from where Wakefield would have been totally inaccessible. As things turned out, Thomas Attlee did not have to move and remained in Wandsworth until his final release in April 1919.

Attlee reconnected with the F.O.R. and was involved in the founding of the International Fellowship of Reconciliation in 1919. In his 1920 booklet, *Man and His Buildings*, he summed up the events of the recent past.

> We have just emerged from a war ... which has knocked the bottom out of the faith of men – not indeed in Christianity, but in a Church which has everywhere surrendered to the state, has degraded itself to the position of claques, applauding each its own actor in the five years tragedy, which has not dared to denounce injustice, except among foreigners, which has submitted to the nationalists today as it submitted to the economists a century earlier.[91]

The family moved to Cornwall to recover from the horrendous scars they had all received from Attlee's period of incarceration. They were looking for a quiet life, far from London, to heal the wounds of the previous years and to build a new life. In 1922, Attlee was able to assist Bernard Walke in a group called the Servants of the Church, helping local tin miners whose industry faced collapse; there were various prayer meetings and political meetings across the county.[92]

The final word in this chapter goes to Kathleen Attlee. Whilst male conscientious objectors were suffering directly the deprivations imposed by the state, their wives and families suffered indirectly in innumerable ways, exacerbated by the public stigma which meant they could not call upon the social solidarity which supported military families with absent husbands or fathers. Kathleen and Thomas Attlee had shared much of their political life together; now the suffering of each would be contemporaneous with but separate from that of the other.

Kathleen Attlee had been active in the Poplar Labour League and in Council business, including being Vice Chairman of the Library Committee. She was an established lecturer for nursing associations and the Oxford University Extension Course. In 1915, she became a mother. With her husband's arrest, she had to juggle motherhood, lectures, council duties, meetings of the Labour Party and the N.C.F., dock-gate peace meetings, and time-consuming prison visiting. Having heard of the illness and death of other imprisoned C.O.s, Kathleen Attlee was afraid Thomas was going to die. Her health was as threatened as his. She was the Honorary Secretary of the Conscientious Objectors' Maintenance Fund, set up by the Poplar and Stepney branch of the N.C.F.. In practical terms, she had the support of the Lansbury family, but finding child-care was the most difficult aspect.[93] With the arrival, in 1917, of her second child, the demands became too great. She allowed her Council membership to lapse and based herself increasingly at the family home in Seaton, Devon. By now, illness was taking its toll on her, and she restricted herself to the occasional lecture and visiting her husband in prison in London when possible. It is not surprising that the thought that he might be transferred to Wakefield filled her with dread. Their younger son would be twenty-one months old before he eventually met his father, by which time the health of both parents was decidedly fragile. Kathleen Attlee had had enough of politics and showed no inclination to return to the politically active life she had led in Poplar. Indeed, they moved further west still, near to Falmouth, almost as far away as possible from the intensity of national politics. Waiting for a conscientious objector husband had been too much. In her journal she noted "Nos Idem Mortales", a poem by M. St Clare Byrne from a 1917 collection, *Aldebaran*.

> When they shall come and tell me you are dead
> I will be very quiet; I shall know
> Instantly then the place where I must go
> The thing that I must do. . . .[94]

10.
Losing "The Manhood of England"

The Peripheral Church of England

In general, the Church of England's response to the war was shameful. Its leaders placed a higher value on the approval of the Government than the imperative of the Gospel. In the week before the outbreak of war, Randall Davidson, the Archbishop of Canterbury turned away a suggestion that he should advocate non-intervention, listening instead to the Prime Minister who, on 31 July 1914, begged him to use his influence to stop any public expression in favour on such a policy.[1] Davidson refused to sign a November 1914 appeal for peace and Christian friendship, made through the World Alliance by Nathan Söderblom, the new Archbishop of Uppsala.[2] Söderblom was convinced that the unity of the churches would make them better able to be instruments of peace in the world; Davidson was yet to be convinced. Even before hostilities were declared, Bishop Moule of Durham circulated every parish advocating war in defence of Belgium.[3] The Archbishop of York declared in October 1914 that there could be no peace "until this German spirit of militarism has been crushed".[4] Even the ageing bishops who had been active in peace affairs (Hicks of Lincoln and Percival of Hereford, who both joined a hastily-formed Neutrality Committee including Gilbert Murray and Ramsay MacDonald) soon distanced themselves from pacifism.[5] Both had been critics of the Boer War, and of imperialist expansion by force, but the invasion of Belgium was German expansion by force and therefore forcible resistance seemed to both of them, as to Gilbert Murray, to be legitimate.[6] Notwithstanding a sermon advocating neutralism, which he preached at Cleethorpes on the Sunday before the war, within a week Hicks was arguing that although he hated war, it seemed as though the Kaiser wanted it.[7] He later called for the overthrow of Prussian militarism.[8] Scott Holland, too, wrote that "War is right when it is fought on behalf of Peace".[9] Edward Talbot, Bishop of Winchester, another figure associated with the Church of England Peace League, having claimed to have "far more sympathy with the Stop-the-War party among the workers" than he had with "Prussian aggressive militarism", then appealed to those same workers to turn from their "self-regarding" pacifism and take part in the war.[10] In the summer of 1916, as C.O.s were facing death for their opposition to the war, all the Archbishop of Canterbury could offer was: "I find as yet no basis on which to encourage or justify our approaching with proposals of peace those with whom we are at war", adding, at his Diocesan Conference, that "So long as they assure us that they are committed irrevocably to principles which I regard as absolutely fatal to what Christ has taught. . . . I should look on it as flimsy sentimentalism were I to say that I want immediate peace".[11]

Caroline Playne's response was highly critical, asking "If the more liberal-minded leaders of the Church had nothing more adequate to the situation to teach than subtleties like these, at the critical moment when they saw 'the house of established order' crumbling about them, was theirs not indeed a lamentable failure?"[12] Her own answer was "Oh! ye of little faith, could ye not have watched one hour (four years as it turned out) in the faith?"She believed that the "failure of many clerics was the failure to believe the faith that should have been theirs".[13]

The failure was not only that of the senior figures. 1,000 London curates of military age signed a petition asking for permission to become combatants.[14] That move that was too much even for the anonymous author of the Preface to *Crockford's Directory*, who argued both that military chaplains were in short supply and that all other available clergy should be reaping the harvest of the National Mission.[15] And so the residual tokens of pre-Constantinian Christian pacifism were defended not on the grounds of principle, but pragmatism and self-interest.

It was not until much later in the war that at least some of the senior figures in the Church of England could rediscover any of their former zeal for peace. Those who had, in times past, been advocates of arbitration, could hardly defend the Government's determination to continue the war until total victory was achieved, especially after 12 December 1916, when the German Chancellor, Bethmann Hollweg, informed the United States that Germany was ready to enter peace talks. A Peace Negotiations Committee presented a petition to the Prime Minister with 200,000 signatures of people who wanted a negotiated peace.[16] For a time, pacifist groups and individuals were hopeful that a peace settlement, brokered by President Wilson, might be imminent. The liberal church journal, *Challenge*, argued that "some attempt at action" should be taken for peace.[17] The prospect of the war coming to an end was no longer remote, especially as Lloyd George had now succeeded Asquith as Prime Minister. Would he even now recall his own opposition to the Boer War? But Lloyd George was set on a fight "to a finish – to a knock out".[18]

Any hopes of an early settlement were thoroughly and finally dashed on 10 January 1917 when the Allies produced such an unrealistically long list of demands that any prospect of meaningful negotiation was dashed. The British Government, despite no sign of immediate military advantage, had refused to take the concept of negotiation seriously and had settled for a long, drawn-out war of attrition, at a cost of hundreds of thousands of lives. Not all the electorate were impressed, and the following month a peace candidate received one quarter of the vote at a by-election in Rossendale. It did not, however, prove to be a strong enough base on which to build. For all the signatures on the petition most peace-by-negotiation candidates at by-elections, although able to present their case vigorously, received only minimal support from the voters.[19] Bizarrely, the International Peace and Arbitration Committee, of all people, even withdrew from membership of the National Peace Council in protest at the N.P.C. promotion of the case for a negotiated peace.[20] At Pentecost 1917, Archbishop Söderblom made a further peace appeal from Church leaders in neutral countries, and the following July saw the founding of the British Council for Promoting an International Christian Meeting, which, as well as a number of Quakers, included Ernest Barnes, Lord Parmoor, William Temple, the bishops of Oxford (Gore) and Southwark (Burge), and others. Söderblom's appeal was linked to such an international meeting, but it eventually had to be confined to Church leaders from neutral countries only. They signed a "declaration of Christian unity" which transcended national values, and considered "what the different churches could achieve in the struggle against war". They made links with the continuation committee of the Edinburgh 1910 conference and proclaimed both "the deep inner unity of Christians" and also "the incompatibility between war and the spirit of Christ".[21]

The consequences of rejecting negotiations were soon to become apparent. On 31 July 1917, General Haig's response to a Reichstag resolution of 19 July calling for "peace without annexations or indemnities", was to order the third battle of Ypres to begin in the mud of Passchendaele, at a cost of hundreds of thousands of human lives.[22] Earlier, many in the Church were shocked at the British Government's policy of reprisals, in particular news of the bombing of Freiburg. On this matter, Archbishop Davidson was prepared to be publicly critical of the Government. He spoke on the subject of reprisals in the House of Lords on 2 May 1917, and a 15 May letter attacking the policy was signed by numerous Church leaders of different denominations, including the bishops of Lichfield (Kempthorne), Lincoln (Hicks) and Soder and Man (Denton Thompson), the Dean of Durham (Hensley Henson), Dick Sheppard and William Temple.[23] Most Anglican leaders, however, dismissed peace proposals made by Pope Benedict XV in August 1917, despite it being hailed by a short-lived group, the Guild of the Pope's Peace.

The final attempt to achieve a negotiated peace followed a letter to the *Daily Telegraph* on 29 November 1917 from Lord Lansdowne, Henry Petty-Fitzmaurice. A private memorandum in similar terms, written to Asquith the previous year, was later seen as a prime cause of the break-up of the coalition Government of that time.[24] His public appeal in 1917 asked for no effort to be spared to bring such a terrible war to an end, recognising that some of the Allied objectives were unrealistic. As cross-party support for Lansdowne grew, attracting fellow peers like Leonard Courtney and Lord Parmoor (Charles Cripps), there was even a suggestion that, with Labour backing, Lansdowne might be able to form a coalition Government. It was an unrealistic expectation, not least because Lansdowne wished to preserve the economic status quo and Labour were desperate to change it. Support for his peace proposals could not be maintained.

Resistance and Repression

Those who opposed the war differed in their attitudes to the limits of campaigning and the respect that ought to be paid to the laws of the military state. Royden, for example, was firmly on the side of constitutional and legal action, for the peace movement as for the suffrage movement, and she regretted the actions of those who deliberately broke the law. She was uneasy about some campaigning done on behalf of conscientious objectors.[25] She disapproved of the W.I.L. lending its secretary, Catherine Marshall, to the N.C.F. to make the latter's campaigning more efficient, because, as she told Marshall, she disapproved of the N.C.F.'s tolerance of law-breaking:

> I have for it much more respect, yet rather the same *kind* of respect, that I had for the best kind of Militant. I think it wrong, though not nearly so wrong, in much the same kind of way. The more I see, both of Militants and political Pacifists, the more I realise that their mistakes are only possible to very fine people. But I still think them mistakes.[26]

Lansbury's view was the contrary. A *Herald* dance in Holborn attracted a number of war resisters who had refused conscription. When the venue was raided by police and soldiers demanding silence, Lansbury lead community singing of socialist anthems for an hour in a deliberate act of obstruction. When the officers left, identity cards were switched to enable those at risk to leave safely. Some people were arrested on the basis of mistaken identity, but these were soon released once their own cards were returned.[27]

Increasingly, the F.O.R. was prepared to face up to hostile public opinion. At Christmas 1916, the F.O.R. and the Society of Friends courted public wrath by distributing Christmas gifts to the families of Interned

Aliens, as a sign of friendship and sympathy.[28] Although, in general, F.O.R. members tended to shy away from overtly political issues, following national publicity given to Lord Lansdowne's proposals to end the war by negotiation a number took part in an April 1917 anti-war march, alongside the I.L.P and other left-wing groups, from Canning Town to Victoria Park, Bow; the subsequent rally was broken up by a mob.[29]

When a regional conference at the Brotherhood Church at Hackney was broken up by violence and the familiar moronic renderings of "Rule Britannia", Henry Hodgkin, who feared for his life but did not join the fighting, was threatened and manhandled.[30] Hearing that those attending refused to be provoked by the violence, Lansbury remarked that he was stronger than ever in his conviction "that force and violence lead nowhere at all".[31] Not for the first time members of the F.O.R. were both the victims of violence and, ironically, liable to be accused of inciting that same violence. F.O.R. leaders were followed by plain-clothes policemen, who also attended their meetings.[32] Police also raided the F.O.R.'s Riverside Village community to take away conscientious objectors awaiting arrest, and to search, unsuccessfully, for a well-hidden printing press.[33]

In autumn 1917 there were police raids on the offices of several anti-war organisations, including the office of the F.O.R., which was first raided on 14 November. Leyton Richards, then F.O.R. General Secretary, offered to assist the police: "I will save you some trouble by giving you straight away the most subversive literature we have in this office", with which he handed over a copy of the New Testament.[34] Richards's comment was especially poignant given that some believed the Government's Regulation 27C (on censorship) meant that even the printing of the Sermon on the Mount would be an offence.[35] Bishop Gore's sympathies for conscientious objectors increased when the sale of his own 1896 book, *The Sermon on the Mount*, was banned by the chief constable of one area, as being likely to undermine the national interest, fuelling rumours that Matthew 5 was contrary to the Defence of the Realm Act.[36]

In July 1918, the W.I.L. attempted to hold a rally in Hyde Park to highlight the case for a negotiated peace. It was a sensitive time and the concept of negotiations was regarded as little less than treasonable. Accordingly, the Government banned the demonstration. Undaunted, W.E. Orchard and Dr Walsh held an impromptu prayer meeting in the park to which those who would have demonstrated were able to go. As well as the W.I.L., the rally was supported by the Christian Peace Crusade, and London branches of the Women's Co-operative Guild, the Independent Labour Party, the Union for Democratic Control and several trade unions.[37]

Another strand of the national women's peace movement, more working-class in its appeal than W.I.L., emerged from Glasgow through the initiative of two socialist women, Agnes Dollan and Helen Crawford, the latter being the Scottish organiser for the W.I.L. Following a local rally of women against the war held the previous year, a Women's Peace Crusade was launched in 1917, with 12,000 people converging on the centre of Glasgow, in separate processions from various parts of the city. Ethel Snowden and Helena Swanwick were among the speakers. By the autumn, thirty three local groups had sprung up, many in Pennine towns and cities. They did not always find things easy. A march of a thousand women in Nelson was faced with a hostile crowd fifteen times that number. Charlotte Despard, who travelled the country speaking at such meetings, faced an early disturbance at a packed meeting in Keighley in January 1918, but was able to continue. A Bradford meeting of the Women's Peace Crusade – see p. 63 – was addressed by Ethel Snowden, Isabella Ford (who was secretary of the Leeds group), Fanny Muir (who was imprisoned for three months for open-air anti-war speeches in Shipley Market Place) and Esther Sandiforth (who had spoken alongside Muir in Shipley). This was one of several women's groups in the city, others being the Wives and Mothers of Conscientious Objectors, and the Bradford Women's Humanity League.[38]

The various strands of the peace movement carefully fostered international connections throughout the war, despite selected pacifists being prohibited from travelling abroad. Bertrand Russell was refused permission to go to the U.S.A. and Marian Ellis was not allowed a passport to visit Scandinavia.[39] The Dutch, Birmingham F.O.R. secretary, Cornelius Boeke, who regularly spoke in front of a munitions factory on Saturday afternoons, was twice arrested. One episode in South Wales led to a fine being paid by confiscation as he was being taken to Swansea jail. Within weeks, he was back in court for an alleged earlier offence at an open air meeting in Birmingham. Charged under the Defence of the Realm Act, for "unlawfully making statements likely to prejudice the administration and discipline of His Majesty's Forces, and intended to interfere with their success", he was again fined and this time he was also deported. Ironically, this was to prove a blessing in disguise as it paved the way for the founding of the International Fellowship of Reconciliation at Boeke's Bilthoven house in 1919.[40]

The Russian Revolution of March 1917 produced a mixed response from pacifists, most of whom could appreciate the aims of the revolution, but few of whom could tolerate the idea of a revolution by force. The British authorities were less equivocal. They viewed revolution with considerable unease. Official harassment of pacifists was commonplace throughout the war, not only because of a misguided feeling that organisations like the F.O.R. were pro-German, but because, in the words of the head of Scotland Yard C.I.D., "Pacifism, anti-Conscription, and Revolution were . . . inseparably mixed".[41] He was not necessarily far from the mark. Fighting ceased on the Eastern front when Russian soldiers stopped fighting and turned for home, showing no mercy to any officers who tried to stop them. In January 1918 the F.O.R. sent a resolution to the new revolutionary Russian Government, "recognising the service which the Russian nation has done to the cause of humanity and of reconciliation".[42] Earlier, the Russian Revolution received popular support at an extraordinary Labour Convention in Leeds on 3 June 1917, after which the 5 June Cabinet meeting agreed "to undertake an active campaign to counteract the pacifist movement".[43]

One aspect of that suppression was the prosecution of the publishers deemed to infringe the Defence of the Realm Act. One such was C.W. Daniel, who had previously been imprisoned for six weeks in 1917 for standing up for free speech, then was tried and fined again in the autumn of 1918, "for making statements in a book entitled *Despised and Rejected* likely to prejudice the recruiting, training and discipline of persons in his Majesty's forces and for having 234 copies of the book in their possession".[44] *Despised and Rejected* was a novel written by Rose Allatini under the pen-name of A.T. Fitzroy. Emerging from an age when homosexuality was not only taboo but illegal, this study of the themes of difference and "abnormality" explored the moral and political issues surrounding pacifism alongside the psychological and sexual issues of female and, especially, male sexuality. The lead character, Dennis Blackwood, a musician with "the soul of a woman in the body of a man", knows himself as "different from the others . . . for ever an outcast amongst men, shunned by them, despised and mocked by them".[45] He was a socialist pacifist who rejected the machinery of the nations "that organised the murder of individuals by individuals who had no personal quarrel with each other", nations that fought for extension of power, consolidation of empire – shifts in the balance of power not worth one man's life-blood, let alone millions. The Russians had committed atrocities; "don't you see", Blackwood said, "that once the 'dogs of war' are loose there's bound to be that sort of thing all round?" These war machines could only produce a sham peace, a lull before another storm: "A lasting peace can never be achieved by war, because war only breeds war". The next generation would have war all over again.[46]

The Blackwood character's greatest fear was not being wounded but "being sent out to inflict death or wounds on others . . . deliberately to maim and shatter the bodies of men as young as himself, the bodies of men as young as Alan [his lover]". He faces the combined challenges of militarism and masculinity, with one accuser exclaiming that "if a man's got no fight in him, he's unnatural".[47]

Herself born in Vienna to a Polish mother and an Italian father, Allatini portrays Blackwood appreciating the diversity of European voices and wanting to meld them together in his music. One pacifist character argues that "it's the sacred duty of everyone who's got the gift of creation to try and keep it intact".[48] Allatini is not a religious writer and, notwithstanding the allusion in the title to Isaiah 53.3, *Despised and Rejected* is in no way a religious book. Perhaps this sentence explains why: "So many of the clergy, who call themselves followers of the Prince of Peace, deny Him, by abuse of their power – by preaching war from the pulpit and joining hands with the misleaders of the people to exhort them to take part in bloodshed and strife".[49]

Blackwood's tribunal verdict is that he should undertake a non-combatant role, something that, as an absolutist, he rejects with surprising venom. The novel ends with the leading character enduring the hardships of prison, despised and rejected for his pacifist ideals and his sexuality too. It is an extraordinary volume for its era, with its exploration of masculinity, machismo and militarism. The whole being of Blackwood rejects war, in his person as much as his political philosophy, a dangerous combination indeed. No wonder the *Times Literary Supplement*'s review of Allatini's book concluded, "it is not to be recommended for general reading".[50]

The F.O.R. and the Churches

For all that it could not avoid controversy and legal backlash, the instinct of F.O.R. members in general was less for promoting political change than in the propagation of a peaceful spirit, a prayerful and reconciling approach to life and theology. Attempts were made to set up an international day of prayer for peace.[51] The F.O.R. was particularly keen for its message to be heard by the Churches, which, with the exception of the Society of Friends, supported the war (albeit "reluctantly") to a greater or less extent. The Church of England was undoubtedly the worst culprit but other Christian traditions – particularly the Roman Catholic Church – were also culpable. Sending 40,000 circulars out to clergy did not prove a fruitful approach for the F.O.R., eliciting as it did a mere 17 "entirely sympathetic" replies, and many that were abusive.[52] More positive were meetings with prominent clergy and supportive friends who were not themselves pacifists. The obvious example was William Temple.

The Rector of St James's Piccadilly since 1914, Temple continued to edit *Papers for War Time* and was very clearly not a pacifist, yet he was invited to attend the Fellowship of Reconciliation General Committee on 19 March 1915 in order to consider the respective positions of pacifists and influential peace-minded non-pacifists, and how it might be possible to work together without antipathy. "The interpretation of secular history in relation to the Kingdom of God" was discussed.[53] The F.O.R. wanted to make some criticisms of Temple, in an atmosphere which would not hamper future co-operation, and Temple wanted to state that he saw peace coming not through disarmament but by an international use of an impartial body of armies, rather implying that, at that time, he accepted that such armies were being used for selfish interest. Temple upheld the decision of the Church at the time of Constantine to move away from relative obscurity and to accept the compromises of having wider influence. There was disagreement over the potential for love in international relations. Temple suggested an evolutionary model whereby a single state could potentially be based on love, but he argued that international affairs had yet to evolve into such a state; it was to be a position echoed a generation later by Reinhold Niebuhr in *Moral Man and Immoral Society*, that the ethical teaching of Jesus applied only to smaller groups, and probably only to individuals, thereby leaving nation states and larger groupings to seek a more "realistic" basis for their actions than the inconvenient ethic offered by Christianity.

On behalf of the F.O.R. Hodgkin countered by pressing for "the infusion of the moral dynamic of those who stand ahead", adding that the continual outbreak of the Divine Order was only possible when people took risks, as Christ did.[54] The parties agreed to disagree, but parted on amicable terms. It was a promising start to a relationship that was to lead to Temple being one of pacifism's fiercest critics, yet respected by many pacifists for his friendship and tolerance for their position.

The respect was apparent in the opposite direction. Despite the hostility of the leadership of the Church of England to the arguments of pacifists, an official Anglican delegation was sent to the 1917 F.O.R. Conference in an attempt to gain the Fellowship's participation in the doomed National Mission for Repentance and Hope.[55]

On the Edge of Establishment: Sheppard and Lansbury

Following that National Mission Temple would become the leading figure, along with Dick Sheppard (Vicar of the neighbouring St Martin-in-the-Fields, Trafalgar Square) of the "Life and Liberty" movement, which questioned the nature of ecclesiastical establishment and worked for the internal reform of the Church of England.

Sheppard was, through and through, a product of the Establishment. He was the son of a Canon of Windsor, and former Secretary to Bishop Lang of Stepney and Head of Oxford House. To the surprise of those around him, he volunteered at the outbreak of war to go to France as an army chaplain. King George V thought his decision reckless, and was reputed to have murmured "Bloody young fool!" [56] For Sheppard, who charged into everything he tried, it was a brief, but formative, experience of the front line. By 17 August 1914 he was writing that "War is awful. More awful than I supposed possible".[57] A few weeks later came the incident that he later described as being the origin of his subsequent peace activity:

> In September 1914 I knelt by a dying soldier. I had just arrived in France. He was the first soldier I saw die. As I bent to catch his painfully-spoken words I discovered that he had little need of my ministry. He was thinking of a life that was still unborn. His wife was expecting a baby about Christmas. And he died thanking God that, if the child was a boy, he would never have to go through the hell of war.[58]

Upon reflection, some years later, Sheppard wrote, "I was not a pacifist in the first year of War: as a professing Christian I ought to have been".[59] That brief experience of battle was an education for Sheppard. In the retreat from Mons he learnt about his own fear, about the soldiers' alienation from a middle-class Church, and about the possibilities for Christian unity that were signalled by chaplains of different denominations working together. "I've held a leg and several other limbs while the surgeon amputated them. I've fought a drunken Tommy and protected several German prisoners from a French mob. I've missed a thousand opportunities and lived through a life's experience in five weeks".[60] He saw German prisoners beaten up and realised that war was hardly likely to deepen spiritual values and lead people to any deeper awareness of God. "We learned as the time passed that men who live constantly in the shadow of sudden death are more apt to turn to the Devil than to God".[61] Sheppard's experience was brief. By mid-October the worn-out chaplain was back in England.[62] One month later, a "prophet aflame for God",[63] he started his ministry at St Martin-in-the Fields. He made it a church that was famous for its twenty-four hour service to tired passing soldiers and the capital's rough sleepers. Even pacifists felt welcome, for, as one pacifist journal reported, "it is the custom to pray for conscientious objectors as well as for soldiers and sailors. We are indeed glad to see that some clergymen, at any rate, are prepared to put into practice the principles of the Sermon on the Mount".[64]

George Lansbury, however, would only give him two cheers. He wished Sheppard had gone further: "What a grander, nobler piece of work would have been done had the Vicar boldly and without reservation declared against war and taken his stand with those who demanded peace. . . . During a war the Churches try to serve the God of War and the God of Peace. It cannot be done".[65]

Such was the context of an offer by Sheppard of a platform to Lansbury, who lived in a small house in Poplar. Sheppard even wondered aloud whether he should move St Martin's Rectory to smaller premises, as an expression of social concern.[66] The following month Sheppard suggested they might issue a joint statement promoting a lay "Crusade" on matters of social concern. Lansbury couldn't see how he could help Sheppard with that.

> You see I so fundamentally disagree with the official church attitude about the war and war in general. It seems to me that, admitting that in the present circumstances – and I don't – humanity is not sufficiently developed for us to trust ourselves unarmed before all nations, yet it seems to me that this is the only ideal Christ would have put before the world. I cannot believe that war does anything else but debase and demoralise mankind. I believe that a triumph won by war and force is simply a triumph of force. To me war is only part of the tremendous problem of social relationships which have their root in the fact that we strive to live our lives for ourselves; and the result is beggaring, both morally, intellectually and spiritually.

Lansbury argued that if the churches were to be saved, they needed to tackle such issues as competition and markets, otherwise for all their hymns and prayer meetings, the great world of humankind would be left untouched.

> And then the persecution of Conscientious Objectors. They may be all wrong but they have upheld what they believe to be right as the men who have stood for right have always stood, buffeted and rebuffed by the leaders of organised religion. . . . When it is labour that is to be crushed, then as a rule the Church is on the side of the State. And at this juncture because the State orders men to go and fight for a country they do not own, it is considered that we must all obey the State and conscience is not allowed to come in. But even if this question were properly dealt with there would still remain the great problem of riches and poverty and this crusade, if it is to be of any worth must have clear-cut opinions as to how the gulf between rich and poor is to be bridged.[67]

Loitering behind Lansbury's outspoken critique was his own growing affection for the message of the Church, if not the flawed agency through which that message was delivered. Without losing his political edge, he warmed more to the spirituality of the F.O.R. the longer the war continued. He reflected on all the wars of his lifetime and realised "that had men loved one another there would have been no war; that envy, hatred, malice, and all uncharitableness has been stirred up by interested men whose god was Mammon and who, for the sake of money, were ready to risk the lives and liberties of millions of their fellow men and women". He told the socialist readership of the *Herald* that he had joined the non-political F.O.R., describing it as a body of men and women who believed that everyone should order their lives, both as individuals and as nations, on the teachings of Christ, "and that instead of being overcome by evil we should overcome evil with good". He stressed the need for Fellowship, "in the workshop and the market-place, in mine and factory", citing the William Morris dictum that fellowship is life, the lack of fellowship hell.[68] On the first anniversary of the war he declared that he was more of a pacifist than he had ever been: "the greatest force in the world is the force exerted by Christ, passive resistance to all wrong doing".[69]

Not that the official organs of the Church of England would have described it in such terms.

The Poetic Critique

Caroline Playne commented that the Church's failure during the war years was that, "It was left to the fighting men to realize that the religion of Christ is incompatible with the brutal savagery of modern warfare".[70] She reported an embarrassed and disgusted railway carriage of soldiers when a clergyman came in and said "So you are going to fight God's war". Far more than that absurd cleric, the soldiers knew only too well that it was not God's war they were fighting.[71]

The marked weakening of allegiance was striking. For every person who, in extremis, was drawn to prayer, there were others for whom the whole experience would lead to the rejection of Church, clergy and faith alike. The Church was in the process of losing a gender and a generation, but it could not see it.[72]

The poets in the front line could. Arthur Graeme West, who died at Bapaume in 1917, came to despise the whole war effort, and everything that contributed to the culture which led to it, including the platitudes of other poets, and of the Church, and the irrelevance, as he saw it, of shallow, naïve Christian faith. He expressed his frustration in the ambiguously titled, *God! How I Hate You*:

> God! How I hate you, you young cheerful men,
> Whose pious poetry blossoms on your graves
> As soon as you are in them, nurtured up
> By the salt of your corruption, and the tears
> Of mothers, local vicars, college deans,
> And flanked by prefaces and photographs
> From all you minor poet friends – the fools –
> Who paint their sentimental elegies
> Where sure, no angel treads; and, living, share
> The dead's brief immortality. . . .

After then recounting in graphic detail the gore and the horror of the sights of war, the "muddy brown monotony/ Where blood's the only coloured thing", West mocks the pieties and inadequacies of religion:

> Yet still God's in His heaven, all is right
> In the best possible of worlds. The woe,
> Even His scaled eyes must see, is partial, only
> A seeming woe, we cannot understand.
> God loves us, God looks down on this out strife
> And smiles in pity, blows a pipe at times
> And calls some warriors home. We do not die,
> God would not let us, He is too "intense,"
> Too "passionate," a whole day sorrows He
> Because a grass-blade dies. How rare life is!
> On earth, the love and fellowship of men,
> Men sternly banded: banded for what end?
> Banded to maim and kill their fellow men –
> For even Huns are men. In heaven above
> A genial umpire, a good judge of sport,
> Won't let us hurt each other! Let's rejoice
> God keeps us faithful, pens us still in fold.
> Ah, what a faith is ours (almost, it seems,
> Large as a mustard-seed) – we trust and trust,
> Nothing can shake us! Ah, how good God is
> To suffer us to be born just now, when youth
> That else would rust, can slake his blade in gore,
> Where very God Himself does seem to walk
> The bloody fields of Flanders He so loves!

It was the same on all sides: Herbert Read, imagining the *Meditation of a Dying German Officer,* noted that "God dies in this dying light". In *The Parson's Job,* Madeline Ida Bedford described the reaction of a bereaved widow ("I hate your religion. . . . I only want my man") to a visiting clergyman:

> What do you want
> Coming to this 'ere 'ell?
> Ain't it enough to know he's dead,
> Killed by a bit o' German lead?
> What! – the Lord means well?. . . .
>
> Get out, or I'll strike you down.
> I'm carrying his kid.
> Do you call that fair?
> Gawd – no wonder I wants to gib;
> Our first-born, and his father – where?[73]

Even whilst still an undergraduate in Oxford, Vera Brittain could anticipate the inevitability of such reaction. In a poem entitled *August 1914* she wrote of God saying "Men have forgotten Me", as a consequence of which they would require redemption through pain: "But where His desolation trod/ The people in their agony/ Despairing cried, 'There is no God.' "[74]

The recognition of the humanity of the enemy (West's "Even Huns are men") was not uncommon among soldiers. Recovering from wounds received in the Battle of the Somme, R.H. Tawney wrote in 1916, that "Hatred of the enemy is not common, I think, among those who have encountered them".[75] The essential humanity of both allies and enemies is a feature of the diaries and reflections of Vera Brittain. She would become a substantive figure in the British peace movement for half a century, first in the League of Nations Union, then, having been converted to pacifism in 1936 by the words of Dick Sheppard, as a prominent Anglican pacifist in the Peace Pledge Union. She became an outspoken campaigner against obliteration bombing in the Second World War (alongside George Bell), and against nuclear weapons thereafter. Her First World War experience as a Voluntary Aid Detachment nurse included a time on the Greek island of Lemnos, tending the wounded from Gallipoli, and at the western front, nursing captured wounded German soldiers. It meant her eyes were open to recognise the breadth of humanity, beyond gender or patriotic divide. Of the (nursing) *Sisters Buried at Lemnos*, she wrote in October 1916:

> Seldom they enter into song or story;
>   Poets praise the soldier's might and deeds of War,
> But few exalt the Sisters, and the glory
>   Of women dead beneath a distant star. . . .
>
> No blazing tribute through the wide world flying,
>   No rich reward of sacrifice they craved,
> The only meed of their victorious dying
>   Lives in the heart of humble men they saved.[76]

In September 1917, she described her experience of *The German Ward* in language that would have seemed incomprehensible to, say, the Bishop of London. It was her nursing of German soldiers that moved her to write:

> And I learnt that human mercy turns alike to friend or foe
>   When the darkest hour of all is creeping nigh,
> And those who slew our dearest, when their lamps were burning low,
>   Found help and pity ere they came to die.

So, though much will be forgotten when the sound of War's
alarms
  And the days of death and strife have passed away,
I shall always see the vision of Love working amidst arms
  In the ward wherein the wounded prisoners lay.[77]

The socialist poet Herbert Read, highly decorated for his exploits in
the Yorkshire Regiment, could also see beyond his own condition. In *The
Execution of Cornelius Vane*, he versed sympathetically the plight of a shell-
shocked deserter, captured and shot by members of his own regiment,
introducing the poem with Arthur Rimbaud's acknowledgement that
"Le combat spirituel est aussi brutal que la bataille d'hommes; mais la
vision de la justice est le plaisir de Dieu seul".[78]

The lives and writings of the First World War poets have been
thoroughly documented elsewhere and they go far beyond the scope
of this volume. Given the huge issues being faced in extreme human
experience and facing up to death and the meaning of life, there is a
surprisingly low proportion of writing using explicitly Christian
imagery. That itself may reflect the distance of the churches from people's
lives in the era before the war. Where Christian imagery is called upon,
it can be used to powerful effect, as in Wilfred Owen's *Parable of the Old
Man and the Young*, when the story of Abraham and Isaac is retold with
the angel appealing to Abraham to slay a ram instead of his son.

But the old man would not so, but slew his son,
And half the seed of Europe, one by one.

Owen's experience as a soldier in the trenches had no points of
contact with the complacent church at home. He "saw God through
mud", and said of his colleagues, that "except you share/ With them
in hell the sorrowful dark of hell,/. . . You shall not hear their mirth'.[79]
Owen would not accept what Ruth Comfort Smith described as those
"tinsel platitudes we've sworn so long",[80] not least "The old Lie: Dulce
et decorum est/ Pro patria mori". It was patriotism that Owen most
rejected, as in *At a Calvary near the Ancre* where he derided "The scribes
on all the people shove/ And bawl allegiance to the state", upholding
instead those who actually lay down their life: "they do not hate".

The concept of military chaplaincy is non-trivial. The Church of
England, in particular, would aim to be visibly present in all areas
of human activity, whether that activity is condoned or condemned;
there is a strong case for the provision of spiritual and pastoral care
for those involved in the trauma of battle, not least to counter "the
temptation for men to be brutalised" whilst maintaining a prophetic
critique of the context.[81] Yet the inadequacies of that ministry in practice,
especially where clergy were unable to communicate with their men,

("Our padre were a solemn bloke,/ We called 'im dismal Jim"[82]) led to a poor reputation for chaplains in general. And prophetic critique was noticeable by its absence. Numerous recent publications have attempted to rehabilitate the reputation of those who donned military uniform and accepted military pay, thereby implicitly (often explicitly) and uncritically accepting and affirming the purposes and means of the military.[83] Added to that, the English class system, which, with all its inequalities, survived the war intact despite some wishful-thinking claims to the contrary, was at its most marked in the relationship between some chaplains and those to whom they ministered. [84] That is why those who deliberately worked to overcome such divisions – most notably the Portsea curate, Philip "Tubby" Clayton, associated with the founding of Toc H at Poperinge ("Abandon rank, all ye who enter here") – were marked as exceptional.

One who overcame those divisions, growing up in the Quarry Hill slum in Leeds where his father was the local priest, was Geoffrey Studdert Kennedy (1883-1929), nicknamed "Woodbine Willie" after the cigarettes he gave away with New Testaments.[85] A master communicator, post-war he would become the voice of the Industrial Christian Fellowship, successor to the Christian Social Union. Enthusiastic for the war in its early days, Father Geoffrey, as he was also known, became a Chaplain to the Forces in France in December 1915, winning a Military Cross for his determination to tend the wounded under fire. It was not long, however, before that enthusiasm waned:

> That poor lad, all blown to bits – I wonder who he was. God, it's awful. The glory of war, what utter blather it all. . . .
> War is only glorious when you buy it in the *Daily Mail* and enjoy it at the breakfast table. It goes splendidly with bacon and eggs. Real war is the final limit of damnable brutality.[86]

Several of Studdert Kennedy's rhymes – he had no pretensions as to their literary merit – implied criticism of other chaplains, and their failure to communicate effectively. He reveals a soldier reflecting:

> Our padre, 'e says I'm a sinner,
>   And John Bull says I'm a saint,
> And they're both of 'em bound to be liars,
>   For I'm neither of them, I ain't.[87]

Constantly drawn to the contrasts and inconsistencies of faith, he asked rhetorically, "How can I reconcile the spirit of those who live to kill, with the Spirit of Him who died to save?"[88] He even asserted, "If God wills War, then I am an atheist, an anti-theist. I am against God. I hate Him".[89] In "The Sorrow of God", essentially a reflection on the passion of Christ, he imagined a soldier expressing,

> Yes, I used to believe i' Jesus Christ,
>   And I used to go to Church,
> But sin' I left 'ome and came to France,
>   I've been clean knocked off my perch.[90]

Similarly exploring "The Religious Difficulties of the Private Soldier" he considers a mock credal confession:

> I believe in God the Father Almighty, and a trench mortar has just blown my pal, who was a good-living lad, to pieces, and God is Love, and they crucified the sergeant-major, and peace on the earth, good will towards men, and I stuck my bayonet through his belly, and Jesus died to save us from sin, and the Boche has been raping women, and this — war never ends.[91]

His writing explores theodicy, the problem of evil, ("And the lovin' God 'E looks down on it all,/ On the blood and the mud and the smell".[92]) along with the all too evident limits of the power of a God of love in the face of human free-will. ("Why don't ye force us to end the war/ And fix up a lasting peace?/ Why don't ye will that the world be still/ And wars for ever cease?")[93] Essentially a pastoral theologian, Studdert Kennedy's apologia for the Christian faith is more convincing for facing up to such inconsistencies.

> God suffers now, and is crucified afresh every day. God suffers in every man that suffers. God, the God we love and worship, is no far off God of Power, but the comrade God of Love: He is on no far off heavenly throne. He is up in the trenches, under the guns.[94]

For a chaplain, the contrasts in life and faith were not only intellectual but emotional. At the front, he would share the men's laughter at the deafening sound of big guns fired at the German lines, only to admit, "But it's damnable, it's a disgrace to civilization. It's murder – wholesale murder. We can't see the other end – ugh – damn all war! They have wives and kiddies like [mine], and they are being torn to bits and tortured. It's damnable".[95]

Such an acute sense of empathy meant that Studdert Kennedy recognised that for some, the legacy of the war would be life-long. He imagined a young wife, longing for a child, receiving home her mangled man. Where once there had been "red 'ot kisses", now "e'll never kiss again,/ 'E ain't got no kissin' in 'im,/ Ain't got nothin' now – but pain". With bitter anger, the young wife declaims,

> But I says – Let them as makes 'em
>   Fight their wars and mourn their dead,
> Let *their* women sleep for ever
>   In a loveless, childless bed.[96]

Called to use his extraordinary communication skills – Dick Sheppard called him "the greatest orator I shall ever hear"[97] – in support of the National Mission, Studdert Kennedy realised that war was never going to lead to a religious revival, far from it; "You don't go out to give your life; you go out to take the other fellow's. You don't go out to save, you go out to kill; and if you don't you are no good as a soldier. . . . Once and for all let me state here my conviction that War is pure undiluted, filthy sin. I don't believe that it has ever redeemed a single soul – or ever will".[98] As he wrote, in 1918,

> Waste of Muscle, waste of Brain,
> Waste of Patience, waste of Pain,
> Waste of Manhood, waste of Health,
> Waste of Beauty, waste of Wealth,
> Waste of Blood, and waste of Tears,
> Waste of Youth's most precious years,
> Waste of ways the Saints have trod,
> Waste of Glory, waste of God –
> War![99]

There is one more poet to consider, one whose background was half Jewish and half establishment Anglo-Catholic. Siegfried Sassoon was like many combatants whose attitude to the war fluctuated. A number of soldiers soon realised that the ends and means for which they had been recruited were not as worthy as they had been led to believe. But protest was virtually impossible, once one had signed up. A handful of men were successful at becoming soldier C.O.s, exchanging military uniforms for those of prisoners undertaking hard labour. Others would have been tortured to conformity by the army, or shot as deserters. In Sassoon's case he met with Bertrand Russell and others in 1917, after which he stated his new understanding that the war which he had originally entered believing it to be "a war of defence and liberation" had become an aggression and a striving after conquest. Having seen the suffering caused to the troops "I can no longer be a party", said Sassoon, "to prolong these sufferings for ends which I believe to be evil and unjust".[100] Like West and Brittain, he acknowledged the humanity of those against whom he was fighting, and their families. In his poem, *Reconciliation*, he wrote:

> When you are standing at your hero's grave,
> Or near some homeless village where he died,
> Remember, through your heart's rekindling pride,
> The German soldiers who were loyal and brave.
>
> Men fought like brutes; and hideous things were done;
> And you have nourished hatred, harsh and blind.

But in that Golgotha perhaps you'll find
The mothers of the men who killed your son.

In his poem *They*, Sassoon mocked the bumbling incomprehension of the English episcopacy.

The Bishop tells us: "When the boys come back
They will not be the same; for they'll have fought
In a just cause: they lead the last attack
On Anti-Christ; their comrades' blood has bought
New right to breed an honourable race,
They have challenged Death and dared him face to face."

"We're none of us the same!" the boys reply.
"For George lost both his legs; and Bill's stone blind;
Poor Jim's shot through the lungs and like to die;
And Bert's gone syphilitic: you'll not find
A chap who's served that hasn't found *some* change."
And the Bishop said: "The ways of God are strange!"

The Church lived in a world of its own.

The National Mission

The Preface to *Crockford's Clerical Directory* is sometimes considered to be a fair snapshot of the dominant opinion and consciousness of the Church of England. In 1916, the verbose author was in bullish mood. How good and satisfying the war was in getting men to consider their mortality; what great opportunities there would be for the Church to cash in!

The Church of England Clergy have not been slow to recognise the opportunity which the war has offered of getting into touch with the manhood of England in the face of circumstances which bring into exceptional prominence all the problems of both the present and future life. It has been matter of regret and constant complaint that our public worship and our meetings for prayer and Christian fellowship have been for a long period very definitely neglected, if not wholly disregarded, by the larger number of our male population.

It must, however, be a cause for much satisfaction to both Clergy and Laity that beings who move in this present sphere of existence only for a limited period should, in view of a probable speedy termination of that period, be brought seriously to consider how and where that existence may be resumed or continued, and with what consequences arising out of the manner in which life here has been utilised or wasted, and whether it will be perpetuation of a state of good or evil.

Denial or neglect of Divine claims upon individual man has been a growing evil for a long period of years. . . . Who can record the numbers who before the war were entirely averse to everything in the nature of religion, but who have through our national difficulties learned that God can "keep him in perfect peace whose mind is stayed upon God because he trusteth in Him"? In the course of this enlightenment, and by the evidence of its results in the arena of war as well as at home, the value of the Church of Christ and of its chosen ministers in the due exercise of their ministry has been abundantly proved, to the edification not only of our armies, but of those whose lot it is to abide at home. A spiritual harvest is gained, the fruit of which can be reaped by those who abode by the stuff as well as by those who bore the burden and heat of the day. If eventually it result in that redemption of our country from sin and indifference which the Church is hoping may be the outcome of the projected National Mission now in course of being organised by our Bishops and Clergy, then shall we have cause for thanksgiving in the midst of the many sorrows which the war entails.[101]

How different that might have been if the war had been opposed. Instead, two years into the hell of war, with the bishops refusing to call publicly for any peace moves, they instead attempted to instigate a morale-boosting National Mission of Repentance and Hope. This was, in effect, an extended version of the Fast Days of previous centuries, the Church rallying in support of the State, even when the State was conducting a war against which a prophetic Church would have protested. At best it was a reflection of the ignorance of the Church leaders at the slaughter of the trenches, at worst it was Erastian collusion.

When the National Mission was announced, Lansbury, not surprisingly, argued that the Church had identified the wrong target. The bishops, he said:

Are much distressed because of vice, immorality, and drunkenness, which, they tell us is more prevalent than before the war.

I suggest to the Bishops that the real social evil to be combated, as the foundation of all social evils, is this one of greed and mammon worship. Why cannot the Archbishop, Bishops, and clergy lead a new crusade to the rich?

Disgusted that the Archbishop of Canterbury had supported the conscription of single men in a speech in the House of Lords, Lansbury urged him to demand the conscription of property instead, not nearly as sacred as a human body: "It is, therefore, the bounden duty of these right Reverend Fathers in God to cease their present policy of siding with the rich, give up sanctioning every kind of evil policy simply because such policy secures the interests of the powerful". If they did that, he wrote, then the people might start to take notice of them as they did Jesus of old, in which case repressive legislation would not be needed and there might arise a speedy way to end the war.[102] There should be an economic dimension to moral argument: "As Christ has taught us, we cannot gather grapes from thistles. Neither can we expect love and comradeship to grow and flourish in the midst of a world of competition and strife".[103] Lewis Donaldson and other Christians on the political left published their critique of the National Mission in the *Herald*, alongside the official response of the Church Socialist League. Stating that the reason Christianity had not brought peace was that people gave only lip-service to the teaching of Christ, Lansbury predicted that the National Mission would be a ghastly failure unless the Churches urged everyone to engage in

> the fight against Mammon and greed, selfishness and lust of power, whether of individuals or nations. The Bishop of London and his colleagues must give up this reliance on brute force and carry the Gospel of the Cross to victory instead. We – all clergy and laity – must humbly and reverently strive to follow the lowly Galilean who, without swords or guns, gathered to Himself a tiny band of men and women who faced and ultimately broke the power of Rome by their rigid adherence to the teaching of their Master. . . . It is time we tried the Gospel of Love, and it is this Gospel which the churches of every denomination ought to be preaching, and especially is it the Gospel which the Church of England should preach to-day if its Mission of Repentance and Hope is to be of any worth.[104]

It transpired that some in high places – principally Temple – were listening to him for an invitation was sent to Lansbury, arch-critic of the Mission, to write one of the official pamphlets. Davidson was very uneasy about Lansbury's involvement, telling Winnington-Ingram that he regarded Lansbury as "unbalanced" and suggesting that he could be a "source of peril, feeling it for example, his duty to raise some big question publically which would cross our mission purposes like a red herring across the trail".[105] Despite the Archbishop's misgivings, in an extraordinary recognition of Lansbury's influence, the radical pacifist socialist was invited to present an official wartime apologia for the mission of the established Church of England.

Although the Mission was theoretically aimed at the "immoral" working classes, Lansbury aimed his paper at those who would in practice engage most with the Mission, existing middle class Anglican church-goers. "I often wonder if those with leisure understand how impossible it is for business men and work people to participate in the daily services of the Church and how out of place a church bell sounds calling men and women to worship at a time when all sweat and labour has to be spent working for the bread that perisheth". He advocated selflessness and castigated the worship of material success "in this sordid, miserable time of competition and greed". Unlike other Mission preachers who blamed morally inadequate working class individuals for the sins of lust and liquor, Lansbury was adamant that there was a social basis for sin. "Where I live, I am surrounded by people for whom life has very few gifts . . . ", so it was not unsurprising for sickness and unemployment and despair to drag people into drink and degeneracy.[106] "Do we realise that we are failing in our duty to God and our Fellows while any of these evils flourish?" The way forward, to counter social sin, was Christian socialism: "God grant that the whole Church of England, rich and poor, old and young, may be drawn together so that the class barriers that divide us may be broken down".[107]

Lansbury notwithstanding, the National Mission was an acknowledged failure, not through lack of effort but because it was based on a catalogue of erroneous assumptions: the social as opposed to the exclusively personal dimension of sin was pointed out by Lansbury; the assumption – as with *Crockford's* – that the working man (and men were the focus) would flock to what the Church was offering if only he had the opportunity to know about it; the Establishment belief that England was still, if it ever had been, its type of Christian; the list continues. Temple and Sheppard temporarily revived ecclesiastical excitement by starting a "Life and Liberty" reform movement, the greatest achievement of which would be the formation of a new Church Assembly.[108]

Following the Mission, the Archbishops set up a number of committees.[109] Lansbury sat on the Committee on Christianity and Industrial Problems, alongside bishops Talbot (the chairman), Gore and Kempthorne, with Bell, R.H. Tawney and others.[110] He did not find it a congenial experience. "Nobody denied capitalism and landlordism were of the devil, but all, except Tawney, jibbed at socialism, he complained.[111] As he saw it, the Church that preached the Magnificat also blessed property and riches:

> Had I the power I would shout from the porch of every church and chapel every day of the week, "Choose ye this day whom ye will serve: ye cannot serve God and Mammon." I tried to get this view expressed by the . . . Archbishop's Committee, but my colleagues were all too clever, too intellectual and more theological than I was, so I was just a voice in the wilderness with the almost solitary exception of Tawney and, on occasions, Bishop Gore.[112]

A memorandum from the Student Christian Movement to the Committee on the Evangelistic Work of the Church, noted that although most students had accepted the arguments for the war, they accurately felt that the Church had nothing distinctive to say to a world at war. "It has done little more than support the State. The result has been a marked weakening of allegiance to the Church since the outbreak of war, and in some quarters a strong desire to see the Church find new leaders".[113]

Maude Royden, Pioneer for Peace

One new leader was emerging, and from an unexpected quarter. Through Maude Royden, as has been seen, the F.O.R. had a connection with the W.I.L. There were also other links between the two organisations. Members of the F.O.R. collected signatures for a W.I.L. petition.[114] Both Marian E. Ellis and Theodora Wilson-Wilson were also on the first W.I.L. executive committee.[115] It was Royden, though, who was the most active, chairing and speaking at countless meetings throughout the war. She held to the opinion expressed by Olive Schreiner, that "No woman who is a woman says of a human body, 'It is nothing' ".[116] In December 1915 she spoke at the Portman Rooms, Baker Street, "To Present the Women's Case Against Conscription". Those present agreed that "the introduction of any form of industrial or military conscription in Great Britain would be a grave blow to liberty and social progress", and "far from contributing to the successful prosecution of the War, it would constitute the greatest victory of German militarism".[117] She gave a series of 1916 addresses at the Fabian Rooms, Westminster, on such topics as: "What has Investment of Money to do with War and Peace?"; "Is it Unpatriotic to be a Pacifist?"; "What has the Woman's Movement to do with Foreign Policy?"; "Patriotism"; "Nationalism, Internationalism and the Churches".[118]

She was not alone in feeling that the Church should be asking for repentance itself before persuading others to repent. She worked alongside Temple and Sheppard in the leadership of the Life and Liberty reform movement.[119] That led Temple to nominate her to Archbishop Davidson for membership of the Mission Council, a body which then urged bishops to find "the best ways of using services and receiving the message of women speakers, whether in Church or elsewhere".[120] The suggestion that women could ever speak in an Anglican Church provoked a response in some quarters little short of the hostility that accompanied the German invasion of Belgium. Even bishops who had found it politic to support the suffrage movement declined to send out any such invitations to women speakers. Royden commented that the National Mission "has come and gone, leaving hardly a ripple on the surface of the water", barring a few committees.[121]

In such a climate, therefore, the request that Royden accepted from the Congregationalist City Temple to preach in March 1917 was a move that was criticised not only by those who felt that Anglican purity was threatened by contact with Nonconformists, but also by those who held that women should not be heard in any church.[122] That was not the view of the long queues that formed both morning and evening to hear her preach. She preached there again in May, then at Kings Weigh House where the Congregationalist pacifist W.E. Orchard was minister.[123] The Rector of St Botolph's, Bishopsgate, G.W. Hudson Shaw, invited her to preach, but she declined to do so without the permission of the Bishop of London.[124] She did, however, agree to take on the specially-created position of "pulpit assistant" at the City Temple. When, on her second week in the post, she baptised four babies, the scandal was too much even for the Life and Liberty Council.[125]

By 1918 Royden was not only preaching regularly at City Temple, but, at St Botolph's, she had with some trepidation become the first woman to read the lessons in an Anglican Church. Her patience, and that of Shaw, with the ecclesiastical authorities finally came to breaking point in late summer that year. On Thursday 19 September, to a packed, standing-room-only church, Maude Royden delivered the address at the midday service. The first woman to preach in an Anglican church preached against war. Her title was "The League of Nations and Christianity", and her text was from Matthew's crucifixion narrative:

> Can we really do nothing but sit down and watch the crucifixion of the youth of the world!
>
> Must we face the returning soldiers after all with empty hands and bankrupt hearts? Must we admit that, after all, their friends have died and they have suffered in vain?
>
> Humanity must change or it will commit suicide. We can go on developing the means of destruction, or we can re-organise the world for peace: 'See I have set before you this day, life and good and death and evil. Therefore choose life that both thou and thy seed may live'.[126]

Revolution and Silence

The soldiers would indeed be returning, after a sudden and unexpected turn of events.

German socialists, upon whom so many hopes had rested in vain in 1914, finally made their presence felt four years later. There had been strikes earlier in the war, in April 1917 and January 1918, but nothing as dramatic as the naval revolt at Kiel in October 1918. With the new Chancellor, Prince Max von Baden, making overtures regarding a negotiated ceasefire, unbeknown to him the German fleet, hitherto trapped in Kiel, received orders to break out and engage in one last sea battle. The sailors at Kiel refused to take part in what would have been a suicide mission and they mutinied. Their action sparked other mutinies and strikes across the country, with the demand for immediate peace and social reform. Kaiser Wilhelm II, grandson of Queen Victoria and cousin of George V, who had been in power since 1888, was forced to abdicate and flee into exile on 9 November. Von Baden resigned too. The guns fell silent two days later.

11.
The Aftermath of War

The Immediate Aftermath

11 November 1918; the war is over.

Except that it wasn't for the bereaved, the wounded, or the broken, whatever their stories. The bodies were still to be retrieved, the war-graves prepared. When Annie and Robert Young, he the fiercely atheist editor of the *Japan Chronicle*, chose the epitaph for their son (2nd Lieutenant Arthur Conway Young of the Royal Irish Fusiliers, slain in France in August 1917) they demanded that the gravestone be engraved, not *"Pro Patria"* or "For King and Country", but "SACRIFICED TO THE FALLACY THAT WAR CAN END WAR". It remains a rare critique among the mass ranks of the fallen in Tyne Cot cemetery near Ieper.[1]

The persecution of conscientious objectors continued well beyond the end of the war. Having called on the Government, in the week of the Armistice, to "SET THE CAPTIVES FREE!", Lansbury was incensed: "whilst we rejoice in the peace, these comrades of ours are dying in prison – for some it is worse than dying; they are gradually being crushed so that they will come out only to a living death".[2] He made it his business to publicise their plight, both inside and outside the Labour movement. In January 1919 an N.C.F. petition, calling for the release of 1,500 men still detained, was signed, *inter alia*, by 15 bishops, and was presented to the Prime Minister by E.W. Barnes and Lord Parmoor, amongst others.[3] A few weeks later Lansbury handed to the Home Secretary another petition of 130,000 signatures collected by the *Herald*, calling for the release of the prisoners.[4] In the short term it had no effect, and tales of health deterioration, and cat-and-mouse arrests, continued. Not until April 1919 did the first releases take place, for those who had been imprisoned longest. Almost all were released by the end of July, the end of the story for the prison system but not for the men of broken bodies but unbroken conscience, who had to try to rebuild their lives in a society which initially despised them. Even those who had been legally awarded exemption were now disenfranchised and much discriminated against by a society that, only later, came to appreciate the principles for which they suffered.

The peace started badly, with the same passion that had advocated pursuing the war to the bitterest of conclusions. The election of December 1918 affirmed Lloyd George and dealt crushing blows to many former M.P.s who had opposed the war, and who would have to wait until 1922 to regain their parliamentary seats. Yet, with a continent in turmoil, a Prime Minister who had once delivered the rhetoric of reparation now began to see the impracticality of such a policy. His French counterparts did not, however, to the cost of the next generation. Many would die as a direct consequence of the greed and desire for vengeance of those behind Versailles and those charged with implementing it. Negotiations began in January 1919, and by the time the treaty was signed on 28 June, parts of German territory – north, east and west – were transferred to neighbouring nations. The Rhineland was neutralised and the population of the Saar valley placed under League of Nations control for fifteen years. German colonies were confiscated and administered by Britain. What remained of Germany had to produce substantial payments in reparation for war losses, on the arguable grounds that Germany alone had been responsible for the start of the war. There was also an enforced disarmament, with the size of the German army restricted to 100,000 men. This was justified on the assumption that it would, in any case, be a prelude to a general disarmament. This assumption constituted the treaty's major failing and allowed the victorious nations to shirk their responsibilities for making the treaty work.

The one ray of hope to emerge from the settlement was the League of Nations, the formation of which was agreed in principle on 25 January. Theory and practice, however, were not the same. Even advocates of the League, like Willoughby Dickinson, admitted that the final form of the institution was far from perfect.[5] Some critics noted that only national governments would be represented and that other groups and institutions would have no voice. The League would not be a worldwide forum but an intergovernmental institution. A door was left open for the possibility of the League imposing sanctions, even military sanctions, on recalcitrant nations. Particularly damaging, especially across the Atlantic, was the linkage of the League with what was perceived as a vindictive and imperialist peace agreement. In November 1919 came the news that the U.S. Senate had refused to ratify the Covenant of the League.[6] That decision, together with the refusal of the Belgian and French Governments to admit the German Government to the League,

The memorial stone of Arthur Conway Young, Tyne Cot Cemetery, Flanders.
"Sacrificed to the fallacy that war can end war".

meant that the new institution for world peace was a pale shadow of what had been promoted by many supporters of the League concept. It would be seen as little more than an alliance of victors in a balance of power.

Could it have worked, despite such shortcomings? There were those with their own reasons for making it enfeebled. No sooner had the League become a reality than campaigning began, especially on the left, for a complete revision of its basis. The League's support group, the League of Nations Union, would initially attract large numbers of pacifists who believed and hoped the League would be the agency to uphold peace and prevent future war. In time, the League's shortcomings would be exposed, and large numbers would defect from the League of Nations Union back into more explicitly pacifist associations. The nature of those societies was also undergoing change.

The Post-War Peace Movement: an International Realignment

The post-war realignment of the peace organisations, almost as dramatic as that of 1914, was significant for its international dimension. Already, by October 1916, the Fellowship of Reconciliation could claim 111 members outside Britain, in 22 different countries.[7] A League for Christian Citizenship had been started in Sweden, and a Dutch Brotherhood of Christ was founded at the end of 1918 by Cornelius "Kees" Boeke, who had visited pacifists in Germany and central Europe in 1915 in an attempt to find grounds for international reconciliation, and who, when he was branch secretary of Birmingham F.O.R., had been deported from England.[8] Following the Armistice, 50 Christian pacifists from 10 countries came together at Boeke's home in Bilthoven, Holland in October 1919, on the invitation of Boeke and Henry Hodgkin.[9] Among those attending were Attlee, Siegmund-Schültze and Pierre Cérésole.[10] Despite being the son of a former President of the Swiss Federation, Cérésole had been imprisoned in his native Switzerland for his refusal to accept military service and his failure to pay the military tax. One of those present in Bilthoven spoke of the mutual strength that came from having no loyalty before loyalty to Jesus. Another spoke of unity and the absence of barriers, saying that "We knew ourselves to be no longer lonely pioneers but part of a great unseen company".[11] Together they agreed to form the Movement Towards a Christian International (M.T.C.I.), a name reflecting their socialist and Christian pacifist aspirations. This was also reflected in their pledge:

> Those who enter such a movement place the claims of Christ and humanity above those of any state, while none the less serving their own nation in every possible way. They cannot, therefore, kill their fellow-men on any pretext whatever, or take any part in military service. They are utterly opposed to Capitalism and Imperialism. The cause of the oppressed is their cause. They are determined on a revolution so radical that, if sought through violence, it would surely fail. They are pledged to a life service for the whole human family.[12]

The message sent out after the meeting showed the deep sense of corporate guilt that the participants felt at being members of a civilisation that had lost its way with such terrible consequences. Yet there was now a rising tide of hope.

> The only way to bring security, justice and joy into the world is the way of Jesus, the way of reconciliation that brings men to their

Father and makes them brothers in one family. . . . Revolution through reconciliation. Jesus is the real revolutionary because He is the real reconciler. If we take His way, we too will be reconcilers and revolutionaries. The path lies open to every man who loves and dares.[13]

Boeke became secretary of the new movement and Cérésole the first international secretary.[14] Cérésole, who continued to be under pressure to pay his military tax, described the founding of the M.T.C.I. to a court official:

We have formed here in Holland, not only spiritually but materially, in a very modest way as yet, an international family of Christians bound by a tacit moral undertaking never to take part in any violent action against one another. The duty to be faithful to this human family supersedes the duty of obedience to the military law, made to defend the limited interest of the State, based on a systematic mistrust of neighbours and coldly envisaging the possibility of murdering them.[15]

Although the M.T.C.I. and the F.O.R. remained technically separate, the relationship between them was close, and in 1923 the M.T.C.I. changed its name to the International Fellowship of Reconciliation (I.F.O.R.).[16]

With the end of conscription, the No-Conscription Fellowship felt that its task was complete, and the members of the organisation finally closed it down in November 1919. However, this left Christian pacifist socialists without a natural home, especially given the lack of campaigning activism within the F.O.R.[17] Concerned at the increasing support for violent revolution amongst some of those on the left, a Crusader group of Christian pacifist socialists, including Lansbury, issued a call for an "Affirmation Against War".[18] This led, in February 1920, to the formation of the No More War International Movement, later known more simply as the No More War Movement (N.M.W.M.).[19] The No More War Movement, described as having "inherited the spiritual idealism of the early Christian Socialists and of the artist-poet-craftmanship school of William Morris", was to be the leading pacifist campaigning group on the political left, sharing many members with the Independent Labour Party.[20]

A delegation, including Wilfred Wellock, attended another Bilthoven gathering in March 1921, with representatives from Germany, Austria and the Netherlands.[21] The result of this meeting was another new international organisation, PACO, after the Esperanto word for peace, pronounced "pahtso". The PACO membership pledge stated, "War is a crime against humanity: I therefore am determined not to support any kind of war, and to strive for the removal of all causes of war".[22] This final clause was to influence the embryonic N.M.W.M., which added to their original "Affirmation Against War" a political obligation "to work for Total Disarmament, the removal of all causes of war and the establishment of a New Social and International Order based on the Pacifist principle of Co-operation for the Common Good".[23] Early in 1923 the secretaryship of PACO passed into the hands of the Congregationalist conscientious objector and N.M.W.M. national committee member, Herbert Runham Brown, from Enfield. The name of PACO was soon changed to War Resisters International (W.R.I.). It proved to be an effective information service about individual war resisters, maintaining the profile of conscientious objectors who continued to be imprisoned in many countries.[24]

Despite the existence of the F.O.R., a number of prominent Christians gave their support to the N.M.W.M. and there was an active ecumenical Churches Committee. Events included Canon Lewis Donaldson, prominent in the Church Socialist League, and W.C. Roberts speaking at a St George's, Bloomsbury event that floated the concept of a Federation of Religious Organisations to Resist War.[25] Donaldson was President of the London Council for the Prevention of War, and in 1925 he issued a passionate message, *War is Anti-Christ!*[26] In December 1926 the N.M.W.M. Churches Committee resolved to urge "the Bishops of the English Church, in their revision of the Prayer Book, to delete the last clause of the 37th Article of Religion – which, it urges, is manifestly contrary to the letter and spirit of Christian teaching".[27] Others involved with the N.M.W.M. included Charles Raven, Maude Royden and the Marquis of Tavistock.

The Post-War Anglican Church: Lambeth 1920

It might have been hailed as "the most famous and best-known of all the Conferences", largely due to its progress on ecumenical relations, but the delayed 1920 gathering of worldwide Anglican bishops was tastelessly triumphalist rather than penitential.[28] The majority of English bishops still had an aristocratic pedigree with its associated myopia, but at least "International Relations" did appear on the agenda. Not even the bishops could ignore the terrible events of the preceding years. Their response, however, was decidedly ambiguous. In one context they even made the astonishing claim that the war was "ennobled", and the forces of nationalism which lay behind the war were actually commended: "We cannot believe that the effect of the coming of the Kingdom of God upon earth will be to abolish nations".[29] At least that meant a positive reception to the Christian basis of the League of Nations, "the most promising and the most systematic attempt to advance towards the ideal of the family of nations which has ever been projected".[30] The League needed not only governments but the hearts and minds of the people in all countries to be behind it.[31] Conference Resolution 4 demanded "the admission of Germany and other nations into the League of Nations at the earliest moment which the conditions render possible".[32]

The Committee appointed to consider and report upon Christianity and International Relations said the League was something "all Christians should welcome with both hands".[33] (The exception was a group of erastian bishops from the United States who, slavishly following their Government's line, would only welcome it half-heartedly.) The Committee was chaired by Archbishop St Clair Donaldson of Brisbane, and included the bishops of Durham (Moule), Lichfield (Kempthorne), Oxford (Burge), Sodor and Man (Thompson), Southwell (Edwyn Hoskyns), Winchester (Talbot) and Worcester (Ernest Pearce).[34] In the work they produced, there is hardly any hint of repentance. There was no indication that the bishops were prepared to admit their own costly errors of the past. There was no rebuke for those guilty of jingoistic speeches; no admission that episcopal statements had fuelled hatred; no acknowledgement that past utterances had been made in comfortable ignorance of the horrifying reality of trench warfare. Indeed, there is more than a hint of self-congratulation for the unhappy role played by the church in the war:

> The nation that had the best trained army in Europe has been defeated. The nation that was the richest in munitions of war has lost, because against her were the moral forces of civilization.[35]

There was certainly no suggestion of awareness that these self-proclaimed "moral forces" might even at that time be in the process of stifling the long-sought-after peace.

The committee commended the World Alliance (soon to meet again in Geneva), the S.C.M. and the League of Nations Union, whilst frustratingly, but somehow unsurprisingly, warning against "the impatience of those who press for immediate disarmament without reference to the facts of the situation".[36] For all that, their analysis was grimly prophetic:

> At the present moment there are two alternatives before the world. On the one hand we may relapse into the old conditions, with an attempted balance of power, and the piling up of armaments with their attendant expenditure, until the world is ready for another and even more hideous war. On the other hand, we may work for the ideal for mankind which shines before us in the pages of the New Testament, guided by the principles which we have learnt from the Lord Jesus Christ. . . . [37]

> If the clauses aiming at the prevention of war are not to be a dead letter, we must preach with all our power, in season and out

of season, in the drawing-room and in the market-place, in the workshop and in the club, the wickedness of hatred. This at the moment is the most appalling barrier in the way of the League of Nations. In every country at the present time the spirit of hatred is hard at work. . . .

We must face the facts. If we wish, whether nation or individual, to enjoy the luxury of hatred, we must pay the price, and the price is another and far more hideous war as soon as ever the nations have sufficiently recovered from their present exhaustion. . . . We must choose between the spirit of hatred and the spirit of the Lord's Prayer.[38]

In many ways the 1920 Lambeth Conference was a step forward in the Church's thinking on issues of war and peace, though that was largely due to the dearth of such thinking in previous Conferences. Many of their hopes and fears were valid. It had taken a Great War to force issues of war and peace on to the Church's agenda; after that there could be no easy return to the ecclesiastical cocoon. Perhaps the most positive feature of the whole Conference was its emphasis on peace-making through Christian unity:

The war and its horrors, waged as it was between so-called Christian nations, drove home the truth with the shock of a sudden awakening. Men in all Communions began to think of the reunion of Christendom, not as a laudable ambition or a beautiful dream, but as an imperative necessity.[39]

It is to an ecumenical conference that we now turn, to find one of the most powerful Christian pacifist statements of the twentieth century, and to meet the principal pacifist theologian for the next generation.

Post-War Churches Acting Together: the C.O.P.E.C. Conference

A Conference Convened

The basis of this Conference is the conviction that the Christian faith, rightly interpreted and consistently followed, gives the vision and the power essential for solving the problems of to-day, that the social ethics of Christianity have been greatly neglected by Christians with disastrous consequences to the individual and to society, and that it is of the first importance that these should be given a clearer and more persistent emphasis.[40]

So began the Basis of the Conference on Christian Politics, Economics and Citizenship (C.O.P.E.C.) held in Birmingham in April 1924. The origins of the Conference can be traced back to a Student Christian

Movement conference at Matlock in 1909, following which an inter-
denominational group (some of whom were to share a common
residential life) was formed to consider social issues. A Quaker and
early member of F.O.R., Lucy Gardner, was the secretary, and William
Temple (a deacon at the time of Matlock) was in the Chair. Another
strand can be traced to the founding of the Anglican Christian Social
Union in 1889. In 1911, an interdenominational conference of such
unions met at Swanwick, the leading figures being Bishop Gore,
the Jesuit Charles Plater (1875-1921), the Congregational minister
Will Reason and Lucy Gardner.[41] The C.O.P.E.C. gathering was
first suggested in 1919. The 4 years of preparation encompassed the
work of 12 commissions and the processing of the results of 200,000
questionnaires. Along with Gardner, the other organising secretary
was Dr Charles Raven, Rector of Bletchingley, and sometime Fellow
and Dean of Emmanuel College, Cambridge. Archbishop Söderblom,
suitably impressed, described their work as a "Conference Obviously
Prepared with Extraordinary Care"![42]

Charles Raven (1885-1964)

John Ray was a seventeenth century naturalist who could not submit to the
Act of Uniformity. His academic biographer, Charles Raven, dedicated
that life story "To All Who Like John Ray Have Sacrificed Security And
Career For Conscience' Sake".[43] No mean naturalist himself, Raven came
to feel that his own preferment had been held back because of his views
on war. As a young man, he felt he had come closer to God on mountain
tops, in a Liverpool boys' club during a year out from college, or grasping
the spiritual experience of a sick friend, than in church worship or the
literalist biblical religion of his Cambridge student peers. He offered
himself for ordination, appreciating the tolerance of Anglicanism: "it
was plain that the Thirty-Nine Articles were rather the trust deeds of
an historic institution" he wrote, "than a code of propositions to each of
which assent must be given".[44] By the time he was twenty-four, he was
Dean of Emmanuel College, Cambridge.

With the coming of war Raven tried, unsuccessfully, to enlist on
several occasions, being turned away on medical grounds before
eventually getting to France in 1917 as Chaplain to the 1st Berkshires.
Within a fortnight he was part of "almost the hottest fight of the war" at
Vimy Ridge.[45] He later recalled:

> a young subaltern joined my battalion in the trenches – a boy
> spick and span as if turned out of a band-box – a boy who had
> spent his last few days with his mother and sisters, being fitted
> out with all that love could offer as equipment for his adventure.
> When twenty-four hours later I buried him, a victim of a casual

bomb on a quiet day, with his own life all unlived, with the hopes and the joys of his home so visibly centred on him, I was ashamed to be alive. I knew then what I might feel and what sometimes one does feel in the face of the Cross of Christ.[46]

He wrote of meeting "the shattered smashed body that once was a husband and a father and one goes through his poor keepsakes – the picture of his wife and babes so similar to that which I carry next my heart".[47]

He had a solidarity with the soldiers around him not unlike that expressed by, say, Wilfred Owen. There was little time for pacifists like Lansbury, though Raven was fast becoming a socialist, soon to write the definitive *Christian Socialism, 1848-1854*. It was the shameful inadequacy of the peace, as much as his experience of war, that led him to reconsider his attitudes, paving the way for his eventual conversion to pacifism. He later described how he, and those like him, had come back to the farcical 1918 election, to an inept Coalition Government, and the disastrous Treaty of Versailles:

> We . . . came back to find our friends dead or maimed, our comrades unemployed, our hopes and ideals openly repudiated, and every position of leadership in Church and State filled by those who had stayed at home and profited by our sufferings.
>
> The poisoning of our own outlook, added to the manifest evidence of a general corruption of private and public life, inevitably convinced us that war was not only wastage and folly, but wickedness and futility. We had been trying to cast out devils by Beelzebub the prince of devils, and they had returned each with seven others worse than himself. There must be, there is, a more excellent way. We had caught a glimpse of it in the naked loneliness of battle; we came to see it revealed plainly in Christ.[48]

The C.O.P.E.C. Commission

The Conference has been described as "one of the most notable efforts ever made to apply Christian principles to contemporary social problems" giving ecumenical activists "a sense of direction which was to prove of first-rate importance in the subsequent history of that Movement".[49]

1,500 delegates (including 80 from outside the British Isles) met in Birmingham Town Hall, and the extraordinary public interest in the proceedings was reflected in the messages of greeting from the King, the Archbishop of Canterbury, the then Prime Minister (MacDonald) and two former Prime Ministers. The F.O.R.'s official roll call read: Walter Ayles, George Maitland, Lloyd Davies, C.H. Dodd, Oliver Dryer, Leyton Richards, Bernard Walke and Gilbert Porteous, with Albert Belden, C.J. Cadoux, James Fraser, Nathaniel Micklem, Mary Phillips, Cecil Wilson and Basil Yeaxlee also present, representing other organisations.[50]

One of the endorsed preparatory volumes for C.O.P.E.C. was entitled *Christianity and War*. It had been produced by a Commission chaired by Alfred E. Garvie, President of the National Free Church Council. Among those on the Commission were: Bertram Appleby, a Congregational Minister who was a member of the National Committee of the No More War Movement; George Maitland Lloyd-Davies, M.P., Assistant Secretary of the F.O.R.; Oliver Dryer, of the United Free Church of Scotland, and General Secretary of I.F.O.R.; and William E. Wilson, Professor at Selly Oak and a founder-member of the F.O.R, whose writings included *Christ and War, Atonement and Non-Resistance* and *The Foundation of Peace*. There were also assorted academics and serving and retired military officers. Gardner and Raven assisted the Commission. Lady Parmoor (Marian Ellis) of F.O.R. and Evelyn Underhill also contributed.[51] The extent of pacifist input to this Commission was remarkable, especially so close to the end of the war. It would have been inconceivable a decade earlier. They were also better able to put their case than they would have been but a few years earlier, partly due to the pacifists' own experience and reflection and partly due to a recent (1919) publication by C.J. Cadoux, *The Early Christian Attitude to War* (soon to be expanded into *The Early Church and the World*) which not only reclaimed Christian pacifist history but also gave pacifism a more coherent theology than hitherto.

Not surprisingly, the diversity of opinion of the members of the Commission meant that full agreement was always going to be difficult. At certain stages in their Report there were different views expressed, in an attempt to satisfy both those who were pacifist and those who could not condemn war in all circumstances. The result was a document with which all felt content and which all realised would have been impossible to achieve just a few years before.

The Commission initially considered the causes and motives of war, including biological, social and religious factors. The sorry conclusion was that:

> it must be confessed that the history of the influence of the Christian Church on war is very sad reading. Men believe, and rightly believe, that the Church should be an international Christian Commonwealth, transcending all smaller divisions, and refusing to be moved from the principles of the Gospel by any lower ideals. That this has not been so historically and is still so far from being so, is the great tragedy of the Christian ages.[52]

In the face of the claim that war was often the lesser of two evils, came the retort that there may be unconsidered alternatives, and that "the victory has not always been to the good cause, and thus war is an uncertain arbiter". More than that, "The war to end war has left Europe in a condition in which, unless the hearts of nations be changed, another war is being prepared".[53]

Anticipating the debates of the next generation, the Commission addressed the false "justification" of war by extrapolation from the demands of social order:

> the use of force in an ordered society is limited as far as possible. Moral obligations to the criminal are recognised. The policeman who uses unnecessary violence is censured by the bench. . . . But in war, not only the use of force, but falsehood, deceit, and the loosening of all moral bonds are justified. . . . Far as the treatment of criminals fails to be what it ought, there is not the remotest analogy between what is done to them to restrain them from wrongdoing, and what is done, justified, and even made a boast of in war.[54]

The concept of national honour was debunked, and the state received a level of critique that would have been beyond the comprehension or competence of the Lambeth Conference, a reflection of the Nonconformist voices on the Commission:

> Patriotism as love of country has to be distinguished from loyalty to the State, and may sometimes demand even defiance and disobedience. . . . For history has shown the State as the wrongdoer, as the enemy of advancement. . . . The individual conscience cannot be relieved of the responsibility of moral judgment and decision by loyalty to the State or love of country, great and enduring as ordinarily is the claim of the State to submission, and of country to any service or sacrifice which conscience allows.[55]

It was not only the duty of individuals to challenge injustice, but also the new League of Nations. Would it be up to the task?

> The League of Nations will perpetuate injustice if it prevents war without removing these conditions which provoke it. If the British Empire were fashioned according to the vision of that school of imperialists who desire to see an exclusive community of nations, sacrificing to its own enrichment the claims of all other peoples, it would become the greatest outrage in human history, a constant summons to war, a defiant negation of the spirit and purpose of Jesus Christ.[56]

Related to that, history and geography teaching were of primary importance, and Cadets and Officer Training Corps were "definitely a preparation for war, and seem to many incompatible with an educational training towards peace as the higher ideal"[57] The Lambeth Conference could never have said such things. Although the Commission echoed Lambeth in commending the World Alliance, S.C.M. and the World Student Christian Federation, it also showered praise on the F.O.R., the No More War Movement, and the Friends' Ambulance Unit. The Commission called on British churches together to foster an international alliance of churches to build up a Christian culture of war resistance. In particular they should:

> unreservedly condemn, and refuse to support in any way, a war waged before the matter in dispute has been submitted to an arbitral tribunal, or in defiance of the decision of such a tribunal. . . .
>
> cultivate such intimate fellowship with the Churches of other lands that through the one Church of Jesus Christ the spirit of reconciliation shall triumph over all national prejudices, suspicions, and enmities, and that the churches of many lands may unitedly formulate a Peace-programme which can be commended to all who profess and call themselves Christian, so that Christ shall reign as Prince of Peace . . . .
>
> hold these principles, not only in times of peace, when their practical denial is not threatened, but that also, when war is imminent, they should dare to take an independent stand for righteousness and peace, even if the Press and public opinion be at the time against them.[58]

On so much, the Commission agreed, yet in other fundamental aspects there was considerable diversity around the table. In an attempt to understand better these varied, even contradictory, approaches and philosophies, the members of the Commission produced two separate statements: "The Position of those who do not accept Pacifism" was stated, followed by a substantive "Statement of the Pacifist Position". The very headings implied that pacifism was the norm from which divergence might take place, rather than the previously assumed opposite. The conscientious objectors of the Great War had achieved more than they realised. This was the first time that a Commission with significant Anglican representation had produced an official report commending Christian pacifism.

The non-pacifist case centred on the desire to preserve and to protect the nation, on the temporal and geographical relativity of Jesus's teaching and example, on the possibility of war as judgment of sin, on human life not having sufficiently evolved to the state where war would be no more, and on the acceptability of self-defence when arbitration had failed. Significantly, considering that the conditions included were not satisfied even in 1939, even the non-pacifists proposed a popular pledge:

> Believing that Law must take the place of War in international disputes, we, the undersigned, solemnly pledge ourselves to withhold service from any Government which refuses to submit

the causes of the dispute to an international Court, or which refuses to accept the decision of such Court. We will fight to defend our country in the event of an attack by another nation which has been offered arbitration, and which has refused it, but in no other circumstances.[59]

The C.O.P.E.C. Pacifist Statement

The "Statement of the Pacifist Position" immediately acknowledged the integrity of the above case. After all, if "Each man must to the best of his powers, using all the light he can get, follow the way that to his conscience appears right, in reliance upon the Spirit of truth who guides into all truth those who sincerely desire to be led", then there must be openness to the possibility that people will be led to believe different things.[60] Neither side would have any right to claim moral superiority. Having said which, the pacifist case was strongly upheld on spiritual and moral grounds.

Spiritual and moral degeneration sets in in all nations engaged in war, said the Statement. There could be no spiritual gain in wholesale slaughter. "When once an appeal to arms is made, passion supersedes judgment, hate is fostered and embittered, love and truth are forgotten. . . . We realise that every decent thing for which Christian civilisation stands is imperilled by it, and that its recurrence will be ever more and more destructive and inhuman".[61] The conduct of war leads the nation whose cause is just to the commission of far more atrocities than its attempted protection of the weak prevents. War does not deliver the goods, but lowers the whole moral standard.[62]

> It cannot proceed without the cultivation of callousness; untruth and deceptive half-truth are essential methods of war-time propaganda, and though the individual has often in war to learn to subordinate himself to the State, a lesson that has perhaps been learnt too well, what is chiefly needed in modern life is the subordination of the nation to the whole of mankind, and war denies this. Even when a nation wages war in a just cause, though the evil passions and ideas that cause aggressive war may be absent from its people, the process of war itself produces the moral degeneration just mentioned, as our own recent experience testifies. . . . The conclusion seems obvious that war is a means that disgraces the holiest cause.[63]

The authors of the statement affirmed the Christian duty to struggle, whilst arguing that certain weapons are forbidden; the Christian "cannot willingly use evil means to achieve good ends: such means do not, in fact, accomplish their purpose".[64] The dictum "Vengeance is mine: I will repay" reflected a pre-Christian conception of God, yet it usefully warned that human beings were not to assume the divine prerogative or exercise a power which only love could rightly use. "Some have claimed that they have killed in war while loving: if there are any who love enough to take so great a responsibility we cannot share their confidence".[65]

In the teaching and example of Jesus Christ there was revealed the way of life necessary to take away the causes of wars and to establish justice on earth. The statement's authors saw in the life and activity of Jesus, and in his death on Calvary, "a method of overcoming evil which, entirely repudiating all means that injure or destroy human life, conquers the evil in it by good, and only by good. . . . They see that returning good for evil and meeting hatred with love hold promise of a victory far greater than has ever been achieved in the world by might of arms".[66]

Such was the ground for believing that Christ's love was supreme, and that society was in need of a "transvaluation", even if that came at a cost:

> The Church exists in order to carry on the work of redemption, in order to love, and if need be for love's sake to suffer. And if the Master would not, surely the Church cannot, contemplate any other method of overcoming evil.[67]

It was for the Christian Church to take the lead, transforming the attitudes of individuals and the actions of society:

> It comes to this, we cannot overcome hatred by hatred or war by war, but only by the opposites of these. Evil can only be effectively overcome by the mightier power of love. . . .
>
> The Church is the custodian of that mighty power, committed unto it by Christ Himself. . . . Men and women of the Christian Church will then seek the expression of these harnessed powers not for ignoble purposes of self-interest, but in a co-operative effort to remove the appalling results of man's sin, and to establish in its place a new social order in which the spirit of war and hate shall be unknown. . . . There must be a wholehearted acceptance of Christ's standard of values, and thus a complete revision of many tragic compromises with the standards of the world.[68]

In language which echoed Maude Royden's earlier vision, the statement called for an alternative to war, "a Great Adventure on the part of the Christian Church". And it was time to set out upon it:

> Is it too much to ask of the Church of Christ to believe that *now* is the accepted time when she should once and for all abandon her reliance on the method of war even to resist the wrongdoer? Let us

not flinch from the consequences which such an Adventure of Faith might involve for us. At the heart of the world's redemption stands a Cross, and to hope that we can fully and fearlessly proclaim the Gospel of Reconciliation without it is to miss that strait and narrow way which leads to Calvary.[69]

The pacifist statement ended with an unattributed quotation:

What greater message of cheer and reconstruction could be brought to mankind to-day than the assurance that all who bear the name of Christ in every land have solemnly resolved to have no part in war, or in the preparation for war, but henceforth to work unitedly for peace by peaceful means alone? Shall we not make this venture of faith together in the love that beareth all things, believeth all things, hopeth all things, endureth all things, and *never* fails? Shall the torch of spiritual heroism be borne by the Church of the living Christ, or shall leadership in the utter rejection of war pass from our hands to men of braver and truer spirit? Which Master shall we who call ourselves Christians be known by all the world to serve, the God of Battles or the Prince of Peace?[70]

Notwithstanding its linguistic flourishes, the extent and depth of this Statement was something that had never before been seen in an official churches' document. Pacifism was now firmly on the agenda of all the Christian churches, not merely that of the Society of Friends. Only a small minority of Christians had been conscientious objectors or F.O.R. activists during the war, yet their prophetic faith and witness had made a substantive impact on the wider church[71]

The Ecumenical C.O.P.E.C. Legacy

One of the distinguished visitors attending C.O.P.E.C. was Archbishop Nathan Söderblom of Uppsala in the Church of Sweden, a pioneer of peace ecumenism. The preparatory written material and the volumes endorsed by the C.O.P.E.C. were used as a valuable work of reference by the major ecumenical "Life and Work" Conference in Stockholm in 1925, which attracted representatives from almost every western church except the Roman Catholic, including Christians from both France and Germany, with all their continuing mutual national tensions. Stockholm was the first international ecumenical conference on social ethics and described as the largest ecumenical conference since the First Council of Nicaea in 325, with 500 delegates attending from 37 countries. The Stockholm Conference "was impressive not only as the first attempt ever made by Christians to discuss internationally the problems of collective life", wrote Raven, later, "but as the first occasion since the war in which victors and vanquished had met as fellow-believers to debate the very issues over which they had so recently been struggling".[72] Echoing the C.O.P.E.C. resolution of the previous year, that "all war is contrary to the spirit and teaching of Jesus Christ", the World Conference stated:

> We believe that war, considered as an institution for the settlement of international disputes, is incompatible with the mind and method of Christ, and therefore incompatible with the mind and method of his Church.[73]

George Bell, Dean of Canterbury, was prominent at Stockholm. He was to steer very similar statements through both the ecumenical Eisenach Conference of 1928 and the 1930 Lambeth Conference. On that occasion, and on most subsequent Lambeth Conferences throughout the twentieth century, the bishops dared to assert that "War, as a method of settling international disputes, is incompatible with the teaching and example of our Lord Jesus Christ".[74] What was to become a famous formula in the Anglican peace tradition was taking shape. It could not have happened without the stand taken by the conscientious objectors of 1916-1918.

12.
The Cast Revisited

I have considered the impact of the war on the churches and on the peace movement as a whole, but what of those individuals whose lives were caught up in the forefront of war resistance? What direction did their stories take in the aftermath of the war? I start with the most significant player of all.

George Lansbury

Lansbury did not actually dislike Lloyd George, though the editor of the *Herald* had been known to refer to the sometime Prime Minister as "the last word in political jugglery and make-believe".[1] Lansbury visited Lloyd George in Paris (he was there for the Peace Conference) in January 1919, to petition for the release of those conscientious objectors who were still imprisoned. Soon afterwards he visited Germany, seeing a country being sucked dry by what Wilfred Wellock called the capitalists' "merciless, soulless Peace, that like a swamp-mist breathed death over everything".[2] Lansbury was taken round children's hospitals,

> to see the ravages our food blockade was making. I saw babies whose bodies were transparent, others whose limbs were twisted and distorted because of malnutrition suffered by their mothers. In the streets I met people whose faces bore the imprint of starvation. The clothing of the people in the streets was very bad. The British troops, who were well fed, often shared their food with children.[3]

The humanity shown by the ordinary soldiers in such circumstances contrasted sharply with the brutal attitudes of the politicians. Lansbury's comment was that "We do not need more of such great men, we need more wisdom and understanding among the masses. It is the few who bring about wars: it is the many who must put an end to the conditions which make wars inevitable".[4]

In his own thinking Lansbury managed to forge a bridge between the Christian pacifist left and the Marxist revolutionary left. In two articles in the summer of 1919 he could write both that "There is no other way by which mankind can be saved but by love",[5] and also that "The class struggle will go on, must go on, till the causes which produce classes and class antagonisms are swept away".[6] He desperately hoped that the revolution in Russia could be made to work, and may have been blind to its abuses as a result. He visited Russia in 1920, before the revolution had turned completely sour, and he saw how external action had made internal repression worse. Seeing a trainload of "broken wounded Russian soldiers" he realised "what horrible suffering is inflicted on innocent people by those who make war", and he understood that those sufferings would never be ended "until all who make wars and support wars are themselves obliged to accept all the risks and sufferings war brings".[7] Whether or not the Bolsheviks were minded to disarm, such a prospect was unlikely while Britain and France were using adjacent states, such as Poland, for launching economic and other attacks on the Soviet Union. Lansbury used the *Daily Herald* to campaign against Churchill's policy of enforcing a military blockade against the Soviet Union.[8] Later in 1920 the headline was "NOT A MAN, NOT A GUN, NOT A SOU" as opposition was successfully aroused to a possible war with Russia.

Back in 1907 Lansbury had helped to arrange finance for the penniless Lenin and Trotsky to come to a conference in London (it was repaid in 1921).[9] In his 1920 visit he met Lenin again and was impressed by his anti-capitalist commitment, though regretting that the Russian was neither religious nor pacifist. Still, Lansbury was able to report back to the *Daily Herald* that "The churches are all open and people going in and out".[10] On his return, Lansbury delivered a message from Lenin to a rally in the Albert Hall:

> If you can bring about a peaceful revolution in England, no one will be better pleased than we in Russia. Keep in your trade union movement; keep in your labour movement. . . . Keep together till you are homogeneous and do not be led into resorting to violence.[11]

That was at a time when the Miners' Federation could threaten a general strike partly on behalf of imprisoned conscientious objectors who had been denied the vote at a general election, and when pacifists in the Independent Labour Party could advocate membership of the (communist) Third International. For Lansbury there was no contradiction, as both Christian pacifism and socialism were based upon the principle of love, which was not a shallow naivety but hard politics. He described Christ as "the lonely Galilean – Communist, agitator, martyr – crucified as one who stirred up the people and set class against class".[12] He was appalled by injustice but distinguished between direct action and violence as means to overcome it, arguing that "the struggle of men and women on strike is passive resistance", and adding, "History records the fact that this is the only effective weapon of the physically weak and those who lack material resources".[13] Lansbury's own highly successful nonviolent revolt was based on Poplarism, a local Council's non-payment of rates to London County Council in response to more lenient demands being made on far richer boroughs. The stand led to Lansbury and other councillors being imprisoned, with over thirty Poplar Council meetings having to be held in Brixton Prison; the successful outcome of their stand came with the introduction of London-wide measures to benefit the citizens of Poplar and other impoverished boroughs.[14]

Lansbury was both hated and needed by the ecclesiastical and political establishment alike. His support for Russia led to attempts being made to prevent him speaking at the Church Congress of 1922.[15] Many in the Labour Party, too, longed for respectability, to be seen to be fit to govern, and their first opportunity came with a minority administration in 1924. Lansbury, who had been elected back to Parliament two years earlier, would have been an obvious cabinet minister, being described by Beatrice Webb in 1920 as "one of the most significant men of today, ranking in his unique position above either the leading trade unionists or the leaders of the I.L.P."[16] When he was only offered a non-cabinet position, which he refused, there was a strong suspicion that the king had directly intervened to make sure that Lansbury was kept out. ("George five should keep his fingers out of the pie".[17]) Lansbury responded by increasing his involvement with the No More War Movement and he was a prominent supporter of Sheffield Brightside M.P., Arthur Ponsonby, whose "Peace Letter" of 1925 was a forerunner of the Sheppard Pledge. When the Government tried to prosecute J.R. Campbell, editor of the Communist *Workers' Weekly*, for a "Don't Shoot" article addressed to troops (an echo of the Tom Mann trial opposed by Hardie and Lansbury in 1910) Lansbury held a massive rally at the Albert Hall in support of the defendant, and made the assembled crowd stand and repeat after him the supposedly offensive appeal. He was treasurer of the committee to defend and support the arrested leaders. The Government dropped the charges in embarrassment, amidst Liberal and Tory condemnation. Within a year the Government had changed again, and Labour was back in opposition.

The years ahead would see Lansbury take over as leader of the Labour Party when it was at its lowest ebb in 1931, only to resign the post over Party policy to support military sanctions. The international status that role gave him meant that he was then able to lead an I.F.O.R. delegation visiting world leaders, and propose a more realistic attempt to renegotiate Versailles and to prevent war than any government was able to manage at that time. As the Conservative Government in Britain was promoting appeasement, tolerating a strong Nazi Germany as a bulwark against communism, Lansbury was trying to the last to prevent war by establishing the means to international justice. Following the debacle of Munich, 1938, it was to Lansbury that President Benes of Czechoslovakia wrote to express his thanks.[18]

C.F. Andrews

The repercussions of the Versailles Conference stretched beyond Europe. Having rejected an appeal by the National Congress for Indian delegates to be elected, the Government made its own appointments. To the fury of C.F. Andrews, the Versailles negotiators then rejected a proposal to include, in the preamble of the Covenant of the League of Nations, a brief statement asserting the principle of racial equality. South Africa and Canada were loudest in their opposition. Andrews unleashed his anger in the *Bombay Chronicle*: "Where was India all this while? Shepherded by the Secretary of State, the representatives of India raised no voice of indignant protest on behalf of the helpless Koreans or the despoiled Chinese, or on behalf of the equality of all races within the Parliament of Man".[19]

Andrews was to see the effects of racism, and the brutal effects of British foreign policy, in the shameful Amritsar Massacre by British troops of unarmed demonstrators in April 1919. On hearing of the carnage, newspaper editors in Lahore asked Andrews to travel to Amritsar. On arrival he was immediately arrested as his presence was deemed to be "not in the public interest".[20] He returned to Tagore, who publicly renounced his knighthood in protest at the British actions. Andrews had to wait until the autumn before he was legally allowed to visit the area, as a member of an investigating Congress.[21] His letters to Gandhi spoke of atrocities which had been even worse than had been reported.[22] Gandhi arrived in the Punjab in mid-October, shortly after which Andrews was refused entry to a local church on the grounds that "This House of God is not for rebels".[23] That November, to a vast Lahore rally of non-Christians, he announced:

> While I have been in Lahore . . . I have gone out each morning . . . and looked up to the sky before dawn, with all its stars. I have watched the sun rise over the great eucalyptus trees, and in the vast silences of Nature there have come to me these words from my own scriptures – the words of Christ my Master: 'Love your enemies, bless them that curse you, that ye may be the children of your Father in heaven; for He makes His sun to rise on the evil and on the good. Be ye therefore perfect, as your Father in Heaven is perfect.' I would urge you not to dwell upon vengeance but rather upon forgiveness; not to linger in the dark night of hate but to come out into the glorious sunshine of God's love.[24]

Drawn to Gandhi's emphasis on *ahimsa*, Andrews became a, not uncritical, ambassador and partner of Gandhi throughout the non-violent campaign for Indian independence. He was charged with making the preparations for Gandhi's visit to Britain in 1931.

Maude Royden

Maude Royden's gift was preaching. She was the first woman invited to preach from Calvin's pulpit in Geneva. Her post-war vehicle of choice for advocating peace was the sermon. Seeing early the injustice and inevitable consequences of Versailles, she preached a Palm Sunday sermon in 1919 entitled "The Passion of Christ". In it, she spoke of,

> the coming destruction that must follow upon the world that *will* not know the things that belong to peace. We are trying to get peace by the methods of hatred, cruelty and revenge. *We do not know the things that belong to peace.* We desire the effect; we *will* not have the cause.
>
> We are worn with war, shattered by the strain and stress of the last four and a half years from 1914 to 1918. We desire peace, but we will not have the things that belong to peace. We know that the laws of nature cannot be broken. We know that if you injure one part of your body the whole of the body suffers. We know that if you injure one nation the others suffer. But we will not accept it. We persist in trying to build our new civilisation on hatred and revenge. And our Lord, looking down upon us, must see what ruin we are bringing on our heads because we will not know the things that belong to peace.
>
> Do you think it belongs to peace to starve a generation of children in Austria? Does it belong to peace to try to hold Ireland against her will? Or to force from Germany what Germany cannot pay? . . .
>
> All I want to say is that you cannot get peace out of war any more than you can get grapes from thistles, because you are trying to do what is impossible, because you are trying to break the laws of nature.[25]

In this sermon she was critical of Lloyd George and those engaged in "the supreme farce, . . . the supreme folly" of trying to injure another nation without injuring oneself. "We cannot spend money on education. Our people live in houses that are slums because we have to prepare for the next war. . . . We prefer Barabbas, and we will not seek the things that belong to our own peace".[26] She considered the "little group of peasants" who stood at the foot of the Cross:

To-day it seems to me as though there were nothing left for most of us but just to pray that we may be found worthy to stand with these. That in a world where the hatred of nations seems undying, where, if it dies, it seems only to give place in men's hearts to a not less cruel hatred of class, that there should be anyone alive who still believes in love, that there should be anyone left at all who perceives in crucified, defeated Christ their God and King is, I think, the only hope for the future of the world. But it is a hope which cannot be conquered, which can never die.[27]

One year on from the end of the war, Royden spoke at the N.C.F. closing Conventions after which she reduced her direct involvement with the F.O.R. and the W.I.L.[28] However, during a conference on International Women's Suffrage in June 1920, she again delivered a sermon on the theme of the League of Nations. It was to become a popular sermon subject for her throughout the decade ahead.[29]

At that time, there was only stumbling progress towards women's ministry in the Church of England. Both W.C. Roberts, at St George's Bloomsbury, and Dick Sheppard at St Martin-in-the-Fields, allowed their churches to be used for rallies by the League of Church Militant, which supported women's ministry. The Lambeth Conference recommended establishing the position of deaconess, but even that was too much for the Church of England's Church Assembly. On two occasions Royden was banned by Winnington-Ingram from delivering Good Friday addresses in an Anglican church. She responded by partnering the liturgist Percy Dearmer in taking over the Guildhouse, a converted Congregational Chapel in central London, which was to become her preaching base. Royden was clear that they were not setting up a new denomination, rather they were engaged in an experiment that "springs from the Church of England, and remains within the Church of England" and, she hoped, would influence the Church of England. There was even the hope that Anglican authorities might encourage the experiment. Behind the scenes, the advisory council reflected both the radical and the Anglican heart of the enterprise by including such diverse supporters as Dick Sheppard, George Lansbury, William Temple, Kathleen Courtney, Louise Creighton, Millicent Fawcett and Bishop Maud of Kensington.[30] In the years that followed there was an impressive list of speakers at the Guildhouse including Norman Angell, G.K. Chesterton, Laurence Housman and Royden's spiritual adviser, the pacifist Father Andrew of Plaistow.[31] Other pacifist speakers included Raven, Siegmund-Schültze and, in 1931, Gandhi. Another Anglican pacifist, Sybil Thorndike, gave poetry readings in support of the Guildhouse.[32] The political awareness of the congregation was shown by the Guildhouse having its own branch of the League of Nations Union.[33] As Royden said in one of her sermons, "The Guildhouse only exists to serve the world, and when it ceases to do that, let it cease to exist at all".[34] Not that there was any chance of that, with Royden's evening sermons drawing (largely female) crowds week by week.

International issues were to the fore. Royden was an active member of the Fight the Famine Council. She called on the Government to keep open food supplies to German children. In a 1921 sermon she spoke of a little Austrian boy staying in her home:

> He was so rickety that he could not walk. . . . That little boy's face was like a little old man's. He had that terrible, anxious, harassed look that is pitiful on any human face, but is heartrending on a child's. He was only two years old when the war ended. He was not born when the war began. His fathers, you will say, made the war. Yes, perhaps. But we made the peace, and it was the war and the peace together that made Freddie look like that.[35]

In another sermon, she supported the Save the Children Fund appeal for money to pay for food for millions of hungry Russians. The amount required was the equivalent to only half the cost of a battleship or half a battalion of troops: "We spent over 100 millions on making war against Russia after war had nominally ceased . . . and now we say we cannot find five millions to keep the people of Russia alive".[36]

Closer to home, Ireland was another concern. On St Patrick's Day, just before Easter 1921, Royden preached on news reports coming from out of Ireland: "It is now certain that the Black and Tans have carried arbitrary shooting and looting, wanton insult and blind futile terrorism to a pitch which we were long unwilling to credit – which we hate to believe. *This disastrous disgrace must be stamped out at any conceivable cost*" [Royden's emphasis.][37]

> Let us abandon the pretence that we are necessary to preserve order in Ireland. We have made a wilderness and no one even dreams that it is peace. Terrorism has accomplished nothing but ruin in Ireland and indelible shame to ourselves. It will never accomplish anything. In the name of God let us abandon it, and now – on the eve of the Passion of our Saviour – cease to put Him to open shame.[38]

When the Lord Chancellor, Baron F.E. Smith of Birkenhead, said that Britain could not govern Ireland by the principles of the Sermon on the Mount, Royden retorted, "What did he govern it by that he made such a mess of it? We cannot govern Europe by the Sermon on the Mount. No? Have we made such a success of it by defying every principle of the Sermon on the Mount?"[39]

Reflecting on the 1922 crisis between Turkey, Armenia and Greece, she asserted once again:

> I am not a believer in war. I do not believe that war settles anything. To me the suggestion that we should go to war for some good purpose seems almost as futile as a proposal to throw oil on a burning house. If you saw a house in flames and innocent people inside it who were obviously finding it very difficult to get out, you would feel a desperate desire to do something, but if your desire to do something translated itself into throwing oil on to the burning house, you might perhaps afterwards regret that you had done anything at all. . . .[40]
>
> Christ at least has not yet been tried and found wanting. He is the only person that has not been found wanting, for – Oh, tragic truth! – He has never yet been tried.[41]

Following the signing of the Locarno Pact in December 1925 and the appointment that same month of a League of Nations Preparatory Commission for a proposed Disarmament Conference, the Women's International League for Peace and Freedom (as W.I.L. became in 1919) suggested a pilgrimage in support of both disarmament and arbitration, under the banner "Law not War". The intention was to set out on seven or eight routes converging on London from across Britain, with a thousand meetings and hundreds of church services on the way, to promote the case for a World Disarmament Conference.[42] The lame Royden joined part of the march from South Wales.

As up to 10,000 women converged on Hyde Park, one eye-witness described the colourful scene:

> Here were the women of the Guild House in blue cassocks and white collars, bearing their banners aloft; behind them walked members of the League of Nations Union, with bannerettes representing various countries of the world. Here was a carriage filled with women graduates robed in black and scarlet and purple; there was a group of miners' wives. At the head of each procession rode a woman in a Madonna-blue cloak on a white horse.[43]

The Guild House banner proclaimed "Better is wisdom than weapons of war".

Charles Stimson

The increasing acceptability of "fashionable" pacifism after 1918 was of no comfort to Charles Stimson; he regarded it as little more than an expression of war-weariness, combined with a middle-class desire for social stability when faced with possible unrest by the workers. In 1920, he and his friend Tom Pickering set out on a second preaching tour without using money to support themselves. After about three weeks they were preaching in the open air outside Leeds Town Hall where they met Jack Harrison and Stanley Creed of the Brotherhood Church, regular preachers at that site.[44] At the end of the preaching tour, Pickering returned to Sheffield and Stimson moved in to the Brotherhood Church.[45] The *Brotherhood* started as a Christian socialist newsletter distributed by a Nonconformist minister, J. Bruce Wallace, from Limavady, Ireland, in 1887.[46] It was just the sort of Christian pacifist anarchist movement Stimson was looking for. Despite its diverse spiritual origins, its rootedness in Tolstoy and the Sermon on the Mount coincided exactly with Stimson's own position. From February 1921 the Brotherhood Church in Leeds expanded to include a farm at Stapleton, Pontefract, where Stimson was based for a time, before becoming parish priest of the tough, Anglo-Catholic parish of St Wilfrid, Newcastle.[47] He took with him three companions from Stapleton, two of whom, Ernest Elworthy (a market gardener) and Leonard Ames (a Ruskin College student) would be with him through the next phase of his life.

Predictably, Diocesan officials were soon unhappy at Stimson's activities and not least because he refused to take the Canonical Oath of Obedience. The Bishop of Newcastle took the dispute to Canterbury, only to be surprised when Lang, recalling his own discussions with Stimson in 1912, came down fully on the side of the radical priest, and produced a special licence which did not require any oath from Stimson. Static parish ministry was never going to be Stimson's taste, however, and he longed to be part of a movement that would still be very much a part of the church, yet with such a radical lifestyle and prophetic message for society that a compromised Church of England could never produce. His solution was to mirror the path taken by George Pilkington, a non-Anglican former Captain of the Corps of Royal Engineers, in the 1830s. Influenced by the Peace Society, but not speaking on their behalf, as there was a suspicion that they were not confident of his reliability, Pilkington travelled the country preaching the unlawfulness of war, and refusing financial collections.[48] On one occasion he had refused to accept money in Pontefract.[49]

On St Francis's Day, 1926, the 700th anniversary of the saint's death, having been inspired by a commemoration service in Newcastle Cathedral, Stimson drew up a rule of life for what was soon to be called the Brotherhood of the Way. The Preamble read:

> It is the conviction of this Brotherhood that the Sermon on the Mount, and similar ethical principles taught by our Lord, are to be regarded as amongst the fundamentals of the Faith. . . . Not to nations, states, or political bodies were the promises made and

the grace given, but to the Church. The Pacifist and non-coercive nature of the Christian ethic make it plain that it was intended to be implemented by a voluntary society of believers.[50]

There were to be three "orders". The First Order of Christian Tramp Preachers was to consist of confirmed and communicant members of the Church of England, respecting other denominations but resisting any moves to form a new sect. They were to follow the injunctions given to the Twelve and to the Seventy in the Gospels to carry with them on their journey only the bare necessities. The Second Order of Communities of the Brotherhood, which could be composed of married or single men and women, would seek to give corporate expression to the principles taught by Jesus. Each community would seek to become a centre of Christian influence and propaganda, with its own self-supporting business. "On no account shall they derive an income from interest on loans, or profits from investments". The third order, which was open to non-Anglicans, would be of local support groups.

They shall abstain from war and the making of munitions, from the police force or from serving as civil magistrates, and from usury in all its forms: they shall pray regularly for the work of the Brotherhood and support it in any way they can. They will obey to the best of their ability the commands of the Sermon on the Mount.[51]

C.F. Andrews later told Stimson that Gandhi had been shown the Brotherhood Rule and had been very impressed: "it was the finest rule of life for a group that he had so far come across".[52] On Shrove Tuesday, 1 March 1927, the date they came to regard as their Passover when they came out of Egypt, Charles Stimson, Leonard Ames and Ernest Elworthy, soon to be joined by Tom Pickering, set out "in much fear and trembling" on their exodus from the "unworkable" compromise between Christianity and the existing economic system in an attempt to discover their Promised Land. It was an age of five-year plans, and the Brothers pledged themselves to each other for five years of open-air preaching and the renunciation of both war and capitalism. The Brotherhood was to sustain this "tramp preacher" ministry for twelve years, before transforming into a residential community based, successively, at Pimlico, Wymondley, then Hoxne.

Bernard Walke

An Anglo-Catholic priest in Cornwall also explored ideas of radical post-war community. Bernard Walke's concern was that, "As pacifists we had rejected war as altogether evil and yet we were content to live in a society which was built largely on fear and distrust of our neighbour."[53] Was it possible, he wondered, to build communities of sharing and openness and trust? He invited people from around the country to St Hilary, to explore this further. They decided to pursue plans for the setting up of Chapters of what Walke described as the Brethren of the Common Table.[54] One attempt was made at St George's Bloomsbury, where W.C. Roberts combined "meals shared in the Rectory kitchen" with "informal discussions as to the obligations of Christians living within a capitalistic society".[55]

Rather more progress was made nearby, in one of the less affluent areas of the capital. In March 1921, a press notice was published originating from three F.O.R. women in East London. One was Mary Hughes, daughter of the Victorian Christian Socialist, Tom Hughes; she was later described as "the angel of the East End".[56] The others were Rosa Hobhouse, daughter of the founder of the National Society for the Prevention of Cruelty to Children (Benjamin Waugh) and Muriel Lester, whom Walke had met at an F.O.R. Conference in 1918. They challenged the public to consider their economic lifestyle.

> We know those who cannot obtain adequate clothing, sheets and warm covering, or necessary food for their children and themselves. The poverty we refer to is commonly known as a state of privation or destitution. But we prefer to call this condition of theirs compulsory want, being brought upon them by force of hard circumstance. Our invitation to you is not into this enforced poverty; but into a very glorious alternative, involving a drastic readjustment in your affairs, called Voluntary Poverty.
>
> We invite you into this condition, that the needs of others, whether in our country or abroad, may generously be supplied by the overflowing of your treasure. We do not here wish to encourage the charity of patronage, but rather the large charity of God, which rejoices in richly providing.

After a meeting at Kingsley Hall, Bow, a group started to work together on a rule of life for a religious community in the East End of London, which Walke suggested they should also call the Brethren of the Common Table.[57] Lester's community consisted of "an heiress or two, a curate, a writer, a teacher, a dog-biscuit packer, an out-of-work carpenter, a dock labourer, a young widow on relief and a journeyman printer". Lester described Walke's approach as being based on the economic significance of the communion table (Lester's phrase), where there would be no specially favoured guest, no head or foot of the table, and where Christ would be the unseen Host of all who care to come. Material things would be regarded as God's gifts, not for ownership but for distributing sensibly.[58] The group that was formed believed that "in order to do their part in making the world a better place to live in they must try, with God's help, to share their goods and give themselves as freely as Christ gave and shared".[59]

They met monthly to give an account to each other of their income and expenditure, with members in credit laying their surplus on the table for redistribution to members with most need. Any still surplus was sent to worthy external causes: the election expenses of a Labour candidate, the international welfare work of the newly formed Save the Children Fund, and other causes. The common pool was handled according to the principle that "The only Christian, the only rational basis for the distribution of goods is need". With growing awareness of the requirements of others, the level of expenditure on luxuries declined; Lester's family thought she was mad when, for example, she resisted the temptation to buy herself a pair of gloves because of the inadequate diet of the dock-labourer's family. There is no record of how long the Brethren continued to meet, but Hughes and, to a lesser extent Lester, retained their personal commitment to voluntary poverty.[60] Lester was an Alderman on Poplar Council with Lansbury during the Poplarism revolt, and she hosted Gandhi at Kingsley Hall during his 1931 visit to London.

In Cornwall, Walke brought refugee children from post-war starvation in Austria to become part of the community at St Hilary. In *The Jolly Tinners*, a disused public house opposite his church, he also set up a small centre for delinquent children, run initially by Grace Costin, later Mother Teresa, F.S.J.M., a project that had F.O.R. support.[61] During the Black and Tans' repression in Ireland, Walke and others met to pray before the Blessed Sacrament in a Roman Catholic church in Truro, the local Irish priest and congregation joining with Anglicans, Nonconformists and Quakers to pray for peace. Cardinal Bourne put an end to that gesture of reconciliation.[62]

There were also tin-miners to help, victims of the collapse of the most significant Cornish industry. Walke had several companions in this work, one of whom was Gerard Collier of F.O.R., a parishioner who had once told Bishop Warman of Truro that "You must repent of your share in the war before you can win the world for Christ".[63] Another was Thomas Attlee, whose family had moved to Cornwall to recover from the effects of his imprisonment as a conscientious objector.[64] The plan was for "an order, under the auspices of the church, in which men might work for the glory of God and the good of their fellow-men", living out a voluntary Christian communism, taking over a deserted mine near Scorrier and work it in a way which would both provide employment and "inspire industry with the spirit of giving". Choosing a specially made ring as their emblem, the first group of 34 adopted the name Servants of the Church, and in June 1922 in Redruth Meeting House were sworn in in the presence of the Bishop of Truro and leaders of five other denominations.[65] A second group was later started in Camborne, but the project failed to attract sufficient backing and had to be abandoned.[66]

Walke, like Sheppard, later became more widely known for being a pioneer of religious broadcasting, producing *Bethlehem*, a village nativity play that was "an act of worship rather than a performance", and which became an annual institution on B.B.C. radio.[67]

Dick Sheppard

The Armistice, ironically St Martin's Day, was a time of extraordinary spontaneous rejoicing at St Martin-in-the-Fields, the central London church that had built up a reputation of serving ordinary people, ordinary soldiers. The church was packed for twenty four hours as one congregation after another poured in for simple services of praise and thanksgiving.[68] Sheppard described their emotions and hopes: "We poured out our hearts in gratitude to God, not so much because He had given us the victory, not even because at long last the killing was over, but because there would be no more war".[69]

A League of Nations committee set up in the parish.[70] As Sheppard said, "I am a passionate believer in the League of Nations – not exactly as it is, but as it can become. . . ."[71] He worked with two of the more influential military chaplains, inviting the orator Studdert Kennedy on to the church staff, and advising P.T.B. ("Tubby") Clayton on the setting up of Talbot House for the founding of TocH.[72] He campaigned for four years to have the new statue of the spy Edith Cavell, situated just outside St Martin's, inscribed with her famous dictum, "Patriotism is not enough – I must have no hatred or bitterness for anyone".[73]

Sheppard's national fame was due to his openness to the new medium of radio broadcasting. His "National Call to Righteousness" service on Armistice Day 1923 in Trafalgar Square was the first religious meeting in Trafalgar Square and the first such meeting to be broadcast. Sheppard designed the service to be as acceptable to Nonconformists as to Anglicans. From the following Epiphany, there were weekly broadcasts from St Martin's, despite opposition from conservative quarters; there was an attempt to get Convocation to ban the broadcasting of services altogether, and one critic even complained that a man might listen to a church service in a pub – with his hat on! – the kind of argument more likely to persuade Sheppard than to dissuade him.[74]

As a result of the broadcasts, Sheppard developed a huge national following, to the extent that when he complained that an inappropriate fancy dress ball was being held in the Albert Hall on Armistice Day 1925, the public clamour was so great that the event was cancelled and Sheppard was asked to lead an "In Memory" meeting there instead, attended by the king and queen, that raised more money than the ball would have done.[75] The General Council of the League of Nations Union gave Sheppard a formal resolution of thanks for the stand that he had made.[76] Arthur Ponsonby, whose book *Now Is The Time: An Appeal For Peace* had just been published and who had just launched a Peace Letter campaign inviting signatures from those who would to fight, told Sheppard:

> To have succeeded single handed in substituting a service for an Albert Hall Fancy Dress Ball is an achievement no one in this country could have done but you . . . I feel my campaign is quite unnecessary. A word from you will stop the next war.[77]

Everyone had heard of Dick Sheppard. He had the ear of the people in a way that no other priest or bishop had. As Ponsonby had suggested, were Sheppard to become a pacifist, then the people would take notice.

The first sign that he was seriously considering this came in 1926, during a period when the asthmatic Sheppard was convalescing between appointments.[78] Inspired by Maude Royden, he started to write a radical manifesto for reforming the Church of England, *The Impatience of a Parson*, which was published the following year. In August 1926 he told Laurence Housman what he was trying to achieve: "I am going out and out for pacifism, disestablishment, the removal of every barrier between sect and sect. . . . " In another short letter to Housman, in February 1927, Sheppard admitted for the first time, "I cannot but identify myself with pacifism, for I am a pacifist and am not prepared to pretend I am anything else."[79] The following week he wrote in more depth, revealing the mind of a man whose thinking was on the move, away from old certainties, towards a new world view: "I believe that a fresh edition of Christianity, with the teaching of the Sermon on the Mount as its creed, is years overdue". He admitted to Housman,

> I myself, am now a pacifist and do not think a Christian can take part in any work of killing or propagating lies, or stirring up passion to kill, or doing anything that he cannot believe that Christ would have done; or for which he cannot ask a blessing 'for Jesus Christ's sake'.[80]

The Impatience of a Parson was published the following October. It expressed Sheppard's dissatisfaction with the Church of England, a too comfortable church, a quiet, devotional society, content to be the upholder of an improper, unjust status quo. Sheppard launched into criticism of its theology, its assumptions, its practice, its sycophantic links with the State, its superior attitude towards other denominations, the way it preached (or did not preach) the Gospel, all of which, he said, revealed a church that had lost its way and which needed change. There was an irony in a comfortable church, preaching a sentimental Jesus, yet which upheld State violence.

We falsify Jesus by too much use of the word gentle, forgetting that much of His teaching was shouted in the teeth of a mob brandishing stones and howling for his life. There was only one weapon that Christ condescended to use – that weapon was love.[81]

New vision was required, and the courage to live that out: "It is far easier to accept the dogmas of Christianity than its ethics".[82] That included the ethics of the "purely bestial and devilish affair" that was war.

> We cannot any more think of war as anything but a damnable arrest of development and decency; it is not only the willingness to suffer agony, it is the willingness to inflict it. War cannot be reconciled with Christianity: there is no such thing as a Christian war. . . .[83]
>
> If war broke out again to-morrow, the Churches would be just where they were in August 1914. They still have no mind on the subject. The Christian Institution should not leave outside organisations like C.O.P.E.C. to do its thinking for it. It should wage a great campaign to end all war before the rumblings of a fresh war are heard on the horizon, and it should wage that campaign solely and simply because Jesus Christ cannot be identified with the bestial brutalities that war produces at the Home Base as well as at the Front.[84]

In a specimen resolution for the next Lambeth Conference, Sheppard suggested that the Anglican Communion should be "obliged to outlaw all war and to demand from its members that they should refuse to kill their brethren".[85]

Senior figures in the Church, not surprisingly, immediately distanced themselves from Sheppard's proposals. The popular press was largely supportive, but a wave of ecclesiastical criticism was directed towards him, including a damning review in the *Times*. Maude Royden commented that "My only consolation is that it is exactly what the *Times* would have written about St Francis". She was a staunch supporter; "I would rather be a door-keeper in the house of Dick Sheppard than dwell in Lambeth Palace", she said, and at the Guildhouse readings from Sheppard even replaced the second lesson.[86]

Sheppard's journey towards pacifism had not been straightforward, partly because he was not drawn to the unattractive, uncompromising harshness of some conscientious objectors and partly because of the high esteem in which he held the common soldier. It was the latter which had drawn him to rejection of war, as he revealed in an Armistice Day broadcast to the nation within days of the publication of *The Impatience of a Parson*. He expressed thankfulness and respect for those who had given so much:

In years to come it will be the glorious task of historians to tell the story of how war was finally abolished from the face of the earth. Surely we are right to think that the ten million who gave their lives in the late War will be thought of and sung of as martyrs, who opened the spiritual eyes of the world and showed by their sacrifice the impossibility of reconciling war either to Christianity or to the best interests of mankind. To me it seems a blasphemy even to suggest that one single life that was laid down was given in vain.

Recognising the popular disillusionment with the quality of the peace, Sheppard believed that those who had passed on would still want those who survived to build a world fit for heroes. He imagined them saying:

Don't bother overmuch about singing our praises; don't set too much store on those granite memorials, they mean little and they signify little to us; but claim for every child adequate education, physical, mental, and spiritual; the decencies of home life; green places in which to play; and reasonable security against standing all the day idle in the market-place when schooldays are over because no man hath hired him. And, as you remember our death in war, see to it, oh, see to it for Christ's sake, that that hell never happens again.[87]

Despite expressing such sentiments in his preaching and his writing, Sheppard was not to speak on a pacifist platform until he appeared at the Albert Hall at Armisticetide 1931. When, in March 1929, Housman proposed a tour of the country to preach pacifism, Sheppard replied, "I am a trifle reluctant to make pacifism my only love".[88] That was to come some five years later. Sheppard had started the journey that would lead to his name being inseparable from the cause of pacifism not only in the Church of England but throughout the country.

13.
Reflection on the Legacy of
1914-1918 War Resistance

The issues did not end on 11 November 1918 and in many ways they are still with us.

Conscientious Objection

The reverberations of the stand of Britain's first conscientious objectors are still being felt around the globe. Lloyd George may have felt he was being uniquely tolerant, beyond the expectations of any other nation, by allowing for the possibility of objection to military service on grounds of conscience. However, his inability fully to comprehend the diverse nature of objections led to brutalities of enforcement that became a cause of national shame and repentance in later years, when it became apparent to many that the C.O.s had been right all along. As Clifford Allen told N.C.F. members at their closing National Convention in November 1919:

> We are proud to have broken the power of the military authority. We have witnessed its brutalities. We have seen the cruel degrading of human personality upon which its discipline depends. We have seen how it leads to contemptible forms of punishment – often men are crucified to gun wheels as a means of breaking the human spirit. We have seen how it deprives its victims of that most sacred right, free judgment in right and wrong, how the system makes men hate each other, bully each other, despise each other, till they become so dehumanised that they can be made even to kill their fellow working men at home. We have defeated it; we will defeat it again if conscription should be continued.[1]

As another speaker put it, "You have won a great victory in so far as you have proved that conscience cannot be forcibly suppressed. . . . But the greater part of your work is still to do. War has not ended war. Satan has not cast out Satan. . . . "[2]

There were still some examples of "cat-and-mouse", immediate re-arrest on release from prison, for conscientious objectors in the Second

World War, but following a strong pacifist movement in the 1930s, C.O.s were generally better understood and there were far fewer grounds for complaint in the treatment they received. In the U.K., conscription itself has been consigned to the dustbin of history. There has now been no attempt to reintroduce it for over half a century.

Could it only have happened in Britain, with its history of religious dissent, the – sometimes reluctant – toleration by the State of dissent, and a growing political awareness as universal education, male (until 1918) suffrage and the rise of socialism all made their mark on society? But these factors were mirrored elsewhere, and the values carried into societies which may or may not have welcomed them. The case for recognition of conscientious objectors spread rapidly after 1918. A Government bill permitting alternatives to military service was introduced in Finland, and in France in 1924 there was a proposal to form a society for the legal recognition of conscientious objectors. In Switzerland, 40,000 people signed a petition demanding alternatives to military service; in 1925 a Union of Anti-Militarist Clergymen was formed there which the following year issued an international Anti-Conscription Manifesto, promoted by seventy distinguished signatories including C.F. Andrews, Gandhi, and Tagore, as well as some less notably religious figures such as Norman Angell, Albert Einstein, Bertrand Russell and H.G. Wells. The manifesto included the assertion, "It is humiliating to human dignity to compel men against their will . . . to sacrifice their lives or to kill others".[3] It is unclear whether that group had any connection with the founding of the International Union of Anti-Militarist Ministers which took place at an Amsterdam Congress in 1928. There, the assembled anti-militarist clergy issued a declaration to the Christian Churches urging them to consider it a sacred obligation "to protect the refusal of military service from conscientious reason as a Christian attitude against the State".[4]

War Resisters International has consistently pushed for conscientious objection to be a human right, recognised universally in legislation. It has long been a contentious issue in international law, with Article 18 of the International Covenant on Civil and Political Rights being deliberately ambivalent, though a Human Rights Committee ruling of 2006 on the position of Jehovah's Witnesses in South Korea indicated that conscientious objectors should be protected. The resistance to military conscription, started by Lilla Brockway in 1914, is close to receiving worldwide recognition. There is still a long way to go to achieve full implementation, however. Given the number of countries which still enforce military conscription, often without so much as an alternative of civilian national service, this remains a live concern, and the 2006 ruling indicates a human right which is still disregarded in many corners of the world. Issues remain even in nations that have abolished military conscription: there are campaigns to enable individuals to divert to charitable use that proportion of direct taxation designated for military purposes, a possible extrapolation of the right to conscientious objection.

The Peace Movement

The post-war shaping of Sheppard, Lansbury, Raven and Royden was itself preparation for the assembling cast of what would, in the 1930s, be some of the headiest days of the British peace movement. Even those future leaders yet to come to the fore had been deeply affected by their war time experiences, not least the novelist Vera Brittain, whose war-time diaries and reflections, especially *Testament of Youth*, contributed to the popular re-evaluation of the First World War that was taking place in literature and on screen.

As the signatories of the Versailles Treaty reneged on their commitment to disarmament, and as international tension increased, Royden attempted to form a civilian peace army, drawing on a concept first floated in pre-F.O.R. days of late 1914, looking to prevent warfare by interposing civilians between fighting forces. Like many military planners, she was preparing for the last war not the next; the first conflict faced by her volunteers was urban warfare between China and Japan, unsuitable for her purposes for reasons both of travel and tactics. The tactic of interposing has occasionally been used in later ages by other peace groups. Nuclear testing in the pacific was hampered by protest boats deliberately sailing into the test area, and some hopeful groups tried to prevent western war against Iraq in the 1990s by congregating in the desert. Given the increasing disregard of civilian casualties, revealed by the growing proportion of civilian deaths in late-twentieth-century wars and beyond, the opportunities to interpose effectively in the future may become more limited still.

Sheppard became leader of the new national peace movement almost by accident. In October 1934, he somewhat casually issued a plea, in the tradition of Burritt and Ponsonby, for men to send him a postcard saying "We renounce war and never again, directly or indirectly, will we support or sanction another".[5] To his astonishment, he soon received over 100,000 replies. The Sheppard Pledge developed an organisational structure and became the Peace Pledge Union (P.P.U.), a major political force at the time. Like every other political influence of that era, it proved insufficient to prevent war, but not for want of trying. As well as those who signed the Peace Pledge for ethical reasons, there were many for whom the motivation was tactical, to reverse Government policy: if enough people stated that they would refuse to fight, then the Government would realise it could not raise an army and would have to change to a non-military foreign policy. The Conservative Government, however, was wedded to a policy of appeasement, tolerating a strong Germany between Britain and its perceived major threat of the Soviet Union, a catastrophic miscalculation which brought about the very war which had been both feared and predicted for twenty years. There no longer being reason for tactical pacifists to belong to the P.P.U., membership numbers fell and, rather like the N.C.F. before it, the movement's energies were diverted to supporting a new generation of C.O.s.

By then, Sheppard was dead, but he had provided the moral and spiritual leadership that was to be a feature of the British peace movement in all its twentieth-century high points. The next wave, in the late 1950s, saw the launch of the Campaign for Nuclear Disarmament (C.N.D.), during which Canon John Collins, back at St Paul's, provided Anglican leadership. For a second wave of C.N.D. activity, in the 1980s, the baton passed to a Catholic priest, Mgr. Bruce Kent. Whenever the peace movement was at its strongest, there was a distinctive Christian presence among the leadership.

Through Lansbury, the International Fellowship of Reconciliation came as close as anyone to preventing further war. I.F.O.R. set up Embassies of Reconciliation, including ambassadors who would argue that the only chance of addressing the causes of likely future war would be a renegotiation of the Versailles Treaty, especially those clauses deemed to be the most punitive. That route just possibly might have provided an economic and diplomatic escape from a path that otherwise seemed to be leading inexorably towards military confrontation. Lansbury, through the Embassies of Reconciliation, consulted with Presidents and Prime Ministers in the U.S.A., France, Belgium, Norway, Sweden, Denmark, Austria, Poland, and Czechoslovakia. In 1937, Lansbury even managed to speak with Hitler. They could not be further apart, and Lansbury was under no illusions about the nature of the man he was meeting:

> I went to Herr Hitler knowing that were I a German citizen or a Jew I would not be allowed to say even in private the things he patiently listened to from me. . . . He did not attempt to deny the suppression of Jews and Bolsheviks. . . . . Again and again as I listened to him I imagined myself listening to speeches that I had heard in our House of Commons defending concentration camps in South Africa and the actions of the Black and Tans in Ireland.[6]

The official statement after their meeting announced that:

> Germany will be very willing to attend a conference and take part in a united effort to establish economic co-operation and mutual understanding between the nations of the world if President Roosevelt or the head of another great country will take the lead in calling such a conference.[7]

That was more than any official diplomacy had achieved, and provided a glimmer of a way forward. But the heads of great countries were not interested and the moment passed.

The vindicated peace movement of 1914-1918 reached its peak in the late 1930s. Many post-1945 histories, perhaps conflating the very different policies of pacifism and appeasement, somehow blame the peace movement for the outbreak of war in 1939. In fact, pacifist civil society came closer to preventing that war than any government channel.

The Churches

Until his death in 1964, Charles Raven would be the leading pacifist academic, intellectual and theologian. He became Regius Professor of Divinity at Cambridge in 1932, and Chair of F.O.R. the following year. The international drive towards Christian unity continued to flourish, partly thanks to George Bell who would soon become even better known for his attempts to stop Britain's obliteration bombing of German civilians. Raven engaged strongly with the "Life and Work" side of the ecumenical movement, not least in its Oxford Conference of 1937 (also attended by Katharine Pierce, soon to become one of the founders of the Episcopal Pacifist Fellowship in the United States).[8] Another, unofficial, American attendee was Reinhold Niebuhr: Raven was appalled by his book *Moral Man and Immoral Society*, "as true only of the herd and not of the fellowship, and as flatly irreconcilable alike with our faith in the church and our experience of the *koinonia*".[9] Some of Raven's best thinking went into his preparations and reflections on this conference, a study of war and peace based around the persons of the Trinity. His conclusions were urgent and all-embracing: "When some great cause, the abolition of slavery or of war, challenged a generation, then the opportunity must be seized, or we are guilty of treason against God".[10] The great cause was a pacifism which, he said,

> is not to be identified with a negative abstentionist policy, but involves a re-examination of the social, economic, and political orders in the light of Christianity as well as a ministry of reconciliation and of evangelism; that, although the concrete problem of war may rightly be made the subject of concentrated and immediate attention, pacifism is only one aspect of Christianity and involves a way of life affecting all relationships; and that the Church, while wholly repudiating war, should press upon its members the duty of constructive peacemaking by giving active support to such movements as seek to remove the causes of strife, or by initiating proposals more drastic than those which non-Christian statesmen think practicable.[11]

For a century, the Peace Society was inter-denominational, as was, even more strongly, the F.O.R. On the one hand, the peace movement was ecumenical, and on the other, the ecumenical movement was itself seen as a peacemaking enterprise, and the development of international ecumenical structures was regarded as one way to build significant international relationships. For all its shortcomings, the World Alliance played an early part, and the personal contributions to ecumenism of both Nathan Söderblom and John Mott earned each of them a Nobel Peace Prize, in 1930 and 1946 respectively.

The Church of England

Reference has already been made to the resolutions on war and peace emanating from the 1930 Lambeth Conference. The influence of these resolutions for the rest of the century cannot be too highly stated, and it is a matter of regret that the most recent Lambeth Conferences have not had the courage to reiterate the 1930 formula. Largely due to Bell's influence and his ecumenical and historical awareness, the Conference, in its Resolution 25, approved the statement that "War, as a method of settling international disputes, is incompatible with the teaching and example of Our Lord Jesus Christ". There were other statements, attempts to wriggle out of the clear meaning of that resolution, but that was the form that lasted, the words that indicated that war resistance was not a tolerated minority vocation for a few but, as in patristic times, at the very heart of Christian identity. That was the form that proved the extent to which the peacemakers had subverted the church. For all its slowly declining authority, exacerbated in part by its response to the war of 1914-1918, the Church of England was still regarded as a significant arm of the state, and the Lambeth formula was latched upon far and wide. Even Quaker wayside pulpits displayed posters announcing the Lambeth text to those who passed by Friends' Meeting Houses.

Sheppard, Lansbury, Royden, Raven and Brittain were all, to greater or lesser extent, linked with a specifically Anglican group, formed in 1937. Thanks largely to the behind-the-scenes efforts of Paul Gliddon, Ursula and W.C. Roberts, and others, the Anglican Pacifist Fellowship (A.P.F.) brought together several thousand pacifists in the Church of England, many of whom have been mentioned above including, *inter alia*, Grace Costin (Mother Teresa), Evelyn Underhill, Father Andrew, Sybil Thorndike, and Ernest Elworthy. In the Second World War there were more Anglican conscientious objectors than during 1916-1918, and A.P.F. not only offered support but also helped to run its own alternative service provision, in a homeless project under Hungerford Bridge in London. By engaging directly with church structures, A.P.F. continued the subversive role of Anglican pacifism. The potential for such subversion to impact on the State was seen in the non-pacifist but anti-nuclear *Church and the Bomb* report of 1982,[12] where Church of England structures came close to condemning the entire nuclear weapons strategy of the British Government.

Peace

The human cost of war in 1914-1918 was, literally, incalculable. 700,000 British young men were killed and at least as many again seriously wounded, many permanently. That was part of a British Empire total of over 1,000,000 military deaths, itself part of a wider *Entente* allies' list of military fatalities that could stretch to 5,000,000 names, depending on the unknown scale of Russian casualties, with maybe double that number wounded; not to mention civilian casualties, including victims of famine, running into seven figures. And that is only one "side". Add the Central Powers – Germany, its colonies and allies – and there is a guesstimate of maybe an additional 4,000,000 military deaths, double that for military wounded, and another 3,000,000 civilian fatalities. The numbers are debatable, with many leaving no trace of the manner of their passing, with records perishing alongside those to whom they referred, with peripheral conflicts and even Spanish flu pushing numbers up or down depending on what is included or excluded. And what about the estimated third of a million people who died of war-related famine in East Africa? What about the unrecorded violence – the mental breakdowns, domestic violence and rapes that inevitably follow the brutalising identified by Samuel Barnett in a previous war?[13]

What was the point of it all, exactly? Was it all a huge mistake, "the greatest *error* of modern history"?[14] Was it, as one Conservative minister has called it, "The greatest disaster of the 20th century".[15] Or was it the honourable upholding of treaties, reinforced by the immediate need to come to the aid of the weak and oppressed, upholding decent values against an overbearing militarism; a liberal intervention? Was it, in short, well-meaning good people motivated to do good things and getting it wrong?

Or, perhaps most terrifying of all, was it both?

Was the First World War the kindness that killed and killed and killed?

If so, it was that era's version of liberal interventionism that brought about such a catastrophe. A century on, it's still liberal interventionism that plagues the international stage, the tempting desire to "do something", to attempt to use violence to overcome violence, that breeds future threats and still kills people in the armed forces with families and nation asking "Why?" The tolerance of war itself is the error, the mistake. As Clifford Allen realised, given the inevitable tide of warlike passions it is simply not possible to wait for conflict to arise, hoping then disinterestedly to

> weigh up the comparative justice of each successive war. That method will never compel our statesmen to put real zeal into framing policies which will preserve peace. They must have a defined conviction that war is fundamentally wrong because it

places men in an immoral relationship to each other. Then and then only will the will to peace really inspire our foreign policy.[16]

Unless and until war is renounced as a means of national policy, then the well-meaning will continue to kill and be killed, again and again.[17]

Even the established Church of England could take a lead in proclaiming the end of war, after all, it does have the historic resources in a Lambeth 1930 resolution. Many of the 1916-1918 conscientious objectors opposed not only the one war, but all war, and they suffered for their insight. Their pacifism was no soft option, but a hard realism. Their arguments are as valid today as they ever were. "Never again" is still possible, but only with a common will.

The goal of peace is a hope, a vision that has inspired millions of people throughout human history. However, the insight of Jesus, with his "Blessed are the peacemakers" (Matthew 5.9), is that the methods of the journey are at least as important as the goal. The end alone cannot justify the means because the means one chooses become the end one achieves. It is as if peace becomes a verb as much as a noun. The methods used *are* the goal; peace is a state of becoming. Christianity was first called "The Way". As Gandhi, who knew Christian scriptures better than many Christians, realized, the issue is not about the most appropriate way to peace, for peace itself is the way.[18] What one sows is what one reaps; war cannot cast out war. Those who wage war create a society where it is assumed at all levels that the most forceful, heavily armed, brutal group will have power and will get their own way. A society or an international order built on violence will itself be inherently violent. The pacifist would argue that only a society built by nonviolent means would stand any chance of producing the nonviolent peace to which its population would aspire. A Christian pacifist would base that approach firmly on the prayer and practice, the teaching and example of Christ.

One argument that can be made for Christian war resistance is eschatological, acknowledging that a divine, eternal timescale can produce a broader perspective than that available in the heat of the moment. What can seem a clear case for military action at the time, the righting of a manifest wrong, can seem more complex and compromised with the passing of time and, it may be admitted, the benefit of hindsight. Unthinking cries of "do something" have led to numerous hasty military interventions in recent times, when wisdom was with the war resisters. Future generations looking back on 1914-1918 can see how, in a highly charged society, an apparently unpatriotic and eccentric anti-war minority was not only vindicated, but was changing national attitudes towards conscription and war for ever. They were not only subversive, they were right.

Endnotes

Preface

1. E.g. Biggar, Nigel, *In Defence of War*.
2. So Martin Ceadel, probably the foremost historian of British peace movements, analyses their strengths and weaknesses from the perspective of an internationalist (or "defencist" – see Ceadel, Martin, "The Peace Movement: Overview of a British Brand Leader", *International Affairs*, 90.2 (2014), p. 351), whose inclination is to view peace activists as shallow and misguided.

1. Introduction: The Nature of the Church of England

1. Neill, Stephen, *Anglicanism*, p. 83.
2. Article Thirty-Seven in this form is an expression of the relationship between civil power, military power and the church. Where relationships differ, the form of the Article differs. Article Thirty-Seven of the protestant Episcopal Church in the United States refers simply to the authority of the civil magistrate in temporal affairs, without any reference to wearing weapons or going to war.
3. Platten, Stephen, *Augustine's Legacy*, p. 28.
4. Hooker, Richard, *Of the Laws of Ecclesiastical Polity*, Book 8.
5. Sykes, Stephen, "The Genius of Anglicanism", in Rowell, Geoffrey, ed., *The English Religious Tradition and the Genius of Anglicanism*, p. 234.
6. Avis, Paul, *The Anglican Understanding of the Church*, 2nd edition, p. 26.
7. Throughout this volume, outside of quotations, "men" will always mean "males". In many historical quotations, however, the usage is intended to convey the meaning "women and men".
8. Rogers, Thomas, *The Catholic Doctrine of the Church of England: an exposition of the Thirty-nine articles*, 1607; Perowne, J.J.S., ed., pp. 350-2.
9. This historical tradition will be considered later, with regard to the First World War.
10. Cited in Hartill, Percy, *Article XXXVII and War*, p. 12. In summer 1939, Hartill attempted to get a motion debated in the Lower House of the Convocation

of Canterbury asking for a declaration "that the English text of the Article should be interpreted in the light of the Latin text, as referring only to 'just wars' (*justa bella*)" and for a committee to be appointed to consider what was meant by "just wars". There was insufficient time for the issue to be debated on that occasion and by the next session, in January 1940, it was decided to adjourn the debate until the close of the Second World War.

11. An Act of Parliament in 1571 only required from the clergy assent to those articles which concerned the true Christian faith and the doctrine of the Sacraments. This was extended by a canon of 1604 which demanded subscription to all the articles. In 1865, convocations with royal assent modified the form of subscription so that assent was once more to the doctrine of the Church of England – echoes of the Elizabethan form – as set forth in the articles, rather than to the articles themselves. Thus clergy from that time could give assent to the general sense of the articles, without regarding each one as being agreeable to the Word of God.

12. *Reconciliation*, April 1937, p. 89. There was also treatment of Article Thirty-Seven in Silverwood, W.J., "War and the Church: Is the 37th Article of Religion Orthodox?", *Reconciliation*, November 1936, pp. 297-9.

13. Sulpitus Severus, *Vita Martini*, 4. "Christi ego miles sum: pugnare mihi non licet".

14. Law was not the last member of the Church of England to take the path from mystical spirituality to pacifism, being followed by Evelyn Underhill nearly 300 years later. Stephen Hobhouse, a First World War conscientious objector, reported that Underhill was among those who regarded Law "as quite the greatest English prose mystic, at least since those of the 14th century". Martensen and Hobhouse, *Jacob Boehme*, p. xii.

15. Flower, in a Preface dated 10 December 1798, commented on Law's *Reflections on War*: "If they have had the same effect on others as they have had on myself, they will lead to the most serious reflections on the present awful degeneracy of the christian world, and to the melancholy conclusion, that however christian nations and churches may be distinguished, or whatever may be the professions of their respective members, they have yet made but little progress in the spirit of christianity, and that, to adopt the emphatic language of our Author – THEY ALL WANT ONE AND THE SAME ENTIRE REFORMATION".

16. Law, William, *An Humble, Earnest and Affectionate address to the Clergy*, pp. 84-5.

17. Ceadel, Martin, *Origins of War Prevention*, p. 167.

18. Williams, John H., *War, the Stumbling-block*, p. 13.

19. Scott's denominational allegiance at the time of writing is unclear, but at least shortly beforehand he had followed various evangelical, mainly Anglican, clergy of Calvinist persuasion. He later moved through Calvinistic Methodism to a more Congregational position. In 1827 the Peace Society described him as Baptist; see Ceadel, Martin, *Origins of War Prevention*, pp. 171-2.

20. Scott, J., *War Inconsistent with the Doctrine and Example of Jesus Christ*, pp. 4-5, reprinted as Tract II of the Society for the Promotion of Permanent and Universal Peace, 1820.

21. Clarkson was one of seventeen eminent foreigners awarded honorary French citizenship by the French Assembly in August 1792. One of the others was Jeremy Bentham who, three years earlier, had proposed a Pacific or Philharmonic Society, on similar lines to the future Peace Society.
22. Wilberforce opposed war in 1794-95, but otherwise opposed pacifism.
23. Clarkson, Thomas, *An Essay on the Doctrines and Practice of the Early Christians as they Relate to War*, p. 24.
24. Rules of the Society.
25. Ceadel, Martin, *Origins of War Prevention*, p. 277.
26. Sixth Annual Report, 1822, p. 6; Seventh Annual Report, 1823, p. 6.
27. Ceadel, Martin, *Origins of War Prevention*, pp. 300-1.
28. Liddington, Jill, *The Long Road to Greenham*, p. 15. Two hundred Olive Leaf women attended the national Peace Convention in Manchester in January 1853 (Ceadel, Martin, *Origins of War Prevention*, p. 496).
29. Elihu Burritt's journal, 21 August 1849, at the start of the 1849 Paris Peace Congress refers to the marching soldiers at the railway station seeming to "tread timidly among the Quakeresses, and the busy crowd of peace men and women as if half ashamed of their muskets" (*The Advocate of Peace*, Vol. 66, No. 8, August 1904, pp. 149-50). [http://www.jstor.org/stable/25752366. Accessed 31 July 2013].
30. *Protection of Commerce* (1836); *Political Writings of Richard Cobden*, pp. 245-6.
31. Ceadel, Martin, *The Origins of War Prevention*, pp. 470-1.
32. Minutes of the Leeds Peace Association, Carlton Hill papers, Quaker Collection, Leeds University.
33. *Herald of Peace*, 1856, p. 71, cited in Ceadel, Martin, *Semi-Detached Idealists*, p. 69.
34. The Representation of the People Acts, 1867 and 1884, led to around 60% of adults males getting the right to vote.
35. Cremer was to be the first Briton to win a Nobel Peace Prize, in 1903.
36. Similarly, in sarcastic tone: "When we find the Prelates of the Established Church presumptuously assuming the countenance of the Deity in our bloody work in the Soudan; to their asseverations "this is the Lord's doing", we may well respond: "and it is marvellous in our eyes" (*Arbitrator*, no. 157/158, February/March 1885, pp. 1, 6).
37. *Herald of Peace*, March 1872, p. 30; January 1873, p. 179; cited in Ceadel, Martin, *Semi-Detached Idealists*, p. 95. International arbitration had a rocky start from a British perspective as one of the first decisions made in Geneva in 1872, over the behaviour of the vessel *Alabama*, found against Britain and in favour of the United States.
38. *Concord*, June 1900, p. 81.
39. *Herald of Peace*, 1 June 1895, p. 209.
40. *Arbitrator*, October/November 1896, p. 91.
41. *Echo*, cited in *Herald of Peace*, 1 March 1890, p. 40.
42. *Arbitrator*, no. 209/210, July/August 1889, p. 3. The *Herald of Peace* quoted a similar phrase from *The Echo*: "The anti-war movement, recently started by Canon Westcott and other representative divines of various churches, has already had the effect of leading several religious bodies to pass resolutions in favour of International Arbitration". The *Herald of Peace* wanted more,

however, asking, "Why do not the whole bench of Bishops take up the matter?" (*Herald of Peace*, 1 March 1890, p. 40).

43. 12 July 1892, printed in *Concord*, 16 August 1892, p. 154. An English translation of von Suttner's work was published in 1892. Von Suttner was responsible not only for suggesting to Alfred Nobel that he might initiate his famous peace prize, but also for persuading Tsar Nicholas II to call together the 1st Hague Conference of 1899. Even the idea of a United States of Europe, promoted by Victor Hugo at the International Peace Congress in Paris in 1849, was gaining ground, as a preparation for the general reduction of armaments. The idea was supported, for example, by Holman Hunt in the *Pall Mall Gazette* (cited in *Herald of Peace*, 11 December 1891, p. 330).

44. *Herald of Peace*, 2 July 1894, p. 81. Two years later the Archbishops of Canterbury and York refused to sign a similar petition (*Herald of Peace*, 1 April 1896, pp. 46-7).

45. *Herald of Peace*, 1 October 1904, p. 276.

46. The other secretary was William Evans Darby (1844-1922), secretary of the Peace Society.

47. *Herald of Peace*, 1 February 1890, p. 14-16.

48. 2 December 1894, printed in *Arbitrator*, January 1895, p. 7.

49. *Herald of Peace*, 1 February 1897, p. 199.

50. Lambeth Conferences are roughly decennial gatherings of Anglican bishops from around the world. The first was in 1867.

51. Annual Report of the Peace Society, 1897-1898, p. 13.

52. Cited in *Herald of Peace*, 1 October 1897, p. 303.

53. *Herald of Peace*, 1 November 1897.

54. Cuthbertson, Greg, "Pricking the 'nonconformist conscience'; religions against the South African War" in Lowry, Donal, ed., *The South African War Reappraised*, p. 170.

55. Bishop of Hereford to Lord Salisbury, 7 September 1899. Salisbury Papers, class H. Cited by Blunden, Margaret, "The Anglican Church during the War", in Warwick, Peter, ed., *The South African War: the Anglo-Boer War 1899-1902*. p. 279.

56. Porter, Bernard, "The Pro-Boers in Britain", in Warwick, Peter, ed., *The South African War: the Anglo-Boer War 1899-1902*. p. 247.

57. From the Pearce Register, of which more later. Hodgson, a 33-year-old Nottingham tobacconist in 1916, spent over two years in prison, much of the time undergoing hard labour, for his refusal to join the army.

58. Blunden, Margaret, "The Anglican Church during the War", in Warwick, Peter, ed., *The South African War: the Anglo-Boer War 1899-1902*, p. 280; Cuthbertson, Greg, "Pricking the 'nonconformist conscience'; religions against the South African War" in Lowry, Donal, ed., *The South African War Reappraised*, p. 172.

59. Allen, Mark, "Winchester, the Clergy and the Boer War", in Parker, S. G., and Tom Lawson, *God and War*, p. 20.

60. Allen, Mark, "Winchester, the Clergy and the Boer War", pp. 24-5.

61. Allen, Mark, "Winchester, the Clergy and the Boer War", pp. 25-6.

62. Allen, Mark, "Winchester, the Clergy and the Boer War", p. 24.

63. Cited by Porter, Bernard, "The Pro-Boers in Britain", in Warwick, Peter, ed. *The South African War: the Anglo-Boer War 1899-1902*, p. 248.

64. Cuthbertson, Greg, "Pricking the 'nonconformist conscience'; religions against the South African War" in Lowry, Donal, ed., *The South African War Reappraised*, p. 173.

65. Munson, J., "The Nonconformists: In Search of a Lost Culture", London, 1991, p.234; cited in Cuthbertson, Greg, "Pricking the 'nonconformist conscience'; religions against the South African War" in Lowry, Donal ed., *The South African War Reappraised*, p. 171.

66. The meeting was chaired by the Rector, G.S. De Sausmarez, and also addressed by another Anglican cleric, W. Paton Hindley. As a result of the meeting, a local Peace Committee was set up (*Herald of Peace*, 1 February 1901).

67. *Herald of Peace*, 1 October 1901, pp. 126-7. He used similar illustrations in a speech two years later, at a "Great Meeting in Queen's Hall" (*Herald of Peace*, 1 January 1904, p. 169).

68. *Herald of Peace*, 1 January 1902, p. 181.

69. *Herald of Peace*, 1 September 1899, p. 274, and 1 June 1900, p. 72.

70. *Herald of Peace*, 1 June 1900, pp. 72-4.

71. Annual Meeting of the Peace Society, 21 May 1901. *Herald of Peace*, 1 June 1901, pp. 77-8.

72. *Herald of Peace*, 2 December 1895, p. 308.

73. Fowler, J.H., ed., *The Life and Letters of Edward Lee Hicks*, p. 118.

74. *Herald of Peace*, 1 February 1902, p. 185.

75. Hampshire Chronicle, 3 February 1900, p. 7. Cited in Allen, Mark, "Winchester, the Clergy and the Boer War", p. 24.

76. *Herald of Peace*, 2 April 1900, p. 47.

77. *Herald of Peace*, 1 June 1904, p. 231.

78. *The Dean of Durham on the War* (Peace Society pamphlet), p. 2.

79. *Peace Year Book, 1911*, National Peace Council, p. 204.

80. *Herald of Peace*, 2 April 1900.

81. Scott Holland, Henry, *A Bundle of Memories*, p. 94. Scott Holland and F.W. Cobb, Rector of St Ethelburga, Bishopsgate Within, made written and spoken contributions, conciliatory but cautious, to the Annual Meeting of the Peace Society, May 1902 (*Herald of Peace*, 2 June 1902, pp. 248-50).

82. The suggestion that the well-educated should live amongst the poor could be traced back to the example of Edward Denison, in 1864. John Ruskin also flirted with the idea. Barnett, however, with his wife Henrietta, was the prime mover, when, as incumbent of the parish of St Jude, Whitechapel from 1878, he considered a variety of education schemes with Arnold Toynbee and other colleagues. Barnett lectured on "Settlements of University Men in Great Towns" in 1883, arguing that "Knowledge, ideas, books, friends, joy . . . are the things which we must share with our brothers". He was the founder and warden of Toynbee Hall, which was regarded as the principal settlement, even though it opened three months after the October 1884 founding of Oxford House, Mape Street, Bethnal Green (Wallis, Jill, *Mother of World Peace*, p. 33). Officially, the aims of Oxford House were "that men may take part in the Social and Religious work of the church in East London; that they may

learn something of the life of the poor; may try to better the conditions of the working classes as regards health and recreation, mental culture, and spiritual teaching; and may offer an example, as far as in them lies, of a simple religious life" (Scott, Carolyn, *Dick Sheppard: A Biography*, p. 30).

83. George Lansbury said the practice of settlements produced bureaucrats and government men who made sure nothing changed the order in which such settlements existed to allow the still rich to be good-hearted to the still poor (Lansbury, Edgar, *George Lansbury, My Father*, p. 159).

84. *Herald of Peace*, 1 June 1899, p. 233.

85. *Herald of Peace,* 1 June 1899, p. 234.

86. *Herald of Peace*, 2 April 1900, pp. 45-6. Barnett was to become a Canon of Westminster in 1906.

87. *Times*, 22 October 1901, cited in Koss, Stephen, *The Pro-Boers*, pp. 228-30.

88. *Concord*, September 1904, p. 135.

89. Wilkinson, Alan, *The Church of England and the First World War*, pp. 24-5. Percival also addressed the 1905 Second National Peace Congress and the 1908 Christian Conference on Peace.

90. Exodus 23.2a.

2. *An Era Ends and a New Pacifism Emerges*

1. Robbins, Keith, *The Abolition of War*, p. 10.

2. *Concord*, April 1905, p. 60.

3. *Arbitrator*, No. 409, June 1913, p. 65.

4. See also the widespread use of "pacificist" by Dick Sheppard and by pacifist correspondents to the *Church Times* in 1935, 1936. Maude Royden (1876-1956) was one who resisted the change of meaning, preferring, in 1917, to return to the pre-war indistinct use of the words. She told the City Temple Executive Committee, "I am more and more convinced that the word 'pacifist' should not be claimed only by those who hold my position, but belongs to all those who hope and work for a time when we shall find some other way of settling international differences than war" (1 July 1917, in Fletcher, Sheila, *Maude Royden: A Life*, pp. 133-4).

5. Taylor is scathing of pacifists, admitting his disregard for peace societies. Taylor, A.J.P., *The Trouble Makers*, p. 51n.

6. The *Biglow Papers* contained poems by the poet Hosea Biglow, the character created by the American poet James Russell Lowell, whose complete works were published in 1897. His perceptive humour was effective in satirising the U.S. invasion of Mexico, 1846-1848. A fuller version of the poem Waldron quoted reads:
   Ez fer war, I call it murder, –
       There you hev it plain an' flat;
   I don't want to go no furder
       Than my Testyment for that;
   God hez sed so plump an' fairly,
       It's ez long ez it is broad,

An' you've got to git up airly
Ef you want to take in God.

'Taint your eppyletts an' feathers
Make the thing a grain more right;
'Taint affollerin' your bellwethers
Will excuse ye in His sight;
Ef you take a sword an' dror it,
An' go stick a feller thru,
Guv'ment ain't to answer for it,
God'll send the bill to you.

7. *Herald of Peace*, 1 July 1902, pp. 265-7, and 1 August 1902, pp. 270-2.
8. That is not to say Tolstoy did not have significant impact on individuals. George Lansbury wrote "I confess that when I first learned about St Francis and his life, and read the teaching of Tolstoi, I wished to live like them" (Lansbury, George, *My Life*, p. 9.)
9. The Second Universal Peace Congress, was in London in 1890, the first having been in Paris in 1889. Other congresses were held in Rome (1891), Berne (1892, also associated with the founding of the Bureau de la Paix), Chicago (1893), Antwerp (1894), Buda Pest (1896), Hamburg (1897), Paris (1900), Glasgow (1901), Monaco (1902), Rouen (1903), Boston (1904), Luzern (1905), Milan (1906), Munich (1907), London (1908), Stockholm (1910), Rome (1911), Geneva (1912) and The Hague (1913). They resumed with the twenty-first Congress being held in Luxembourg in 1922, with meetings most years until Zurich (1939).
10. *Herald of Peace*, 1 August 1902, p. 273.
11. For a full list see *The Advocate of Peace*, Vol. 66, No. 8, August 1904, p. 50. http://www.jstor.org/stable/25752367 [accessed 31 July 2013].
12. Having started in Manchester (1904), future National Peace Congresses took place at Bristol (1905), Birmingham (1906), Scarborough (1907), Cardiff (1909), Leicester (1910), and Edinburgh (1911).
13. The National Peace Council Year Book, 1910. Formal structures were not established until 1908; see Ingram, Kenneth, *Fifty Years of the National Peace Council, 1908-1958*. Among the clergy associated with the National Peace Council, but not otherwise mentioned in the text, were: R.W. Cumming, Owthorne, Withernsea; F.L. Donaldson, St Mark, Leicester; Dean Govett of Gibraltar; John Grundy, St Stephen, South Lambeth; Dundas Harford, Emmanuel, West End; Stewart Headlam, Wavertree, Twickenham; H.W.G. Henrick, Holy Trinity, Hoxton; E.N. Hoare, Oakhill Park, Anfield, Liverpool; E. Grose Hodge, Holy Trinity, Marylebone; Walter Horne, St Saviour, Brixton; A.E. Lait, St Augustine, Bermondsey; Canon Joseph McCormick, St James, Piccadilly; P.W. Sparling, Home, Near Runton, Norfolk; F.D. Vaughan, Emmanuel, Camberwell; Revd Veazey, St Mark, Southeast London; Revd Vine, Lymington; and A.M. Williams, Burtonwood, Newton-le-Willows. There were also two wives of clergy: Mrs Sanders, Rothley, Leicester; and Mrs Vine, Lymington.
14. Resolution 52, cited in Grane, W.L., *The Passing of War*, MacMillan, p. xli.
15. Wilkinson, Alan, *The Church of England and the First World War*, p. 26.

The brother of a liberal politician, Masterman was to become Bishop of Plymouth in 1922. He was not greatly respected by the peace movement of the 1930s.

16. Peace Society Annual Reports: 1909-10, pp. 2-5; 1910-11, pp. 2-5; 1912-13, pp. 2-5. The 1912 Council also included the Rt Revd J.E. Mercer of Hobart.

17. Peace Society Annual Report, 1909-10, pp. 14-15.

18. One of Angell's critics suggested that he had only addressed the question of whether usurers should go to war. Ceadel, Martin, *Living the Great Illusion*, p. 120.

19. Gooch, G.P., *The History of Our Time: 1885-1913*, (London, 1913), pp. 248-9; cited in Gregory, Adrian, *The Last Great War*, p. 9. Another, somewhat sneering, critique suggests that Angell was principally seeking to influence German public opinion, the argument being that Angell was a liberal imperialist editor of Northcliffe's *Continental Daily Mail*, and that his motives were to show specifically that it would be irrational for Germany to attack the British Empire (Ferguson, Niall, *The Pity of War*, p. 22). Hence Angell stating, "[W]hat do you, Germans, hope to get from attacking us?", cited in Ceadel, Martin, *Living the Great Illusion*, p. 109. Unfortunately for Angell, the first German translation of his work was substandard.

20. Grane, W.L., *The Passing of War*, p. 3.

21. Grane, W.L., *The Passing of War*, p. xxxiv. He was quick to point out, however, that such criticism was no reflection on the soldier's calling.

22. Grane, W.L. *The Passing of War*, p. 123.

23. *On War*, bk. i, ch. i, cited in Grane, W.L. *The Passing of War*, pp. 175, 182.

24. Cited in Grane, W.L., *The Passing of War*, p. 158.

25. Grane, W.L., *The Passing of War*, p. 159.

26. Grane believed in "the now practically simultaneous development of ideas in all civilised lands" (*The Passing of War*, third edition, p. 236) which would allow moral education to be worldwide.

27. Note on the American Civil War, in Grane, W.L., *The Passing of War*, p. 297.

28. den Boggende, G.G.J., *The Fellowship of Reconciliation, 1914-1945*, p. 20.

29. Robbins, Keith, *The Abolition of War*, p. 25.

30. den Boggende, G.G.J., p. 22.

31. Playne, Caroline E., *Society at War 1914-1916*, pp. 185, 188. By "clerics" she meant all spiritual leaders, philosophers and opinion-formers.

32. Even the Quakers were divided. Reduced emphasis on the historic peace testimony during the nineteenth century meant that nearly one third of the Society of Friends joined the army in 1914-1918.

33. Thus, a N.P.C. statement in 1915 stressed the need to uphold treaties to preserve a neutral and independent State, a clear reference to Belgium, without actually saying explicitly that Britain was right to be at war. The main thrust of the statement was towards the nature of a post-war peace (*Goodwill*, Vol. 1, No. 1, 1 June 1915, pp. 133-4).

34. *The Advocate of Peace*, Vol. 74, No. 7, July, 1912, p. 164. http://www.jstor.org/stable/20666493. Accessed 31 July 2013.

35. *Herald of Peace*, July 1912. Cited in Robbins, Keith, *The Abolition of War*, p. 13.
36. *Herald of Peace*, October 1917, cited in Robbins, Keith, *The Abolition of War*, p. 134.
37. When specific tasks were required, such as supporting conscientious objectors or campaigning for a negotiated peace, separate umbrella organisations were formed, in these cases the Joint Advisory Committee and, in April 1916, the Peace Negotiations Committee. Dunnico was Secretary of the latter (*Herald*, 15 July 1916), which brought together representatives from the Quakers, I.L.P., Fellowship of Reconciliation, No-Conscription Fellowship, Union of Democratic Control, Women's International League and the Peace Society (Robbins, Keith, *The Abolition of War*, p. 96). Dunnico later became Labour M.P. for Consett, 1922-1931, and was also an Honorary Director and Vice-President of the International Peace Bureau, Geneva (*Peace News*, 16 October 1953, p. 1). He continued as Secretary of the Peace Society until his death, aged 77, in October 1953, by which time the Society, though technically extant, was well and truly defunct, having "not been very active in recent years" (*Peace News*, 16 October 1953, p. 1).
38. National Peace Council Year Book, 1911, p. 92 cited the foundation date as 5 October 1910. The 1912 Year Book cites the foundation date as 4 October 1910.
39. M.H. Huntsman, from Hampstead, had been Assistant Secretary of the National Peace Council since 1907, the editor of *Peace Bibliography*, and had taken an active part in the seventeenth Universal Peace Congress in London (National Peace Council Year Book, 1914, p. 229).
40. Other Vice-Presidents included: the bishops of Oxford (Charles Gore), Hereford (John Percival), Southwark (Hubert Burge), Northern & Central Europe (Herbert Bury), and Kilmore, Elphin & Ardagh (William Richard Moore); the deans of Carlisle (William Barker), Lincoln (Thomas Fry) and Worcester (Moore Ede); Canons Samuel Barnett (Westminster), John W. Horsley (Southwark; he was an authority on British snails!), Joseph McCormick (St James's Piccadilly), J.H.B. Masterman and Hardwicke D. Rawnsley; Prebendaries James Jeakes (St Paul's) and Harmer W. Webb-Peploe; the clergy Walter H. Frere, Thomas.J. Lawrence (an authority on international law) and William Temple; and the laity Henrietta Barnett, Louise Creighton, and Richard Cornthwaite. Lambert, M.P. (National Peace Council Year Book, 1917, p. 54).
41. National Peace Council Year Book, 1912, p. 156. In summer 1914 Johnson visited the editor of the *Manchester Guardian*, C.P. Scott, to see if there was any way of preventing the war (Johnson, Hewlett, *Searching for Light*, p. 51). Johnson "verged on pacifism" (Hughes, Robert, *The Red Dean*, p. 41), and claimed that he was, and always had been "ninety per cent Pacifist" (Johnson, H., p. 57). Johnson was described by Edith Rylie Richards (widow of Leyton Richards) as "also a pacifist but a milder and more benign variety than Leyton" (Richards, E.R., *Private View of a Public Man*, p. 68).
42. Cited in Playne, C.E., *Society at War 1914-1916*, p. 184.
43. den Boggende, G.G.J., p. 18.
44. The Church of England Peace League did, however, make direct appeals to

Anglican conscientious objectors. A membership form was sent to Thomas Briggs when he was incarcerated in Mill Hill Barracks in 1917 (Letter from Walter Hohnrodt to Lester Smith, 26 December 1917, in the Peace Pledge Union archive. I am grateful to William Hetherington for drawing my attention to this.)

45. National Peace Council Annual Report, 1917, pp. 16-7.
46. National Peace Council Annual Report, 1917, p. 4.
47. National Peace Council Year Book, 1921, p. 67.
48. One of the leaders of the World Student Christian Federation, John Mott, chaired the 1910 World Missionary Conference in Edinburgh; he would later (1946) be awarded a Nobel Peace Prize.
49. Wilkinson, Alan, *The Church of England and the First World War*, p. 282.
50. Wilkinson, Alan, *The Church of England and the First World War*, p. 14.
51. Wilkinson, Alan, *The Church of England and the First World War*, p. 52.
52. Other F.O.R. figures linked with the S.C.M. included Cecil John Cadoux (1883-1947, Congregationalist), Richards, Malcolm Spencer (1877-1960) and Lilian Stephenson (1871-1960). She wanted "Militant Pacificists" to form a new group, "something like the Franciscan tertiary Order – i.e. relating to all of life" (den Boggende, G.G.J., p. 72). Later S.C.M./F.O.R. personalities included Kees Boeke (1884-1966), Lucy Gardner (1863-1944), Herbert Gray (1868-1956), Charles Raven (1885-1964), Roger Soltau (1888-1953), Alex Wood (1879-1950), and the Quaker theologian H.G. Wood (1879-1953). At one time the F.O.R. appointed McEwan Lawson, a Congregationalist minister, specifically as its S.C.M. representative (den Boggende, G.G.J., p. 34). Albert D. Belden, Cecil John Cadoux, Lucy Gardner, Herbert Gray, Stephen Hobhouse, Henry Hodgkin, John S. Hoyland, William E. Orchard, Gilbert Porteous, Richard Roberts, Malcolm Spencer and other F.O.R. figures were also involved at one time or another in the Swanwick Free Church Fellowship, founded in 1911, in response to Free Church complacency on social problems (den Boggende, G.G.J., pp. 35-6). A further influential group was the Socialist Quaker Society, founded in 1898, which included amongst its members Corder Catchpool and Alfred and Ada Salter; it held that war was an adjunct of capitalism and that people needed liberation from both (den Boggende, G.G.J., p. 29-31).
53. *Goodwill*, Vol. 1, No. 1, January 1915, p. 3. Also Brittain, Vera, *Rebel Passion*, London, 1964, p. 27. Earlier moves included an Anglo-German Conciliation Committee, for whom Archbishop Davidson expressed support in 1905, and a British Committee for the Study of Municipal Institutions which invited a party of German mayors to visit Britain in 1906. In 1907, some of the Germans were in a Congress delegation received at Buckingham Palace. The British party in 1908 were received by the Kaiser.
54. Brittain, Vera, *Rebel Passion*, pp. 27-8.
55. Wilkinson, Alan, *The Church of England and the First World War*, p. 22.
56. The Archbishop of Canterbury was President and the Archbishop of York a Vice-President (National Peace Council Year Book, 1911, p. 91).
57. Wilkinson, Alan, *The Church of England and the First World War*, p. 23.
58. Cited in Ceadel, Martin, *Living the Great Illusion*, pp. 98-9.
59. Cited in Grane, W.L., pp. 99-100.

60. Robbins, Keith, *The Abolition of War*, p. 18.
61. *Goodwill*, Vol. 1, No. 1, January 1915, p. 4; also Wallis, Jill, *Valiant for Peace*, p. 3.
62. The intention had been to have 153 delegates from twelve nations and representing some thirty-three religious bodies (*Goodwill*, Vol. 1, No. 1, January 1915, p. 4).
63. The station-master at Constance laughed scornfully when he heard that the departing delegates had been part of a Peace Conference (*Goodwill*, Vol. 1, No. 1., January 1915, p. 6).
64. *Goodwill*, Vol. 1, No. 1, January 1915, p. 6.
65. *Goodwill*, Vol. 1, No. 1, January 1915, p. 5.
66. Robbins, *The Abolition of War*, p. 18. *Goodwill*, Vol. 1, No. 1, January 1915, p. 4.
67. *Goodwill*, Vol. 1, No. 1, January 1915, p. 7.
68. *Goodwill*, Vol. 1, No. 1, January 1915, p. 2.
69. *Goodwill*, Vol. 1, No. 1, January 1915, p. 2.
70. *Goodwill*, Vol. 1, No. 1, January 1915, p. 20.
71. *Goodwill*, Vol. 1. No. 6, 29 July 1915, p. 137.
72. Wilkinson, Alan, *The Church of England and the First World War*, p. 199.
73. *Goodwill*, Vol. 3, No. 6, 31 March 1919, pp. 269-70.
74. Though not, apparently, in the same carriage (den Boggende, G.G.J., p. 55).
75. Wallis, Jill, *Valiant for Peace*, p. 4; Brittain, Vera, *Rebel Passion*, p. 30.
76. den Boggende, G.G.J., details the various letters and statements of that time (pp. 55-6). The friendship between the two men contributed to the founding of the International Fellowship of Reconciliation in 1919.
77. Cited in den Boggende, G.G.J., p. 57. 475,000 copies were printed in England and 50,000 in the U.S.A.

3. 1914 – A New Peace Movement

1. *Daily Herald*, 28 July 1914, p. 1.
2. *Daily Herald*, 29 July 1914, p. 5.
3. Bevan, Edwyn, *German Social Democracy During the War*, pp. 8-10.
4. "By far the greatest calamity wrought by the war has been the death of Jaurès, who was worth more to France and to Europe than ten army corps and a hundred Archdukes". Shaw, George Bernard, *Common Sense about the War*, Section 3.
5. *Daily Herald*, 30 July 1914.
6. *Daily Herald*, 1 August 1914.
7. *Daily Herald*, 31 July 1914.
8. Hardie's Independent Labour Party had always been anti-militarist, more likely to advocate a general strike than a violent revolution. Many socialists believed, or at least hoped, that the spread of humanitarian values and international socialist solidarity would be enough to make war impossible; socialist would refuse to kill socialist and there simply would not be enough people willing to fight. The British Section of the International, whose manifesto "DOWN WITH WAR" was signed by Hardie and Arthur

Henderson (1863-1935), urged organised Labour to "hold demonstrations everywhere" (*Herald*, 1 August 1917). The Daily Herald League had originally only called Londoners to the Trafalgar Square rally, and the resolution passed referred to "this mass meeting of London citizens" (*Daily Herald*, 31 July 1914).

9. *Daily Herald*, 1 August 1914. In the same issue, C. Langdon Everard scorned those excited by war: "Here come the troops. Cheer ye patriots! Wave your little flags. Sing your music hall ditties. These men are marching to Death, and you will march bravely with them to the railway station".

10. *Daily Herald*, 3 August 1914. In the same edition Lansbury wrote in more general terms that "It is not this war only against which we make our protest. History brings countless witnesses to the futility of empires built on force. The old truth is to-day more true than ever that they who take the sword perish by the sword". The following day's editorial was couched in religious language, speaking of the workers having a common creed that was not entirely material, but which had a greater, spiritual side, a dream of "a mystic splendour in the knowledge of brotherhood", from which came the assertion: "We need peace; we must have peace; our children will thank us if we make possible the realisation of its promise" (*Daily Herald*, 4 August 1914).

11. *Daily Herald*, 31 July 1914.

12. Jowitt, J.A.,"Bradford and Peace 1800-1918", in Rank, Carol, ed., *City of Peace*.

13. *Daily Herald*, 3 August 1914.

14. *Hull Daily Mail*, 3 August 1914, p. 3; cited in Gregory, Adrian, *The Last Great War*, pp. 20-1.

15. *Cambridge Daily News*, 4 August 1914, p. 4; cited in Gregory, Adrian, p. 21.

16. Groves, R., *Conrad Noel and the Thaxted Movement*, p. 156.

17. *The Bower Chalke Parish Paper*, cited in Gregory, Adrian, p. 21. See also http://history.wiltshire.gov.uk/community/getcom.php?id=23 [Accessed 5 August 2013].

18. Gregory, Adrian, p. 72.

19. Thomas, Anna Braithwaite, *St Stephen's House*, Emergency Committee, London, c.1921, pp. 11-13.

20. Cited in Robbins, Keith, *England, Ireland, Scotland, Wales, The Christian Church 1900-2000*, p. 110.

21. *Goodwill*, Vol. 2, No. 8, 23 June 1917, p. 232.

22. The Chairman was Willoughby Dickinson (Robbins, Keith, *The Abolition of War*, p. 53). Two years later the Archbishop of Canterbury was prepared to speak in Central Hall on its behalf (Robbins, Keith, *The Abolition of War*, p. 131). A second (anti-German) pressure group, the League of Free Nations Association was formed early in 1918. The two merged late in 1918 to form the League of Nations Union. This was to become the most numerically successful of any peace-minded organisation, advocating arbitration and multilateral disarmament. Following the Locarno Treaties, it reached its peak in the late 1920s, when it embraced close on one million supporters (Ceadel, Martin, *Pacifism in Britain, 1914-1945*, pp. 61-2).

23. Robbins, Keith, *The Abolition of War*, pp. 107-9.

24. den Boggende, G.G.J., p. 79; Wallis, J., *Valiant for Peace*, p. 7; Ceadel, M., *Pacifism in Britain, 1914-1945*, p. 61; Robbins, K., *The Abolition of War*, pp. 38-45. There was some overlap of membership; Leyton Richards, for one, was a founder member of the N.C.F. as well as being active in the F.O.R. The Independent Labour Party was also a focus for opposition to the war; Marian Ellis was the F.O.R.'s unofficial representative at the I.L.P. (den Boggende, G.G.J., p. 169).

25. *Daily Herald*, 10 August 1914. Not surprisingly, the editorial commends MacDonald for his stance.

26. Robbins, K., *The Abolition of War*, p. 45.

27. Royden contributed to the U.D.C. anthology, *Towards a Lasting Settlement* (1915). There was not family unanimity on these matters: her brother, Thomas Royden, was Deputy Chairman of the Cunard Line, and was advising the Government on the most efficient way to transport forces and supplies to France.

28. Fenner Brockway acknowledged that it was his wife's idea in "The Story of the N.C.F." in No-Conscription Fellowship, *Troublesome People*, Central Board for Conscientious Objectors, London, 1940, p. 14. Lilla Brockway became the *de facto* secretary of the movement. Many of the N.C.F. branches would be run by women, especially after the introduction of conscription when male N.C.F. members became conscientious objectors. The Pearce Register (C.O. Support section), see below, lists twenty-five N.C.F. branches with female secretaries.

29. Kennedy, Thomas C., *The Hound of Conscience*, p. 43.

30. Hobhouse, Margaret, *I Appeal to Caesar*, p. 19.

31. Graham, John W., *Conscription and Conscience*, 1922, p. 174.

32. Allen, Clifford, "The Faith of the N.C.F." in No-Conscription Fellowship, *Troublesome People*, pp. 5-6.

33. Russell, Bertrand, *Autobiography of Bertrand Russell, Volume II, 1914-1944*, p. 25.

34. Reprinted as Salter, Alfred, "The Religion of a C.O." in No-Conscription Fellowship, *Troublesome People*, pp. 9-13.

35. Graham, John W., p. 45.

36. Graham, John W., pp. 174-5.

37. Brockway, A. Fenner, "The Story of the N.C.F." and Brown, H. Runham, "The Women of the C.O. Movement" in No-Conscription Fellowship, *Troublesome People*, pp. 16, 55-6.

38. Fisher, David, "Just War and The First World War: Where was the Just War Tradition when it was needed? (or how moral theology could have saved the world)", in *Crucible*, Hymns Ancient and Modern, Norwich, April-June 2014, p. 28. Fisher argues after the event, p. 33, that "A just war critique of World War one would have raised the level of ethical debate about the war and lent greater urgency to the quest for alternative strategies and tactics. It could thus have saved many lives". Listening to the pacifists of the time would have done the same.

39. For a Marxist analysis of "just" war changes see Manokha, Ivan, "The History of Modern Military Humanitarianism Revisited" in Durward, Rosemary and Lee Marsden (eds.), *Religion, Conflict and Military Intervention*, pp. 129-46.

40. For "just" war theory and analysis see, *inter alia*: Adeney, Bernard T., *Just*

War, Political Realism, and Faith; Regan, Richard J., *Just War, Principles and Cases*; Zook, Darren C. and Cady Duane L., "Just War", *The International Encyclopedia of Peace*, edited by Nigel Young, Volume 2, pp. 546-54.

41. Freiburg was bombed as an act of reprisal following German attacks against British non-combatant targets. The Bishop of Ely (Frederic Chase) and the Free Church Council spoke out against any policy of reprisals. Bell, Stuart, "The Church and the First World War", in Parker, Stephen G. and Tom Lawson, eds., *God and War*, p. 43.

42. For one overview of *Jus Post Bellum* see Sharma, Serena K., " 'Just Peace' or Peace Postponed" in Durward, Rosemary and Lee Marsden, eds., pp. 167-82.

43. *Herald of Peace*, October 1914, cited in Robbins, Keith, *The Abolition of War*, p. 31.

44. Robbins, Keith, *England, Ireland, Scotland, Wales, The Christian Church 1900-2000*, p. 103.

45. Winnington-Ingram to Royden, 13 August 1914, cited in Fletcher, Sheila, p. 112.

46. Winnington-Ingram to Royden, 28 January 1915, cited in Fletcher, Sheila, p. 126.

47. *Arbitrator*, no. 422, July 1914, p. 75.

48. This is a controversial accusation, challenged by later apologists for Winnington-Ingram. Roland H. Bainton, in *Christian Attitudes to War and Peace*, p. 207), claimed that the Bishop of London, in a sermon in Westminster Abbey on 28 November 1915, called with "brutal candor" on Young England to "Kill Germans – to kill them, not for the sake of killing, but to save the world, to kill the good as well as the bad. . . . " When later challenged to produce the text of the sermon, Bainton could only refer to a secondary source from 1934. Bainton accepted that the bishop could distinguish between combatant and non-combatant, and was acknowledging that on the battlefield it was not possible to distinguish between a good combatant and a bad combatant. However, Bainton argued (*Theology*, Vol. LXXIV, January 1971, no. 607, pp.32-3) that there was nothing in the quotation which Winnington-Ingram might not have said, and that he would retain the quotation noting only that the preacher would instead have delivered it "regretfully but candidly".

49. *Challenge*, 21 August 1914, cited in Fletcher, Sheila, p. 110.

50. *Challenge*, 2 October 1914, p. 616, cited in Fletcher, Sheila, p. 111.

51. Royden to Murray, 17 October 1914, cited in Fletcher, Sheila, p. 111.

52. Wallis, Jill, *Valiant for Peace*, p. 5.

53. Cited in den Boggende, G.G.J., p. 64. Other Anglicans involved in the *Papers for War Time* group included Percy Dearmer, Archdeacon Gresford Jones, W.H. Moberly and J.H. Oldham (den Boggende, G.G.J., p. 86).

54. The first papers suggested an acceptance by most of the group of Britain's honourable intentions in taking part in the war, although moderate papers were written by Richard Roberts, Gray and Orchard. The basis for publication of later papers went even further, stating that Britain should "carry the war to a decisive issue" (Playne, Caroline E., p. 193; den Boggende, G.G.J., p. 67).

55. Cited by den Boggende, G.G.J., pp. 58-9. The five were future F.O.R.

members G.H.C. Angus, M.S. Lawson, Nathaniel Micklem, William Paton and R.D. Rees.

56. den Boggende, G.G.J., pp. 68-9.
57. den Boggende, G.G.J., pp. 69-71. The Collegium was Lucy Gardner's home in St George's Square (Wallis, Jill, *Valiant for Peace*, p. 8).
58. Cited in den Boggende, G.G.J., p. 71.
59. Cited in den Boggende, G.G.J., p. 71.
60. Thompson, Andrew C., *Logical Nonconformity? Conscientious Objection in the Cambridge Free Churches after 1914*, Journal of the United Reformed Church History Society, Vol. 5, No. 9, November 1996, p. 550; den Boggende, G.G.J., p. 72.
61. Leeds University, Liddle Collection, GS1121.
62. Leeds University, Liddle Collection, GS1422.
63. Diary of Spence Sanders, 25 December 1914. My thanks to Andrew Sanders for providing me with this.
64. Leeds University, Liddle Collection, GS0527.
65. Diary of Spence Sanders, 1 January 1915.
66. Maude Royden in Fry, Joan M., *Christ and Peace*, pp. 38-40.
67. Maude Royden in Fry, Joan M., p. 42.
68. Maude Royden in Fry, Joan M., p. 43.
69. *Worker*, December 1914, cited in Schneer, Jonathan, *George Lansbury*, p. 140.
70. Lansbury, George, *My Life*, p. 211.
71. A General Committee was elected to promote the new F.O.R. Members included Phillips and Royden, along with C. Franklin Angus, Roderick K. Clark, Marian Ellis (1878-1952, a Quaker; she later became Lady Parmoor), Lucy Gardner (honorary secretary), W. Fearon Halliday, J. St G. Heath, Henry T. Hodgkin (chairman), McEwan S. Lawson, W.E. Orchard, Richard Roberts and Lilian Stevenson (Fry, Joan M., *Christ and Peace*, p. 107). Lansbury later declined to join, but he did agree to write a pamphlet, *Why I Joined the F.O.R.* (den Boggende, G.G.J., p. 176).
72. Wallis, Jill, *Valiant for Peace*, pp. 7-8.
73. General Principles of Propaganda, 1. Fry, Joan M., p. 106. Presumably this was the "indefiniteness" of which Lansbury complained.
74. Fry, Joan M., pp. 104-5.
75. General Principles of Propaganda, 2. Fry, Joan M., p. 106.
76. Robbins, Keith, *The Abolition of War* p. 193.
77. F.O.R.'s forays into the world of social work were not a success. Late in 1915 a Social Service Committee was formed. In February 1916 it was agreed to support a colony of young offenders, providing kindness and patience instead of the traditional regime of birch and corporal punishment. Royden was one of the members of the Commune Committee appointed, and in June the Riverside Village experiment was started at Syonsby Knoll in Melton Mowbray. It was not a positive initiative, with complaints to the police from nearby residents about the conduct of the delinquent children sent to Riverside by the Probation Service, with financial difficulties, overworked staff and a lack of both industrial and religious training. A damning Home Office report led to the temporary closure of Riverside, and when it reopened in 1919 the emphasis changed to being a small Co-

operative Industrial Society, living in community (den Boggende, G.G.J., pp. 202-4; Wallis, Jill, *Valiant for Peace*, pp. 23-4). Once again, at the start, there were some delinquents involved, but the new scheme was hardly more successful than its predecessor, falling apart in 1921 and being finally discontinued in 1925 (den Boggende, G.G.J., pp. 332-3). Equally short-lived, but more successful while it existed than its predecessor at Riverside, was Grace Costin's Fairby Grange centre at Hartley in Kent.

78. "Printed by special request" in the *Herald*, 6 February 1915.

4. The Pen is Mightier Than the Sword: George Lansbury

1. Lansbury, George, *My Life*, pp. 37-8.
2. Lansbury, George, *My Life*, p. 39. One example was his Russian contacts. He was involved with a 1905 demonstration in Trafalgar Square protesting against the Tsar's Winter Palace shootings, and successfully opposing a visit to Britain by the Tsar. Two years later he helped to get funds for a penniless Lenin and Trotsky to attend a London conference. They repaid the money in 1921.
3. Lansbury, George, *My Life*, p. 83.
4. Shepherd, John, *George Lansbury: At the Heart of Old Labour,* pp. 78-9; Postgate, Raymond, *The Life of George Lansbury*, p. 53.
5. Cited in Shepherd, John, p. 80.
6. *Arbitrator*, May 1892, cited in Schneer, Jonathan, pp. 131-2.
7. Miles, Susan, *Portrait of a Parson: William Corbett Roberts,* Allen and Unwin, London, 1955, p. 16. The parish was St Mary, Stratford, Bow, once the territory of Chaucer's Prioress, who spoke "French", "After the school of Stratford-atte-Bowe;/ French in the Paris style she did not know." Roberts and Lansbury would both have abhorred her anti-semitism, but would have had rather more sympathy with the condemnation of the "foul lucre" of usury.
8. He recounted the spiritual impact of his first service he attended on his return in *The Herald*, 1 December 1917.
9. Lang subsequently noted: "He was a secularist lecturer, by name Lansbury, who seemed to be feeling his way back to the church. He came to Bow Church, very shamefacedly, and sat in the back behind a pillar. After supper, he poured out doubts, questions, desires, as out of a long-corked-up bottle; and I was much moved by his sincerity. Thereafter, he threw in his lot with the church, taking St Francis of Assisi as his ideal Christian. . . . Shortly after our talk at Bow Rectory, I asked him if he would give his witness to the Christian faith at a big men's meeting to be held at Bow Baths. He said it would not be easy, but he would do his best. It was advertised that he would speak. There was a great crowd – hundreds of the collarless men not usually seen at such meetings. They listened quietly to me but when Lansbury rose there was an outcry – shouts of 'Traitor!', 'Judas!', and so forth. I shall never forget the way

in which Lansbury turned on them – 'Is this the freedom of speech you claim for yourselves?' etc – and gave his witness and impelled silence" (Lockhart, J.G., *Cosmo Gordon Lang*, pp. 160-1.) W.C. Roberts set up that public meeting.

10. He had already tentatively started to go to church again, at Barkingside (Postgate, Raymond, p. 55).

11. Lansbury's political allies were not always sympathetic towards his attempts to enlist the Church of England in campaigns against poverty. For them, "whatever they may think of the teachings of the founder of Christianity, the Church of England itself stands for privilege and monopoly, riches and power" (Edgar Lansbury, p. 5.)

12. Schneer, Jonathan, p. 133.

13. Lansbury was involved in an almost identical "Don't Shoot" campaign fifteen years later, involving J.R. Campbell, editor of the Communist *Workers' Weekly*.

14. Both Conrad Noel, the vicar of the parish, and Lady Warwick, the patron, contributed articles in the early years.

15. Chesterton, who had been Pro-Boer, was still Anglican at that time; he did not convert to Roman Catholicism until 1922. Gould would travel with Lansbury to France and the western front (Shepherd, John, p. 147). Scurr, and his suffragette wife Julia, were to be close allies of Lansbury in Poplar politics in the decade ahead.

16. E.g. "Socialism After the War", by Ramsay MacDonald (*Herald*, 22 April 1916). Only the *Herald* would have had the nerve and the social critique to publish two lavish menus from a top hotel: "How They Starve at the Ritz" (24 November 1917) and "Still Starving at the Ritz" (15 December 1917).

17. *Herald*, 15 May 1915, p. 3.

18. A Lansbury editorial remarked that "The spirit of democracy, in fact, plays as slight a part to-day in the general life of Europe as practical Christianity" (*Daily Herald*, 10 August 1914).

19. *Daily Herald*, 28 August 1914.

20. The first warnings were in the *Daily Herald*, 18 August 1914.

21. *Daily Herald*, 14 August 1914.

22. "Hymn After Battle", a poem by A. St John Adcock, *Daily Herald*, 6 August 1914.

23. *Herald*, 30 January 1915.

24. *Herald*, 13 February 1915 and 1 January 1916 when it was stated that there was a flourishing women's peace movement, and that the minority peace party with the Social Democrats was growing.

25. Lansbury admitted that he admired the spirit of the men, even though he hated and detested the war (*Herald*, 21 November 1914).

26. *Herald*, 21 November 1914.

27. *Herald*, 15 May 1915.

28. *Herald*, 9 March 1918.

29. *Herald*, 9 March 1918.

30. Lansbury, George, *My Life*, pp. 183-5. He had met some French socialists, but "got little pacifist change from them". Later, Lansbury wrote the Introduction to *Reflections from France*, a volume by columnist Chris Massie, serving in France with the R.A.M.C. (*Herald*, 23 September 1916).

31. *Herald*, 19 December 1914. That issue also contained an evangelistic short story by John M. Maillard, as well as other articles highly critical of Christianity. A poem, "Christmas, 1914" by "L.S." included the stanzas:

> Mourn, ye Mortals, for your Sin,
> War is raging 'twixt the Kin,
> Mocking Christmas and Our Lord,
> Worshiping the evil Sword,
> Silence, bells, your jeering song,
> Peace is only for the Strong,
> Christ is laughed at. Peace is dead.
> Justice! Honour! Truth! Have fled . . .
>
> Yet again this Christmas morn
> Unto us The Child is born.
> Peace He brings to us, an[d] we will
> Bid the dogs of war be still.
> May His message be our guide,
> Bring us Peace by Eastertide:
> So next year upon the Earth
> We may sing glad songs of mirth.

32. *Herald*, 26 December 1914.
33. *Daily Herald*, 7 August 1914 and *Herald*, 4 October 1917.
34. *Daily Herald*, 6 August 1914.
35. *Daily Herald*, 16 September 1914.
36. *Herald*, 24 October 1914.
37. *Herald*, 4 March 1915 and 15 May 1915. It was noted that the International Conference of Socialist and Labour Women had passed a resolution sympathetic to the women meeting at The Hague (*Herald*, 10 April 1915).
38. Postgate, Raymond, p. 163. See also Lansbury, George, "Why we say 'Yes!'", (*Herald*, 30 December 1916).
39. For Henry Ford's expedition, see Kraft, Barbara S., *The Peace Ship*, Macmillan, New York, 1978.
40. Expressing their intention to take their demonstration to other London churches, the organisers said that "those who honour the Prince of Peace in church should honour Him still more by doing His work in the world" (*Herald*, 22 September 1917). Hopes for peace by Christmas (*Herald*, 18 October 1917) proved unfounded.
41. *Herald*, 9, 11 and 16 November 1918.
42. *Daily Herald*, 13 July 1914.
43. *Daily Herald*, 6 August 1914.
44. *Daily Herald*, 6 August 1914.
45. *Daily Herald*, 8 August 1914; *Daily Herald*, 6 February 1915; *Herald*, 3 April 1915; *Herald*, 23 June 1917.
46. *Herald*, 29 January 1916. She provided an Easter message on 30 March 1918, and contributed to a Herald Book Service publication, *Equal Pay and the Family*.
47. *Herald*, 16 August 1916.
48. *Herald*, 3 June 1916.
49. *Herald*, 13 May 1916.

50. Benedict XV, Apostolic Exhortation, *To the Peoples Now at War and to Their Rulers,*28 July 1915 (*Herald*, 7 August 1915).
51. *Herald*, 7 August 1915.
52. *Herald*, 13 May 1916.
53. *Herald*, 25 May 1917.
54. For example, *Herald*, 19 December 1914 and an open letter to the churches by Wilfred Wellock, *Herald*, 17 April 1915.
55. *Herald*, 25 December 1915.
56. *Herald*, 26 February 1916.
57. *Herald*, 16 September 1916 (see also Schneer, Jonathan, pp. 139-40).
58. 28 May 1916 (*Herald*, 27 May 1916).
59. *Herald*, 1 December 1917 (see also Schneer, Jonathan, p. 139).
60. *Herald*, 30 December 1916.
61. *Herald*, 23 December 1916.
62. *Herald*, 26 January 1918.
63. *Herald*, 30 March 1918.
64. *Herald*, 10 August 1918.
65. *Herald*, 2 November 1918. Lansbury did not always find hope easy. On the first post-war Christmas in Britain, he realised the guns were still booming in Russia and recalled a verse from *Christmas Bells*, by H.W. Longfellow (1807-1882):

    Then in despair I bowed my head.
    There is no peace on earth, I said,
    For hate is strong and mocks the song
    Of peace on earth, goodwill to men.

    Yet still he was able to take heart from the final verse from that poem,

    Then pealed the bells more loud and deep
    Love is not dead nor doth it sleep.
    The wrong shall fail, the right prevail,
    With peace on earth, goodwill toward men.
                            (*Herald*, 28 December 1918).
66. *Herald*, 7 April 1917; also Postgate, Raymond, pp. 167-8.
67. *Herald*, 7 June 1917.
68. *Herald*, 11 August 1917.
69. Bolsheviks discovered, in the Tsar's records, clandestine agreements from 1915 and 1916 to allow the allies to acquire the spoils of war: Constantinople to Russia, part of Persia to Britain, part of Austria to Italy, and so on. The *Herald* published them in a special edition on 11 May 1918, which sold a record quarter of million copies.
70. Lansbury, George, *My Life*, p. 209.

5. *Women for Peace*

1. *Christian Pacifist*, October 1939, p. 256. In 1916 Philips wrote that "Long before Belgium was invaded, people were weak and helpless in the grip of the industrial machine of every civilised country" (*Venturer*, Vol.1, No. 6, March 1916, p. 182) and "The war, too, has taught us that things are

not ours in the way that we thought they were. . . . The rich need to learn how to live efficiently on less, and the poor how to live wisely on more" (*Venturer*, no. 12, September 1916, pp. 369-71). In 1933 Philips wrote *The Responsibility of the Christian Investor*.

2. den Boggende, G.G.J., p. 150. At first the Committee met at the Collegium, but this was proving to be too small for F.O.R. purposes. As a result, the F.O.R. moved its base to new premises at 17 Red Lion Square (den Boggende, G.G.J., p. 175). The property had an artistic heritage, having been associated with Dante Gabriel Rossetti, Edward Burne-Jones and William Morris. That was not inappropriate given Morris's assertion that, "Fellowship is heaven, and lack of fellowship is hell: fellowship is life, and lack of fellowship is death: and the deeds that ye do upon the earth, it is for fellowship's sake that ye do them" (*The Dream of John Ball*, ch. 4).

3. *Venturer*, vol.1, no.12, September 1916, pp. 369-70. Cited in den Boggende, G.G.J., pp. 126-7.

4. Cited by den Boggende, G.G.J., p. 208.

5. den Boggende cites "open diplomacy, free trade, international parliaments, arbitration, disarmament, co-operation between capital, management, labour and consumer, limitations of individual incomes, education for all and of the whole person and the abolition of capital punishment"(p. 210).

6. den Boggende, G.G.J., pp. 211, 224.

7. Friends' House, Miscellaneous Papers.

8. Royden, Maude, *The Great Adventure*, pp. 9-10.

9. Maude Royden to Kathleen Courtney, 17 October 1899 L.M.H.

10. Maude Royden to Kathleen Courtney, 5 April 1900. L.M.H.

11. Maude Royden to Kathleen Courtney, 5 April 1900. L.M.H.

12. Maude Royden to Kathleen Courtney, 3 July 1900. L.M.H.

13. Fletcher, Sheila, p. 31.

14. Maude Royden to Kathleen Courtney, 19 June 1900. L.M.H.

15. Maude Royden to Kathleen Courtney, 29 December 1900. L.M.H.

16. Wiltsher, Anne, *Most Dangerous Women*, p. 4.

17. Wiltsher, Anne, p. 72. Differences between women's groups as well as between Christians in their attitudes to war are evident from the personal diary of one (unknown) woman in the North of England. On 15 February 1915 she recalled that, "At the time the war started I had not considered these matters much, but I was vaguely a pacifist. In the first months I must admit that the constant fire of calumny against our enemies nearly bowled me over, until I recognized that it was part of the trick. I also mildly believed in the slogan, 'War to end War', until I realized that war can never end war, but can only breed more war, and this because it involves, justifies and glorifies every crime which in normal times we abhor. Then I definitely repudiated war, and felt I could understand and admire the attitude of the conscientious objector better than that of those who fought and died for God, King and country. . . . " (Playne, Caroline E., p. 132). She had met with the local Suffrage Society on 4 August 1914 and had been astonished at the differences between the members with regard to the war. "Only the Quaker members supported me in my anti-war attitude". She spoke regretfully of the way in which women had been mobilised, not only for

work in munitions factories, but for knitting clothing for soldiers, or for raising money through flag-days, or for making sand-bags or gas-masks: "Hardly any of my friends seemed alive to the more momentous task of keeping alive the ideals of Christianity and safeguarding the future against a recurrence of this dire state of affairs. This, however, was the aspect which appealed most to me. I went for my spiritual food not to the Church, but to the various societies I had joined. When I expressed my views to those around me it was as a voice crying in the desert" (Playne, Caroline E, p. 133.) In June 1916 she spoke of the wrath of one of her friends who discovered that she would support the War Savings campaign but was instead intending to sign the memorial to the Prime Minister in favour of peace by negotiation. The accuser asked "Do you think the middle of a great war is the time to bleat your ideals?" The diarist was unmoved and did sign the memorial: "for I felt very clear in my reasoning that the only way to promote a just and lasting peace was by applied Christianity in all relations between nations. Reason, good will and conciliation versus revenge, reprisals, hatred and blind force" (Playne, Caroline E., pp. 133-4).

18. *Common Cause*, 30 April 1915, p. 46, cited in Fletcher, Sheila, p. 118.
19. Fletcher, Sheila, pp. 175-6.
20. Royden, Maude, *The Hour and the Church*, pp. 38-9.
21. Royden, Maude, *The Hour and the Church*, p. 41.
22. Royden, Maude, *The Hour and the Church*, pp. 43-4.
23. Royden, Maude, *The Hour and the Church*, p. 94.
24. Fletcher, Sheila, pp. 102-4.
25. Fletcher, Sheila, p. 140.
26. Fletcher, Sheila, pp. 143-4.
27. Anon. *Militarism Versus Feminism*, p. 62. The co-authors were actually Mary Sargant Florence and Charles Ogden. See Kamester, Margaret and Jo Vellacott, eds., *Militarism Versus Feminism: Writings on Women and War; Mary Sargant Florence, Catherine Marshall, C.K. Ogden*, p. 138.
28. Wiltsher, Anne, p. 8.
29. Bussey, Gertrude and Margaret Tims, *Pioneers for Peace*, p. 17.
30. Liddington, Jill, *The Long Road to Greenham*, p. 95.
31. Bussey, Gertrude and Margaret Tims, p. 18.
32. Liddington, Jill, "The Women's Peace Crusade", in Thompson, Dorothy, ed., *Over Our Dead Bodies*, p. 184.
33. Liddington, Jill, "The Women's Peace Crusade", in Thompson, Dorothy, ed., *Over Our Dead Bodies*, p. 185.
34. *Manchester Guardian*, 20 April 1915, cited in *Militarism Versus Feminism* (1987 edition), p. 154.
35. Wiltsher, Anne, p. 84.
36. Wiltsher, Anne, p. 89.
37. Liddington, Jill, *The Long Road to Greenham*, p. 102.
38. *Daily Express*, 27 April 1915, cited in Wiltsher, Anne, p. 89.
39. Bussey, Gertrude and Margaret Tims, p. 19.
40. Bussey, Gertrude and Margaret Tims, pp. 20-1.
41. *Annual Report*, cited in Liddington, Jill, *The Long Road to Greenham*, p. 106.
42. *W.I.L. Yearly Report*, 1916, p. 2.

43. Cited in Royden, Maude, "War and the Woman's Movement", in Buxton, Charles Roden, ed., *Towards a Lasting Settlement*, p. 135.
44. *W.I.L. Yearly Report*, 1916, pp. 8-9. Also Fletcher, Sheila, p. 136.
45. Royden to Marshall, 10 August 1916. Cited in Fletcher, Sheila, pp. 136-7.
46. Kennedy, Thomas C., p. 199.
47. Royden, Maude, "War and the Woman's Movement", pp. 133-46.
48. *W.I.L. Yearly Report*, 1916, pp. 9-10.
49. *W.I.L. Yearly Report*, 1917, p. 11.
50. *W.I.L. Yearly Report*, 1916, p. 12.
51. *W.I.L. Yearly Report*, 1917, pp. 10-24.
52. *W.I.L. Yearly Report*, 1918, pp. 17-8.
53. Royden, Maude, *Women and the Sovereign State*, pp. 131-2.
54. Royden, Maude, *The Great Adventure*, p. 13.
55. Macfadyen, Dugald, *Life and Letters of Alexander Mackennal, D.D.*, p. 257, cited in Royden, Maude, *The Great Adventure*, p. 3.
56. Royden, Maude, *The Great Adventure*, p. 4. One strand of Christian pacifism, for example that later followed by Evelyn Underhill, would have taken more literally the command of Matthew 5.39, not to resist an evildoer.
57. Royden, Maude, *The Great Adventure*, p. 6.
58. Royden, Maude, *The Great Adventure*, p. 7.
59. Royden, Maude, *The Great Adventure*, pp. 8-9.
60. Royden, Maude, *The Great Adventure*, pp. 9-10.
61. Scarborough had been bombarded.
62. Royden, Maude, *The Great Adventure*, pp. 11-12.
63. Royden, Maude, *The Great Adventure*, pp. 11-12.
64. Membership by that time had already risen to nearly two thousand (den Boggende, G.G.J., p. 168).
65. The account of Constance Coltman (née Constance Todd) and Claude Coltman, cited in Fletcher, Sheila, p. 129.
66. den Boggende, G.G.J., p. 182. Her appointment had been announced in May (den Boggende, G.G.J., p. 187).
67. Possibly Constance Todd, soon to be the first woman minister of the Congregational Church (*Mansfield Reporter*, 23 July 1915; cited in Fletcher, Sheila, p. 131).
68. Coltman, Claude, "1915 – Mission to England", *Reconciliation*, February 1964, p. 26.
69. On 4 August the *Daily Express* described Royden's *Great Adventure* as "Peace Crank's Mad Plea". It appealed for details in advance of any anti-war meetings, presumably with the aim of creating derision if not disruption (Fletcher, Sheila, p. 131).
70. Coltman, Claude, pp. 26-7.
71. Coltman, Claude, p. 27. The events were used in the plot of Theodora Wilson-Wilson's novel, *The Last Weapon*. The owner of the caravan, one William Cook, demanded £300 compensation (den Boggende, G.G.J., p. 182).
72. Coltman, Claude, p. 27.
73. Wallis, Jill, *Valiant for Peace*, p. 14.
74. Fletcher, Sheila, pp. 131-2.
75. The chief advocate was Claude Coltman (den Boggende, G.G.J., p. 162).

Least enthusiastic was the pacifist and Congregationalist theologian C.H. Dodd (1844-1973) who preferred a quieter form of campaigning.

76. Cited by Wallis, Jill, *Valiant for Peace*, p. 14.
77. den Boggende, G.G.J., p. 175.
78. Wallis, Jill, *Valiant for Peace*, p. 15.
79. Wallis, Jill, *Valiant for Peace*, p. 27.
80. Wallis, Jill, *Valiant for Peace*, p. 29.
81. den Boggende, G.G.J., p. 152.

6. Clergy in the Front Line of Resistance

1. Wilkinson, Alan, *The Church of England and the First World War*, p. 53.
2. Palmer, Bernard, *Men of Habit*, p. 136.
3. Palmer, Bernard, p. 137.
4. Palmer, Bernard, p. 137. Later he founded a short-lived religious community at Westcote, in the Cotswolds, and was influential in starting the Village Evangelism movement, which conducted missions across the country. Another military chaplain in difficulty was Stuart Denton Morris (1890-1967), believed to have been stationed at an airfield in Yorkshire in 1915, following a curacy in Walworth, East London and presumably prior to his next appointment as Domestic Chaplain to Bishop Robberds of Brechin, the Primus of Scotland. The Morris family oral tradition is that he experienced the tensions of the time wondering whether the pilots would ever return from their missions. According to the tradition, he was eventually asked to resign from his chaplaincy because of his pacifist sermons (Hilda Morris in conversation with Clive Barrett, 12 December 1992; also, Morrison, Sybil, *I Renounce War*, p. 12). Morris would become the public face of the Peace Pledge Union after the death of Dick Sheppard in 1937.
5. *Herald*, 23 September 1916.
6. Miles, Susan, *Portrait of a Parson, William Corbett Roberts*, pp. 42-3.
7. Miles, Susan, *Blind Men Crossing a Bridge*, p. 469.
8. Part of the story may be an allusion to a gang's threat to break rectory windows at Crick made when Roberts allowed farmers to give groceries, rather than cash, as Christmas charity offerings. The recipients were angered that they were not thus able to spend the money on alcohol (Miles, Susan, *Portrait of a Parson*, p. 31).
9. Wilkinson, Alan, *The Church of England and the First World War*, pp. 53-4.
10. Harford, J.B. and F.C. MacDonald, *Handley Carr Glynn Moule*, pp. 273-6, cited in Wilkinson, Alan, *The Church of England and the First World War*, p. 54.
11. Pickering had used some of the legacy from his late uncle, Bishop Moorhouse of Manchester, to pay for a Durham University education, which he left after one year. Returning to Sheffield, he spent the remainder of the bequest on the hostel.

12. Stimson, Charles C., *The Price to be Paid; "The Tramp Preachers"*, p. 29. Stimson thought that Christ's teaching was "more or less explicitly denied in the Thirty Nine Articles" (p. 53).

13. Letter from the Brotherhood Church to Philip Dransfield, 14 September 1965.

14. This Rule was later to be developed into the Rule for the Brotherhood of the Way. One clause of that later Rule interpreted part of the Sermon on the Mount: "In our struggle with evil, to abandon the appeal to brute force – or to the law, which rests on brute force – that is, to throw away the sword and rely on the Cross as our weapon" (Stimson, Charles C., *The Price to be Paid*, p. 173). It would have been a similar sentiment on the youth club mantelpiece in 1914.

15. Stimson, Charles C. *The Price to be Paid*, pp. 95-7. Herford, a supporter of the F.O.R., later advocated a revival of Franciscanism (*Reconciliation*, November 1933, p. 215). In a Philip Dransfield typescript of the *Manchester Evening News*, 13 January 1931, Pickering claims to have been ordained in 1918 by a Syrian Bishop of the Orthodox Church, because the state church would not accept conscientious objectors. Pickering eventually consented to Anglican ordination in 1940 (deacon) and 1941 (priest).

16. Stimson, Charles C. *The Price to be Paid*, p. 55.

17. Dorothy Stimson in conversation with Clive Barrett, 31 October 1992.

18. Stimson, Charles C., *The Price to be Paid*, p. 17.

19. Stimson, Charles C., *The Price to be Paid*, p. 41.

20. Stimson, Charles C., *The Price to be Paid*, pp. 39-46.

21. *Reconciliation*, 1935, p. 252.

22. Walke, Bernard, *Twenty Years at St Hilary*, pp. 61-2.

23. Walke, Bernard, pp. 63-64.

24. Walke, Bernard, p. 84.

25. Walke, Bernard, p. 109.

26. Wallis, Jill, *Valiant for Peace*, p. 48.

27. Walke, Bernard, p. 110.

28. Walke, Bernard, pp. 111-6.

29. Boulton, David, *Objection Overruled*, p. 11.

30. *Times*, 8 October 1917, reported in *Tribunal*, 11 October 1917. The bishop distinguished between religious and political objectors. The former, he argued, should be freed and treated as good citizens with fanatic views: "no one would ask the Mahomedan to eat pork or the Hindu to kill the sacred cow, and so no sane man would suggest that either a Quaker or a Christadelphian, or any other Nonconformist pacifist should have anything to do with war". (He did not include "Anglican" in that list.) Beyond that, however, Cecil had no time for political objectors. A man who refused to take part in organised murder on the grounds that it was a crime against humanity should be regarded as "an enemy of our commonwealth", said the bishop.

31. Walke, Bernard, pp. 120-1.

32. Walke, Bernard, p. 154.

33. Walke, Bernard, p. 145.

34. Walke later became known for putting on annual broadcast nativity plays,

and for a public clash with Kensitites opposed to his ritualism. Contracting tuberculosis in the 1930s, he was helped in his parish duties by various Anglo-Catholic clergy travelling down from London and the south east (*Church Times*, 6 January 1933, p. 10). The unlikely significance of this episode for pacifism was that it was from within a similar group of parish clergy that the seeds of organised Anglican pacifism were sown later in that decade. W.C. Roberts was one of those priests, and he said admiringly of Walke, "here is a Christian who has learnt to love his enemies" (*Reconciliation*, 1935, p. 252).

35. Barnes, John, *Ahead of His Age*, p. 59.
36. Barnes, John, p. 60.
37. Barnes, John, p. 66.
38. Wilkinson, Alan, *The Church of England and the First World War*, p. 46.
39. Barnes, John, p. 96. After the October Revolution of 1918, Bolshevik brutality was also denounced by Barnes (p. 99).
40. Barnes, John, p. 97.
41. Barnes, John, pp. 100-1.
42. Barnes, John, p. 111.

7. World War, Worldwide War Resistance

1. Andrews, C.F. in Radhakrishnan, Sarvepalli, ed., *Mahatma Gandhi: Essays and Reflections*, pp. 50-3.
2. Andrews, C.F., *What I Owe to Christ*, pp. 101-3.
3. Andrews, C.F., *What I Owe to Christ*, pp. 140-3.
4. Andrews, C.F., *What I Owe to Christ*, p. 152.
5. *India in Transition* (1910), cited in Chaturvedi, Benarsidas and Marjorie Sykes, *Charles Freer Andrews*, p. 63.
6. Andrews, C.F., *What I Owe to Christ*, p. 169.
7. Andrews, C.F., *Christ in the Silence*, p. 18.
8. Andrews, C.F., *Christ in the Silence*, p. 18.
9. Andrews to Mahatma Munshi Rama, cited in Chaturvedi, Benarsidas and Marjorie Sykes, p. 89.
10. Chaturvedi, Benarsidas and Marjorie Sykes, p. 92.
11. C.F. Andrews, *What I Owe to Christ*, p. 267.
12. Chaturvedi, Benarsidas and Marjorie Sykes, pp. 90-3.
13. Hoyland, J. S., *C.F. Andrews: Minister of Reconciliation*, p. 36.
14. Chaturvedi, Benarsidas and Marjorie Sykes, pp. 92-3.
15. Chaturvedi, Benarsidas and Marjorie Sykes, p. 94.
16. Clark, I. D. L., *C.F. Andrews – Deenabandhu*, p. 31.
17. 6 January 1914; cited in Chaturvedi, Benarsidas and Marjorie Sykes, p. 98.
18. Andrews, C.F., *What I Owe to Christ*, p. 239; Chaturvedi, Benarsidas and Marjorie Sykes, p. 100. Another racial dimension to the First World War was apparent in the persistent parliamentary questions of ship-owner Robert Houston, who succeeded Maude Royden's father, Thomas Royden, as Conservative M.P. for West Toxteth in 1892. He wanted to know why (presumably more expendable) "coloured men", especially from South Africa, could not be drafted into the

Front Line in large numbers, thereby releasing British soldiers to return home safely, where they could then work in the shipyards. One aspect was economic, as was shown by the earnings of those already in the army. The rate of pay of a British Private was 3s11d; for an Indian labourer it was 0s11d. HC Deb 17 January 1918 vol 101 c508W, http://hansard.millbanksystems.com/written_answers/1918/jan/17/coloured-men#column_508w; also HC Deb 18 January 1918 vol 101 cc603-4 http://hansard.millbanksystems.com/commons/1918/jan/18/labour-battalions#column_603 [accessed 17 January 2014]. See also, Chaturvedi, Benarsidas and Marjorie Sykes p. 100.

19. *Friend*, 3 March 1939, p. 169.
20. Andrews, C.F., *What I Owe to Christ*, pp. 246-7.
21. Clark, I.D.L., p. 33.
22. Andrews, C.F., *What I Owe to Christ*, p. 251.
23. Andrews, C.F., *What I Owe to Christ*, pp. 257-8.
24. Chaturvedi, Benarsidas and Marjorie Sykes, p. 108. In 1932 Andrews described his relationship with the Anglican Church. "I have remained throughout a communicant of the Anglican Communion wherever I have gone in distant lands, and I have accepted occasional invitations to preach and administer the Sacrament whenever Christian fellowship demanded. I have done the same for other Christian Communions also, without any distinction. From that day to this, the thought has been present with me that the true ministry for which I was fitted and prepared by God was prophetic rather than priestly, and that He had brought me back, through all my own futile wanderings, to the right way by which I should go" (Andrews, C.F., *What I Owe to Christ*, 1937, pp. 269-70).
25. Part of *The Palms at Santiniketan*, cited in Chaturvedi, Benarsidas and Marjorie Sykes, p. 326.
26. Andrews, C.F., *What I Owe to Christ*, p. 276.
27. Andrews, C.F., *What I Owe to Christ*, pp. 275-7.
28. Andrews, C.F., *What I Owe to Christ*, p. 297.
29. Andrews, C.F., *What I Owe to Christ*, p. 277.
30. Andrews, C.F., *What I Owe to Christ*, p. 279.
31. Andrews, C.F., *What I Owe to Christ*, p. 280.
32. Andrews, C.F., *What I Owe to Christ*, p. 280.
33. Andrews, C.F., *The Inner Life*, p. 103.
34. Cited in I.D.L. Clark, pp. 40-1.
35. Andrews, C.F., *What I Owe to Christ*, p. 286.
36. Clark, I.D.L., p. 37.
37. In the years ahead, Andrews would negotiate on behalf of the Indian population in both South Africa and East Africa.
38. *The Churchman*, April 1934, cited in Pierce, Nathaniel W. and Paul L. Ward, *The Voice of Conscience: A Loud and Unusual Noise?*, p. 2.
39. Melish, John Howard, *Bishop Paul Jones: Witness for Peace*, revised edition edited by Peter Eaton, pp. 22-3.
40. He had previously cited such texts as Romans 12.17-21, the peaceable wisdom of James 3.17, the command of 1 Peter 3.9 to bless and not to render evil for evil, and the accusation of 1 John 4.20 that those who claim to love God but do not love their brothers are liars.

41. Cited by Melish, John Howard, p. 54.
42. *The Record*, Episcopal Diocese of Michigan, October 2002.
43. Melish, John Howard, p. 22.
44. Pierce, Nathaniel W. and Paul L. Ward, pp. 87-90.
45. Report of the second Committee of Bishops to the House of Bishops of the Episcopalian Church, 12 December 1917 (cited in Pierce, Nathaniel W. and Paul L. Ward, p. 89).
46. 20 December 1917. The House of Bishops, upholding the Commission's conclusions but embarrassed by its language, declined to accept that letter from Jones. It preferred a second letter (dated April 1919) with a single sentence presenting "my formal resignation as Bishop of the Missionary District of Utah". They could then claim the dismissal was due to Jones's "impaired usefulness" without being open to criticism of obstructing free speech (Melish, John Howard, pp. 24-5; Pierce, Nathaniel W. and Paul L. Ward, p. 90).
47. Bishop Jones farewell address to the Diocese of Utah, 30 January 1918 (Pierce, Nathaniel W. and Paul L. Ward, p. 90).
48. "The Meaning of Pacifism", taken from Devere Allen, ed., *Pacifism in the Modern World*, p. 6.
49. Allen, Devere, ed., p. 11.
50. Allen, Devere, ed., p. 10.
51. Melish, John Howard, p. 47.
52. "The Doubting Pacifist", reproduced in Scudder, Vida Dutton, *The Privilege of Age*, pp. 164-6.
53. Scudder, Vida D., *Introduction to Bede's Ecclesiastical History*, p. x.
54. Scudder, Vida D., *The Church and the Hour; Reflection of a Socialist Churchwoman*, chapter 1. Taken from a paper read at the Church Congress, Norfolk VA, May 1916, and reprinted from *The Yale* Review, January 1917. Reproduced online by Project Canterbury: http://anglicanhistory.org/socialism/scudder/hour/01.html [accessed 1 August 2013].
55. Scudder, Vida D., *The Church and the Hour; Reflection of a Socialist Churchwoman*, chapter 1.
56. Scudder, Vida D., *The Church and the Hour; Reflection of a Socialist Churchwoman*, chapter 6, "The Sign of the Son of Man".
57. Mr Justice Brandeis, Case 252 US 239. Pierce et al v United States No. 234, Argued November 18 and 19, 1919. Decided March 8, 1920.
58. My thanks go to Ted Mellor for this quotation.
59. Case 252 US 239. Pierce et al v United States No. 234, Argued November 18 and 19, 1919. Decided March 8, 1920.
60. Tucker, Irwin St John, "The Price We Pay", *The World*, Oakland, California, 584, 1 June 1917, p. 6ff. See also, www.marxisthistory.org./subject/usa/eam/index.html [accessed 1 August 2013].
61. U.S. Supreme Court, Pierce v U.S., 252 U.S. 239 (March 8, 1920). The ruling, which includes the entire transcript of *The Price We Pay*, is available online at both http://caselaw.lp.findlaw.com/scripts/getcase. pl?court=US&vol=252&invol=239 and http://www.vlex.us/caselaw/U-S-Supreme-Court/Pierce-v-United-States-252-U-S-259-1920/2100-20019426,01. html [both accessed 1 August 2013]. Tucker remained a parish priest in

Chicago, with a particular penchant for poetry. His early political poems and lectures (*Poems of a Socialist Priest*, 1915; *Internationalism*, 1918; *Sangreal*, 1919; *The Chosen Nation*, 1919; *A History of Imperialism*, 1920; *Now it Must be Done*, 1920) broadened in scope in later years. He wrote over the nom de plume "Friar Tuck" for the *Chicago Tribune*; twenty years on, it was reported that "Lank, bushy-browed Friar Tuck is a copyreader, feature-writer and religion editor for the Sunday Herald and Examiner". His Bishop declared Rector Tucker to be the official poet laureate of the Chicago diocese. At that time, Tucker had for eleven years been in charge of the rather eccentric St Stephen's Church in Chicago, a minor tourist attraction known as the "Poets' and Artists' Church". The walls were lined with paintings, sculpture and poets' manuscripts. Amongst its oddities, apparently, was a font made from a broomstick and a bread bowl (*Time Magazine*, 3 October 1938).

62. Shaw, Amy J., *Crisis of Conscience: Conscientious Objection in Canada During the First World War*, University of British Columbia Press, Vancouver, 2009, pp. 32-3. Pacifists of German heritage – Mennonites and Hutterites – were regarded with particular suspicion, assumed to be part of an international German spy network. Socknat, Thomas P., *Witness Against War; Pacifism in Canada 1900-1945*, p. 87.
63. Graham, John W., pp. 133-4.
64. "Spectator", "From Week to Week", *Canadian Churchman*, 3 October 1918, p. 683, cited in Shaw, Amy J., p. 103.
65. Cited in Shaw, Amy J., pp. 107-8.
66. Taken from tables in Shaw, Amy J., pp. 166-95.
67. Bollard, Robert, *In the Shadow of Gallipoli*, 2013, p. 31.
68. Graham, John W., p. 353.
69. Bollard, Robert, p. 67.
70. Bollard, Robert, pp. 65-6. Archbishop Kelly's action was motivated by the Government's refusal to give seminarians exemption from the call up.
71. Bollard, Robert, p. 57.
72. Compulsory Military Training also galvanised the peace movement with a number of organisations being formed in opposition to it, including the Anti-Militarist league, the Freedom League, the New Zealand Peace Council, and the Passive Resisters' Union. There were nearly five thousand convictions of young men for refusing Compulsory Military Training by the start of the war in 1914, and many were in detention. See http://www.teara.govt.nz/en/conscription-conscientious-objection-and-pacifism/page-2 [accessed 10 January 2014].
73. Graham, John W., p. 361.
74. For a numerical breakdown, see Holland, H.E., *Armageddon or Calvary*, p. 8; also available at https://archive.org/details/armageddonorcalv00holliala [accessed 10 January 2014].
75. Graham, John W., p. 361.
76. http://www.nzhistory.net.nz/war/first-world-war/conscientious-objection/maori-objection (Ministry for Culture and Heritage) [accessed 10 January 2014].
77. Holland, H.E., p. 15.

78. Cited in Holland, H.E., p. 16. Holland himself wrote to the Prime Minister at the time, saying that Massey, "seems to think that the possession of a conscientious principle is a matter to be determined by Act of Parliament or War Regulations. For the first three centuries of the Christian era the Christians generally held similar views to those held by the Christian Conscientious Objectors of to-day; then the conscience men (and women) were flung to the lions or nailed to the cross. Mr Massey makes a law which refuses to the Catholic, the Anglican, the Presbyterian, the Methodist, the Salvationist or the Socialist, the right to hold a conscientious objection to military service, and having made his law, he then pronounces his victims 'conscienceless' ". Holland, H.E., p. 43.
79. Bizarrely, this policy ultimately led the Government itself to establish a Commission which urged imprisoned C.O.s to claim such "religious" status, in order to ameliorate their plight.
80. Holland, H.E., p. 17. Parliament still went ahead with the legislation, but the Minister of Munitions provided a certificate of exemption for each Christian minister on application by his Church.
81. http://www.nzhistory.net.nz/war/first-world-war/conscientious-objection, (Ministry for Culture and Heritage) [accessed 10 January 2014]. A list of the names of many of the C.O.s is in Holland, H.E., pp. 105-6.
82. Arriving at Plymouth, they heard one officer respond to their group, "Conscientious objectors! What on earth does New Zealand mean, sending conscientious objectors here? As if we hadn't enough to do with our own!" Baxter, Archibald, We Will Not Cease, p. 76. Also available online at http://nzetc.victoria.ac.nz/tm/scholarly/tei-BaxWeWi.html [accessed 10 January 2014].
83. Baxter's own account in Holland, H.E., p. 76. See also Grant, David, Field Punishment No. 1, pp. 41-64.
84. Grant, David, p. 81. Briggs tells his own story in Holland, H.E., pp.54-75.
85. Baxter, Archibald, pp. 127-8; Graham, John W., p. 133.
86. Graham, John W., pp. 128-9.
87. Baxter, Archibald, p. 136.

8. Conscience Versus the Military State

1. Wallis, Jill, Valiant for Peace, p. 18.
2. Boulton, David, p. 89. Sir John Simon, who, as Home Secretary upheld their sentences, was not himself a supporter of conscription. Indeed, he resigned his post in protest at the legislation.
3. Graham, John W., pp. 59-61.
4. Allen, Clifford, "The Presidential Address to the Concluding Convention". in No-Conscription Fellowship, Troublesome People, Central Board for Conscientious Objectors, London, 1940, p. 59.
5. Taken from "The Only Way", dated June 1915. From the collection, Ewer, W.N., Five Souls and other War-Time Verses, published by the Herald, 1917, pp. 10-11. The title poem, from October 1914, had considered working people from across Europe, with the refrain (pp. 7-8), "I gave my life for freedom

– This I know/ For those who bade me fight had told me so". Ewer was not a pacifist, as seemed to be evident in his poem "To Any Pacifist", which urged Britain to fight on, whatever the sacrifice, until there is planted in Gallipoli (my italics show Ewer's mockery), "The freedom-bringing banner *of the Czar*" (p. 42).

6. *Herald*, 1 January 1916.
7. *Herald*, 8 January 1916.
8. *Herald*, 22 January 1916, and *Herald*, 12 February 1916.
9. The officers were Robert Smillie, F.W. Pethick Lawrence and B.N. Langdon Davies, with other Executive members including, inter alia, Margaret Bondfield, Dr John Clifford, Dr Henry Hodgkin and Clifford Allen (*Herald*, 22 January 1916). Significantly, not all these were opposed to the war, but all were opposed to conscription.
10. *Herald*, 22 January 1916. Further attacks were reported in the 5 February 1916 edition.
11. *Herald*, 29 January 1916.
12. *Herald*, 22 January 1916. The legislation inspired others to form F.O.R. groups, e.g. George Dutch in Tunbridge Wells.
13. *Herald*, 22 January 1916 and 4 March 1916 ('Bravo! Philip Snowden!').
14. *Herald*, 25 March 1916.
15. *Herald*, 8 April 1916.
16. *Herald*, 11 March 1916. The author may have been John Scurr.
17. Kennedy, Thomas C., p. 117.
18. *Labour Leader*, 13 April 1916, cited in Shepherd, John, pp. 169-70. Lansbury commended others on the platform – Snowden, Clifford, Helena Swanwick and Robert Mennell for their "magnificent speeches" (*Herald*, 15 April 1916).
19. Lansbury, George, *My Life*, pp. 208-9. With his daughter-in-law Minnie, Lansbury was also sympathetic to the families of those who had agreed to join the armed forces. They were both associated with the League of Rights for Soldiers' and Sailors' Wives and Relatives, a body with which Sylvia Pankhurst and the East London Federation of Suffragettes was involved, which agitated for proper pensions and for allowances for families left at home without breadwinners.
20. On the first day of the Somme, 1 July 1916, there were 60,000 British casualties, of whom 20,000 were killed. Of 2,000 Bradford Pals, 1,770 were casualties before lunchtime. The Leeds Pals lost 750 out of 900, the Accrington Pals had 584 casualties out of 720, and so on. These were community tragedies, as the men in these regiments had all been recruited from the same neighbourhoods.
21. A last minute addition promoted by two Quaker M.P.s, T. Edmund Harvey and Arnold Rowntree (Wallis, Jill, *Valiant for Peace*, pp. 18, 251).
22. Gregory, Adrian, p. 101.
23. Gregory, Adrian, p. 155. Gregory notes that in this case it is the proven heretic who is released.
24. *Herald*, 4 March 1916.
25. Chamberlain, W.J., p. 48.
26. *Herald*, 11 March 1916.

27. Graham, John W., pp. 70-1.
28. Adrian Stephen in Bell, Julian, ed., *We Did Not Fight*, pp. 380, 386.
29. *Nation*, cited in Playne, Caroline E., p. 272.
30. Rae, John, *Conscience and Politics*, p. 60.
31. Ceadel, Martin, *Pacifism in Britain, 1914-1945*, p. 39. Almost all were Quakers.
32. Ceadel, Martin, *Pacifism in Britain, 1914-1945* p. 43. The most thorough breakdown of such religious groups is in Rae, John, pp. 73-8.
33. See, for example, Graham, John W., pp. 84, 87-8. Also, Bibbings, Lois S., *Telling Tales About Men*, pp. 62-3.
34. There were divisions of opinion within the N.C.F., though not within the F.O.R., about the validity or adequacy of those who were not Absolutists. In practice, most objectors were not, but the demands of those who refused any compromise with the state, for whatever reason, were to have the most lasting impact.
35. Harold Bligh, Congregationalist, the first husband of the Anglican pacifist Margaret Eurich (Tom Scrutton, sometime Chairman of the Anglican Pacifist Fellowship, was the second), worked in the sanitary section of the R.A.M.C. but came to argue that "the Pacifist should avoid any sort of work wh. assists in the working of the whole military machine" (den Boggende, p. 195). Despite the work of the Friends' Ambulance Unit, many Absolutists came to view any ambulance work, and certainly the R.A.M.C., with greater rather than less unease. For example, when E.H. Marsh, the Secretary of the First British Ambulance Unit for Italy (i.e. British Red Cross), wrote to A. W. Evans on 14 December 1915 noting that the R.A.M.C. was full and that the Red Cross Society was clearing out of its number those fit for military service, not even for transfer into the R.A.M.C., the consequence was that Evans came to see the R.A.M.C.'s job as keeping up the supply of fighting men in the trenches (Leeds University, Liddle Collection, CO/FAU, CO 030). Opposition to the N.C.C. can be seen in the *Herald*, 18 March 1916.
36. *Herald*, 18 March 1916.
37. The surviving graffiti in the cells of Richmond Castle remains a powerful testimony to those imprisoned. One example is the verse written by Ernest Lawson in cell 1:
    Come at me with your scorn
    Strike me with your rod.
    Though I be slain a thousand times
    I will not fight my God.
38. Rae, John, pp. 250-1. "An Anglican theological student provided the test case of whether an essentially political objection could be regarded as conscientious within the meaning of the Act" (Minutes of the Central Tribunal, 2 May 1916). Rae, p. 79, does not name the ordinand in question, but he could be referring to H.F. Runacres, see below.
39. The conditions of a Quaker with Anglican roots, Stephen Hobhouse, became a cause célèbre, and led to a campaign for prison reform. See chapter 9.
40. Raven, Charles E., *Alex Wood: The Man & His Message*. F.O.R. 1952, cited in Ceadel, Martin, *Pacifism in Britain, 1914-1945*, p. 37.

41. Whereas the Friends' Ambulance Unit was a 1914 initiative, the Friends' War Victims' Relief Committee (F.W.V.R.C.) was technically a 1914 revival of a body that had functioned in the Franco-Prussian war of 1870. The main undertakings were construction work – housing, or agricultural machinery – in France. The Pearce Register identifies over 1,300 C.O.s who spent some time in France. As well as those imprisoned, there were far more in the N.C.C., the R.A.M.C. and the F.W.V.R.C.

42. Graham, John W., p. 349. A more detailed breakdown (p. 350) indicates:

Absolutists	
released April 1919 after at least two years	843
released July 1919	221
released on medical grounds after Dec. 1917	334
incomplete records	55
deserted while awaiting court martial	49
other deaths	14
released in exceptional circumstances	19
released on medical grounds before Dec. 1917	8
ABSOLUTISTS TOTAL	1543
Home Office Scheme	3750
Accepting combatant or non-combatant service	351
Discharged on medical grounds	267
Deserted	21
Released in exceptional circumstances	12
Deported	2
Evading or on indefinite furlough at time of general release	45
Records incomplete	270
TOTAL	6261

So only a small number, 351, of those arrested were ultimately persuaded to join the armed forces, and many of those would have entered the N.C.C. Graham's figure for deaths (14) does not tally with his list of names (10) on p. 323. The total for Absolutists could be reduced by up to 285, being the 158 (up to 30 July 1917) deemed "not genuine" by the Central Tribunal – e.g. anarchists who did not recognise the authority of the tribunal, or those whose presentation was inconsistent – and thus ineligible for the Home Office Scheme. There were also around 127 imprisoned at the end for various other reasons. Graham estimated that an accurate total for Absolutists would be around 1,350.In general, Cyril Pearce's latest research, see next chapter, endorses the overall accuracy of these figures, though future analysis of Pearce's Register will inevitably allow them to be refined."

43. A Conscientious Objector: Founded on Fact", published in the *Herald*, 16 September 1916. After the war, S. Gertrude Ford wrote a number of articles for children's magazines.

44. *Herald*, 15 July 1916.

45. Wilkinson, Alan, *The Church of England and the First World War*, p. 47. In Margaret Hobhouse's study of 307 prisoners in 1917, seventeen were Anglicans (Hobhouse, Margaret, pp. 16-17). See also Walke, Bernard, chapter 6, for a

description of his visit to conscientious objectors imprisoned in Dartmoor.

46. *Herald*, 24 June 1916. Earlier there had been tributes to the bishops of Oxford (Gore), Winchester (Talbot) and Lincoln (Hicks) who had been more supportive of conscientious objectors (*Herald*, 8 April 1916).

47. Rae, John, pp. 78-9.

48. Adrian Stephen in Bell, Julian, ed., p. 386.

49. Adrian Stephen in Bell, Julian, ed., pp. 389-90.

50. *Herald*, 29 April 1916; see also 17 June 1916.

51. *Herald*, 16 September 1916.

52. Reported by John Scurr in the *Herald*, 18 March 1916. See also the *Oxford Chronicle*, 10 March 1916, describing the tribunal of 6 March (the same tribunal faced by Maude Royden's pilgrimage associate Claude Coltman and Lansbury's future son-in-law Raymond Postgate). Runacres's experience did not persuade him to change his mind. In 1935, when he was Vicar of the parish of St Wilfrid, Leeds, he wrote that "War is not an action of the righteous man against a criminal; it is the instrument of the national sovereign State, putting [scientific] weapons at the disposal of the private economic adventures of those who control the State. Ultimately, the national sovereign State becomes Fascist War is totalitarian". He held that once war had started, "No protest of a hundred Bishop Gores against any of its methods will be of the slightest avail" (*Church Times*, 25 October 1935, p. 448).

53. "Gross Injustice at Oxford", *Tribunal*, 23 March 1916, 30 March 1916; referred to me by William Hetherington, Peace Pledge Union archivist, 10 September 2004. See also *Venturer*, vol. 1, no.7, p. 218. Gore, Temple, A. Clutton Brock and other supporters of the "war on behalf of freedom" signed a 30 March 1916 letter to the *Daily News*, *Daily Chronicle* and *Manchester Guardian* expressing concern over the tribunals, that "in many cases the examination has not been conducted with the fairness and respect for sincerely held opinions, which Englishmen demand and respect. . . . Conscience, however mistaken, ought not to be a subject for public ridicule. We desire to affirm our conviction that the preservation of freedom of conscience is a vital religious principle" (reported in *Tribunal* no.5, 6 April 1916, p. 1).

54. William Hetherington to Clive Barrett, 7 September 2004.

55. Graham, John W., p. 74. The three letters to the *Times* appeared on 14 March, 30 March and 4 April 1916 respectively (Kennedy, Thomas C., pp. 103-4).

56. *An Appeal to Christians*, 20 May 1916. Friends' House archive.

57. *F. Sheehy Skeffington's Speech from the Dock in 1915*, Skeffington Memorial Committee, New York, 1917. http://digital.library.villanova.edu/Item/vudl:121564. Accessed 3 August 2013.

58. Manuscript diary for 8 May 1916 by Jack Foister (Leeds University, Liddle Collection, CO/FAU, CO 032). Others managed to get hastily scribbled letters out at Basingstoke.

59. *N.C.F. Souvenir*, p. 39.

60. Stanton, Harry Edward, *Will You March Too?*, unpublished manuscript by one of the men sent from Harwich to France (Leeds University, Liddle Collection, CO/FAU, CO 098). Brewster's and Hicks's denominational affiliation (H.E.

Stanton, *Will You March Too?*, p. 60) is confirmed by the address book of Norman Gaudie, a Congregationalist sent from Richmond Castle to France (Leeds University, Liddle Collection, CO/FAU, CO 038). Much of Brewster's story is well documented by Stanton, as the two were close.

61. Stanton, H.E., p. 49.
62. Stanton, H.E., p. 50.
63. Stanton, H.E., p. 55.
64. Statement in the papers of Alfred W. Evans, from Southall, the only Roman Catholic in the group (Leeds University, Liddle Collection, CO/FAU, CO 030).
65. Of the seventeen, three were members of the Society of Friends: Cornelius Barritt and Howard Marten, both from Pinner, and Howard Stanton. Four, though not members at the time, were associated with the Society of Friends: Adam Priestley, Oscar Ricketts, Frank Shackleton, Rendel Wyatt. Jack Foister and John Ring described themselves as Socialist, and H.J. Wilson as Christian Socialist. H.W. Scullard was Congregationalist and H.G. Lief a Presbyterian. Fred Bromberger belonged to the Brethren and Bernard Bonner the International Bible Students Association. As stated above, Evans was a Roman Catholic, with Brewster and Hicks both members of the Church of England (Stanton, H.E., p. 60).
66. Stanton, H.E., p. 57.
67. Rae, John, p. 154.
68. Letter from Fred Gaudie to W.J. Chamberlain, 22 May 1916; Leeds University, Liddle Collection, CO/FAU, CO 038, Gaudie N. The Captain (Gorst? Or Guest?) was the officer in charge of a separate group of conscientious objectors at Richmond Castle, in the Non-Combatant Corps.
69. Graham, John, pp. 112-3. Numbers do not tally exactly with Hubert Peet in the *N.C.F. Souvenir*, 1919, p. 39, which records 37 men taken to France, 30 of whom received the death sentence. The *Herald*, 22 July 1916, is clear that 34 men were sentenced to death.
70. The manuscript diary of Norman Gaudie, p. 14 (Leeds University, Liddle Collection, CO/FAU, CO 038).
71. The manuscript diary of Norman Gaudie, p. 12.
72. Pearce Register, 1.
73. Gaudie diary, 12 May 1916. Leeds University, Liddle Collection, CO/FAU, CO 038.
74. Ellsworth-Jones, Will, *We Will Not Fight*, p. 159.
75. There was one amusing incident en route when "the never-bashful Wyatt" signalled to a woman sewing by her window that the passing group was thirsty. She promptly presented prisoners and guards alike with copious quantities of cider! (Jack Foister diary, Tuesday 9 May 1916; Leeds University, Liddle Collection, CO/FAU, CO 032).
76. Stanton, H.E., pp. 75-6.
77. Stanton, H.E., p. 78. Also Foister's diary, pp. 16-17; Leeds University, Liddle Collection, CO/FAU, CO 032.
78. *N.C.F. Souvenir*, p. 42.
79. Stanton, H.E., pp. 90-1
80. Stanton, H.E., pp. 83-5.

81. *N.C.F. Souvenir*, p. 44. Under the Defence of the Realm Act, H. Runham Brown was prosecuted for circulating copies of this letter (Graham, p. 198).

82. Ellsworth-Jones, Will, pp. 167-8.

83. Stanton, H.E., pp. 126-8.

84. Stanton, H.E., p. 129; Graham, John W., p. 115. In the *Friend*, 25 August 1967, p. 1067, Marten himself confirms these names and points out that David Boulton is wrong to include Cornelius Barritt in this first group. The dramatic personal account from one of the men in *N.C.F. Souvenir*, pp. 45-6, erroneously refers to "Monday, the 9th June", which date did not exist. The account probably refers to a separate episode on Monday 19 June.

85. Wallis, Jill, *Valiant for Peace*, also includes Rendel Wyatt from Cambridge, who had been involved in setting up the meeting that founded the F.O.R., and who was among those taken to France, but his Court Martial took a different turn and he was not among those sentenced to death (see Graham, pp. 115-6), being one of three men imprisoned instead. The fullest accounts are in the Liddle Collection memoirs of H.E. Stanton and Norman Gaudie.

86. Graham, John, pp. 114-5.

87. Death sentences were pronounced on: Jack Foister, Howard C. Marten, John R. Ring, Harry W. Scullard, Cornelius Barritt, Harry E. Stanton, Geoffrey E. Hicks, Adam T. Priestley, O.G. Ricketts, Harold F. Brewster, Bernard M. Bonner, Herbert G. Law, William ("Billy") E. Law, Leonard Renton, Charles H. Senior, Charles R. Jackson, Clarence Hall, Stafford Hall, Clifford Cartwright, Ernest S. Spencer, John W. Routledge, Charles Cryer, Alfred Myers, Robert Lown, John "Bert" Brocklesby, Alfred Martlew, Norman Gaudie, Alfred W. Taylor, Wilfred T. Frear, George H.S. Beavis, Edwin H. Walker, Frank Arthur Walling, James F. Murfin and Philip B. Jordan. Immediate sentences of imprisonment were pronounced on: Rendel H. Wyatt, John B. Lief, Arthur Helsby, and Oliver Rowlands. Alfred W. Evans's court-martial was deferred, as was Frederick C. Bromberger's promulgation of sentence.

88. *N.C.F. Souvenir*, pp. 45-6, based on Stanton, H.E., pp. 134-6. Brewster was the first one of the group who were sentenced individually on Monday 19 June. When the men's story became known publicly there was a fierce parliamentary exchange, with Philip Snowden and Philip Morrell forcibly putting the case for the C.O.s (*Herald*, 1 July 1916).

9. The Cost of Resistance

1. The Pearce Register of British Conscientious Objectors, http://www. livesofthefirstworldwar.org. A preliminary copy of the Register is lodged with the Peace Museum, Bradford.

2. Fourteen of the Anglican sample indicated a leaning toward the Society of Friends. Movement was not all one way: Harry Adams left the Church of England to join the Quakers, whereas Howard Bull left the Quakers to join the Church of England. Pearce Register, 7435, 7437.

3. Thomas Lusher, a schoolmaster from South Shields, who joined the R.A.M.C. Pearce Register, 15687. Paul Gliddon also indicated he was vegetarian.

4. Pearce Register, 18004, 18006.

5. Pearce Register, 12286.

6. Pearce Register, 3575.

7. Pearce Register, 14577.

8. F.O.R. members at Dartmoor included: Lewis Batley, Harold Brewster, Archie Hobart, John Routledge and William Wells. Several Anglican C.O.s joined the F.O.R. at Dartmoor: Alfred Goodfellow, Herbert Kneale, Richard Lowe, Harold Moxham, Lawrence Parrett, George Pearson and Edward Weston. Other F.O.R. Anglicans included: John Baker, Willie Jermy and Bertram Somner, who worked for the F.O.R. after his employer dismissed him.

9. For example, Percy Davies and Henry Wilson, both active on the political left. Pearce Register, 2010, 3545.

10. At the moment there is a strong Welsh bias in the numbers, see below. English Anglicans in the R.A.M.C., some of whom transferred from the N.C.C., included: Hugh Attlee, Charles Day, George Glazebrook, George Hopkinson, Thomas Lusher, Andrew Milligan, Cuthbert Morson, Thomas Snow, Ernest Turner.

11. Pearce Register, 5267 and 9155.

12. Pearce Register, 7917.

13. Pearce Register, 12145.

14. Pearce Register, 10100. Ernest Shorter from Lewisham, was another Anglican in the N.C.C. who was court-martialled at Rouen. Pearce Register, 10099.

15. Pearce Register, 15655.

16. Pearce Register, 15671.

17. Pearce Register, 4200. Those in the F.A.U. included: Harry Adams, Howard Bull, Edward Mowbray Mandale, William Riley, Albert Tomkins, Stephen Wilson.

18. Pearce Register, 811, 2087, 3543. Parliamentary questions were also asked concerning the cases of Charles Gooding, Archie Hobart, Cuthbert Morson, Ernest Prevost, and Ethan Shallcross. Pearce Register, 6180, 15655, 1011, 2796, 795.

19. Pearce Register, 2646, 9859.

20. Pearce Register, 4755, 10670, 565, 599, 733, 8749, 8750.

21. Pearce Register, 70. Herbert Sears was also a fatality, contracting influenza in the N.C.C. and dying at Gravesend Military Hospital in 1918. Pearce Register, 5903.

22. Pearce Register, 354, 533, 565, 733, 936, 1353, 1873, 2267, 2568, 3323, 3543, 6180, 7993, 9167, 9288, 9835, 9934, 10338.

23. Pearce Register, 9148. The regime at Étaples was notoriously brutal; the military base there was the scene of one of several mutinies and revolts by British troops, quickly suppressed in September 1917. For more on British army mutinies see Lamb, David, *Mutinies 1917-1920*. The most significant French army rebellion was at Chemin des Dames, west of Reims, in May 1917. The revolt spread and up to 30,000 men were involved, of whom 23,000 were convicted at courts martial. The mutiny affected 40% of French forces. There was a smaller Italian revolt in autumn 1917. For a

comprehensive bibliography of literature on British military mutinies see http://www.marxists.org/history/etol/revhist/backiss/vol8/no2/part4-intro. html [accessed 9 May 2014].

24. Pearce Register, 2052, 8749.
25. Pearce Register, 9054. George Wells and Horace Herbert also had links with Friends' War Victims Relief Service. Pearce Register, 3323, 9288.
26. William Chapman, T. Davies, W.K. Davies, Gwilym Davies, Norman Edwards, Owen Jones, Henry Lewis, John Morris, Thomas Tossell, John Thomas, W.B. Williams, David Williams, R.B. Williams, John Winston, Thomas Evans. Pearce Register, 17871-5, 17877-85, 18036. Gwilym Davies, Jones, Morris, Thomas and Evans all worked with the R.A.M.C. in Salonika, as did Tom Evans, a teacher from Troedyrhiw, Merthyr Tydfil and Harold Williams, a student from Normal College, Bangor, who died of pneumonia in Salonika in January 1919. Pearce Register, 17876, 18037. Walter Poutin (or Pontin), another Anglican student at Normal College, Bangor, and a Manchester-born teacher, Henry Jones, were also in the R.A.M.C. (Welsh Company). Pearce Register, 18032, 18038.
27. Pearce Register, 11162.
28. Pearce Register, 10077, 10237.
29. Pearce Register, 3521, 9892.
30. Pearce Register, 9893.
31. Pearce Register, 9910.
32. Pearce Register, 9835.
33. Pearce Register, 2310; Army Order 203/16, cited at http://www.1914-1918. net/reserve.html [accessed 6 January 2014].
34. Pearce Register, 2979.
35. Pearce Register, 8648, 8657.
36. Pearce Register, 18.
37. Pearce Register, 1502.
38. Pearce Register, 4346.
39. Pearce Register, 10248, 10249.
40. Pearce Register, 10025.
41. Pearce Register, 10170.
42. Pearce Register, 2560.
43. Pearce Register, 9322, 10217, 10024, 10076, 10329.
44. Cited in den Boggende, G.G.J., p. 192.
45. den Boggende, G.G.J., p. 217.
46. Robbins, Keith, *The Abolition of War*, p. 75. This organisation was soon to become the National Council for Civil Liberties, though not connected with a later organisation of the same name (Wallis, Jill, *Valiant for Peace*, p. 20). Lansbury, who was too old to be called up himself, said he would probably have demanded non-combatant service; he attended various tribunals, including that of Clifford Allen, and visited a number of imprisoned conscientious objectors including the hunger-striking Francis Meynell.
47. Graham, John W., p. 123. According to Peet (*N.C.F. Souvenir*, p. 44), Meyer was not himself a pacifist but a supporter of liberty of conscience.
48. *Herald*, 8 July 1916.
49. *Herald*, 22 July 1916.

50. den Boggende, G.G.J., p. 219.
51. Walter Ayles, Joan Fry, Leyton Richards, Ada and Alfred Salter, and Theodora Wilson-Wilson were all F.O.R. members on the National Committee of the N.C.F. (Graham, John W., p. 182).
52. Principally at Dr. Alfred Salter's Fairby Grange property at Hartley, Kent, later to be used as a centre for delinquent girls, run by Grace Costin (den Boggende, G.G.J., pp. 334-5).
53. Pearce, Cyril, *Comrades in Conscience*, p. 284.
54. Graham, John W., p. 221. See also, Attlee, Peggy, *With a Quiet Conscience*, p. 56.
55. *Tribunal*, 17 August 1916, cited in Graham, p. 222
56. From "The Philosophy of Alternative Service" by Herbert F. Runacres, in *The Granite Echo: Organ of The Dyce C.O.'s*, Vol. 1 no. 2, November 1916, edited by Guy Aldred; pictured in Goodall, Felicity, *A Question of Conscience*, p. 47; also in Goodall, Felicity, *We Will Not Go to War*, seventh page of photographs inserted at p. 114. An article in *Scotland*, 23 May 1999 (Susan Lumsden, "Horrific treatment of Great War 'conchies' is revealed at last"), cites a letter from Runacres at Dyce, 24 October 1916, "It is true that a physically fit theological student could become a useful navvy; it is also true that an intelligent navvy could in time translate the Greek testament, but a business government would not seek to carry out either transformation". I am grateful to William Hetherington, Peace Pledge Union archivist, for tracing these references (William Hetherington to Clive Barrett, 7 September 2004).
57. *The Granite Echo*, op. cit.
58. Graham, John W., pp. 224-5.
59. Graham, John W., pp. 229.
60. Graham, John W., p. 247. Of those who had earlier been sent to France, all but three (H. Stuart Beavis, Frederick J. Murfin and Alfred W. Taylor) accepted the Home Office Scheme, but a small group (including Barritt, Stanton and Wyatt) refused to continue and returned to prison where they stayed until April 1919.
61. Wallis, Jill, *Valiant for Peace*, p. 22. He was Walter Roberts of Stockport (Graham, John W., pp. 312-3).
62. So, on 17 May 1917, a general meeting of Dartmoor men, of which Howard Marten was secretary, was "prepared to perform the work provided in a reasonable spirit, but protests against the penal character of the work imposed by the Home Office Committee and demands civil work of real importance with full civil rights". They, and C.O.s at other camps, vehemently denied fabricated press claims of slacking (Graham, p. 246).
63. Stanton, H.E., p. 213.
64. Graham, John W., pp. 241-2.
65. Some of those who had earlier been sent to France, returned from Dyce to Wakefield Prison, where they led the refusal to co-operate with the Home Office Scheme (Stanton, H.E., pp. 210-20)
66. Hobhouse came from an extremely well-connected family. His great-grandfather, Richard Potter – brother of Thomas Potter, the founder of the *Manchester Guardian* – had been M.P. for Wigan in the 1830s. Hobhouse's

cousin Emily, the daughter of a Church of England clergyman, had revealed the horror of British concentration camps in South Africa (Koss, S., pp. 198-207). Stephen Hobhouse's mother was Margaret Hobhouse (née Potter: her sisters included Beatrice Webb, Catherine Courtney and Theresa Cripps, wife of Charles and mother of Stafford Cripps). His father, Henry (a nephew of Baron Hobhouse, a traveller with Byron) had been a M.P., 1885-1906, and an Ecclesiastical Commissioner. After being brought up as an Anglican at Eton, taking a full part in the Corps, wearing the uniform of an Old Etonian who was to be killed in South Africa, Stephen Hobhouse read Tolstoy's *How I Came to Believe*, and *My Religion*, one Oxford vacation in 1902. "The result was instantaneous and catastrophic – the whole edifice of my conventional patriotism and Anglican religious practice collapsed like a pack of cards" (Bell, Julian, ed., p. 158). After seeing militarism taught in German schools in 1908, he became a Quaker and a lifelong pacifist. Following his own release from prison, he campaigned for prison reform.

Margaret Hobhouse co-ordinated opposition to cat-&-mouse detentions when her son was imprisoned, highlighting the plight of conscientious objectors by publishing in 1917 the highly influential *"I Appeal Unto Caesar": The Case of the Conscientious Objector*. She even managed to get the pro-war Gilbert Murray to write a supportive introduction. Jo Vellacott has suggested that much of the text was actually written by Bertrand Russell; see Kennedy, Thomas C., p. 189.

Stephen Hobhouse later listed his own influences as William Law, Böhme, Quakers, Sheppard and Gandhi. In World War II, he wrote several pamphlets for F.O.R., including *Retribution and the Christian* (1942) in which he was critical of Temple, whom he would have known from an early date, either through F.O.R. or the World Alliance. Nonetheless, when Hobhouse's 1941 pamphlet, *Christ and Our Enemies*, was revised and reprinted in 1944, Temple magnanimously wrote a foreword. Thus Hobhouse ultimately influenced Temple's attitude to pacifists, or more accurately, to conscientious objectors whose freedoms he supported though whose opinions he disagreed with. In June 1953, the Anglican Pacifist Fellowship Newsletter referred to "Our member, Stephen Hobhouse".

67. *Challenge*, Anglican Pacifist Fellowship journal, Vol. II, No.4, March 1963, pp. 13-4. Gliddon was to be the prime mover in the 1937 founding of the Anglican Pacifist Fellowship, of which he soon afterwards became the secretary.
68. Graham, John W., pp. 322-5, said there were seventy-one deaths, but he gave seventy-three names. The *N.C.F. Souvenir* listed sixty-nine names (pp. 48-9).
69. Graham, John W., p. 250.
70. Graham, John W., pp. 294-5.
71. Hobhouse, M., pxvi.
72. Hansard, XXV, col. 333, cited in Wilkinson, Alan, *The Church of England and the First World War*, p. 50. The wording in Hobhouse, M., pp. 12-3 is slightly different.
73. Wilkinson, Alan, *The Church of England and the First World War*, p. 50.
74. Iremonger, F., *William Temple*, p. 388.

75. *Tribunal*, 8 November 1917.
76. Walter Ayles, in *N.C.F. Souvenir*, p. 67.
77. Walter Ayles, in *N.C.F. Souvenir*, p. 67.
78. Stanton, H. E., p. 210.
79. *Tribunal*, no. 326, 26 September 1918, pictured in Brock, Peter and Nigel Young, *Pacifism in the Twentieth Century*, p. xxiv; also cited in Graham, John W., pp. 302-3.
80. Attlee, Peggy, *With a Quiet Conscience*, p. 26. The hostel was named after the Christian socialist F.D. Maurice, and had recently been opened by Scott Holland.
81. Clement Attlee's political journey started with him became secretary of Toynbee Hall, 1909-1910, and led to him becoming Labour Prime Minister in 1945.
82. Attlee, Peggy, p. 36.
83. Attlee, Peggy, p. 38.
84. Attlee, Peggy, p. 48.
85. Cited in den Boggende,G.G.J., pp. 214-5.
86. den Boggende, G.G.J., pp. 129-30, citing F.O.R. *Newssheet* insert, 25 August 1916. For five years from 1918 the F.O.R. produced a series of booklets entitled "The Christian Revolution Series". Attlee wrote one of these booklets, *Man and His Buildings*, 1920. He showed great sympathy for crafts and small shopkeepers (den Boggende, G.G.J., p. 346).
87. Attlee, Peggy, p. 52.
88. A footnote dealt with the expulsion of the moneychangers from the temple.
89. Attlee, Peggy, pp. 48-51.
90. Attlee, Peggy, p. 63.
91. Cited in Attlee, Peggy, p. 74.
92. Walke, Bernard, p. 206. They were assisted by Gerard Collier of the F.O.R., one of Walke's parishioners, who had once told Bishop Warman of Truro that "You must repent of your share in the war before you can win the world for Christ" (Walke, Bernard, p. 176).
93. Attlee, Peggy, p. 57.
94. Attlee, Peggy, p. 62.

10. Losing "The Manhood of England"

1. Wilkinson, Alan, *The Church of England and the First World War*, p. 18.
2. Wilkinson, Alan, *The Church of England and the First World War*, p. 226.
3. Wilkinson, Alan, *The Church of England and the First World War*, p. 27.
4. *Daily Chronicle*, 12 October 1914, cited in Playne, Caroline, p. 192.
5. Wilkinson, Alan, *The Church of England and the First World War*, p. 27.
6. Wilkinson, Alan, *The Church of England and the First World War*, p. 24.
7. Wilkinson, Alan, *The Church of England and the First World War*, p. 27.
8. *The Church and War*, cited in Wilkinson, Alan, *The Church of England and the First World War*, p. 27.
9. Cited in Fletcher, Sheila, p. 112.
10. Playne, Caroline, p. 190.
11. *Tribunal*, 29 June 1916.

12. Playne, Caroline, p. 190.
13. Playne, Caroline, p. 191.
14. Playne, Caroline, p. 208.
15. Preface, *Crockford's Clerical Directory 1916-1917*, p. iv.
16. Robbins, Keith, *The Abolition of War*, p. 114.
17. Cited in Playne, Caroline, p. 337.
18. Playne, Caroline, p. 334.
19. Robbins, Keith, *The Abolition of War*, p. 119.
20. Robbins, Keith, *The Abolition of War*, p. 121.
21. See Söderblom's 1930 Nobel Peace Laureate Lecture: http://www.nobelprize.org/nobel_prizes/peace/laureates/1930/soderblom-lecture.html [accessed 9 August 2013].
22. Robbins, Keith, *The Abolition of War*, pp. 138-9.
23. *Goodwill*, Vol. 2, No. 8, 23 June 1917, pp. 203-9.
24. Dictionary of National Biography entry for Henry Charles Keith Petty-Fitzmaurice, 5th Marquess of Lansdowne.
25. Kennedy, Thomas C., p. 199.
26. Royden to Marshall, 10 August 1916 (cited in Fletcher, Sheila, pp. 136-7).
27. Lansbury, George, *My Life*, p. 210.
28. Wallis, Jill, *Valiant for Peace*, p. 25.
29. By the end of 1917 the F.O.R. was becoming more overtly political, placing confident policy advertisements in the *Herald*, claiming that the precepts of Jesus were "the only practical rules which can save us from THE EVILS OF THE PRESENT CAPITALISTIC SYSTEM", that philanthropy was not enough to make slums disappear, that often "crime is caused by the evils of our social system" and that a greater power than appeal to force of arms was that of self-sacrificing love (*Herald*, 1 December 1917).
30. den Boggende, G.G.J., p. 165. *Tribunal*, 11 October 1917, referred to incitement by a national newspaper promising "entertainment" at the Brotherhood Church at the time of a conference there.
31. *Herald*, 4 August 1917.
32. Wallis, Jill, *Valiant for Peace*, pp. 29-30.
33. Wallis, Jill, *Valiant for Peace*, p. 30.
34. Richards, E.R., p. 71.
35. Wallis, Jill, *Valiant for Peace*, p. 30.
36. Wilkinson, Alan, *The Church of England and the First World War*, p. 51. The same regulations were used to prosecute the publishers of the F.O.R. journal, *Venturer*, after it included a letter by an imprisoned conscientious objector, G.M. Davies to his wife (Wallis, Jill, *Valiant for Peace*, p. 30).
37. *W.I.L. Yearly Report*, 1918, p. 16.
38. Liddington, Jill, "The Women's Peace Crusade", in Thompson, Dorothy, ed., *Over Our Dead Bodies*, pp. 190-1; Woods, Mike, Angela Woods and Tricia Platts, "Women, Peace and Politics" in Woods, Mike and Tricia Platts, eds., *Bradford in the Great War*, pp. 166-9. For an earlier reference to the Women's Peace Crusade see the *Herald*, 24 October 1914.
39. den Boggende, G.G.J., p. 172.
40. den Boggende, G.G.J., pp. 165-6.
41. Basil Thomson, cited in den Boggende, G.G.J., p. 164.

42. Wallis, Jill, *Valiant for Peace*, p. 31.
43. Responding to stories of violence in Russia, Lansbury called for nonviolent means of revolution, but complained that "the churches and religious teachers with few exceptions are striving to do the impossible – that is, to prove that violence, force, poison gas, reprisals, and all the necessary equipment of war are right when used in a certain way, but wrong when used by the masses against their oppressors" (*Herald*, 9 March 1918).
44. Smith, Angela K. ed., "Introduction", *British Literature of World War 1*, volume 4, p. xv.
45. Fitzroy, A.T. (Rose Allatini), *Despised and Rejected*, in Smith, Angela K. ed., p.57.
46. Fitzroy, A.T. in Smith, Angela K. ed., pp. 81-2, 109.
47. Fitzroy, A.T. in Smith, Angela K. ed., pp. 81, 108.
48. Fitzroy, A.T. in Smith, Angela K. ed., p. 111.
49. Fitzroy, A.T. in Smith, Angela K. ed., p. 148.
50. *Times Literary Supplement*, 6 June 1918, p. 266, cited by Smith, Angela K. ed., p. xiv.
51. den Boggende, G.G.J., p. 201. One suggested date was Easter Day 1916, ironically the date on which the Republican rising in Dublin took place.
52. Wallis, Jill, *Valiant for Peace*, pp. 31-2.
53. den Boggende, G.G.J., p. 156.
54. F.O.R. General Committee Minutes, 19 March 1915. Box 1/1, pp. 40-5.
55. Wallis, Jill, *Valiant for Peace*, p. 32.
56. Roberts, R. Ellis, *H.R L. Sheppard: Life and Letters*, p. 8.
57. Roberts, R. Ellis, p. 78. The letter was to Alison Carver, one of Shepherd's former Grosvenor House congregation, and soon to become his fiancée.
58. Sheppard, H.R.L., *We Say 'No'*, p. 1.
59. Sheppard in Preface to Bell, Julian, ed., pvii.
60. Sheppard to Lang, cited in Scott, Carolyn, p. 64.
61. Scott, Carolyn, p. 63.
62. Temple later unjustly criticised pacifists of being Pelagian, of trying to work their own salvation. In Sheppard's case, he may have had a point.
63. *Church of England Newspaper*, cited in Scott, Carolyn, p. 68.
64. *Tribunal*, 8 November 1917.
65. Lansbury, George, *My Life*, p. 222.
66. Lansbury's reply of 11 November 1916 (Richardson papers), exactly two years before the war ended, indicated both the differences between the two men and the basis for their future friendship. " 'Sell all thou hast' in all probability was the right thing two thousand years ago but the right thing to do now is to reiterate and reiterate till people believe it, that there is more than enough for everyone if labour were organised on the lines of service. It is not less comfort that we need, it is more comfort; it is not smaller houses, but bigger houses; it is not less food but more food that the great mass of people need; and they can all have it and still leave more than enough for the rest of the community".
67. Lansbury to Sheppard, 18 December 1916. Richardson papers. In the last line, before "rich and poor" Lansbury had written and crossed out "men and women".

68. *Herald*, 10 July 1915.
69. *Christian Commonwealth*, 11 August 1915, cited in Shepherd, p. 168.
70. Playne, Caroline, p. 215.
71. Playne, Caroline, p. 216.
72. For discussion on the accelerated gendering of religious observance see Gregory, Adrian, p. 182.
73. The widow ends by expressing the scathing platitude, "Gawd bless yer, Parson. . . . Teach me – 'ow – to pray". Reilly, Catherine, ed., *Scars Upon My Heart*, pp. 8-9.
74. Brittain, Vera, *Verses of a V.A.D.*, p. 15; Brittain, Vera, edited by Mark Bostridge, *Because You Died*, pp. 3, 214-5.
75. Tawney, R.H., "Some Reflections of a Soldier", in *"The Attack" and Other Papers*, p. 27; cited in Biggar, Nigel, *In Defence of War*, p. 82.
76. Brittain, Vera, *Verses of a V.A.D.*, pp. 29-30; Brittain, Vera, edited by Mark Bostridge, *Because You Died*, pp. 24-5, 217.
77. Brittain, Vera, *Verses of a V.A.D.*, pp. 37-40; Brittain, Vera, edited by Mark Bostridge, *Because You Died*, pp. 38-9, 219.
78. "The spiritual struggle is as brutal as human battle, but the vision of justice is enjoyed by God alone". There is also a sympathetic study of *The Deserter* by Winifred M. Letts; Reilly, Catherine, ed., pp. 61-2.
79. Owen, Wilfred, *Apologia Pro Poemate Meo*.
80. "How much longer, O Lord, shall we bear it all? / How many more red years?" *He Went for a Soldier* by Ruth Comfort Mitchell in Reilly, Catherine, ed., pp. 75-6.
81. G.A. Studdert Kennedy, *Rough Talks by a Padre*, pp. 31-2, cited in Holman, Bob, *Woodbine Willie*, p. 45. Much of Studdert Kennedy's ministry was based in Worcester; for a Worcester-centred view of his life, see Grundy Michael, *A Fiery Glow in the Darkness*.
82. Studdert Kennedy, G.A. (Woodbine Willie), "Well?", in *Rough Rhymes of a Padre*, p. 11.
83. Defence of chaplaincy has been made, inter alia, by: Snape, Michael and Edward Madigan, *The Clergy in Khaki*, Ashgate, Farnham, 2013; Madigan, Edward, *Faith Under Fire*, Palgrave Macmillan, London, 2011; Snape, Michael, *God and the British Soldier*, Routledge, London, 2005; Parker, Linda, *The Whole Armour of God*, Helion, Birmingham, 2009; Howson, Peter, *Muddling Through*, Helion, Birmingham, 2013.
84. See Bell, Stuart, "Collapsing Class barriers – another Myth of the Trenches?" in *Crucible*, April-June 2014, pp. 35-42.
85. Holman, Bob, *Woodbine Willie*, p. 32.
86. Cited by Walters, Kerry, (ed.), *After War, Is Faith Possible?*, *G.A. Studdert Kennedy, An Anthology*, p. 41.
87. Studdert Kennedy, G.A. (Woodbine Willie), "Sinner and Saint", in *Rough Rhymes of a Padre*, p. 27-9.
88. G.A. Studdert Kennedy, *Rough Talks by a Padre*, 1918, pp. 26-8, cited in Walters, Kerry, ed., p.10.
89. G.A. Studdert Kennedy, *Lies!*, 1919, p. 6, cited in Walters, Kerry, ed., p. 22.
90. Studdert Kennedy, G.A. (Woodbine Willie), "The Sorrow of God", in *Rough Rhymes of a Padre*, pp.19-26.

91. Cited by Walters, Kerry, ed., p. 65.

92. Studdert Kennedy, G.A. (Woodbine Willie), "The Sorrow of God", in *Rough Rhymes of a Padre,* pp.19-26.

93. Studdert Kennedy, G.A. (Woodbine Willie), "The Sorrow of God", in *Rough Rhymes of a Padre,* pp.19-26.

94. Studdert Kennedy, G.A., "The Religious Difficulties of a Private Soldier", in Macnutt, F., ed., *Church in the Furnace,* p. 391, cited by Stuart Bell, "The Church and the First World War", in Parker, Stephen G. and Tom Lawson, eds., *God and War,* p. 47.

95. Cited by Walters, Kerry, ed., p. 37.

96. Cited by Walters, Kerry, ed., pp. 54-5.

97. Sheppard, Dick and Laurence Housman, *What Can We Believe?,* pp.138-9.

98. Cited by Walters, Kerry, ed., pp. 61-2.

99. Cited by Walters, Kerry, ed., p. 50.

100. Wilkinson, Alan, *The Church of England and the First World War,* p. 52.

101. Preface, *Crockford's Clerical Directory, 1916-1917,* pp. iii-iv.

102. *Herald,* 19 February 1916.

103. *Herald,* 2 December 1916.

104. *Herald,* 16 September 1916 (see also Schneer, Jonathan, pp. 139-40).

105. Davidson to Winnington-Ingram, 28 February 1916, Lambeth Palace, Davidson Papers, vol. 360; cited in Gregory, Adrian, p. 326.

106. Gregory points out (Gregory, Adrian, pp. 278-9, 283, 336) that in nearby Lambeth, not the poorest working class suburb, children's death rates in 1913 were double that of adult males in the armed forces during the war. Lansbury was, in effect, pointing his readers to an even bigger war, on his readers' doorstep. Similarly, the likelihood of a miner being killed in his regular working life was the same as a soldier on 1 July 1916, the first day of the Somme.

107. Lansbury, George, *Faith and Hope,* cited in Gregory, Adrian, pp. 166-7.

108. For Sheppard's role, see Roberts, R. Ellis, p. 119.

109. There were some pacifists on ecclesiastical committees, but their influence was peripheral on issues relating to the war. E.W. Barnes sat on the Committee on The Teaching Office of the Church, with such figures as Scott Holland, Gore, Temple, inter alia (Wilkinson, Alan, *The Church of England and the First World War,* p. 81).

110. Wilkinson, Alan, *The Church of England and the First World War,* p. 86.

111. Lansbury, George, *My Life,* pp. 220-1.

112. Lansbury, George, *My Life,* p. 222.

113. Cited in Wilkinson, Alan, *The Church of England and the First World War,* pp. 85-6.

114. Wallis, Jill, *Valiant for Peace,* p. 28, and Brittain, Vera, *Rebel Passion,* p. 42.

115. *W.I.L. Yearly Report,* 1916, p. 2.

116. Cited by Royden in Buxton, C.R., ed., p. 135.

117. *W.I.L. Yearly Report,* 1916, pp. 8-9; also Fletcher, Sheila, p. 136.

118. *W.I.L. Yearly Report,* 1916, pp. 9-10. Lansbury also gave two of the talks in these series, on "War and the Journalist" and, at Christmas, on "Peace to Men of Goodwill" (*W.I.L. Yearly Report,* 1917, p. 11). Royden and Lansbury were signatories, along with Lewis Donaldson (Rector of St. Mark's,

Leicester), the Bishops of Hereford (John Percival) and Lincoln (Edward Hicks), and others, supporting a suffrage letter to Asquith in June 1916 (*W.I.L. Yearly Report*, 1916, p. 12).

119. Fletcher, Sheila, pp. 167-71.

120. Fletcher, Sheila, pp. 145-6.

121. Royden, Maude, *The Hour and the Church*, p. 83.

122. Fletcher, Sheila, p. 152.

123. Royden was both a committed Anglican and an ecumenist. In 1918 she stated categorically that "The Church of England is the Church of my baptism. I am her child by temperament and by conviction as well", (Royden, Maude, *The Hour and the Church*, p. 26), a sentiment she later expanded upon: "In ecclesiastical matters I am 'a soul naturally Anglican. Too Anglican to care for the rigid logical completeness of either High or Low Church extremes, or for the intellectualism of the Broad Church, I want something of all of them, and am convinced that the Church of England is the place where I ought to be able to have them and can have them all" (Royden, Maude, *I Believe in God*, p. 3). At the same time she recognised the gifts of other traditions: "We have opened our eyes to the existence of holy men and women in other Churches than our own, unnourished by our sacraments, unguided and unblest by our priests. They are not of the Church of England; yet, too clearly for denial, they are of Christ" (Royden, Maude, *The Hour and the Church*, p. 23). She longed for a united Christianity with the order and beauty of Anglicanism, the freedom of Nonconformity and the silent worship of the Quaker (Royden, Maude, *The Hour and the Church*, p. 84).

124. Royden spent most of her life in close platonic relationship with Shaw. As early as 1906, she had written of him, "I do want him – often – but hunger is not the same as loneliness. . . . I am never <u>lonely</u> when I am with Mr Shaw" (Letter to Kathleen Courtney, 23 July 1906, L.M.H). She did eventually marry him, in October 1944 when he was a widower over 80 years old (*Times*, 31 July 1956).

125. Royden, Maude, *The Hour and the Church*, 1918, p. 61. When Life and Liberty wanted to meet at Cuddesdon in 1917 the Principal – later Bishop Seaton of Wakefield – refused to allow her to sleep under the theological college roof, in protest at her Temple activities (Wilkinson, Alan, *The Church of England and the First World War*, p. 92). Ultimately, the modest achievement of the Life and Liberty movement, which by then no longer had the benefit of Royden's contribution, was the formation in 1920 of the Church Assembly – to which Royden was the first woman elected (Fletcher, Sheila, p. 236) – through the Enabling Act of 1919. Tissington Tatlow of the S.C.M. was one of the few Anglicans to speak up for Royden, acknowledging her unique influence among young people (*Challenge*, 19 October 1917, cited in Fletcher, Sheila, p. 173). Winifred Holtby remarked on Royden's preaching that "the gracious tolerance of the sermon struck a responsive chord in the developing mind" (Brittain, Vera, *Testament of Friendship*, Virago, London, 1980, p. 68).

126. Cited in Fletcher, Sheila, p. 179.

11. The Aftermath of War

1. Robert Young had a portrait of the militant atheist Charles Bradlaugh in his office in Kobe. His son was named after Moncure Conway, who once presided over what later became the South Place Ethical Society in London. There is contempt for both religion and war in the headstone's use of the language of "sacrifice". War-grave reference for A.C. Young: Tyne Cot IV G. 21.
2. *Herald*, 16 November 1918, front page banner headline; *Herald*, 18 January 1919.
3. The bishops were from: Barrow (Campbell West-Watson), Bath & Wells (George Kennion), Bristol (George Nickson), Chelmsford (John Watts Ditchfield), Ely (Frederic Chase), Gloucester (Edgar Gibson), Guildford (John Randolph), Kingston (Samuel Taylor), Lichfield (John Kempthorne), Lincoln (Edward Hicks), Liverpool (Francis Chavasse), Llandaff (Joshua Pritchard Hughes), Oxford (Charles Gore), Peterborough (Frank Woods), Ripon (Thomas Drury), Southampton (James Macarthur) and Wakefield (George Eden). Other clerical signatories included C.C.B. Bardsley (Secretary of the Church Missionary Society), E.W. Barnes, J.W. Horsley, Gresford Jones (Archdeacon of Sheffield), Sheppard, Temple, Tissington Tatlow (Secretary of S.C.M.) and H.W. Webb-Peploe (Prebendary of St Paul's). *Tribunal* no. 140, 9 January 1919, p. 3.
4. *Herald*, 15 March 1919.
5. Robbins, Keith, *The Abolition of War*, p. 184.
6. Robbins, Keith, *The Abolition of War*, pp. 185-6.
7. den Boggende, G.G.J., pp. 277, 300. The principal countries were India (22 members), South-Africa (12), New Zealand and China (10 each), and Canada and France (9 each).
8. Stevenson, Lilian, *Towards a Christian International*, pp. 4-6.
9. The F.O.R. appointed fourteen delegates to attend if they were able, including Thomas Attlee, together with Walter Ayles, Gerard Collier, Oliver Dryer, Joan Fry, Carl Heath, Henry Hodgkin, Muriel Lester, Lord Parmoor, William Paton, Leyton Richards, Lilian Stevenson, Wilfred Wellock and Theodora Wilson-Wilson (den Boggende, G.G.J., p. 300).
10. Siegmund-Schültze had only narrowly avoided execution in Berlin for his pacifist stance (Wallis, Jill, *Mother of World Peace*, p. 49).
11. Stevenson, Lilian, p. 7.
12. Cited in Rigby, Andrew, *A Life in Peace*, p. 31.
13. Stevenson, Lilian, p. 8.
14. In the months that followed, Boeke moved steadily towards an anarchist position, and in 1921 he was asked to step down as secretary. Within a year the post of secretary of the M.T.C.I. was shared with the secretary of the F.O.R., Oliver Dryer, and transferred to London.
15. A further Bilthoven gathering in 1920 led to a reconstruction project in Verdun and the birth of the Service Civil International (S.C.I.), following an initiative by Cérésole (Anet, Daniel, *Pierre Ceresole, Passionate Peacemaker*, pp. 53-81). In Britain this was known as International Voluntary Service (I.V.S.), following an international work camp at

Brynmawr, South Wales, in 1931, organised by Cérésole, Jean Inebnit of Leeds University and Peter Scott, a Quaker (Perry, Harry, *50 Years of Workcamps*, pp. 5, 6).

16. den Boggende, G.G.J., p. 281.
17. Rigby, Andrew, p. 37.
18. Ceadel, Martin, *Pacifism in Britain, 1914-1945*, p. 72.
19. The name came from German posters bearing the inscription *Nie Wieder Krieg!* A similar German organisation was founded at about the same time (Chamberlain, W.J., *Fighting for Peace*, p. 124).
20. Wellock, cited in Rigby, Andrew, p. 39. The *Crusader* changed its name to *No More War*, with Fenner Brockway appointed as its first editor. The first Chairman of the N.M.W.M. was W.J. Chamberlain. By the summer of 1925, membership had risen to 2,000, with 13,000 signatures collected in a petition calling for the British Government to implement total disarmament by example (Rigby, Andrew, pp. 46-7).
21. Wellock had started the *New Crusader* – as it was first called – an occasional Christian pacifist broadsheet, on 25 March 1916. When he was imprisoned as a conscientious objector the broadsheet was taken over by an editorial committee of F.O.R. activists, principally Theodora Wilson-Wilson – later to be the originator of the "Affirmation Against War" (Chamberlain, W.J., p. 118) – together with W.E. Orchard, Muriel Lester, W.J. Chamberlain, Helen Ward and Stanley James (Rigby, Andrew, p. 25).
22. Rigby, Andrew, pp. 37-8.
23. Chamberlain, W.J., p. 124.
24. The first international conference of W.R.I. brought 95 delegates from 18 countries to the Hoddesdon base of S.C.M. in 1925 (Rigby, Andrew, p. 47). At a second conference, in Sonntagberg, Austria, in 1928, there were affiliated organisations from 21 countries represented. Brown was to remain in his post with W.R.I. until his death in 1949 (Rigby, Andrew, pp. 37-9).
25. No More War Movement Annual Report, 1926-27, p. 19.
26. *No More War*, Vol. V, No. 3, December 1925, p. 1.
27. No More War Movement Annual Report, 1926-27, p. 30. The N.M.W.M. regretted that their resolution did not appear to have had any influence upon those to whom it was directed (p. 19).
28. Stephenson, Alan M.G., *Anglicanism and the Lambeth Conferences*, p. 128.
29. *Lambeth Conferences, 1867-1930*, p. 23; also, Davidson, Randall, *The Six Lambeth Conferences, 1867-1920*, pp. 9-10. Conference resolutions, but not committee reports, can be found at http://www.lambethconference.org/resolutions/1920/ [accessed 6 December 2013.]
30. *Lambeth Conferences, 1867-1930*, p. 31; Davidson, Randall, pp. 19-20.
31. *Lambeth Conferences, 1867-1930*, p. 31; Davidson, Randall, p. 20.
32. *Lambeth Conferences, 1867-1930*, p. 37; Davidson, Randall, p. 25.
33. *Lambeth Conferences, 1867-1930*, p. 57; Davidson, Randall, p. 54.
34. *Lambeth Conferences, 1867-1930*, p. 55; Davidson, Randall, p. 51.
35. *Lambeth Conferences, 1867-1930*, p. 57; Davidson, Randall, p. 53.
36. *Lambeth Conferences, 1867-1930*, p. 60-1; Davidson, Randall, pp. 57-8

37. *Lambeth Conferences, 1867-1930*, p. 55; Davidson, Randall, p. 51.
38. *Lambeth Conferences, 1867-1930*, pp. 57-8; Davidson, Randall, pp. 54-5.
39. *Lambeth Conferences, 1867-1930*, p. 24; Davidson, Randall, p. 11.
40. C.O.P.E.C. Commission, *Christianity and War*, p. iv.
41. Raven, Charles E., *War and the Christian*, p. 30.
42. Nathan Söderblom, cited in Dillistone, F.W., *Charles Raven*, p. 118.
43. Raven, Charles E., *John Ray: His Life and Works*, p. v.
44. Raven, Charles, *A Wanderer's Way*, p. 104.
45. Raven to S.W. Burgess, 30 April 1917. My thanks to Faith Raven for access to this correspondence.
46. Raven, Charles E., *Our Salvation*, p. 64.
47. Raven to S.W. Burgess, 29 July 1917. Faith Raven collection.
48. Raven, Charles E., "We Will Not Fight", in Macaulay, Rose, H.R.L. Sheppard, et al, *Let Us Honour Peace*, p. 48.
49. Dillistone, F.W., p. 117. Iremonger, F., p. 335.
50. den Boggende, G.G.J., p. 264.
51. C.O.P.E.C. Commission, pp. ix-x.
52. C.O.P.E.C. Commission, p. 23.
53. C.O.P.E.C. Commission, p. 39.
54. C.O.P.E.C. Commission, p. 38.
55. C.O.P.E.C. Commission, pp. 29-31.
56. C.O.P.E.C. Commission, p. 86.
57. C.O.P.E.C. Commission, p. 87.
58. C.O.P.E.C. Commission, pp. 99-100.
59. C.O.P.E.C. Commission, p. 59.
60. C.O.P.E.C. Commission, p. 59.
61. C.O.P.E.C. Commission, p. 69.
62. C.O.P.E.C. Commission, pp. 61-2.
63. C.O.P.E.C. Commission, pp. 62-3.
64. C.O.P.E.C. Commission, p. 67.
65. C.O.P.E.C. Commission, p. 67.
66. C.O.P.E.C. Commission, p. 64.
67. C.O.P.E.C. Commission, p. 66.
68. C.O.P.E.C. Commission, pp. 70-1.
69. C.O.P.E.C. Commission, p. 72.
70. C.O.P.E.C. Commission, pp. 72-3.
71. One immediate side-effect of C.O.P.E.C. was a marked increase in the numbers subscribing to the F.O.R. journal *Reconciliation*. den Boggende, G.G.J., p. 236.
72. Raven, Charles E., *War and the Christian*, p. 25.
73. Cited in Raven, Charles E., *Is War Obsolete?*, p. 22, p. 22; Jasper, Ronald C.D., *George Bell, Bishop of Chichester*, p. 94.
74. Resolution 25, Lambeth Conference 1930.

12. The Cast Revisited

1. Lansbury, George, *My Life*, pp. 211-2.

2. *Crusader*, 20 February 1920, cited in Rigby, Andrew, p. 32.

3. Lansbury, George, *My Life*, p. 219.

4. Lansbury, George, *My Life*, p. 220.

5. 17 May 1919, cited in Schneer, Jonathan, p. 148.

6. 26 July 1919, cited in Schneer, Jonathan, p. 148.

7. Lansbury, George, *My Life*, p. 234.

8. The paper resumed its daily editions from 31 March 1919. Having survived the war on a shoestring, at the height of its power it had a readership exceeding 3,250,000. Lansbury was to stay with the paper until February 1925, "one of the most worrying and happy episodes in my life" (Lansbury, George, *My Life*, p. 170). Adding to his influence on the left was the independent *Lansbury's Labour Weekly*, first published on 28 February 1925, which had a circulation of 172,000 and joined with the I.L.P.'s *New Leader* in July 1927 (Postgate, Raymond, pp. 230-1).

9. Lansbury, George, *My Life*, p. 245.

10. Lansbury, George, *My Life*, p. 235. One Bolshevik he met, Georgy Chicherin, told him that in his experience the churches had been one of the curses of mankind which had made capitalism possible (Lansbury, George, *My Life*, p. 242). Lansbury's report was significant as the British press had claimed that the churches had been closed down.

11. Postgate, Raymond, p. 207.

12. *Daily Herald*, 27 August 1921, cited in Schneer, Jonathan, p. 1.

13. *Daily Herald*, 4 October 1919, cited in Schneer, Jonathan, p. 149.

14. For the full story see Branson, Noreen, *Poplarism, 1919-1925*.

15. Lansbury, Edgar, p. 121.

16. *Diary*, vol. 3, 24 February 1920, p. 356, cited in Schneer, Jonathan, p. 150.

17. Postgate, Raymond, p. 251.

18. *Embassies of Reconciliation*, I.F.O.R. pamphlet, 1938, p. 16.

19. 5 August 1919, p. 134.

20. Chaturvedi, Benarsidas and Marjorie Sykes, pp. 131-2. Ironically, the examining Commissioner who sent him back to Delhi had been a contemporary of his at Pembroke College, Cambridge.

21. Clark, I.D.L., p. 43.

22. Gandhi, Mohandas K., *An Autobiography: The Story of My Experiments with Truth*, p. 396. Andrews toured the local villages with Gurdial Mallik who regarded C.F.A. as standing for "Christ's Faithful Apostle" (Chaturvedi, Benarsidas and Marjorie Sykes, p. 136).

23. Chaturvedi and Sykes, p. 137.

24. *Tribune*, 16 November 1919, cited in Chaturvedi, Benarsidas and Marjorie Sykes, p. 137. Three years later, Andrews returned to Amritsar to urge Sikh reformers to work nonviolently when challenging their religious leaders (Clark, I.D.L., p. 50; Chaturvedi, Benarsidas and Marjorie Sykes, pp. 186-7).

25. Royden, Maude, *Political Christianity*, pp. 37-8.

26. Royden, Maude, *Political Christianity*, pp. 40-1.

27. Royden, Maude, *Political Christianity*, p. 42.

28. Graham, John W., p. 341.
29. Fletcher, Sheila, pp. 207-8.
30. Fletcher, Sheila, pp. 210.
31. Fletcher, Sheila, pp. 215.
32. Fletcher, Sheila, pp. 216.
33. Fletcher, Sheila, pp. 227.
34. Royden, Maude, *Political Christianity*, pp. 87-8.
35. *Church Militant*, (Supplement), July 1921, cited in Fletcher, Sheila, p. 206.
36. Royden, Maude, *Political Christianity*, pp. 81-6.
37. Cited in Royden, Maude, *Political Christianity*, pp. 78.
38. Royden, Maude, *Political Christianity*, pp. 71-81.
39. Royden, Maude, *Our Policy in the Near East*, p. 10.
40. Royden, Maude, *Our Policy in the Near East*, p. 3.
41. Royden, Maude, *Our Policy in the Near East*, p. 14.
42. Liddington, Jill, *The Long Road to Greenham*, pp. 144-5.
43. Cited in Bussey, Gertrude and Margaret Tims, p. 51. One prominent figure was the Anglican pacifist Sybil Thorndike who carried a banner embroidered with doves
44. Higgins, Alfred G., *A History of the Brotherhood Church*, p. 54.
45. Letter from the Brotherhood Church to Philip Dransfield, 14 September 1965.
46. Higgins, Alfred G., p. 2.
47. Higgins, Alfred G., p. 53.
48. Pilkington, George, *The Doctrine of Particular Providence*.
49. Pilkington, George, *Travels Through the United Kingdom in Promoting the Cause of Peace on Earth and Goodwill Towards Men*, pp. 59-60.
50. Stimson, Charles C., pp. 168-9. The three Orders were later described by Pickering as preachers, guilds and workers (Dransfield typescript of the *Scotsman*, 3 January 1928. I am grateful to Philip Dransfield for introducing me to details of this story).
51. Stimson, Charles C., pp. 169-71.
52. Stimson, Charles C., pp. 143-4.
53. Walke, Bernard, p. 145.
54. Walke, Bernard, p. 148.
55. Miles, Susan, *Portrait of a Parson*, p. 61.
56. Wallis, Jill, *Mother of World Peace*, p. 37.
57. Wallis, Jill, *Mother of World Peace*, pp. 51-2.
58. Lester, Muriel, *It Occurred to Me*, p. 66.
59. Lester, Muriel, p. 193.
60. Wallis, Jill, *Mother of World Peace*, pp. 52-3.
61. Wallis, Jill, *Valiant for Peace*, p. 49.
62. *Reconciliation*, 1935, p. 252,
63. Walke, Bernard, p. 176.
64. Walke, Bernard, p. 206.
65. Wallis, Jill, *Valiant for Peace*, p. 48.
66. Walke, Bernard, pp. 207-12; also *Reconciliation* 1935, p. 252.
67. Walke, Bernard, pp. 241-6; also *Reconciliation*, 1935, p. 252.
68. *We Do Not Forget*, an article in the *Sunday Times*, cited in Sheppard, H.R.L., *God and My Neighbour*, p. 190.

69. Sheppard, H.R.L., *We Say "No"*, p. 2.
70. Scott, Carolyn, pp. 107-8.
71. Scott, Carolyn, p. 120.
72. Roberts, R. Ellis, pp. 116-8.
73. Scott, Carolyn, p. 109.
74. Scott, Carolyn, p. 129.
75. Roberts, R. Ellis, p. 145.
76. Scott, Carolyn, pp. 141-2.
77. In the two months to December 1925 some 40,000 supporters had signed this forerunner to the Sheppard Peace Pledge (Brock, Peter, *Twentieth-Century Pacifism*, Van Nostrand Reinhold, New York, 1970, p. 127). Vera Brittain claimed Ponsonby's appeal ultimately attracted 128,770 signatures (Brittain, Vera, *Rebel Passion*, p. 46). Ponsonby himself later claimed 140,000 in an unpublished, undated tribute to Dick Sheppard in the Richardson papers. A similar document was in circulation in Germany, and in Saxony alone over 200,000 signatures were collected (Chamberlain, W.J., p. 127.) See also Ceadel, Martin, *Pacifism in Britain, 1914-1945*, pp. 80-3; Scott, Carolyn, p.142.
78. Sheppard's next appointment was to follow George Bell as Dean of Canterbury, a position again cut short because of his health. He then accepted an invitation to become a Canon of St Paul's. At the time, there was a young minor canon at St Paul's, John Collins, who would lead the peace movement alongside Bertrand Russell a quarter of a century later.
79. Sheppard to Housman, 4 February 1927. Housman, L., ed., *What Can We Believe?*, p. 82.
80. Sheppard to Housman, 12 February 1927; Housman, L., ed., pp. 85-9.
81. Sheppard, H.R.L., *The Impatience of a Parson*, pp. 121-2.
82. Sheppard, H.R.L., *The Impatience of a Parson*, p. 37.
83. Sheppard, H.R.L., *The Impatience of a Parson*, p. 52.
84. Sheppard, H.R.L., *The Impatience of a Parson*, p. 170.
85. Sheppard, H.R.L., *The Impatience of a Parson*, p. 216.
86. Scott, Carolyn, pp. 159-62.
87. McCormick, Pat, H.R.L. Sheppard, et al, *St Martin-in-the-Fields Calling*, pp. 106-12.
88. Sheppard to Housman, 12 March 1929. Housman, L., ed., p. 139.

13. Reflections on the Legacy of 1914-1918 War Resistance

1. Allen, Clifford, "The Presidential Address to the Concluding Convention", in No-Conscription Fellowship, *Troublesome People*, p. 60.
2. Edward Grubb, cited in No-Conscription Fellowship, *Troublesome People*, p. 4.
3. Brittain, Vera, *Rebel Passion*, p. 46.
4. *War Resister*, No. 21, October 1928, p. 22.
5. The text was based on an Armisticetide sermon by Harry Emerson Fosdick, Minister of the Riverside Church, New York (Morrison, Sybil, *I Renounce War*, p. 8). The sermon was preached on 12 November 1933.

6. Lansbury, George, *My Quest For Peace*, pp. 134-5, 138.

7. Lansbury, George, *My Quest For Peace*, p. 139.

8. Pierce, Nathaniel W. and Paul L. Ward, *The Voice of Conscience: A Loud and Unusual Noise?*, p.7.

9. Raven, Charles E., *War and the Christian*, p. 82. This volume sold 25,000 copies in its first three months (*Reconciliation*, September 1938, p. 265.)

10. Raven, Charles E., "The Religious Basis of Pacifism", in Oldham, J.H., ed., *The Universal Church and the World of Nations*, Church Community and State Series volume 7, p. 307.

11. Raven, Charles E., "The Religious Basis of Pacifism", in Oldham, J.H., ed., p. 315.

12. A.P.F. member Paul Oestreicher was a key member of the group which produced this report.

13. Even a century later, there are those who argue that "it" was worth it, and would still have been worth it even if far more people had been killed, (Biggar, Nigel, *In Defence of War*, pp. 129, 144), that too much fuss is made about casualties, and that war is disproportionate "if one thinks only in terms of the number of lives" saved or lost (Biggar, Nigel, p. 139; Biggar argues that intent is more important than consequence, so if those conducting a war are well-meaning, the cost of their actions is a secondary concern, even to the point of "virtuous callousness"– the planned destruction of hundreds of thousands of one's own troops, pp. 147-8).

14. Ferguson, Niall, *The Pity of War*, p. 462.

15. Kenneth Baker, *The Times*, 11 November 1996, p. 15, cited in Gregory, Adrian, *The Last Great War*, p. 4.

16. Allen, Clifford, "The Presidential Address to the Concluding Convention", in No-Conscription Fellowship, *Troublesome People*, p. 61.

17. See Gregory, Adrian, *The Last Great War*, p. 296: "The same urge to support military interventions will be present until war is renounced, either through a genuine conversion to absolute and unconditional pacifism or a self-centred decision to forego any military action whatsoever on the grounds that it cannot serve our interests or most hopefully and perhaps least likely, through the establishment of an orderly world in which aggression has ceased. Then and only then we can finally state with justified confidence that we have fought the last war".

18. A phrase popularised by the American pacifist, A.J. Muste.

Bibliography

Cited Texts

Relevant Periodicals and Journals Included:

Advocate of Peace
Arbitrator
Challenge
Church Times
Concord
Daily Herald
Goodwill
Herald
Herald of Peace
Reconciliation

Archives or Papers of Organisations or Individuals:

Anglican Pacifist Fellowship archive held by Clive Barrett
Charles Raven papers held by Faith Raven
H.R.L. Sheppard papers held by the late Lady Richardson of Duntisbourne
Leeds Peace Association, Carlton Hill papers, Quaker Collection, University of Leeds
Diverse First World War papers from the Liddle Collection, University of Leeds
Maude Royden correspondence with Kathleen Courtney, Lady Margaret Hall, Oxford
Vera Brittain papers, McMaster University, Hamilton, Ontario
Pearce Register of British Conscientious Objectors, a preliminary copy of which is held at the Peace Museum, Bradford
Society of Friends, Friends' House Library, London

Archives, complete and partial, and diverse papers held at the British Library of Political and Economic Science, London, including:
Fellowship of Reconciliation

International Arbitration League
National Peace Council
Peace Society
Women's International League
Workman's Peace Association

Cited Volumes, Articles and Theses Included:

Adeney, Bernard T., *Just War, Political Realism, and Faith*, ATLA, Metuchen NJ, 1988

Allen, Clifford, "The Faith of the N.C.F." in No-Conscription Fellowship, *Troublesome People*, Central Board for Conscientious Objectors, London, 1940

Allen, Clifford, "The Presidential Address to the Concluding Convention", in No-Conscription Fellowship, *Troublesome People*, Central Board for Conscientious Objectors, London, 1940

Allen, Devere, ed., *Pacifism in the Modern World*, Doubleday Doran, Garden City NY, 1929

Allen, Mark, "Winchester, the Clergy and the Boer War", in Parker, S.G., and Tom Lawson, *God and War*, Ashgate, Farnham, 2012

Andrews, C.F., *What I Owe to Christ*, Hodder and Stoughton, London, 1932

Andrews, C.F., *Christ in the Silence*, Hodder and Stoughton, London, 1933

Andrews, C.F., *The Inner Life*, Hodder and Stoughton, London, 1939

Anet, Daniel, *Pierre Ceresole, Passionate Peacemaker*, Macmillan, Delhi, 1974

Attlee, Peggy, *With a Quiet Conscience*, Dove and Chough, London, 1995

Avis, Paul, *The Anglican Understanding of the Church*, 2nd edition, SPCK, London, 2013

Bainton, Roland H., *Christian Attitudes Toward War and Peace*, Hodder and Stoughton, London, 1961

Barnes, John, *Ahead of His Age*, Collins, London, 1979

Baxter, Archibald, *We Will Not Cease*, Caxton Press, Christchurch, New Zealand, 1965

Bell, Julian, ed., *We Did Not Fight*, Cobden-Sanderson, London, 1935

Bell, Stuart, "The Church and the First World War", in Parker, Stephen G. and Tom Lawson, eds., *God and War*, Ashgate, Farnham, 2012

Bell, Stuart, "Collapsing Class barriers – another Myth of the Trenches?" in *Crucible*, Hymns Ancient and Modern, Norwich, April-June 2014

Bevan, Edwyn, *German Social Democracy During the War*, Allen and Unwin, London, 1918

Bibbings, Lois S., *Telling Tales About Men*, Manchester University Press, Manchester, 2009

Biggar, Nigel, *In Defence of War*, Oxford University Press, Oxford, 2013

Blunden, Margaret, "The Anglican Church during the War", in Warwick, Peter, ed., *The South African War: the Anglo-Boer War 1899-1902*. Harlow, Longman, 1980

Bollard, Robert, *In the Shadow of Gallipoli*, New South, Sydney, 2013

Boulton, David, *Objection Overruled*, MacGibbon and Key, London, 1967

Branson, Noreen, *Poplarism, 1919-1925*, Lawrence and Wishart, London, 1979

Brittain, Vera, *Verses of a V.A.D.*, Erskine MacDonald, London, 1918

Brittain, Vera, *Rebel Passion,* Allen and Unwin, London, 1964

Brittain, Vera, *Testament of Friendship*, Virago, London, 1980

Brittain, Vera, edited by Mark Bostridge, *Because You Died,* Virago, London, 2008

Brock, Peter, *Twentieth-Century Pacifism*, Van Nostrand Reinhold, New York, 1970

Brock, Peter, *Freedom From Violence,* Toronto University Press, Toronto, 1991

Brock, Peter and Nigel Young, *Pacifism in the Twentieth Century*, Toronto University Press, Toronto, 1999

Brockway, A. Fenner, "The Story of the N.C.F." in No-Conscription Fellowship, *Troublesome People,* Central Board for Conscientious Objectors, London, 1940

Brown, H. Runham, "The Women of the C.O. Movement" in No-Conscription Fellowship, *Troublesome People,* Central Board for Conscientious Objectors, London, 1940

Bussey, Gertrude and Margaret Tims, *Pioneers for Peace,* WILPF, London, 1980. Originally *Women's International League for Peace and Freedom, 1915-1965,* George Allen and Unwin, London, 1965

Buxton, Charles Roden, ed., *Towards a Lasting Settlement,* George Allen and Unwin, London, 1915

Cady, Duane L., "Just War", *The International Encyclopedia of Peace,* edited by Nigel Young, Oxford University Press, New York, Oxford, 2010

Ceadel, Martin, *Origins of War Prevention,* Clarendon, Oxford, 1996

Ceadel, Martin, *Pacifism in Britain, 1914-1945,* Clarendon, Oxford, 1980

Ceadel, Martin, *Semi-Detached Idealists,* Oxford University Press, Oxford, 2000

Ceadel, Martin, *Living the Great Illusion,* Oxford, Oxford University Press, 2009

Ceadel, Martin, "The Peace Movement: Overview of a British Brand Leader", *International Affairs,* Vol. 90, No. 2, 2014

Chamberlain, W.J., *Fighting for Peace,* No More War Movement, London, 1928

Chaturvedi, Benarsidas and Marjorie Sykes, *Charles Freer Andrews,* George Allen and Unwin, London, 1949

Clark, I.D.L., *C.F. Andrews – Deenabandhu,* ISPCK, Delhi, 1970

Clarkson, Thomas, *An Essay on the Doctrines and Practice of the Early Christians as They Relate to War,* Peace Society; 1817

Cobden, Richard, *Political Writings of Richard Cobden,* Cassell, London, 1886

Coltman, Claude, "1915 – Mission to England", *Reconciliation,* February 1964

C.O.P.E.C. Commission, *Christianity and War,* Longmans Green, London, 1924

Cuthbertson, Greg, "Pricking the 'nonconformist conscience'; religions against the South African War" in Lowry, Donal, ed., *The South African War Reappraised,* Manchester, Manchester University, 2000

Davidson, Randall, *The Six Lambeth Conferences, 1867-1920,* SPCK, London, 1929

den Boggende, Gijsbert Gerrit Jacob, *The Fellowship of Reconciliation, 1914-1945,* Ph.D., McMaster University, Hamilton, Ontario, 1986

Dillistone, F.W., *Charles Raven,* Hodder and Stoughton, London, 1975

Durward, Rosemary and Lee Marsden, eds., *Religion, Conflict and Military Intervention,* Ashgate, Farnham, 2009

Ellsworth-Jones, Will, *We Will Not Fight,* Aurum, London, 2007

Ewer, W.N., *Five Souls and other War-Time Verses,* Herald, London, 1917

Ferguson, Niall, *The Pity of War,* Penguin, London, 1998

Fisher, David, "Just War and The First World War: Where was the Just War Tradition when it was needed? (or how moral theology could have saved the world)", in *Crucible*, Hymns Ancient and Modern, Norwich, April-June 2014

Fitzroy, A.T., *Despised and Rejected*. See Smith, Angela, ed., British Literature of World War 1, volume 4

Fletcher, Sheila, *Maude Royden; A Life*, Blackwell, Oxford, 1989

Fowler, J.H., ed., *The Life and Letters of Edward Lee Hicks*, Christophers, London, 1922

Fry, Joan M., *Christ and Peace*, Headley, London, 1915

Gandhi, Mohandas K., *An Autobiography: The Story of My Experiments with Truth*, Jonathan Cape, London, 1966

Goodall, Felicity, *A Question of Conscience*, Sutton, Stroud, 1997. Reissued as *We Will Not Go to War*, History Press, Stroud, 2010

Graham, John W., *Conscription and Conscience*, George Allen and Unwin, London, 1922; reprinted by Augustus M. Kelley, New York, 1969

Grane, W.L., *The Passing of War*, MacMillan, London, 1912

Grant, David, *Field Punishment No. 1*, Steele Roberts, Wellington, New Zealand, 2008

Gregory, Adrian, *The Last Great War*, Cambridge University Press, Cambridge, 2008

Groves, Reg, *Conrad Noel and the Thaxted Movement*, Augustus M. Kelley, New York, 1968

Grundy Michael, *A Fiery Glow in the Darkness*, Osborne, Worcester, 1997

Hartill, Percy, *Article XXXVII and War*, Anglican Pacifist Fellowship, 1940

Hartill, Percy, *Into the Way of Peace*, James Clarke, Cambridge, 1941

Higgins, Alfred G., *A History of the Brotherhood Church*, Brotherhood Church, Stapleford, 1982

Hobhouse, Margaret, E., *I Appeal to Caesar*, Allen and Unwin, London, 1917

Holland, H.E., *Armageddon or Calvary*, H.E. Holland, Wellington, New Zealand, 1919

Holman, Bob, *Woodbine Willie*, Lion, Oxford, 2013

Hooker, Richard, *Of the Laws of Ecclesiastical Polity*, 1593

Housman, L., ed., *What Can We Believe?*, Jonathan Cape, London, 1939

Hoyland, J.S., *C.F. Andrews: Minister of Reconciliation*, Allenson, London, 1940

Hughes, Robert, *The Red Dean*, Churchman, London, 1987

Ingram, Kenneth, *Fifty Years of the National Peace Council, 1908-1958*, National Peace Council, London, 1958

Iremonger, F., *William Temple*, Oxford University Press, London, 1948

Jasper, Ronald C.D., *George Bell, Bishop of Chichester*, Oxford University Press, London, 1967

Johnson, Hewlett, *Searching for Light: an Autobiography*, Joseph, London, 1968

Jowitt, J.A., "Bradford and Peace 1800-1918", in Rank, Carol, ed., *City of Peace*, Bradford Libraries, Bradford, 1997

Kamester, Margaret and Jo Vellacott, eds., *Militarism Versus Feminism: Writings on Women and War; Mary Sargant Florence, Catherine Marshall, C.K. Ogden*, Virago, London, 1987

Kennedy, Thomas C., *The Hound of Conscience*, University of Arkansa Press, Fayetteville AR, 1981

Koss, Stephen, *The Pro-Boers*, University of Chicago Press, Chicago IL, 1973

Kraft, Barbara S., *The Peace Ship*, Macmillan, New York, 1978

Lamb, David, *Mutinies 1917-1920*, Solidarity, London, 1977

Lambeth Conferences, 1867-1930, SPCK, London, 1948

Lansbury, Edgar, *George Lansbury, My Father*, S. Low, Marsden, London, 1934

Lansbury, George, *My Life*, Constable, London, 1928

Lansbury, George, *My Quest For Peace*, Michael Joseph, London, 1938

Law, William, *The Works of the Reverend William Law, A.M.*, nine volumes, London, 1789

Lester, Muriel, *It Occurred to Me*, Kingsley Hall, Sarratt, 1942,

Liddington, Jill, "The Women's Peace Crusade", in Thompson, Dorothy, ed., *Over Our Dead Bodies*, Virago, London, 1984

Liddington, Jill, *The Long Road to Greenham*, Virago, London, 1989

Lockhart , J.G., *Cosmo Gordon Lang*, Hodder and Stoughton, London, 1949

Lothian, Marquess of, et al, *The Universal Church and the World of Nations*, George Allen and Unwin, London, 1938

Lowell, James Russell, *The Biglow Papers*, Trübner, London, 1861

Lowry, Donal, ed., *The South African War Reappraised*, Manchester, Manchester University, 2000

Macaulay, Rose, H.R L. Sheppard, et al, *Let Us Honour Peace*, Cobden Sanderson, London, 1937

McCormick, Pat, H.R.L. Sheppard, et al, *St. Martin-in-the-Fields Calling*, Athenæum, London, 1932

Manokha, Ivan, "The History of Modern Military Humanitarianism Revisited" in Durward, Rosemary and Lee Marsden, *Religion, Conflict and Military Intervention*, Ashgate, Farnham, 2009

Martensen, H.L. and S. Hobhouse, *Jacob Boehme*, Rockliff, London, 1949

Melish, John Howard, *Bishop Paul Jones: Witness for Peace*, revised edition edited by Peter Eaton, Forward Movement, Cincinatti, Ohio, 1992

Miles, Susan, *Blind Men Crossing a Bridge*, Constable, London, 1934

Miles, Susan, *Portrait of a Parson, William Corbett Roberts*, Allen and Unwin, London, 1955

Morrison, Sybil, *I Renounce War*, Sheppard Press, London, 1962

Musto, Ronald G., *The Catholic Peace Tradition*, Orbis, Maryknoll NY, 1986

Neill, Stephen, *Anglicanism*, Penguin, Harmondsworth, 3rd Edition 1965

No-Conscription Fellowship, *NCF Souvenir*, 1919; reprinted as *Troublesome People*, Central Board for Conscientious Objectors, London, 1940

Nuttall, Geoffrey F., *Christian Pacifism in History*, World Without War Council, Berkeley CA, 1971

Oldham, J.H., ed., *The Universal Church and the World of Nations*, Church Community and State Series volume 7, George Allen and Unwin, London, 1938

Palmer, Bernard, *Men of Habit*, Canterbury Press, Norwich, 1994

Parker, S.G., and Tom Lawson, *God and War*, Farnham, Ashgate, 2012

Pearce, Cyril, *Comrades in Conscience*, Francis Boutle, London, 2001

Perowne, J.J.S., ed., *Thomas Rogers: The Catholic Doctrine of the Church of England, 1607*, Parker Society, Cambridge, 1854

Perry, Harry, *50 Years of Workcamps*, International Voluntary Service, Leicester, 1981

Pierce, Nathaniel W. and Paul L. Ward, *The Voice of Conscience: A Loud and Unusual Noise?*, Episcopal Peace Fellowship, Washington D.C., 1989

Pilkington, George, *The Doctrine of Particular Providence*, Effingham Wilson, London, 1836

Pilkington, George, *Travels Through the United Kingdom in Promoting the Cause of Peace on Earth and Goodwill Towards Men*, Edmund Fry, London, 1839

Platten, Stephen, *Augustine's Legacy*, DLT, London, 1997

Playne, Caroline E., *Society at War, 1914-1916*, George Allen and Unwin, London, 1931

Porter, Bernard, "The Pro-Boers in Britain", in Warwick, Peter, ed. *The South African War: the Anglo-Boer War 1899-1902*, Harlow, Longman, 1980

Postgate, Raymond, *The Life of George Lansbury*, Longmans Green, London, 1951

Radhakrishnan, Sarvepalli, ed., *Mahatma Gandhi: Essays and Reflections*, George Allen and Unwin, London, 1949

Rae, John, *Conscience and Politics*, Oxford University Press, London, 1970

Rank, Carol, ed., *City of Peace*, Bradford Libraries, Bradford, 1997

Raven, Charles E., *Our Salvation*, Martin Hopkinson, London, 1925

Raven, Charles E., *A Wanderer's Way*, Martin Hopkinson, London, 1929

Raven, Charles E., *Is War Obsolete?*, George Allen and Unwin, London, 1935

Raven, Charles E., "We Will Not Fight", in Macaulay, Rose, H. R. L. Sheppard, et al, *Let Us Honour Peace*, Cobden Sanderson, London, 1937

Raven, Charles E., *War and the Christian*, SCM, London, 1938

Raven, Charles E., "The Religious Basis of Pacifism", in Oldham, J.H., ed., *The Universal Church and the World of Nations*, Church Community and State Series volume 7, George Allen and Unwin, London, 1938

Raven, Charles E., *John Ray, Naturalist: His Life and Works*, Cambridge University Press, Cambridge, 1942

Regan, Richard J., *Just War, Principles and Cases*, Catholic University of America, Washington DC, 1996

Reilly, Catherine, ed., *Scars Upon My Heart*, Virago, London, 1981

Richards, Edith Ryley, *Private View of a Public Man*, George Allen and Unwin, London, 1950

Rigby, Andrew, *A Life in Peace*, Prism, Bridport, 1988,

Roberts, R. Ellis, *H.R.L. Sheppard: Life and Letters*, John Murray, London, 1942

Robbins, Keith, *The Abolition of War*, University of Wales Press, Cardiff, 1976

Robbins, Keith, *England, Ireland, Scotland, Wales, The Christian Church 1900-2000*, Oxford University Press, Oxford, 2008

Rogers, Thomas, *The Catholic Doctrine of the Church of England*, 1607; see Perowne, J.J.S.

Royden, Maude, *The Great Adventure*, Headley, London, 1915

Royden, Maude, "War and the Woman's Movement", in Buxton, Charles Roden, ed., *Towards a Lasting Settlement*, George Allen and Unwin, London, 1915

Royden, Maude, *Women and the Sovereign State*, Headley, London, 1917

Royden, Maude, *The Hour and the Church*, George Allen and Unwin, London, 1918

Royden, Maude, *Our Policy in the Near East*, H.B. Trustees, London, 1922,

Royden, Maude, *Political Christianity*, G.P. Purman, London, 1922

Royden, Maude, *I Believe in God*, Harper, London, 1927

Russell, Bertrand, *The Autobiography of Bertrand Russell, Volume II, 1914-1944*, George Allen and Unwin, London, 1968

Salter, Alfred, "The Religion of a C.O." in No-Conscription Fellowship, *Troublesome People*, Central Board for Conscientious Objectors, London, 1940

Schneer, Jonathan, *George Lansbury*, Manchester University Press, Manchester, 1990

Scott, Carolyn, *Dick Sheppard: A Biography*, Hodder and Stoughton, London, 1977

Scott Holland, Henry, *A Bundle of Memories*, Wells Gardner, London, 1915

Scott, J., *War Inconsistent with the Doctrine and Example of Jesus Christ*, 1820

Scudder, Vida Dutton, *Introduction to Bede's Ecclesiastical History*, J.M. Dent, London, 1910

Scudder, Vida Dutton, *The Church and the Hour*, E.P. Dutton, New York, 1917

Scudder, Vida Dutton, *The Privilege of Age*, J.M. Dent, London 1939

Sharma, Serena K., " 'Just Peace' or Peace Postponed" in Durward, Rosemary and Lee Marsden, eds., *Religion, Conflict and Military Intervention*, Ashgate, Farnham, 2009

Shaw, Amy J., *Crisis of Conscience: Conscientious Objection in Canada During the First World War*, University of British Columbia Press, Vancouver, 2009

Shaw, George Bernard, *Common Sense about the War*, Statesman, London, 1914

Shepherd, John, *George Lansbury: At the Heart of Old Labour*, Oxford University Press, Oxford, 2002

Sheppard, H.R.L., *The Impatience of a Parson*, Hodder and Stoughton, London, 1927

Sheppard, H.R.L., *We Say "No"*, John Murray, London, 1935

Sheppard, H.R.L., *God and My Neighbour*, Cassell, London, 1937

Smith, Angela K., ed., British Literature of World War 1, volume 4, Pickering and Chatto, London, 2011

Socknat, Thomas P., *Witness Against War; Pacifism in Canada 1900-1945*, University of Toronto Press, Toronto, 1987

Stanton, Harry Edward, *Will You March Too?*, unpublished manuscript, Liddle Collection, Leeds

Stephenson, Alan M.G. *Anglicanism and the Lambeth Conferences*, SPCK, London, 1978

Stevenson, Lilian*Towards a Christian International*, International Fellowship of Reconciliation, Paris, 1936 edition

Stimson, Charles C., *The Price to be Paid; "The Tramp Preachers"*, Peaceprint, Pontefract, 1988

Studdert Kennedy, G.A. (Woodbine Willie), *Rough Rhymes of a Padre*, George H. Doran, New York, 1918

Studdert Kennedy, G.A. (Woodbine Willie), and Walters, Kerry (editor), *After War, Is Faith Possible: An Anthology*, Lutterworth Press, Cambridge, 2008

Sykes, Stephen, "The Genius of Anglicanism", in Rowell, Geoffrey, ed., *The English Religious Tradition and the Genius of Anglicanism*, Ikon, Wantage, 1992

Taylor, A.J.P. , *The Trouble Makers*, London, Hamish Hamilton, 1957

Thomas, Anna Braithwaite, *St. Stephen's House*, Emergency Committee, London, c.1921

Thompson, Andrew C. , *Logical Nonconformity? Conscientious Objection in the Cambridge Free Churches after 1914*, Journal of the United Reformed Church History Society, Vol. 5, No. 9, November 1996

Tucker, Irwin St. John, "The Price We Pay", *The World*, Oakland, California, 584, 1 June 1917

Walke, Bernard, *Twenty Years at St. Hilary*, Methuen, London, 1935

Wallis, Jill, *Valiant for Peace*, Fellowship of Reconciliation, London, 1991

Wallis, Jill, *Mother of World Peace*, Hisarlik, Enfield Lock, 1993

Walters, Kerry, ed., *After War, Is Faith Possible?*, G.A. Studdert Kennedy, An Anthology, Lutterworth, Cambridge, 2008

Warwick, Peter, ed., *The South African War: the Anglo-Boer War 1899-1902*. Harlow, Longman, 1980

Wilkinson, Alan, *The Church of England and the First World War*, SPCK, London, 1978 (reprinted by Lutterworth Press, Cambridge, 2014)

Wilkinson, Alan, *Dissent or Conform? War, Peace and the English Churches, 1900-1945*, SCM, London, 1986 (reprinted by Lutterworth Press, Cambridge, 2010)

Wiltsher, Anne, *Most Dangerous Women*, Pandora, London, 1985

Woods, Mike, Angela Woods and Tricia Platt, "Women, Peace and Politics" in Woods, Mike and Tricia Platts, eds., *Bradford in the Great War*, Sutton, Stroud, 2007

Zook, Darren C., "Just War", *The International Encyclopedia of Peace*, edited by Nigel Young, Oxford University Press, New York, Oxford, 2010

Quotations

Index

You may also be interested in

The Church of England and the First World War

By Alan Wilkinson

Print ISBN: 978 0 7188 9321 7

Newly reprinted, this classic work of social history explores the complex and multifacted role played by the Church of England in British society during World War One. *The Church of England and the First World War* (first published in 1978) explores in depth the role of the Church during the tragic circumstances of the First World War using biographies, newspapers, magazines, letters, poetry and other sources in a balanced evaluation.

Canadian Churches and the First World War

Edited by Gordon L. Heath

Print ISBN: 978 0 7188 9358 3

A selection of essays discussing the responses of the Christian churches in Canada to the First World War, providing an invaluable introduction to a neglected area of Canadian social and religious history. Most accounts of Canada and the First World War either ignore or merely mention in passing the churches' experience. *Canadian Churches and the First World War* redresses this surprising neglect, exploring the marked relationship between Canada's 'Great War' and its various churches in intricate detail.

Available now with more excellent titles in Paperback, Hardback, PDF and EPUB formats from **The Lutterworth Press**

www.lutterworth.com